PERIPHERAL VISIONS

CHICAGO STUDIES IN PRACTICES OF MEANING

A series edited by Jean Comaroff, Andreas Glaeser, William Sewell, and Lisa Wedeen

ALSO IN THE SERIES:

Inclusion: The Politics of Difference in Medical Research
BY STEVEN EPSTEIN

Producing India: From Colonial Economy to National Space
BY MANU GOSWAMI

Bengal in Global Concept History: Culturalism in the Age of Capital
BY ANDREW SARTORI

Parité!: Sexual Equality and the Crisis of French Universalism
BY JOAN WALLACH SCOTT

Logics of History: Social Theory and Social Transformation
BY WILLIAM H. SEWELL, JR.

Bewitching Development: Witchcraft and the Reinvention of Development in Neoliberal Kenya
BY JAMES HOWARD SMITH

The Devil's Handwriting: Precoloniality and the German Colonial State in Qingdao, Samoa, and Southwest Africa
BY GEORGE STEINMETZ

PERIPHERAL VISIONS

PUBLICS, POWER, AND PERFORMANCE IN YEMEN

LISA WEDEEN

THE UNIVERSITY OF CHICAGO PRESS • CHICAGO AND LONDON

LISA WEDEEN is professor of political science at the University of Chicago and author of *Ambiguities of Domination: Politics, Rhetoric, and Symbols in Contemporary Syria*.

The University of Chicago Press, Chicago 60637
The University of Chicago Press, Ltd., London

Printed in the United States of America

17 16 15 14 13 12 11 10   2 3 4 5

ISBN-13: 978-0-226-87790-7 (cloth)
ISBN-13: 978-0-226-87791-4 (paper)
ISBN-10: 0-226-87790-6 (cloth)
ISBN-10: 0-226-87791-4 (paper)

Library of Congress Cataloging-in-Publication Data

Wedeen, Lisa.
Peripheral visions : publics, power, and performance in Yemen / Lisa Wedeen.
p. cm. — (Chicago studies in practices of meaning)
Includes bibliographical references and index.
ISBN-13: 978-0-226-87790-7 (cloth : alk. paper)
ISBN-13: 978-0-226-87791-4 (pbk. : alk. paper)
ISBN-10: 0-226-87790-6 (cloth : alk. paper)
ISBN-10: 0-226-87791-4 (pbk. : alk. paper) 1. Yemen (Republic)—Politics and government. 2. Political participation—Yemen (Republic) 3. Nationalism—Yemen. I. Title.
JQ1842.A58W43 2008
320.9533—dc22

2008005222

∞ The paper used in this publication meets the minimum requirements of the American National Standard for Information Sciences—Permanence of Paper for Printed Library Materials, ANSI Z39.48-1992.

If I have exhausted the justifications I have reached bedrock,
and my spade is turned. Then I am inclined to say:
"This is simply what I do."

Ludwig Wittgenstein,
Philosophical Investigations, par. 217.

CONTENTS

CHAPTER FIVE
PIETY IN TIME:
CONTEMPORARY ISLAMIC MOVEMENTS IN NATIONAL
AND TRANSNATIONAL CONTEXTS

CONCLUSION
POLITICS AS PERFORMATIVE

Illustrations follow page 102.

LIST OF MAPS

ACKNOWLEDGMENTS

How do I begin to thank those who have contributed to this project? In Yemen, I am grateful to so many people for their kindness. In particular, special thanks are owed to 'Alī Sayf Ḥasan, Muḥammad Qaḥṭān, Dr. Muḥammad 'Abd al-Malik al-Mutawakkil, Qabūl al-Mutawakkil, and Dr. Inṭilāq al-Mutawakkil, the late Jār Allāh 'Umar and his family, Mujāhid al-Quhālī, Nabīl al-Ṣūfī, and Muṣṭafā Nu'mān for their extraordinary hospitality and intellectual generosity. I am also grateful to Muḥammad Ghālib, Muḥammad al-Mikhlāfī, Wahbiyya Ṣabrā, Muḥammad Saqqāf, the al-Madwahī family, the Isḥāq family, staff at al-Ayyām newspaper, the villagers of Kuhhal and the townspeople of Shibām in the Ḥaḍramawt for their thoughtfulness. Special acknowledgment also goes to 'Abd al-Ḥakīm al-Sa'da, Consul of Yemen in Detroit for his assistance over the years. I also thank all those unnamed members of the Yemeni Socialist Party, al-Iṣlāḥ, and the General People's Congress who helped me during my fieldwork, as well as to the various poets I encountered through the Center for Yemeni Studies under the directorship of Dr. 'Abd al-'Azīz al-Maqāliḥ. I remain indebted to everyone who gave time and energy to this project.

At the University of Chicago, I have been fortunate to find an intellectual community that is inspirational and tough-minded. I am grateful to my colleagues at 3CT (Chicago Center for Contemporary Theory). Jean and John Comaroff read the manuscript from beginning to end and provided me with superb suggestions in the margins of every page. They also took care of me in South Africa, at a time when I was badly in need of a break, and for their friendship and movie-going proclivities, I remain truly thankful. William H. Sewell, Jr., read countless drafts of particular chapters and tried to teach me to write the historical chapter like a historian, an endeavor at which I fear I was only partially successful. He also read the entire manuscript and offered me overall recommendations that were truly transformative. Dipesh Chakrabarty listened to so many versions of chapter 3 that I'm not sure he or I will ever be the same again. At 3CT, I would also like to thank Andreas Glaeser, Patchen Markell, and Danilyn Rutherford for their comments during our sessions on my book. Thanks are also owed to the late Iris Marion Young, to Carles Boix, Robert Gooding-Williams, John McCormick, and Dan Slater for helpful suggestions that pushed the book along. For their friendship and intellectual companionship, I am particularly indebted to Jennifer Cole and Rochona Majumdar, both of whom read drafts of specific chapters and encouraged me to exercise my body as well as my mind. Jennifer Cole's scholarly advice and elegant editorial suggestions for the introduction, conclusion, and chapter 5 were enormously useful. Michael Dawson has been a true friend and exceptional interlocutor throughout this process. I am particularly grateful for his insightful comments on multiple (and I mean *multiple*) drafts of all chapters. This book could not have been written without his patience and unstinting dedication to our friendship and to the book. My colleagues in the Department of Political Science more generally deserve acknowledgment for their faith in the project and for their helpful interventions during workshop events. Conversations in the Comparative Politics workshop and in the interdisciplinary Political Communications workshop were especially productive, and thanks are due to Susan Gal and Michael Silverstein for their contributions to the latter.

At the Institute for Advanced Study, I thank Joan Scott, whose hospitality and intellectual acuity helped make our seminar sessions worthwhile. Rosalind C. Morris's readings of my work during the 2006-7 year challenged me in unexpected and pleasurable ways, and she has become a friend and an inspiration in the process. I was not able to incorporate all of her suggestions or entertain all of her invitations for elaboration, but I do not stop thinking of how they might enhance whatever I do next. Susan

Lehman made her apartment in New York available to me every week while I was in Princeton. She is my BFF, my gal pal for life. And I thank her children too, Zack, Annie, and Max, for giving up their usual sleeping arrangements to accommodate me so often. I am particularly lucky to have another best friend in Nadia Abu El-Haj, whose friendship and astute readings of my work I have treasured over the years. She too made commuting from Chicago to the East Coast as delightful as such an ordeal can be. And I am grateful to Nadia's immediate family, Amer Bisat and Aya, for welcoming me into their household on many occasions. For their constancy, even when my own has wavered, I thank my friends Gaston Alonso Donate and Betsy Andrews. For his indefatigable decency, wit, and common sense, I am forever indebted to Al Ravitz.

This project has benefited from terrific research assistants. Thanks are owed to Adria Lawrence, Sevag Kechichian, Aram Shahin, and Rohit Goel for their tireless efforts at various stages of this project. They have tracked down articles, checked citations, and read drafts of chapters. Thanks especially to Aram Shahin for his meticulous handling of transliterations and for his erudition on issues Islamic. And especial appreciation is due to Rohit Goel, whose creative readings of countless drafts improved the text immeasurably. I remain grateful to both Rohit and Aram for their assistance in preparing the final manuscript, and to Anita Chari, Jessica Greenberg, Loren Goldman, Todd Hall, Kabir Tambar, and João Gonçalves for their substantive comments. Students, not all of whom are mentioned here, are also acknowledged in endnotes for particular contributions they have made to the work. I also register my gratitude to my own teachers, particularly to the late Michael Rogin, whose originality and imagination continue to inspire my own efforts, and to Hanna Pitkin, who remains my intellectual muse. I am also fortunate to have had extraordinary guidance from scholars knowledgeable about and appreciative of Yemen. Thanks to Renaud Detalle, Engseng Ho, Jillian Schwedler, Shelagh Weir, John Willis, and Anna Würth for their help and suggestions, and especially to Sheila Carapico, who read every word of the book at one point in its metamorphosis and provided incisive comments and enduring emotional support. I am also grateful to Paul Dresch, who responded to queries via email with dispatch and uncommon erudition, and to Selma Al-Radi, who provided companionship and encouraged distractions from politics during our overlapping stays in Yemen. This book was also assigned to two exceptional reviewers, both of whom revealed their identities to me during the course of my significant revisions. Both Brinkley Messick and Steven C. Caton did what one hopes for in reviews—offer honest, critical, perceptive assessments designed to make the manuscript as insightful, polished, and true as it can be.

The book benefited from the comments and criticisms colleagues at other universities also provided. I thank the audiences at New York University, Columbia, the New School, Northwestern, the University of Pennsylvania, Yale, Harvard, Rutgers, Princeton, the University of California at Los Angeles, the University of California at Santa Barbara, and the Center for the Study of Developing Societies in Delhi for feedback. Julia Paley, Elizabeth Perry, and Linda Zerilli deserve thanks for spending considerable time on parts of the manuscript, pointing out weaknesses and shoring up its strengths. Thanks also to my copyeditor John Raymond, and to Rodney Powell, Michael Koplow, and especially the wonderful John Tryneski, all from the University of Chicago Press.

This project was supported by generous research leaves from the University of Chicago. I began writing the book at Chicago's very own Franke Institute for the Humanities, directed by the indomitable Jim Chandler. Jim's comments and support for the project and our growing friendship have helped to make Chicago a rewarding place to be. Thanks as well to the American Institute of Yemeni Studies, the Institute for Advanced Study at Princeton, the breathtakingly beautiful Rockefeller Center in Bellagio, and the George A. and Eliza Gardner Howard Foundation for their generous support. Chapter 2 is a revised version of an essay published in *Comparative Studies in Society and History*, October 2003. A shortened version of an earlier version of chapter 3 was published in *Public Culture*, winter 2007.

I am once again grateful to my family—to my parents Helen and Harvey Wedeen, to my sister Laura Wedeen and her family, and to my partner Don Reneau and our son, Zack Reneau-Wedeen. Don has endured this project, its joys and frustrations, its demands and rewards, and its inestimable sorrows. He is my love, and among my most demanding readers. This book belongs to him as much as it does to me.

Peripheral Visions is dedicated to the memories of Jār Allāh 'Umar and Rick Hooper. I miss their world-enlivening presence every day. Rick died in the bombing of the United Nations building in Baghdad in August 2003, a casualty of the war he loathed and a UN presence he condemned. And Jār Allāh was assassinated in December 2002 after a speech registering possibilities for a united opposition in Yemen. Both men believed that the only way to bring about a freer politics was to start enacting it, and to encourage others to do so as well. They were engaged on a daily basis with the basic political question, "what shall we do?" and they also knew that the "we" and "do" were problematic categories—ones open to interpretation, disagreement, contestation, and change. I miss their critical engagement, their love of the world, their sense of boldness, their willingness to acknowledge mistakes, and their delight in relating to people. Yet in the shadow of death, there is continued life, and so I also dedicate this book to my son Zack, who reminds me of the day's affirming pleasures, of playful abandon and enduring connection.

INTRODUCTION

President ʿAlī ʿAbd Allāh Ṣāliḥ has been in power for over twenty-five years, as the leader of North Yemen since 1978, and of unified Yemen since its inception in 1990. Yet in spite of the regime's durability, the Weberian fantasy of a state that enjoys a monopoly on violence—legitimate or otherwise—is not remotely evident. Yemen, according to a 2003 report by Small Arms Survey, is one of the world's "most heavily armed societies."[1] The state, moreover, is incapable of providing welfare, protection, or education to the population. Complaints are heard with incantation-like regularity all over Yemen about the absence of "security" (*amān*) and "stability" (*istiqrār*), the inability of the state to guarantee safe passage from one region to another, to put a stop to extralegal justice, and to disarm the citizenry. And to the extent that a sense of membership coherent and powerful enough to tie people's political loyalties to the nation-state does exist, there is little evidence that the incumbent regime is responsible for creating it.

Yet Yemen is not to be categorized with such countries as the former Yugoslavia or Rwanda, where violence has destroyed communities and shattered fragile political arrangements previously in existence. In an era when some nation-states are being challenged by ethnic conflict and the fragmentation of previously unified multinational political communities, and others are undermined by transnational patterns of migration and capital accumulation, a never-before-united Yemen has emerged and has endured despite markedly weak institutional capacities and a peripheral location in the global political and economic order.[2]

This book analyzes the making of national attachments when state institutions are "weak"—incapable of controlling violence or distributing adequate goods and services within a demarcated territory. What makes a Yemeni a Yemeni in the context of the state's fragilities, and why does Yemen hold together to the extent that it does? More generally, how does nationalism operate, and how do claims of national belonging articulate with other experiences of solidarity? How important is national loyalty for political order anyway? The objectives of this book are to specify the mechanisms by which national identifications are established in the absence of effective state institutions; to investigate how national affiliations work in relation to two other forms of identification (democratic and pious);[3] to examine the effects of weak state institutions on all three forms of solidarity (national, democratic, and pious); and conversely, to assess the impact of these affiliations on political order, on the modes of compliance, and on the practices of activism central to political life. Finally, I demonstrate how a theory of politics as performative adds value to political analyses.

Yemen is ideal for a scholarly analysis of the making of national attachments and their relationship to political order for at least four reasons. First, unlike other recent instances of unification such as Vietnam and Germany, before 1990 North and South Yemen had never been united in a single nation-state. In this sense, the Republic of Yemen is not an instance of "reunification," but a new experiment in nation-state formation. Or, put differently, although nationalist identification with the state requires ongoing work in any context, in Yemen there were no prior political arrangements that regulated membership in a territorially determinate association of citizens who, as "a people," could identify themselves with an existing common political authority.

Second, this nationalist experiment was accompanied by what analysts typically call "a transition to democracy," or at least a substantial gesture in that direction. Openly contested elections for Parliament, a wide array of critical newspapers, and a plethora of political parties in the early 1990s made Yemen one of the only Middle Eastern countries to tolerate peaceful, adversarial politics. A brief civil war in 1994 altered these conditions of democratic possibility, however, transforming a democratic partnership into an authoritarian, northern-dominated politics that continues to this day.[4] However, the persistence in both north and south of vibrant political activism, often in the form of peaceful, quotidian activities of deliberation and debate, makes apparent the mechanisms through which rulers and ruled navigate their political lives, raising important theoretical questions about the nature of democracy and the practices through which a democratic politics can be enacted in quasi-autocratic circumstances. Of particular note in this regard is the understanding I develop in chapter 3 of Yemenis' gatherings around *qāt*—a leafy stimulant chewed daily in the context of afternoon socializing. These "*qāt* chews" provide the occasion for a broad range of discursive interaction among friends and acquaintances as well as strangers, including intensive discussions of manifestly political matters. In this way, *Peripheral Visions* shows how social science scholarship can benefit theoretically and empirically from attending to democratic phenomena that exist outside of electoral and other formal organizational confines.

Third and relatedly, the ineffectiveness of Yemen's state institutions means that national solidarities—to the extent that they exist—tend not to be generated through institutions usually credited with inculcating national values, but through the ordinary activities undertaken by men and women in pursuit of their daily lives. The same can be said of democracy: in the absence of fair and free elections, democratic persons are nevertheless produced through quotidian practices of deliberation.[5] These acts are not embellishments of a democracy independently existing. They are the thing itself.[6] Contrary to the literature on civil society, I argue that the democratic nature of this deliberation is a function of the activity's very form rather than of deliberation's ultimate institutional effects (e.g., as a promoter of contested elections). The minipublic of the *qāt* chew operates concurrently with other minipublics (such as those associated with mosque sermons and lessons, newspapers, radio broadcasts or television) to produce lively communities of argument, distinct modes of democratic being and acting in which participants often orient their addresses to and receive information as part of a broader public of anonymous citizens (Warner 2002). The example of Yemen thus brings into stark relief how democracy and national solidarity can work as ongoing, performative practices, as ties that are produced and reproduced by a given population as a function of diffuse points of shared reference (Brubaker and Cooper 2000). Not all performative practices produce either national consciousness or democratic persons, of course. This book explores the questions of which ones are likely to do so and how we know when they do.

Fourth, by foregrounding Yemen's experiment in national unity, *Peripheral Visions* uses the case to advance our understandings of identity formation more generally. The multiplicity of Yemeni identifications and their availability for political mobilization invite a detailed analysis of the conceptual and empirical concerns to which the vast literature on "identity" refers. The Yemeni example presents a varied array of sub- and transnational allegiances, operating sometimes compatibly with and sometimes in opposition to the regime. Loyalties to tribe and region, occupational caste distinctions, identifications with Shāfiʿī (Sunnī) or Zaydī (Yemeni Shīʿī) denominations, migrant laborers' exposure to the practices of piety in oil-producing Gulf states, and family connections to Ethiopia, Eritrea, India, Indonesia, or Singapore complicate people's experiences of Yemeni-ness. Both official and unofficial declarations of Yemeni authenticity function ambiguously and simultaneously with local and transnational experiences of identification.

As may already be obvious, my approach to the study of nationalism is to view the nation as a contingent category rather than as a substantial thing. The sociologist Rogers Brubaker has perhaps said it best: "Instead of focusing on nations as real groups, we should focus on nationhood and nationness, on 'nation' as practical category, institutionalized form, and contingent event. . . . To understand nationalism, we have to understand the practical uses of the category 'nation,' the ways it can come to structure perception, to inform thought and experience, to organize discourse and political action" (Brubaker 1996, 7). In this spirit, I want to do more than simply assert that the nation is not a biological or transhistorical fact, an assertion widely accepted in academic circles. I want to show how understanding "the nation" as a contingent category enriches our analyses of political life, and how neglecting to do so leads to error.

Scholars today tend not to agree on what a nation is or, consequently, on when (or where) nationalism first emerged. Arguments about the origins of nationalism locate its genesis variously in "New World" Latin American independence movements and the exigencies of print capitalism (Anderson 1991), in the political and structural transformations associated with industrialization (Gellner 1983; Nairn 1996), in the effects of expanding communication and transportation networks (Deutsch 1953; Seton-Watson 1977; Hroch 1993), in the processes of state-formation (Kohn

1967; Weber 1978; Hobsbawm 1990; Mann 1993; Breuilly 1994; Marx 2003), in the changing notions of community initiated by France's revolutionary actors (Sewell 2004), or in new international arrangements produced in the aftermath of World War II (Kelly and Kaplan 2001).[7] Underlying these divergent views is a consensus about the nation form being distinctly modern in character—closely associated with the political, economic, and social transformations of recent times—but it is less well elaborated in the scholarship what this modernity implies for nationalism's particularity as an ideology.[8]

I want to begin redressing that neglect by investigating the novelty of nationalism as Benedict Anderson (1991) and those inspired by his ideas perceive it. As I show below, Anderson helpfully specifies what distinguishes nationalism from other forms of solidarity, although the Yemeni case also unsettles well-established Andersonian claims about what nationalism entails and how it works. Following this theoretical interlude, I turn to an explanation of practices as performative. I then discuss briefly the methods and source materials used in the book, as well as how subsequent chapters are organized. I end by adumbrating *Peripheral Visions*' key arguments.

THEORIZING NATIONS AND NATIONALISMS: TERRITORIAL SOVEREIGNTY AND MULTIPLE TEMPORALITIES

Although there has been a myriad of work criticizing Anderson, and it is arguable that little more can or should be said, I have three reasons for bringing him into conversation with the case of Yemen. First, I want to make a methodological intervention into studies of nationalism by underscoring a neglected distinction in Anderson. In his discussion of how national citizens are constituted, he differentiates discourses that are specifically nationalist in content from other ways in which national imaginings happen independently of this rhetoric. This distinction has implications for how we identify the various mechanisms that have made nationalist imaginings plausible. Second, I want to highlight the qualities specific to "the nation," a term that resembles concepts connoting older solidarities of kinship and shared piety but is not coterminous with them. The example of Yemen—where a notion of *Yaman* is ancient, yet does not come to be understood in explicitly nationalist terms until the 1920s and 1930s—invites us to identify the "ingredients" of nationalism, the modern doctrines and practices differentiating it from other forms of collective representation. Whereas some scholars use "nation" to mean any form of community—Walker Connor (1972), for example, writing influentially of "nation-building" requiring "nation-destroying" where "nation" means any community in which othering takes place—specifying more precisely what nationalism is permits us to understand its particular logics and implications for political identifications and state sovereignty. It allows us to be conceptually clear about when we are referring to nationalism and when we are studying other group affiliations. The added value of identifying nationalism's particularities as an ideology is often methodological as well as substantive, helping us to pinpoint when nationalism emerged in a particular place, preventing us from retrospectively misidentifying movements as "protonational" or from conflating all communal imaginings with national ones. This exercise is less an effort to produce a rule-bound definition than to look historically at the nation form's "family resemblances" (Wittgenstein 1958, par. 67), identifying the overlapping and crisscrossing "network of similarities" among nationalisms over time (ibid., par. 66).

Third and finally, this section foregrounds significant problems with Anderson's theory, revealing his indebtedness to a modernization story that conceives of nationalism as a complete linear progression from one master narrative of communal imagining to the next. As a consequence he neglects other processes of subject formation, ways in which people can and do experience their worlds through multiple and hybrid spatial, temporal, and political frameworks. In particular, nationalism and secularism do not necessitate each other, as some scholars beholden to Anderson suggest (e.g., Asad 1993, 2003; Taylor 2004; Agrama 2005). These scholars mistake a historical connection between nationalism and secularism for a constitutive one. Here I am not only arguing that the same person can be both nationalist and devoutly pious, calling into question the purportedly intrinsic connection between secularism and nationalism. I am also contending that there are movements that can be correctly understood as both religious and nationalist despite the seeming theoretical contradictions such movements bring to the fore.[9] Or to put it differently and perhaps less contentiously, the observable empirical overlap of pious and nationalist sensibilities requires us to theorize how the distinct notions of being and acting each imply can inflect one another to produce novel political possibilities.[10]

Anderson's *Imagined Communities* helpfully distinguishes between the content of nationalist discourses and the fact of people's shared experience in time, which allowed individuals living in disparate areas to imagine themselves as inhabiting a world in common with like-minded, anonymous others. This distinction has methodological implications Anderson does not discuss but that inform my own approach. It is possible, on the one hand, to think about the words and concepts that index "the nation"—phrases such as "the people" or "my fellow Yemenis." On the other hand, we can also analyze the various practices that exemplify and produce specific assemblages of fellow readers and listeners who, whatever the content of their discourses, nevertheless have come to share (or be perceived to share) the everyday experiences of others within a limited, territorially sovereign space. Maintaining the distinction between the rhetoric of nationalism and shared practices rooted in spatial contiguity helps expose the multiple ways in which actors can be "hailed" or "interpellated" (Althusser 1971), brought into being as a national community—at least some of the time.

Second, there are the "ingredients" that make nationalism different from other forms of communal imagining. In the scholarly literature inspired by Anderson, nationalism is viewed historically as situated in specifically modern, abstract notions of "horizontal fraternity" and "homogeneous, empty time."[11] Other kinds of communities are also assuredly "imagined" by their members, but nationalist discourses posit a form of fellowship predicated specifically on the sovereignty of "a people" whose existence presupposes a worldly past and territorially bounded understandings of space (Anderson 1991, 11; Asad 2003, 193). The modern nation-state and the ideologies of eighteenth- and nineteenth-century nationalism are in this view fundamentally different from their medieval antecedents, and nationalism is implicated historically in the processes of capitalism, state formation, and secularism.[12] In *Time, Labor, and Social Domination*, a particularly insightful discussion of Marx's analysis of value in capitalist society, Moishe Postone (1993) clarifies how capitalism relates to modern conceptions of time. He differentiates between concrete time (e.g., the time it takes to cook pasta or say one's prayers) and abstract time, the "uniform, continuous, homogeneous 'empty' time" that is "independent of events" (202). Concrete time can be linear or cyclical, sacred or profane; it refers to and is apprehended through "natural cycles and the periodicities of human life as well as particular tasks or processes" (201). Abstract time, by contrast, involves units that are universally commensurable, interchangeable, constant, and invariable (202–9). Its roots can be discerned in the late Middle Ages, but the idea as such became hegemonic only with the spread of the "commodity-determined" forms of social relations inherent to capitalism in the West.[13]

This modern notion of time was important for nationalism because it entailed a new sense of simultaneity, one that permitted people who were distant from one another to conceive of themselves as part of a shared world of concomitant events. Anderson famously writes that the nation is "imagined because the members of even the smallest nations will never know most of their fellow-members, meet them, or even hear of them, yet in the minds of each lives the image of their communion" (Anderson 1991, 6). Of course, other practices—e.g., of piety, to name an example to be explored in detail later on—also require anonymous members to imagine the collectivity's "communion" and to do so simultaneously. What makes nationalism distinct is that this simultaneity, enabled initially by technological innovations such as those related to print capitalism, the proliferation of personal clocks, and ultimately by railroad schedules,[14] produced assemblages of people who could share a sense of clock-oriented, calendrical time *within a boundary-oriented, limited, sovereign, self-governing space.*

In this sense, it is arguably state institutions, with their increasing powers to record, educate, and police populations, that prove critical for the emergence of nationalist imaginings as such, not only because advances in communication associated with state formation enabled ideas to travel more quickly and widely but also because the content of nationalism tied state sovereignty to ideas of a *territorially* located, explicitly political community. Or to put it differently, nationalist ideology presumes a congruency between "the people" and state institutions.[15] And images of the political community's historical relationship to territorially delimited states in Europe and the Americas had consequences for later nationalist imaginings of time, space, and collectivity (even in places where state institutions remained fragile and industrial capitalism less relevant). As Manu Goswami notes in reference to the state:

> The consolidation of the inter-state system as a nation-state system, the generalization of the doctrine of self-determination, and the progressive naturalization of the tie between nation and state dynamically reconfigured the discursive terrain. . . . Nationalisms had to confront either existing state structures and seek their transformation or aspire to their own sovereign national states. In either instance, the spatial correspondence between a people, economy, culture, territory, and state consti-

> tuted the institutionalized ideal and horizon for legitimate collective struggle. (Goswami 1998, 614)

In contrast to classical theological communities, nationalism relates to the powerful organizing influences of "sovereignty" as a doctrine whose principles include "constitutional independence, non-intervention, territorial integrity, and formal reciprocity" (Scott n.d., 3). Such principles are bound up, according to some authors, with ideas of the modern state as an "irreducibly singular and secular moral-legal entity," one that is fundamentally different from the *universitas* of Christendom or Islam (ibid.). As Talal Asad notes in reference to the Islamic *umma*, it is not "a total political society, limited and sovereign like other limited and sovereign nations in a secular (social) world. The *ummat al-muslimīn* [community of Muslims] is ideologically not 'a society' onto which state, economy, and religion can be mapped." Unlike nation-state nationalisms or Arab nationalism's notion of *al-umma al-'arabiyya* (often translated as the pan-Arab nation), the Islamic umma "can and eventually should embrace all of humanity" (Asad 2003, 199).

Nationalism, in this view, is not only joined to the histories of capitalism and state formation but is also connected to the project of secularism. But what exactly does this latter relationship entail? For Asad, the imagined community implied in nationalism differs from the ancient notion of the Islamic community (*umma*) in ways that further identify the specificity of nationalism as a discourse, and in many ways this contrast is helpful. In terms of temporality, for example, classical Islamic chronicles articulating the idea of the umma derive from *ḥadīth* accounts (records of the sayings and doings of the Prophet) on which the Sunna is based,[16] and they express the political and theological conflicts among the faithful as seen through an explicitly Qur'ānic worldview (Asad 2003, 197). Islamic chronicles do not claim to "have a history" in the way that nationalist accounts of "the nation" do (ibid., 197). The theological view of the term *umma* also presupposes notions of space, collectivity, and personhood that differ from those in a nationalist episteme. Asad echoes Anderson's take on these abstractions:

> The Islamic *umma* in the classical theological view is thus not an imagined community on a par with the Arab nation waiting to be politically unified but a theologically defined space enabling Muslims to practice the disciplines of *dīn* [conventionally translated as religion] in the world. Of course the word *umma* does also have the sense of "a people"—and

> "a community"—in the Qur'ān. But the members of every community imagine it to have a particular character, and relate to one another by virtue of it. The crucial point therefore is not that it is imagined but that what is imagined predicates distinctive modes of being and acting. The Islamic *umma* presupposes individuals who are self-governing but not autonomous. The *sharī'a,* a system of practical reason morally binding on each faithful individual, exists independently of him or her. (2003, 197)

Not all nationalist ideologies presuppose autonomous individuals, as fascist versions of nationalism remind us, and surely many citizens experience secular law as existing "independently of him or her." But the contrast between the national community and the Islamic umma *does* highlight the distinct manner in which each operates—under a different logic of spatiotemporal boundedness.

The distinctions Asad notes between the national community and the umma thus suggest an elective affinity between secularism and the properties that make a movement identifiably nationalist.[17] As I shall show below, however, this should not be taken to imply, as it does for Anderson and his adherents, a linear shift from theological imaginings to national ones. Nor should it mean, as it often does, that there is a *necessary* relationship between nationalism and secularism.

To summarize thus far: the "national community," as opposed to other forms of communal imagining, implies a recognizably distinct understanding of time as abstract and uniform; of space as territorial, sovereign, and circumscribed by both the reach of state institutions and by the formalities of international recognition; and of political personhood as premised on notions of a "people"—which is sovereign by virtue of a horizontal camaraderie that is fundamentally political, humanly fashioned, and, at least in theory, protected by law. Even when discourses do not explicitly refer to nationalist ideas, people unknown to one another can come to share knowledge about events, actors, and places in ways that allow them to imagine themselves as members of discrete homogeneous collectivities, existing in calendrical clock time within a spatially demarcated territory. To put it differently, it is possible for assemblages of people to be created and organized independently of the content of nationalist discourses, but in ways that reinforce nationalism's ideological premises. These insights bear directly on the widespread portability of nationalism, or what Anderson calls its "modularity"—its availability "for pirating by widely different, and sometimes unexpected, hands" (Anderson 1991, 67). Some scholars charge Anderson with misunderstanding the specificity of anticolonial movements by insisting on nationalism's modularity, but in doing so these critics misread or disregard the most promising part of the argument.[18] Nationalism is a highly particular ideology with identifiable frames of reference that are recognizable and transposable, even under conditions dramatically different from those under which nationalism originated.

Yet bringing the Yemeni example to the fore allows us not only to deepen this analysis but also exposes the limitations of an approach too reliant on Anderson or other secularization theses. For Anderson fails to appreciate how radically modular nationalism has turned out to be, so that the relations among the components he and others took for analytical necessities now appear to have the form of historical contingencies. It is in these terms that Yemen spotlights the possibility, and indeed the empirical appearance, of nonsecular nationalisms. The aim here, taking up the third point in this section, is to specify more precisely what is involved in the constitution of contemporary nationalisms, as the condition for an adequate understanding of the ongoing processes of political subject formation.

For example, it might be tempting to see the reign of Imām Yaḥyā (1904–48), arguably the first modern state-builder of North Yemen, as gradually enabling a transition from a theologically based notion of community to a national one, and early opposition to the Imām was often framed in language accusing him of acting like a king at the head of a state (*dawla*). But this reading of a transition from one kind of community to another misleads in the Yemeni case, and it forecloses theorizing more generally about how competing understandings of time, space, community, and personhood might coexist within the heterogeneous contexts of modern nation-states.

A view that posits a comprehensive, fully realized succession from classical theology to a specifically secular nationalism fails to recognize more heterogeneous forms of collective imagining. The officially sponsored regime newspaper *al-Īmān* (1926–57), published in North Yemen, exemplifies how theological and national visions coalesced in official representations of new state institutions. In particular, the paper routinely listed new state activities, such as governmental appointments and the establishment of public works projects, but it also reported the state's application of Islamic *ḥudūd* punishments for a variety of crimes (including theft, murder, adultery, and alcohol consumption).[19] What made this paper "national," at least in part, was its geographical coverage of events and people in the context of state practices. In the application of *ḥudūd*, for example, the newspaper advertised the extent of the state's power by chronicling punishments not only in the capital of Ṣan'ā' but in the Tihāma region by the Red Sea, in the northern highlands, in Lower Yemen's city of Ta'izz, and even in Qa'ṭaba on the border of the Aden Protectorate (Willis 2007, 51). To the extent that these punishments were in fact being carried out on behalf of a state whose executive reach was becoming increasingly tenable, the newspaper both specifies and produces the national community—*and it produces the community through its specification*. It does the latter by both presuming an audience with a common knowledge of territory and generating a readership that acquired that knowledge by consuming the news. In other words, the state's institutional practices *and* the fact that they were reported by an official newspaper helped to create a distinct assemblage of fellow readers who understood the paper's references and could imagine the state's activities as part of a growing world to which readers belonged. This world was both national and theological, combining the new activities of the state with the state's enforcement of an explicitly Islamic moral order. Although it is unclear whether readers actually experienced multiple time orientations or "temporalities" in reading the newspaper, an analysis of the newspaper's content does tell us that reforms in territorial administration associated with state building were working to produce new notions of space, generating territories with legally specified jurisdictions that were conceptually and perhaps organizationally increasingly homogeneous. It also tells us that such understandings of space operated in tandem with theological justifications for state punishment, which themselves presupposed the *possibility* of sacred and clock-oriented time coexisting.

The national and the theological also coincided in the international arena. On the one hand, the North's Imām Yaḥyā and his ministers were gradually integrating Yemen into an international order through international agreements, which entailed accepting North Yemen's status as one nation-state among others. On the other, the Imām was also attempting to affirm Yemen's position, and arguably the position of the Zaydī (Shī'ī) denomination (*madhhab*), in the community of Muslim and Arab countries. In a letter to his emissary in Cairo in 1928, Imām Yaḥyā stressed his authority over Muslims everywhere:

> Further it is recognized and well-known that the Mohammedans, in accordance with the provisions of God's book, are all brethren, and there-

> fore it is of importance to us here to be able to know everything about the welfare of our brethren the Mohammedans in distant countries and we therefore order you to carry out the exhortations above referred to, and in addition to appeal to them to contribute what is due from them to the descendants of the Prophet, prayers be upon him, as a duty and as a sign of their loyalty and devotion to us owing to our lineage—such an assistance to us from the Mohammedans has been ordained by God himself, who prescribed the "Zakāt" from the income of all Moslems.[20]

But in practice Imām Yaḥyā focused on migrants living abroad, authorizing his emissary to collect the *zakāt* taxes on the grounds that the imām was the spiritual leader of Yemenis—inhabitants of both the North and the South—and the protector of their families. Such appeals were not always successful in getting people to give up income, but they laid bare the ways in which claims to a Yemeni people were conjoining with norms of moral propriety to reinforce simultaneously both a national and a pious notion of citizenship. Although it is true that a *sharīʿa* politics based on religious denominational (*madhhab*) categories gradually shifted to make a nation-state politics more prominent, novel conceptions of citizenship did not entail the total eclipse of pious ideas or practices. Nor did it mean, in North Yemen's case, the simple relegation of religion to the private sphere, as secularizing projects generally imply (although it did tend to mean that in the South). The point is that these and subsequent changes cannot be described as stages in the linear development of a fully realized secular sensibility, but rather enabled new combinations both rhetorically and institutionally of piety and national collectivity.[21]

The Yemeni example underscores the problems with a theory of nationalism that posits a complete shift, as if homogeneous empty time proceeded from messianic time as "pure succession."[22] Conflating nationalist, modernist formulations of time with an analysis of how time actually gets reconceived, such theories thereby participate in the linear narration of history they seek to interrogate. An Andersonian formulation of national identity also suggests a comprehensive transformation from familial, kin-based persons to autonomous individuals. Those inspired by Anderson sometimes go further, presuming that a national subject is necessarily a liberal one (see Asad 2003; Agrama 2005). But assertions of horizontal fraternity do not in themselves imply, nor do political developments suggest, that nationalism necessarily presumes autonomous, liberal individuals.

Moreover, although distinctions between nation and umma are instructive, the latter concept should not be seen as synechdochic with or analogous to piety in general. There are forms of piety in Yemen and elsewhere that cohere more easily with national logics than the notion of an Islamic umma does. Ministries of religious affairs (or sometimes, of religious guidance) across the Middle East, for example, speak not to the entire umma but to the country-specific Muslim citizen, a form of address that inspires denunciations by some Islamic organizations.[23] And certain ideas of piety, as we shall see in later chapters, have become conceivable only within a nationalizing project.

To put my argument in schematic terms: (1) Anderson helps us understand what makes the "nation form" distinctive. What distinguishes nationalism from other forms of collective belonging is the way in which national solidarities imply a specific relation to space and time, one that is inextricably tied to modern notions of sovereignty—invested in a people and realized (ideally) through common state institutions. (2) But Anderson and scholars inspired by him fail to distinguish adequately between this generic aspect of nationalism and its historical dimension, which is to say that they overgeneralize the historical connection in the West between the idea of the nation and the project of secularism in particular. Some historians have pointed out that even in the West this historical connection may not be as neat empirically as Anderson tends to suggest.[24] The ideas of time, space, sovereignty, personhood, and collectivity implied by nationalism as a secular project could outlive or become modular even when secularism proved less totalizing than it was in some Western liberal countries. (3) By overgeneralizing the relationship between secularism and nationalism, scholars miss certain critical implications of their own work. Discourses, whether they concern piety or national solidarity, evolve. And because identities are fluid and contextual, human beings can and do experience their lives in terms of multiple temporalities or time frames. Thus, nationalism often develops in tandem with other ideologies or master narratives, and sometimes combines with them. Many theorists of nationalism, not simply Anderson, exaggerate the primacy of nationalist imaginings, as if once indulged, they are all-consuming.

THE PERFORMATIVE POLITICS OF WORDS AND OTHER DEEDS

By emphasizing the nation as a historically contingent category, *Peripheral Visions* specifies the "work" particular discourses do—how the use of words, the understanding of abstract concepts, and the enactment of everyday practices produce specific logics and generate observable political effects. References throughout this book to the "work" performed by discourses are meant to refer both to their observable political effects, when evident (especially in the ethnographic sections), and to their specific logics, when a more analytic approach is called for. These logics do not imply that scholars can know what actors' intentions are; rather, the term "logics" denotes how words and concepts make sense in specific contexts; their intelligibility comes from the ways in which language and institutions are embedded in a social world of iterative actions and performative practices.

This focus on performative practices requires some elaboration. Practices are actions or deeds that are repeated over time; they are learned, reproduced, and subjected to risk through social interaction.[25] Practices are also, in the sense I use the term, unique to human beings. Like actions (as opposed to "behaviors"), they involve "freedom, choice, and responsibility, meaning and sense, conventions, norms, and rules" (Pitkin 1993, 242). They may be self-consciously executed, but they need not be. They tend to be intelligible to others in context-dependent ways. Practices are ultimately "dual," composed both of what "the outside observer can see and of the actors' understandings of what they are doing" (Pitkin 1993, 261; also discussed in Wedeen 2002). As this book argues, the importance of everyday practices to nationalism (as well as to other kinds of political imaginings) does not reside simply in the meanings they signify to their practitioners, but also in the ways in which they constitute the self through his or her performance as an explicitly national (or, in chapter 3, democratic) person in the absence of a strong state or an institutionalized, procedural democracy.

The word "performative" was initially invoked by J. L. Austin to describe particular kinds of speech acts in which the utterance is the act itself: "I promise" or "I protest" or "I bet" are examples of performatives.[26] Derrida's use of "performativity" to refer to an "iterable practice" (1988) has been adopted by subsequent theorists to articulate a theory of self formation in which the iterative character of speech and bodily activities constitute individuals as specific kinds of social beings or "subjects." Through the repeated performance of practices, in this view, the person's desires, understandings, and bodily comportment come to acquire a particular, recognizable form (Butler 1993, 1997; Mahmood 2005, 162–63; see also

Bourdieu 1991).[27] *Peripheral Visions* takes from this literature an appreciation for the ways in which the category of the national citizen, for example, is actualized through the performance of norms associated with nationalism. Nationalist actions, in this light, may be understood as performatives because they enact that which they name, a national self or "subject."[28]

The concept of "performativity" as I am using it here needs to be distinguished from other genealogies of performance in anthropology.[29] Performatives refer to a structural logic, while performance refers to an event.[30] Some events or performances have this structural logic—the act that brings into being the very thing invoked—while others do not. Analyzing this logic in any particular situation requires specifying issues of context. Thus, although many theories of performativity do not operate in sociological terms, there is nothing about such arguments that precludes thinking contextually.[31] In the Yemeni case, for example, a poet who declares himself as a proud Yemeni thereby helps constitute himself as one, just as a politician who addresses an audience of the "Yemeni people" summons that assemblage into being through the declaration.[32] As we shall see, some performatives are explicit enunciations, while others are actions indexing a particular concept (such as nationalism, democracy, or piety, to name relevant examples for this book). I can act patriotically, thereby constituting myself as a patriot without overtly calling myself a patriot, for instance. The same can be said for concepts as diverse as bravery, bachelorhood, piety, and so forth.

Emphasizing practices as "performative" relates to my treatment of issues of "identity" throughout this book. Rather than think of identities as antecedent facts about people that help determine their actions, I follow Hannah Arendt in understanding identities as what results from public speech and action; *through* public words and deeds, actors "make their appearance" in the world (Arendt 1958, 179; also discussed in Markell 2003, 13). As Patchen Markell notes, "one important consequence of this is that identity, for Arendt, is not something over which agents themselves have control. Because we do not act in isolation but interact with others, who we become through action is not [simply] up to us; instead, it is the outcome of many intersecting and unpredictable sequences of action and response, such that 'nobody is the author or producer of his own life story' " (Markell 2003, 13; Arendt 1958, 184). By emphasizing the "performative" aspects of identity formation, I show not only that nationalism is actualized in nationalist practices but also that national persons themselves are formed by the speech and bodily acts associated with nationalism. Similarly, to take another example, it is not simply that democratic virtues cause or are realized in particular kinds of democratic acts but also that democratic persons are themselves constituted through the doing of democratic deeds.[33]

This approach to practices does not imply that nationalist persons believe in nationalism or that people acting democratically are necessarily committed to democracy. If, in interpreting actions in this way, I privilege intelligibility over deep-seated meanings, I do so for the following reason: Intelligibility does not presuppose grasping an inner essence or getting into the heads of informants understood as captive minds of a system, but rather is centered on the ways in which people attempt to make apparent, observable sense of their worlds—to themselves and to each other—in emotional and cognitive terms. In stark contrast to grasping an inner essence, this conceptualization of meaning requires us to discover what in fact we know (that children are saluting a flag or ballots are being checked and counted, for example) and what we need to know (what work this flag salute or ballot tallying is doing in the context in which it is happening). Such an inquiry then prompts us to ask questions about the conditions under which specific material and semiotic activities emerge, the contexts in which they find public expression, the consequences they have in the world, and the irregularities they generate in the process of reproduction. By focusing on the logics of a discourse and its political effects in material practices, we can specify how ideas relate to institutions; how group identities are summoned into existence; and how publics—national, deliberative, pious, and transnational—get made.

METHODS, SOURCES, AND CHAPTER ORGANIZATION

Recent research in political science has championed the use of "multi- or mixed methods," advocating the combination of sundry quantitative methods with "narrative" ones.[34] *Peripheral Visions* also employs multiple methods, but all of them are recognizably *interpretivist* in orientation.[35] I adopt a practice-oriented approach to language and other symbolic systems, while blending participant observation techniques with careful readings of texts. In preparing the book, I have conducted more than eighteen months of fieldwork throughout Yemen, from 1998 to 2004. This has entailed in-depth ethnographic work as well as open-ended interviews with ordinary men and women from diverse regions and class backgrounds, including politicians from various political parties.[36] Ethnographic work tends to imply an enmeshment in the social, semiotic world under investigation. I participated in the daily life of Yemenis through ordinary conversations and interaction, by observing and sometimes taking part in activities (including social gatherings, regime-run electoral events, and protests), examining gossip, jokes, and other informal speech acts, and recording this data in field notes. Open-ended interviews lasted between one and four hours. I approached people through what social scientists call "snowball sampling," whereby initial contacts generate new ones.

The processes of national belonging this project examines include the development of a "historical consciousness"—the purportedly collective memories, national myths, and Qur'ānic references in which understandings of Yemeni-ness come to the fore; the political procedures of unification; narratives and ongoing observation of regime coercion and co-optation; and phenomena associated with "globalization" (e.g., the end of the cold war, neoliberal economic reforms, and new patterns of migration). Source materials therefore include cassette tapes of Friday mosque sermons, regional poetry and songs, intellectuals' conferences and social gatherings, historical narratives of Yemen's ancient origins, newspapers, biographies of political figures, political iconography, official spectacles, maps, published data on migratory patterns, and nongovernmental organization (NGO) surveys. These materials offer perspectives that have allowed me to understand the importance of both everyday practices *and* extraordinary events, not only for establishing group solidarities of various kinds but also for occasioning acts of deliberative democracy in the absence of contested elections. Almost all conversations were in Arabic and all of the translations are my own unless otherwise specified.[37]

The book is organized into five chapters. Each chapter can be read as a discrete essay or as part of a sustained, cumulative set of arguments. Chapter 1 explains the dynamics of national belonging in the making. Combining historical synthesis with some ethnography and interviews, the chapter considers the imaginative status of Yemen historically and the conditions under which actual unification took place, the role of radio and poetry in the 1950s, and the ways in which even a fragile state can instill in its citizenry intermittent attachments to a national community. Chapter 2 is primarily ethnographic, discussing three exemplary events in Yemen to dramatize the relationship between state power and the experience of citizenship in the aftermath of national unification in 1990. It demonstrates how national belonging may actually be shared in the breach of state authority—in the moments when large numbers of citizens, unknown to each other, long for its protection. Chapter 3 operates as a hinge chapter, exploring more fully a proposition introduced in chapter 2, that in fragile authoritarian states (with weak capacities to generate national loyalty) opportunities for widespread political activism and critical, public discussion may be enhanced. It too is ethnographic, using the example of quotidian *qāt* chews to show how everyday practices of political contestation outside electoral channels confound aspects of both minimalist conceptions of democracy as contested elections and a Habermasian story about the origins of and conditions for public spheres. The chapter demonstrates how specific performative practices can create distinctly democratic publics, some but not all of which can also be understood as national ones. Chapter 4 focuses on the recent battles between the regime and the organization Believing Youth (Shabāb al-Mu'minīn) to advance our understandings of identity formation more generally. Using newspaper reports, religious and political pamphlets, open-ended interviews, and some ethnographic work (outside the immediate conflict zone), I look at the evolving Islamic "discursive tradition"[38]—the changing ways in which adherents relate to and are constituted through their engagement with sacred texts. By examining how this tradition articulates with the history of contemporary nation-states and the changing forms of nationalist movements themselves, this chapter exposes certain problems with prevailing classifications and explanations while attending to local debates about scriptural interpretation, national solidarity, party politics, and the permissibility of rebellion. Chapter 5 situates contemporary pious solidarities in terms of broader historical, political, and economic processes, while also using the Yemeni case to refine our general theorizations about both the reasons for the Islamic revival and the forms of circulation through which it works.

THE MAIN ARGUMENTS

Studying political identity formation yields the following interrelated propositions about nationalism. First, there is no necessary connection between idioms of national solidarity and the likelihood of political stability, as such national imaginings can be used to challenge existing regimes as well as to naturalize them. Second, national solidarities are rarely as all-encompassing as students of nationalism presume; they can happen episodically, be conveyed anonymously, and solidify suddenly, only to collapse once again in apathy or discord. Third, in the absence of a robust network of state institutions, traumatic political events and the public discussions they inspire can produce conditions in which a putative "nation" of citizens takes shape in the form of a demand for a state capable of protecting them.

Public sphere activities facilitate nation-ness to the extent that they create specific assemblages of fellow participants who have come to share the everyday experience of communicating with others within the limited, territorially sovereign space of the nation-state. But the content of these discussions does not necessarily presume a national identity or use vocabulary suggestive of one. The Yemeni example shows too that the public addressed in quotidian social gatherings can be both broader and more indeterminate, or narrower and more specifically local, than a national one. Thus, the significance of these public interactions also resides in their profoundly political character, in the ways in which they make possible an addressing of others in terms that connect actors' diverse and contentious interests to a common venture (see Pitkin 1993, 216; Arendt 1958, 52). In this light, I contrast entrenched minimalist formulations of "democracy" as contested elections with civic participation and the formation of "public spheres," arguing that the latter must be understood as activities of democratic expression in their own right. In shifting attention away from the formal dimensions of electoral competition to the substance of participatory politics, this study explores how public sphere practices occasion the performance of an explicitly democratic "subjectivity" (or presentation of self)—one that relishes deliberation—without producing specifically liberal debates or forms of personhood. These deliberative practices, as they reveal themselves in Yemen, have arisen under conditions fundamentally different from the ones that Habermas (1996) and others have identified as seminal to the Western European experience. Analyzing the example of Yemen is thus an exercise in theory building. It requires us to question not only what we mean by democracy but also to consider anew the factors conducive to the cultivation of democratic practices, even in the absence of a democratic regime.

By foregrounding Yemen's experiment in national unity and attending to the everyday practices of deliberative contestation, this book also provides the context needed to investigate how contemporary expressions of piety operate in relation to nationalist imaginings. For anthropologists, my findings suggest that nationalism and piety can and do coalesce in ways that not only demand decoupling nationalism from secularism[39] but also necessitate unsettling assertions about the historical relationship between "neoliberal" reforms and the proliferation of piety movements. For political scientists, my arguments require abandoning the assumption that pious solidarities are deleterious for nationalist ones or pose strict alternatives to them. Such claims may be missing how weak states can benefit from the assumption of welfare services by charitable organizations.[40] By considering what sermons and pamphlets say, moreover, this book grounds an understanding of current pious movements in the political-ethical dilemmas of the present.

As is perhaps obvious, the title of the book plays on the dual meaning of "peripheral visions." On the one hand, the term "peripheral" means located in or constituting an outer boundary or periphery. Yemen is in many ways a peripheral country in the current global configuration, one of the poorest countries in the world, and a country geographically situated on the outer boundary of the Arabian Peninsula. In this sense, "peripheral visions" refers to perspectives offered by those residing at the economic, political, and geographic margins. On the other hand, "peripheral vision" refers to the activity of perceiving near the outer edges of the field of vision, of seeing out of the corner of one's eye. In this sense, the book invites its readers to see in unconventional ways, to question comfortable assumptions, and to catch a glimpse of nationalism and democracy not as linear, perhaps even teleological, processes to which individuals subscribe, but as a series of ongoing practices that people enact.

CHAPTER ONE

IMAGINING UNITY

On the eve of unification in 1990, what is now the Republic of Yemen consisted of two distinct polities with different histories, ideological underpinnings, and loyalty claims. This chapter considers the imaginative status of a unified Yemen historically and explores the conditions that made unity conceivable and practical. In what ways did a sense of Yemeni-ness precede political unification? Where did ideas about Yemen as a nation come from? If Yemeni nationalism is a constructed phenomenon, as much of the scholarship on nationalism would presume, then constructed out of what? And how do ideas about Yemeni-ness articulate with other claims to solidarity, ones based on piety, neighborhood, or Arab ethnicity, to name just a few?

My goal in this chapter is twofold: to relate a brief history of the circumstances under which the existence of a unified nation-state became possible, and to intervene in key theoretical debates about the nature of nationalism and the social, historical, and political processes associated with it. Part 1 begins with a historical analysis. It not only identifies some of the changing meanings of *Yaman* but also specifies the background conditions under which two respective "geographies of rule" (Willis 2004) came to exist in the two independent nation-states established in the 1960s. Part 2 examines the multiple meanings of *Yaman* current in the period when nationalist ideas came to the fore. It highlights the critical role of communications technology, as well as that of preexisting cultural forms, especially poetry, in expressing and disseminating the idioms of national, affective connection (both Yemeni and pan-Arab) in the 1950s and 1960s. Part 3 discusses the circumstances precipitating formal unification in 1990. It illustrates how strategic interests are constructed through a semiotic world in which national unification could already be seen as desirable and commonsensical.

As I suggested in the introduction, the historical situation characterizing the recent development of nationalism in Yemen is in many ways unlike the one in which the idea of the "nation" originated. In particular, this history has transpired under conditions in which state institutions proved incapable of inculcating national values. Yet even in places such as Yemen where robust state institutions were absent, the idea of the "nation form" (Balibar 1991) proved remarkably portable, and like others around the world, Yemenis came gradually to imagine themselves as a people, located in a territorially determinate space with seemingly like-minded, anonymous others.[1] The Yemeni example nevertheless also makes clear that nationalist imaginings do not necessarily proceed in a linear way or in complete succession from older (e.g., sacred or familial) conceptions of belonging.

In this chapter, I demonstrate how understandings of the nation find expression in and overlap with other solidarities; how they get generated through textual practices and social interaction; and how conflicts about specific imagined worlds become provisionally settled through the combined effects of violence, elite "pacts," and the iteration of ordinary activities.

PART ONE:
HISTORICAL BACKGROUND

Scholars of Yemen tend to emphasize the ways in which the modern space of nineteenth- and early twentieth-century Ottoman and imamate control in the North, and British colonial administration in the South, were products of innovative organizational and technical capacities for managing populations, ones that also introduced new legal, moral, and social categories of rule.[2] These scholars reaffirm Michel Foucault's understanding of modern power as generative, as having the capacity to produce particular kinds of "subjects," or selves.[3] In this view the law, to take one prominent example, plays a central role in constituting the subject as citizen by specifying what counts as citizenship. Similarly, the law creates wives and husbands by defining who can be married and who cannot. According to Foucault, the traditional liberal understanding of the individual seeking representation before the law, as a subject who literally comes prior to and is the author of the law, is misguided. Citizens do not make the laws; laws, in part by codifying the legal categories of belonging, make citizens. The importance of classificatory practices is also underscored in Foucault's well-known discussion of the appearance of marginal or "perverted" sexualities and their scientific categorization into specific types in the West. It was not that the activities to which these classifications referred had not existed before, but that their categorization brought them into being in a new way, one that marked a shift in the understanding of sexuality from an unconnected series of acts to the expression of a deeply rooted identity.[4] That identity derived from the ways in which such classifications were invoked, institutionalized, and internalized. When Foucault discusses how "power constitutes the subject," he is referring to the ways in which, in our case, the modern nationalist emerged as a particular type of person. In Ian Hacking's summary, new categories of people generate "new ways for people to be" (Hacking 1986).

In the following, I do not contend that the reach of the British colonial administration in the South (1839–1967) was as extensive as a strict Foucauldian account might imply. Nor was the Ottoman occupation of the North (1872–1918) a fully coherent or all-encompassing project. In fact, Ottoman occupation over parts of North Yemen coexisted with local imamate rule over other parts, and under Imām Yaḥyā's rule (1904–48) Ottoman control gradually ceded territory and jurisdictional authority to him, even before the Ottomans' formal withdrawal in 1918. What I want to demonstrate here is how political circumstances in all three regimes, British colonial, Ottoman, and imamic, drew upon prior, conventional understandings while also generating new categories of collectivity and subjectivity. These categories, both old and new, combined with everyday practices of cross-border communication to make possible novel and conflicting conceptions of *Yaman*, ones that authorized competing yet explicitly national political imperatives. The changing meanings of *Yaman* and *Yamanī*, as we shall see, were inflected by historical circumstances, including the modes of classification associated with British colonial and Ottoman rule in the South and North, respectively, the concomitant dynamics of early state formation in the North's ruling imamate, the emergence of borders, and the introduction of nationalist ideas in the 1920s and 1930s.

In considering the historical conditions that made unification of North and South thinkable, it is worth noting that the term Yemen (*Yaman*) is considerably older than identifiable aspirations for a single nation-state or the emergence of the two separate Yemens in the 1960s, which is to say that the idea of Yemen as a single *political* entity preceded the establishment of two independent nation-states in the 1960s, or formal unification in 1990.[5] Important historical antecedents to Yemen's twentieth-century "imagined unities" include repeated invocations of the term *Yaman* in the *ḥadīth* (Traditions of the Prophet) to indicate the territory south of Mecca, and the centuries-old identification of various local literatures and practices as explicitly *Yamanī* (Dresch 2000).[6] In the mid-seventeenth century, the Qāsimī dynasty controlled much of the territory associated with the current Republic of Yemen, and nationalists could retrospectively point to that history to demonstrate Yemen's coherence. So too could they highlight the fact that there was no formal border between North and South until 1905 (although there were and continue to be geographical markers, such as mountain passes—the *naqīl yislaḥ* or the *naqīl sumāra*—that separate northern highlands from southern lowlands).

In short, nationalist movements beginning in the 1920s and 1930s, as well as the poetry, songs, and stories they fostered, drew on, but also invested novel political significance in, specific background conditions. Under colonial, Ottoman, and imamic rule, people and texts had circulated interregionally as a result of the exigencies of trade and labor. Contact had been facilitated by the travels of scholars and workers, the circulation of goods via camel and beginning in the 1950s through trucking links, and the dissemination of newspapers, literature, and legal writings. By the 1950s, Aden, in particular, became a gateway for inhabitants in both territories to gain access not only to one another but to regional and global sources of information (Douglas 1987; Messick 1993, 30; see also Carapico 1998, especially 23–26; Dresch 2000, 74). Key figures in what was to become the socialist People's Democratic Republic of Yemen (PDRY) in the South after independence from British colonial rule in 1967 originated from the North, and politicians in the North's Yemen Arab Republic (YAR), established in 1962, hailed from the South. Complementing this circulation of people and goods were existing understandings of a place called *Yaman*,

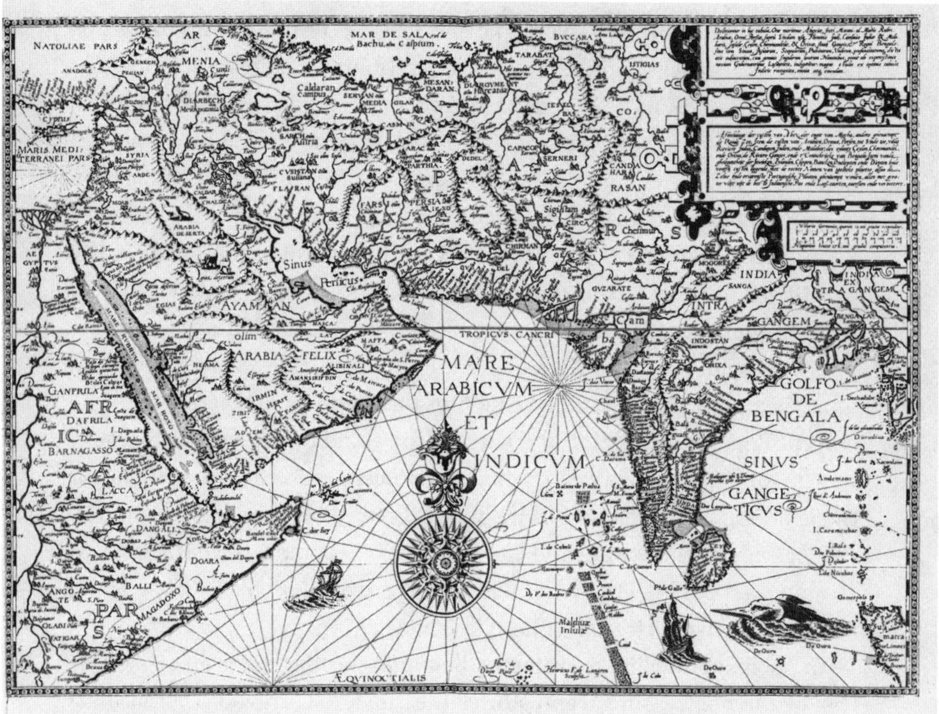

Map 1.1: Map covering the area from Oxus to Sumatra and from the Nile Valley to the coast of Burma, produced by Henricus Langren to depict the travels of the explorer Jan Huyghen van Linschoten (1596). Inspired by Giacomo Gastaldi, credited with producing the first modern map of Arabia, this illustration situates Arabia in the broader worlds of the Indian Ocean and Horn of Africa. Among geographers of the ancient world, Arabia was conventionally divided into three main zones: the region bordering the Indian Ocean (including the relatively fertile area of modern Yemen) denoted as Arabia Felix (or happy Arabia), the Arabia Deserta (desert interior), and Arabia Petraea (the zone controlled from Petra in modern-day Jordan). Copied from G. R. Tibbetts, *Arabia in Early Maps: A Bibliography of Maps Covering the Peninsula of Arabia Printed in Western Europe from the Invention of Printing to the Year 1751* (Cambridge: Falcon-Oleander, 1978), 55.

Map 1.2: Map of the Kingdom of Yemen in Arabia Felix (1716). Illustrated to portray the explorer Jean de La Roque's travels, Guillaume de L'Isle's map shows jurisdictional divisions among areas controlled by the sharīf of Medina, the sharīf of Mecca, the kingdom of Yemen, the kingdom of Muscat, and the kingdom of Fartach. Note that Yemen here covers the entire southern part of the Arabian Peninsula, with the exception of the kingdom of Fartach. Copied from Tibbetts (1978, 135). Local geographers of Yemen provided rich descriptions of life and climatic conditions, but they did not tend to draw maps.

a word indexing a territory that, in the context of nationalist discourses, could be made the object of attachment for an imagined people.

Notions of Yemen as a single political entity notwithstanding, likewise in train were processes leading to the formal creation in the 1960s of two separate and independent nation-states. Given the presence of nationalist discourses advocating the establishment of a single Yemen by the 1930s and the historical ambiguities over jurisdiction, which might have made several small states viable, the founding of two nation-states requires some explanation in its own right. Unification in the 1990s cannot be understood

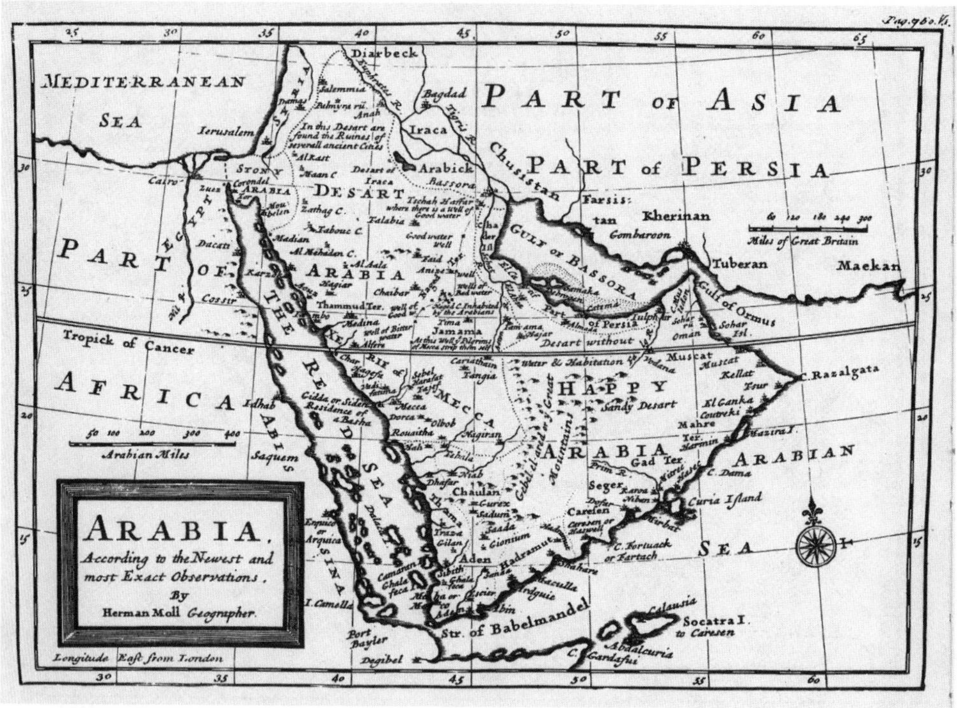

Map 1.3: Map of the Arabian Peninsula by Herman Moll (1712). Note here how the peninsula is understood as a whole and not in terms of nation-state distinctions. Copied from Tibbetts (1978, 130).

without exploring the conditions that made two states realizable in the 1960s. And this earlier history also underscores some of the key theoretical claims of the book: that the nation is a contingent category rather than a substantial thing; that its conceptual portability as a structuring idiom for political imaginings in the twentieth century is tied to notions, if not the actual fact, of territorial sovereignty; that the nation form's distinctiveness has to do with the particular visions of community, time, space, and personhood that nationalism as an ideology brought to the fore; that nationalism often combined with other understandings of solidarity and subjectivity to produce hybrid experiences of political belonging; and that the effects of official classifications, colonial or otherwise, were to presuppose and thereby summon into existence new groups, opening up novel possibilities for political being and action, even under conditions of weak internal control.

Colonial Classifications: British Rule in the South

In the South, the British constructed a colonial administration along a familiar pattern: British authorities separated Aden from its hinterland, self-consciously adopting different modes of rule based on the categorical distinction between "city" and "tribes" (Willis 2004, 120).[7] In 1850, Aden was declared a free port, with the explicit aim of increasing trade and strengthening a new commercial class that, according to the statements of British administrators, would provide the basis for a British-friendly civil society (Willis 2004, 121). The Aden Act of 1864, in turn, created a court system inspired by Indian legal procedures, restricting religious law to issues of inheritance and personal status. The effect of these measures in Aden, as elsewhere in the empire, was to grant "religion" a public existence as a private phenomenon. "Religion," while produced by and subject to repeated administrative interventions, was a legal category that relegated piety to private life (Asad 2003, 230–31).

If Aden was the locus of new legal frameworks and new conceptions of what the law could and should do, colonial policy in the South's hinterland had the stated objective of protecting Aden from disorder and was therefore not subject to the same legal or secularization measures.[8] The British constructed elaborate fortifications and policed immigration from the hinterland into Aden. British colonial administrators also sought to preserve what they identified as political practices specific to the hinterland by promoting policies termed "nonintervention" and "indirect rule" there.[9] The paradox of such policies, however, is that although they aimed ostensibly at protecting traditional ways of social and political life, they also produced new forms of community, new political interests on the part of local elites and their constituencies, and a new body of knowledge around the social category of the "tribe." This colonial discourse took shape and evolved in relation to local realities and social actors, of course, but it also helped to transform them, organizing, at least formally, existing social and political relationships into a system that was comprehensible and legible to colonial rulers.

In other words, the self-understandings of colonial officials generated the need for new modes of intervention and forms of knowledge. These in turn had the unintended consequence of posing novel challenges to colonial administration on the ground. For example, in an effort to secure the hinterland, the British identified nine tribes, sometimes termed "cantons": the 'Abdalī, 'Aqrabī, 'Alawī, Amīrī, 'Awlaqī, Faḍlī, Ḥawshabī, Ṣubayḥī, and Yāfi'ī, thereby collapsing other forms of association into this dominant classificatory grid (Gavin 1975; Willis 2004). Inhabitants' own practices of belonging, however, rarely conformed neatly to the categories under which they were officially grouped, and in many instances the use of the terms "tribe" or "chief" obscured the political realities it was intended to illuminate (Gavin 1975, 201). In particular, the word "tribe" was used to indicate a political or administrative unity that often did not exist.[10] British reliance on local leaders also led to complications because local leaders—created by the British or empowered by them—had a tenuous allegiance to the colonial project and were often less capable of ensuring stability than colonial officials had assumed. Rival leaders in the hinterland made alliances with the Ottomans or with the imām against the British. In short, colonially constructed "tribes" did not turn out to be cohesive units with stable leaderships (Willis 2004). Nevertheless, activities such as the geographical survey of 1891–92 and the subsequent Anglo-Turkish Boundary Commission of 1902–05 located inhabitants in a particular geographical landscape, helping to shape the contours of postcolonial rule. Colonial domination was also to produce felicitous conditions for the emergence of an explicitly national liberation struggle beginning between 1920 and 1940, one that derived inspiration from other nationalist movements in British, French, Dutch, and Belgian territories.

British colonialism's effects were thus mixed. On the one hand, Foucauldian scholars or others who focus primarily on colonial discourses are likely to exaggerate the success of colonial "hegemony," mistaking the stated claims or "will to power" of colonial rulers with colonialism's actual consequences. But this would be a mistake, and Yemen is no anomaly in this respect. The Yemeni case dramatizes a form of colonial rule apparent in much of Africa as well (see Herbst 2000), one in which administrative efforts to map territory proved particularly important in establishing a security grid to protect commercial interests, without requiring expensive formal systems of administration. Nevertheless, and pace scholars who contend that colonialism's effects were minimal, in Yemen the creation of classificatory systems that divided port town from countryside, the determination of what counted as a relevant "tribe," the empowerment of some local leaders and the diminution of the authority of others, the promulgation of legal codes that relegated religion to the private domain, and ultimately the formation of boundaries between a north and a south were to have a lasting, if not all-determining, impact on postcolonial politics, helping both to shape the form that nationalist imaginings took and to define the nature of political struggle.

The Copresence of Ottomans and the Imamate in the North

The North's specific "geography of rule" is best exemplified by the copresence of Ottoman rule with the institution of the imamate. North Yemen was primarily a land of peasant sharecroppers and independent farmers and herders in which tribute collection coexisted with modes of communal production. It was characterized by a different ordering logic than the South, one in which the Ottoman Turks vied for territory and jurisdiction with Zaydī rulers of the local imamate. Spiritual and temporal authority were justified, despite theological differences, in terms of each party's defense of the *sharīʿa* (Messick 1993, 50; Willis 2004).[11]

The Ottomans occupied North Yemen twice, first when they absorbed parts of the North in the sixteenth century only to be driven out in the seventeenth by a particularly powerful dynasty, the Qāsimīs; second when troops belonging to Muḥammad ʿAlī Pāshā, the Ottoman governor of Egypt, acquired the southern highland province of Taʿizz in Yemen in 1837. According to the historian Khaled Fahmy (1997), Muḥammad ʿAlī Pāshā's conquests bespoke his own ambitions to reconfigure the Ottoman order from the province of Cairo.[12] This was not a "proto-nationalist" project to build a territorially bounded nation-state of Egypt, but an effort to expand imperial authority (Mitchell 2002b, 180).[13] In the context of an ensuing great power rivalry between the British and the Ottomans provoked in part by Muḥammad ʿAlī's independent initiatives and British responses to them, the Ottomans took Ṣanʿā', the capital city of present-day Yemen, and created an administration whose coexistence with local rulers of the imamate lasted until the empire's demise in 1918.

During the course of their rule, the Ottomans established small, regular military detachments in towns and constructed barracks, a move that would later inspire Yemenis to shift from quartering soldiers in homes to housing a professional army in dedicated facilities (Messick 1993, 248; see also Zabāra 1956, vol. 3, 13; Nājī 1976; al-ʿInān 1983, 8–18). This second

Ottoman occupation also introduced document registration, which had the effect of creating a state archiving system for legal documents such as wills and land deeds (Messick 1998, 48). The Ottomans set up a local bureaucracy staffed by inhabitants of northern Yemen, and many judges and administrators spoke Turkish. The Ottomans were also able to co-opt local notables in Lower Yemen (the southern part of North Yemen), but they had difficulty subduing the populations northwards.

The partial conquest of North Yemen by the Ottomans from 1872 to 1918 did bear *some* resemblance to British imperial policies in the South, allowing us to consider the connections between colonial orders and competing notions of Yemeni-ness over time: Ottoman bureaucrats and intellectuals stressed the cultural inferiority of the local population and depicted the conquest as a civilizing mission that would ultimately enable locals to be assimilated into the empire as citizens (Kühn 2002, 192). As in British and French colonial cases, visions of assimilation were also counteracted by narratives emphasizing North Yemen's status as a colony, the inhabitants of which were not meant to be integrated but simply ruled (Kühn 2003, 5). And competing understandings about the local population revolved largely around ideas of governance similar to those employed by the British, presupposing that a conquered population could be ruled effectively if "accurate" knowledge about their "culture" could be ascertained (ibid.). In the case of the Ottomans, this knowledge relied critically on a denominational distinction between Zaydīs/Shīʿīs and Shāfiʿīs/Sunnīs. On the one hand, this distinction obscured important ways in which the Zaydī imamate had already been redefined in Sunnī terms in the eighteenth century by the exceptionally influential jurist al-Shawkānī (Haykel 2003; al-Shawkānī 2000).[14] On the other, Ottoman claims to rule nevertheless *did* tend to be stronger in regions designated as Sunnī/Shāfiʿī in Lower Yemen, as evidenced by the relative success of Ottoman efforts to impose institutions in those areas, collecting *zakāt* (Islamic taxes) and establishing religious schools.

Despite similarities between British colonial rule and Ottoman occupation, there were also key divergences. First, Ottoman rulers and intellectuals understood Yemenis explicitly as Muslims and made appeals to rule on the basis of a purportedly shared connection to Islam, which committed adherents (at least in principle) to common practices of moral propriety. Second, Ottoman rule competed with the growing strength of Imām

Yaḥyā, to be discussed below, and was hobbled by the empire's troubles elsewhere. Therefore, many of the modernizing ambitions of the Ottoman administration remained unfulfilled: plans for cadastral surveys, censuses, and other strategies to organize the population frequently were not carried through, and an agreement in 1911 with the Ottomans gave Imām Yaḥyā significant autonomy over key parts of North Yemen.[15] Given that the British colonial project in the South was a minor enterprise in comparison to British efforts in other places, Ottoman colonial rule in the North seems to have been even more superficial. With the empire's growing weakness, Ottoman rulers often seemed less interested in maintaining a durable administration than in acquiring quick wealth through extortionist tax-gathering methods (Farah 2002, 212). And although there were some attempts to instill a sense of "Ottomanism" in members of the learned elite, Yemenis trained by Ottoman Turks were not expected to make the administrative rounds in the rest of the empire, in part because Yemenis were understood to be particularly backward. In this the Ottoman project as implemented in Yemen differed from the way it was organized elsewhere (Kühn 2003).

Coincident with Ottoman rule was the imamate. The imāms of North Yemen, like other leaders in the Middle East historically, ruled in the name of Islam. In addition to being a free adult, sound in mind and body, pious, and generous, the imām also had to be both a *mujāhid*, a warrior in the name of religion, and a *mujtahid*, a skillful, scholarly interpreter of Islamic law (*sharī'a*) (Willis 2004, 128; Messick 1993, 38; Wenner 1967, 31). In theory, a learned man became the imām through his summons to allegiance (*da'wa*) and his willingness to rise against illegitimate rule (*khurūj*) (Haykel 2003). In actuality, this meant that an imām's authority was frequently contested and precarious, for in both principle and practice there could be and were many claimants to the imamate. Oaths of allegiance could be withdrawn as well as given, and the very nature of the imām's moral authority presupposed a land of disorder or impiety in need of being "returned to the domain of obedience" (*ḥaẓīrat al-ṭā'a*) (Willis 2004). That return generally necessitated the presence of an imām or his troops.[16] As Messick argues, the space of the old imamic administration "was, in part, created through the movements of the imām and his armies through the countryside" (Messick 1993, 248). The local existence of this administration was constituted by the presence of officials who made their daily rounds in the markets and streets, by the extension of his person through his sons occupying provincial posts, and by the circulation of texts bearing his seal (ibid.). These practices of officialdom helped actualize imamic rule by making the imām's person and the signs of his bureaucratic and coercive power visible to the population.

There were several claimants to the imamate when the Ottomans arrived in Ṣan'ā' in 1872, but by 1904 Imām Yaḥyā had successfully assumed the mantle, gradually gaining control of large swaths of territory in the North under a power-sharing arrangement with Ottoman officials.[17] Imām Yaḥyā's initial claims to rule blended expressions of Islamic piety with what might retrospectively be termed "proto-national" sentiments. But these statements differ significantly from later nationalist rhetoric in illuminating ways. Consider, for example, Imām Yaḥyā's reply to a mission of religious scholars from Mecca sent by the Ottomans to mediate in 1906–07:

> The land of Yemen was in the hands of our ancestors, the most noble family [i.e., the Prophet's kin], from the third century [of Islam] to the present, and never has there not been a claimant to that right, whether ruling all Yemen or part of it, as is known from the chronicles of Yemen. There were constant battles between our ancestors and those who opposed them, thus opposing the wish of the people (*ahl*) of Yemen to be ruled by their lords and the sons of their Prophet, may God be pleased with them. . . . They have no desire save to order the right and extirpate what is loathsome and reprehensible, to establish the sharī'a, set straight he who strays, and advise the ignorant. (al-Wāsi'ī 1991, 304–5; also cited in Dresch 2000, 6; from al-Wāsi'ī, 1928 edition, 213)

The anthropologist Paul Dresch notes that "the ordering of what is right" is part of the Zaydī discursive tradition.[18] The invocation of dates "from the third century to the present" could be interpreted as both modern and dynastic; as a literary convention, such figures of speech were first employed by Yaḥyā's father in an attempt to elide territorial control with morally authoritative rule (Dresch 2000, 7). And the invocation of the Prophet's kin suggests a genealogical connectedness, one that was particularly important to the imamate's justifications for rule. To my mind, and in this light, it is Imām Yaḥyā's use of the word *ahl*, rather than the nationalist *sha'b*, that is revealing. The former can mean people or a native population, but its etymological connotations index family, kin, or adherents of a group. *Sha'b*, by contrast, also means "people," but its modern connotations are explicitly national or racial, or both. The notion of a specific people bound together by a common history is adumbrated here, but the nationalist idea of rights-bearing subjects enjoying popular sovereignty within a specified, bounded, internationally recognized space emerges more consistently only in the 1920s and 1930s. At that time, the phrase "people of Yemen" came to signal the attempt to override old *madhhab* or denominational categories distinguishing Zaydīs and Shāfiʿīs and to question the moral right of the Prophet's descendants, in particular, to rule.[19] The use of the phrase in this later period also reflects a growing awareness among Yemeni intellectuals in both North and South of the rise of Arab nationalist movements in Syria and Iraq (Messick 1993, 52, 278; see also al-Wāsiʿī [1927–28] 1991, 243–44).[20]

The institution of the imamate—both the local Qāsimī dynasty's rule over most of modern-day Yemen in the seventeenth century and the early efforts at state building by Imām Yaḥyā in the first two decades of the twentieth—differs from later expressions of territorial nationalism in critically instructive ways. The rulers of North Yemen tended to exercise what Peter Sahlins calls, in the early-modern European context, "jurisdictional sovereignty."[21] Jurisdictional sovereignty implies first and foremost a personal relationship of allegiance between the ruler and his subjects.[22] Similar to early-modern Europe, relations between rulers and ruled in North Yemen under the imamate were defined through, and reaffirmed in, the oaths of loyalty sworn by individuals and groups to the leader. Jurisdictional sovereignty also entailed a mode of management that gave precedence to jurisdiction over territory. Sovereignty, in this light, implied the exercise of authority over military affairs, taxation, religious policies, and commerce in ways that anticipate modern states. But the domains subject to central jurisdiction often failed to coincide with what would otherwise seem to be the territorial boundaries of the dynasty. Jurisdictional sovereignty also meant that rulers acquired and ceded areas of control in the form of villages or trade routes as a result of wars and treaties, without being overly concerned with specifying territorial boundaries.

Mapping the Border

In the early twentieth century, with two empires and an imamate ruling over the territories comprising what is now the Republic of Yemen, the circumstances favoring jurisdictional sovereignty began to change. Internal

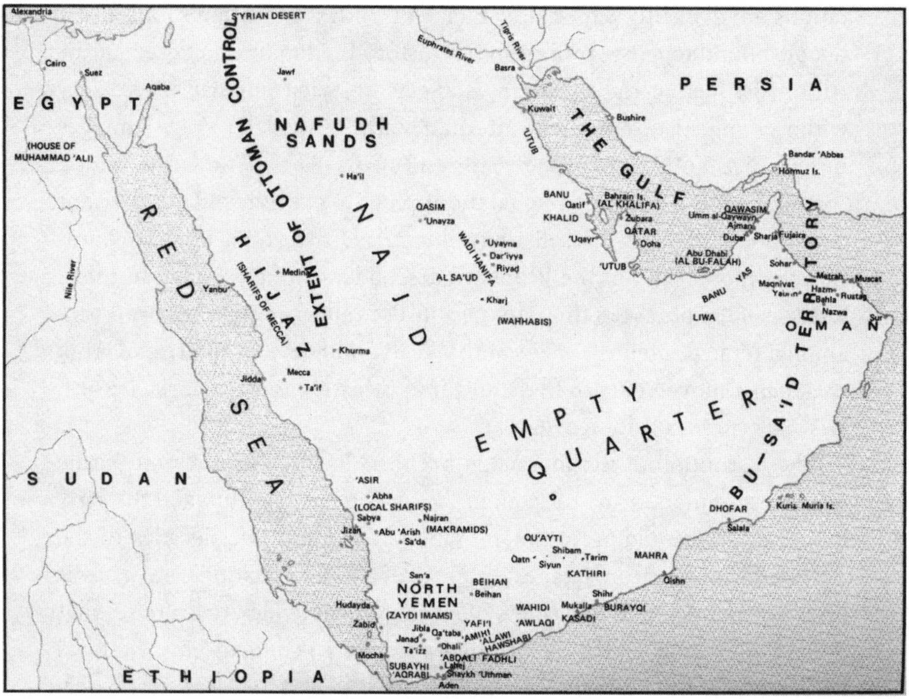

Map 1.4: Map of Arabia, ca. 1903, on the eve of the Ottoman-British partition. Copied from Kamal Salibi, *A History of Arabia* (Delmar, N.Y.: Caravan Books, 1980), 186.

political struggles throughout the area, difficult to manage in part because of ambiguities over jurisdiction in both North and South, led the British to insist in 1905 on demarcating the boundary, a practice colonizers were pursuing in East Asia and Africa as well. Judging from colonial documents, it was precisely anxieties about disorder in the hinterland and the urgency of protecting Aden's port that prompted the British to establish an Anglo-Turkish commission to draw a border.

The diplomatic process of constructing that boundary laid bare serious disagreements between the British Home Office and the Indian imperial government (the latter formally administering Aden and the hinterland) and between British and Ottoman negotiators.[23] Only following military skirmishes, a contentious cadastral survey, and protracted diplomatic negotiations among London, Aden, Delhi, and Istanbul was an agreement reached.[24] This procès-verbale of 1905, ratified at the Anglo-Turkish convention of 1914, marked the culmination of British efforts to secure the Aden port by preventing surrounding populations from being subjected to either the Ottomans or the local rulers of the North (Little 1968, 14).

The border of 1905 was thus a political construct of the colonial era, its demarcation a product of diplomatic wrangling and military conquest. But it connected populations to territory in ways that also helped make both a North and a South Yemen increasingly thinkable. There was nothing given or obvious about this arrangement of North and South, of course. In times to come many Yemeni nationalists would see the delimiting line as an aberration, an artificial boundary that severed natural or historical connections among a coherent people. Yet this is surely a retrospective view, and other historical conditions might well have involved one Yemen or several territorial units instead of the two. Borders are by definition artificial, artifacts of historical events, power relationships, and political considerations.

It may be tempting to interpret the conflicts that emerged over demarcating the boundary, including Ottoman claims to "the whole of Southern Arabia,"[25] as implying that *Yaman* already was a coherent political entity or enjoyed the imaginative status of nationhood before the interwar period. But although the term *Yaman* existed, there was no notion of a Yemeni citizenry, and legal texts continued to specify affiliation in *madhhab*, or denominational categories, of Zaydī or Shāfiʿī membership, rather than in a legislated code invoking Yemenis as "a people." In the North, both the Ottomans and Imām Yaḥyā had expansionist designs on parts of what came to be the southern People's Democratic Republic of Yemen at independence. Imām Yaḥyā even made claims to a "Greater Yemen" (*al-Yaman al-kubrā*),[26] as did the official newspapers he supported. Even so, these appeals were not generally expressed in terms of nationalist idioms. Moreover, as a practical matter, and following several attempts to intervene in the British Protectorates, Imām Yaḥyā ended up abandoning whatever hopes he had of conquering the British-held South in favor of consolidating his holdings in the North, transforming areas over which he had periodic jurisdiction into territories subject to state authority. The treaty of Ṣanʿāʾ in 1934 formalized an agreement between the British and Imām Yaḥyā to establish an administrative frontier, one adhering to the 1905 border between North and South. Notably, though, even this treaty simply recognized what it described as the "status quo," while leaving the final status of the boundary to be negotiated at a later date. Even with the creation of the two separate, independent states in the 1960s, despite the border as defined in 1905 and formalized in 1934, some boundaries remained undemarcated. By the 1960s, however, borders were being contested in a way that jurisdictional sovereignty per se did not occasion, so that now the lack of clear boundaries had come to signal an explicit preoccupation with competing territorial claims, framed in terms of a unified people who belonged to a land and were represented by its rulers.

Conclusion

In summary, the difficulties of imposing an Ottoman or British colonial project onto the territories that were to become in the 1960s the Yemen Arab Republic (YAR) and People's Democratic Republic of Yemen (PDRY), respectively, suggest the problems with a strict Foucauldian approach, not so much because Foucault's own narrative is tied to European historical forms (although that may be true), but because those inspired by him tend to confuse the stated or projected aspirations of imperial rulers with the actual effects of empire. Imperial power was not as saturating as theorists of colonialism tend to claim.[27] To recognize the limitations of colonialism is not to argue that there were no consequences, however. In both North and South, different regimes emerged partly in response to perceived problems of disorder in the nineteenth century. In the South, colonial administrators diagnosed the problems of dissension as specifically "tribal." In the North, disorder tended to be portrayed by the imamate (and by the Ottomans) less as a battle between tribes and the state and more as a struggle over moral propriety (Willis 2004). Indeed, many of the skirmishes between the imām and his subjects took place in the agricultural, non-tribally identified parts of Lower Yemen. (In chapter 4 I will return to the notion of "tribe"—a much used [and abused] term in Middle Eastern studies.)

For now, the key point is that the organization, classification, and management of territory differed markedly in the imamate-controlled North and the British-administered South, as well as from the ways in which space was understood when borders were fixed or claimed on the basis of an appeal to the nation-state.[28] In the colonially administered South, the production of space ultimately made possible a territorially grounded understanding of the nation-state, one that facilitated at least two different visions of an explicitly national economy and "culture": the first vision was confined to the British-imposed borders that after independence became the People's Democratic Republic of Yemen;[29] the second vision was of the more expansionist "Greater Yemen" (*al-Yaman al-kubrā*). Arguably, too, in the North Imām Yaḥyā's state-building efforts and territorial conquests generated the terms for a North Yemen nation-state. But official rhetoric in the imamate never abandoned claims to a Greater Yemen either, and these claims, as we shall see, were taken up by self-identified nationalists, some of whom enjoyed state patronage, while others opposed the imām's regime, seeking a different moral ground for rule.

PART TWO: PERFORMING NATIONALISM

Intellectuals and the Production of Nationalist Ideas

As in most other examples of nationalism, state-sponsored intellectuals in Yemen played a key role in asserting the continuous presence of a Yemeni nation, as well as in offering divergent understandings of what Yemen meant.[30] Imām Yaḥyā established a "history commission" in 1937 to sponsor scholarly studies, making Yemen a coherent object of historical inquiry and analysis. These studies tended to privilege the succession of imāms from "the third century [of Islam] to the present" (Dresch 2000, 50), imposing in their historical accounts a single overview on what was otherwise a set of fragmented, often distinctly regional accounts (Messick 1993, 122–24).[31] The chronicler ʿAbd al-Wāsiʿ ibn Yaḥyā al-Wāsiʿī's 1927–28 *Tārīkh al-Yaman* (History of Yemen) is instructive here. At times, the language denoting "Greater *Yaman*" is clear. In the context of discussing the population of Yemen, for example, the author assures his reader that he has consulted experts—foreigners and learned men from Ḥaḍramawt—to estimate the number of people in "all of Yemen, its east, west, north, and south" (*jamīʿ al-Yaman mashāriqihā wa maghāribihā wa shamālihā wa janūbihā*).[32] At other times, the language is more ambiguous, as, for example, in the phrase the "land of *Yaman*" (*arḍ al-Yaman*),[33] which could designate both North and South but could also mean simply North Yemen. North Yemen is at other times explicitly identified: "all of the centers of *Yaman* where there were Turks" (*jamīʿ marākiz al-Yaman allatī fīhā al-Atrāk*)[34] names the areas occupied by the Ottomans. "Lower Yemen" (*al-Yaman al-asfal* or *asfal al-Yaman*) refers to the southern parts of North

Yemen but could also include parts of the South.[35] Explicit invocations of the South tend to name specific areas, such as Aden and Ḥaḍramawt.[36] Al-Wāsiʿī's book is nevertheless a "history of *Yaman*," and its inclusion of areas of the South in its various discussions presupposes a "Greater Yemen," as do the words used to qualify the North's distinctly Ottoman history and Aden's British occupation.

Not surprisingly, Yemeni nationalist narratives from the late 1920s onward come to follow conventional primordialist or perennialist views of history, depicting the Yemeni nation as an ancient civilization whose members settled in the fertile southwest part of Arabia several millennia ago. The historic kingdoms of Maʿīn, Saba', and Ḥimyar are part of a linear genealogy linking contemporary Yemenis to a putative South Arabian ancestry (al-Wāsiʿī 1928, 1991; see also Halliday 1997).[37] Étienne Balibar notes that such understandings of the nation entail "believing that the generations which succeed one another over centuries on a reasonably stable territory, under a reasonably univocal designation, have handed down to each other an invariant substance." Members of a nation are the "culmination of that process," which appears both inevitable and predestined (Balibar 1991, 86). Ronald Suny, borrowing from Ernest Gellner, refers to this position as the "Sleeping Beauty" view, according to which nations wake up and attain consciousness of their preexisting, naturally shared language, culture, history, and destiny (Suny 1993, 3). Like most nationalist discourses, Yemeni ones stress the people's antiquity, their continuous occupation of a territory coincident with unified Yemen, and the sacrifices that "the people" (or particular heroic figures) have made in the effort to achieve national unity.

Yet not all intellectuals endorsed such coherence. Or, rather, what counted as *Yaman* or "national" remained an openly contested matter throughout the period under consideration here. Aḥmad Faḍl ʿAbdalī of Laḥj in the South, a notable from a leading sultanate family, wrote a history both presenting himself as Yemeni and repudiating the idea of Yemen as a single entity (Dresch 2000, 50).[38] In Ḥaḍramawt, new forms of historical writing privileged a distinctively Ḥaḍramī collective identity, one already foregrounded in the Ḥaḍramī moralizing narratives of the nineteenth century. In both Ḥaḍramī historical writing and fictional tales, Java and Singapore figure more prominently than North Yemen, which is marginal when invoked at all.[39] The Aden Association advocated a policy of self-rule for Aden, adopting the slogan "Aden for the Adenis" to underscore the exclusion of outsiders (often referred to as "Yemenis") from political decision making in the colony. In addition to historical chronicles in which Yemen became an object encoded in calendrical, abstract time, newspapers began to emerge, putting forth unified, if varying, conceptions of what Yemen meant.[40] For example, *Fatāt al-jazīra* (Youth of the Peninsula), a newspaper that began publication in 1940, understood "South Arabia" to mean Yemen as a culturally cohesive entity, but its writers, who came from the South, tended to view the North as both particularly authentic and problematically backward.[41] In the official northern newspaper *al-Īmān*, sometimes the term *Yaman* referred to both North and South Yemen, whereas at other times *Yaman* connoted the North.[42]

These historical chronicles and newspapers demonstrate both the multiple significations of *Yaman* and the ways in which nationalist discourses coincided with pious ones. They also register the gradually expanding (albeit imperfect) reach of state institutions. But they did more than merely exemplify a nationalist imaginary. They also helped to produce one by constituting an audience that, through the shared practice of reading, was beginning to have the experience of knowing about and participating in a common political project. Leading reformers worked to promote education, with one such reformer, Muḥammad Luqmān, establishing the first Arab secondary school in Aden as early as the 1930s; he also sent students to Baghdad and Cairo for further study, many of whom returned bearing ideas of Yemeni and Arab nationalism.[43] Other educational movements linked literate Yemenis to one another, promoting the informal dissemination of books such as *Ṭabā'i' al-istibdād* (The nature of oppression), by the Islamic reformer 'Abd al-Raḥmān al-Kawākibī, which some present-day Yemeni intellectuals liken in importance to Rousseau's works for the French Revolution (Dresch 2000, 55; Douglas 1987, 32–33). The routine movement of intellectuals between North and South entailed the exchange of ideas on both Arab and Yemeni nationalisms,[44] even as the British military base in Aden contributed to the same development by drawing in workers from throughout the region during World War II. These workers also forged connections to disparate parts of Yemen, establishing village associations linking Aden with "Lower Yemen" in the North and with Yāfi' and Ḥaḍramawt in the South.

The prevalence of historical chronicles, the existence of newspapers, the travel of intellectuals and workers, and the reach of state institutions are critical aspects in the proliferation and dissemination of nationalist ideas and practices. But it is easy to overstate their importance, in particular as regards the efficacy (as opposed to the ideal) of state institutions or the impact of intellectuals. As the Yemeni example shows, and as I suspect is true more generally in non-Western contexts, other forms of cultural production were doing the work that key institutions (e.g., schools) did in Europe and the Americas. Illiteracy rates were extremely high in the 1940s and 1950s in Yemen, and what primary schools did exist privileged Qur'ānic training over nationalist ideology. Even today, an estimated 50 percent of men and 70 percent of women are unable to read. Although inhabitants of Aden have historically had greater access to education than most of their urban counterparts in the North or other southerners from the hinterlands, even there the numbers of readers remained small. Compounding the problem of literacy was the limited distribution of newspapers and books. One former nationalist leader remembers that when he was a student in Ta'izz in the 1950s, probably the most politically vibrant town in North Yemen at the time, there were no bookstores or places to buy newspapers. The first bookstore in Ta'izz opened, to the best of his recollection, only in 1960–61.[45] Moreover, although the Ottomans had introduced newspapers into Yemen at the end of the nineteenth century and the first printing press in Ṣan'ā' went into use in 1872, this remained the only press in the capital until 1970, when a gift bestowed on the government by the Chinese in 1963 was finally made operational (al-Mutawakkil 1983, 18). We thus have to look additionally at other media in order to grasp how understandings of national commonality happened.

Popular Expressions of Nationalism(s): Radio and Poetry

In many ways, it was radio that functioned to disseminate ideas about both Arab and Yemeni nationalisms the way "print" purportedly did in Western Europe in an earlier period.[46] Radio cultivated in people living in disparate geographical spaces the sense that others were listening to the same broadcasts, acquiring the same information, and experiencing similar affective connections. Just as print languages for Creole American populations and in Western Europe allowed for "unified fields of exchange and communication below Latin and above the spoken vernaculars," radio gave modern standard Arabic what Anderson describes in the Creole American context as a "new fixity, which in the long run helped to build that image of antiquity so central to the subjective idea of the nation" and "created languages-of-power" that were closer to some dialects and farther from others (Anderson 1991, 44, 45).

In the Middle East, as in Creole America, the language community being addressed was more expansive than the individual nation-states that emerged. Ṣawt al-ʿArab (Voice of the Arabs) began broadcasting on July 4, 1953, in an explicit attempt to manufacture a pan-Arab public, one whose political consciousness and emotional affect were directed, at least ideally, toward struggling for national liberation from colonial rule, redistributing wealth through land reform, and creating the conditions for Arab unity. Voice of the Arabs and the already established Radio Cairo were the two most influential services; they were probably the most effective means of communicating with and cultivating supporters of Egyptian president Jamāl ʿAbd al-Nāṣir (Gamal Abdel Nasser) in other Arab countries prior to the 1967 war.[47] They also worked to portray (and perhaps to sustain) multiple national commitments. Radio Cairo supported pan-Arab dissent against the British, for example, routinely referring in the 1950s and 1960s to local Yemeni notables at odds with the British as "*mujāhidīn*" dedicated to the cause of pan-Arab "revolution." In keeping with Nāṣir's stated goals of combating reaction and imperialism, Egyptian radio also permitted Muḥammad al-Zubayrī, a leader of the Yemeni Union (al-Ittiḥād al-Yamanī, 1952–62), to broadcast a program calling for political reforms in Yemen. The existence of the newly founded National Liberation Front (NLF), which was eventually to take over South Yemen, could be announced on North Yemen's own Radio Ṣanʿāʾ in 1963 (Lackner 1985, 37–38).[48] North Yemen's national broadcasts after the 1962 revolution were rife with Yemeni national and pan-Arab vocabulary; they also combined the theological with the national, including a ten-minute, twice-daily *Barnāmaj Fatāwā* (Fatwa program) (Messick 1996, 311). This blend of the national and theological transformed both. While not eliminating the immediate, face-to-face relationship in which Islamic judges (*qāḍīs*) and supplicants secured "the authoritative transmission of knowledge," radio did provide a way of delivering fatwa messages by broadcasting them to an abstract, distant mass audience, the "characteristic citizenry of a nation-state" (ibid., 320).

The ultimate failure of Arab nationalism to produce a permanent countermovement to more provincial nationalisms had something to do with the historical context of its emergence, in which the circumscribed nation-state had already become the worldwide idiom for political solidarity.[49] The colonial demarcation of boundaries also helped inscribe the specific contours of nation-state nationalisms, establishing the discursive and institutional basis for local political resistance in the form of nationalist independence movements, beginning in the mid-1930s with the Free Yemeni Movement in the North and with the development of various political movements in Aden in the 1950s.[50] Members of the various organizations associated with the Free Yemeni Movement initially called for political transformations in the North exclusively, but after the defeat of an uprising against the imamate in 1948, leaders who escaped to Aden came to advocate union with the "occupied South" and to include "all Yemenis," not just those from the imām's domains, in their calls for political change. As the prominent Free Yemeni nationalist al-Zubayrī stated on Radio Cairo in the 1950s, "When we began to draft the constitution of the society, we had the common feeling that we all belonged to one homeland. We paid no attention to the political barriers which separated our countries."[51] What is remarkable about the Yemeni case, as some of these movements dramatize, is that colonial borders could be challenged by an imagined community that extended beyond the territorial arrangements of North and South—offering up the possibility of a nationalism located conceptually in between the grand reach of Arabism and the particularistic visions of the two Yemens.[52]

Radio represented one way in which Yemenis experienced themselves as part of a wider Arab world—both because of Arab nationalist programming and because people throughout the Arab world were sharing the experience, or could imagine themselves as simultaneously listening to the same programs with anonymous others. Yet, for many, a crucial means through which explicitly *Yemeni* nationalist commitments could be imagined was poetry. Poetry, as Steven C. Caton writes, has the status of a "key cultural event," a part of the region's "central political, social, and religious institutions" (1990, 4–5), and as nationalist idioms gained currency poetry played an important role in generalizing a sense of national possibility without obliterating regional distinctions. Poetry's content could be expressive of visions of Yemeni unity, but it was also important to nationalism because of poetry's increasing circulation—first by word of mouth, informal performances, and radio broadcasts, and then in the 1970s and 1980s through audiocassettes. These modes of communication created an audience that could imagine specific references—whether to a family, a political event, or a mountain—as part of a growing spatiotemporal world to which the listener also belonged. According to a group of northern Yemeni nationalists,[53] it was through poetry specifically in the 1950s that they first learned to think of the nation (*al-waṭan*), of "Greater Yemen," and of Yemenis "as a people" (*sha'b*). Many of these men were children at the time, attending local *kuttāb*s (Qur'ānic schools), and the imām's poets would travel through the villages reciting *zawāmil*—a form of oral poetry. In this way, poetry provided local villagers with ways to imagine the nation that were independent of printed forms and available even before radio emerged as a new communications technology. Poetry's role in making nationalist ideas accessible to a largely unlettered population qualifies the emphasis on material and technological advances that Anderson, Deutsch, and others ascribe to the nation. Poetry, at least initially, was face to face and oral; it involved travelers moving on foot on unpaved roads, and yet it nevertheless was the genre through which national ideas became familiar to a generation who self-identified as nationalists.

By the 1960s nationalists benefited from the prevalence of transistor radios, so even written poetry could be broadcast to broader audiences, becoming a pervasive medium for establishing the commonality of and interpreting political events. A case in point is the work of the preeminent poet al-Baraddūnī, which aired on the radio and whose verses were subsequently recited by villagers to one another. The following poem, inspired by the North's 1962 revolution, when the imamate was eliminated and the military established a self-described "republican" order to take its place, is a typical example:[54]

> The homeland will never surrender or submit.
> Spirit in revolt, she fills her breast with pure air.
> See how she lifts her head and moves forward,
> Trampling with disdain these foolish idols. . . .
>
> What is North? And what the South?
> Two hearts whose joy and pain are joined
> Were united by hate and suffering,
> By history and by God.
> Shamsān will soon meet its brother Nuqum.

A precise instance of the shared knowledge assumed and exploited by the poet in cultivating this national imaginary is the invocation of Shamsān and Nuqum in the closing line, which are mountains on the outskirts of Aden and Ṣan'ā', respectively.

Oral poetry did not even require a radio, however, and it continued to be a potent means of expressing political concerns after these technologies had arrived in the countryside. In the following example "Binā" refers to a valley in Yemen, "red" is meant to be understood as "bloody," and the "we" who "left" refers to men from the countryside who had gone to Ṣan'ā' to organize politically or had fled to Aden:[55]

Oh Binā, how have you been since we left?
  And you, alone, facing the shots.
Tell them, oh Binā, that we left but will return.
  And we shall ignite the revolution—red and relentless.

Many poems work as exchanges, clever ripostes between two poets registering divergent views about political life. Poems are rhetorical appeals, tailored variously to persuade audiences of religious elites, peasants, the urban bourgeoisie, or self-identified tribesmen to support an established policy or to protest against it.[56] In the context of the North's 1962 "revolution" against the imamate and the South's independence movement against British colonial rule in 1967, these poems could operate as a recruitment technique, as a way to affirm and invigorate anticolonial political loyalties by calling for material and emotional support, as well as for actual participation (Caton 1990; interviews, July 2001). The idea of Yemen is evident in this poetry, even while local identifications or contested political positions often figure more prominently than the notion of a unified nation—whether Yemeni or Arab. The civil wars that wracked North Yemen from 1962 to 1970 pitted colonial and "royalist" forces supported by Saudi Arabia against "republicans" and revolutionaries buttressed by Egyptian military manpower and arms. Political fault lines found expression in poetic exchanges, as in the following village poem. (Mount al-Ṭiyāl is in the eastern area of the country known as Khawlān. Ḥasan and al-Badr refer to royalists.)

The First Poet:[57]

Mount al-Ṭiyāl called and every proud Yemeni declared his response:
  "We will never become republican even if we are banished from the earth forever."
Even if yesterday returns today or the sun rises from Aden.
Even if the earth lights on fire or the sky rains bullets.

The Reply:

> What will the Sharp do? Or the M1, with the helicopter, and the fighter jet?
> Nājī . . . Tell Ḥasan and Badr that silver has become brass[58] and we shall not become royalist even if we are banished from the earth forever.

Among the noteworthy features of this poem, I want to draw attention here to two. First is the way in which the poem indicates that general political battles are waged on local, intimate levels. The audiences for this poem, as well as countless others like it, are Yemenis from a distinct geographical area, participants who know the references to places and the personalities of a particular regional, historically specific moment. Second, this regional familiarity is complicated by another imaginary, one that sees Yemen as more encompassing, extending perhaps to Aden. And Yemenis in both North and South became familiar with versions of this poem because it circulated widely.

Poems of this kind also routinely hint at another important qualification about nationalist discourses. Nationalist discourses imply that in times of crisis the collective vulnerability of this entire community overrides parochial, sectional, or more intimate organizations of solidarity such as the family (Calhoun 1997, 39). Yet, in actuality national identifications are more complex and perhaps less dramatic than this demand for collectivity presumes. Loyalties among Yemenis differ among distinct social groups, and national identity is evoked contextually, often serving local interests. Moreover, adopting national identities (even during times of crisis in which passions may be pronounced) does not necessarily require abandoning local ones. As we shall see, Yemeni nationalists often espoused and continue to create new, more encompassing identifications without abandoning their local interests, their divergent political allegiances (as royalists, republicans, and socialists), or their sense of place.[59]

Over the decades separating independence in the 1960s and unification in 1990, poetry continued to do important political work. As an avenue for self-expression, poetry focused on issues construed as "national," as well as on local or regional concerns (the resolution of conflict between the warring "tribes" of Ḥāshid and Bakīl in the northern highlands, for example), on love (*ghazal* poetry), or on the problems of corruption in the regimes of North and South. There were poets who saw themselves as advising leaders,[60] and others who recorded audiocassettes castigating them (Caton 1990; Miller 2007). Poetry remained important because the exchange and circulation of cassettes allowed poets and audiences formally separated by the borders of two often clashing nation-states to communicate with one another (Miller 2007). Arguably, poems also increasingly narrated a specifically historical, worldly past (without necessarily abandoning other notions of time), and regional histories were often linked to national spatial imaginaries, ones that put forth an understanding of Yemen extending across the official boundaries of North and South. Poetry constituted a background circumstance, one of the felicitous conditions that made a unified Yemen thinkable, especially for those whose access to formal media was limited. At the same time poetry worked as a performative, summoning into being nationalists by evincing the commonalities that could create them.

In short, narrowly drawn institutional histories of unification fail to capture the often subtle forces at work in making a unified territorial nation-state of Yemen conceivable in the first place. As we have seen, intellectuals' chronicles, radio broadcasts, and poetry were more or less informal but important modes of political expression. Poetry, in particular, was a widespread popular medium, celebrating instances of local valor and ancestral prowess, while also revealing a cartographic imaginary that transcended the boundaries of North and South (Miller 2007, 388–89). More generally, discourses that put forth an image of unified Yemen not only reflected transformations in political understandings already under way; they also helped to produce or constitute national "subjects." By "producing national subjects," I mean that discourses about Yemen disseminated the content of a specifically national imaginary and also created the various assemblages of individuals who could increasingly conceive of themselves as sharing the same experiences with unknown others. Innovations in technology, such as the proliferation of trucks and transistor radios, as well as the increasing (albeit often exaggerated) institutional capacities of both the British colonial authorities and the imamate are part of the story. As we have seen, these technologies were combined with preexisting cultural forms to generate and spread multiple and sometimes contradictory notions of a nation called *Yaman*. External events also played a role, including the rise of Saudi Arabia in the 1920s and its border war with North Yemen in 1934, the emergence of the Palestine question in the 1940s, and the Egyptian revolution of 1952.[61] Yemenis often disagreed on what territory *Yaman* included or whether other regional areas such as Ḥaḍramawt were a stronger locus for collective solidarity than Yemen, yet the more critical factor is that people increasingly fought out those differences on grounds that presupposed the concept of "the nation."

PART THREE: FORMAL UNIFICATION

An emphasis on categories and their circulation is not meant to imply that institutions do not matter. Rather, I suggest that we think of the relationship between discourses on nationalism and institutions (such as political parties, labor unions, nationalist organizations, media outlets, the imamate's growing state apparatus, and the British colonial administration) in ways that might be termed "dialectical." By "dialectical" I mean a relationship in which discourses and institutions—or more generally, the terms on either side of a divide often coded as "material" versus "ideational"—do more than merely influence each other. Discourses and institutions are defined and generated in reference to each other, and yet can come into conflict, both conceptually in their meanings and causally in the world, so that the only way of handling such material is by considering their analytic synthesis—that is, by maintaining an overview that includes each without stifling the conflict or denying their logical incompatibilities (see Wedeen 2002).[62] Or to put it somewhat differently: to think dialectically about discourses and institutions is to be sensitive to the ways in which they are reciprocally determining, that is, mutually implicated in the changes that each undergoes through time. Apprehending theoretically how discursive and institutional factors are dialectically related to one another allows us to develop an empirically rich, more accurate description of political reality and action.

A dialectical approach also suggests that conventional formulations, in which "political entrepreneurs" or elites use nationalist rhetoric as a way of manipulating constituencies, mislead in important ways.[63] The conventional view assumes that elites (or states) exist outside of the historical and ideological conditions that produce and affect ordinary citizens (or "society").[64] It is undoubtedly true that the process of determining a standard or official national narrative in conditions of flux generally requires efforts to achieve discursive coherence. Achieving this coherence often entails portraying the present within an authoritative framework that includes positive assessments of past events and actors (Asad 1993). But elites are also part of their societies, so that such authority is a collaborative effort between narrators and audiences who are coformed by the discourses they produce and consume.

In the following, I want to explore how the events precipitating the creation of unified Yemen in 1990—despite their obviously contingent character, and over and above considerations of political expediency—were linked to the histories of nationalist thought and practice outlined above. Persistent calls for the national integration of North and South in the aftermath of independence in the 1960s, constitutionally mandated appeals for unification, and failed unity agreements were inspired and made possible by this earlier history. They were fueled as well by the problem of centralized state control within the two Yemens. The aims of this section are thus twofold: to describe the precipitating reasons for formal unification in a context in which nationalist categories organized and continue to suffuse political processes and institutional relationships; and to discuss some of the practical problems and political effects of unification.

The Background to Unification: Enduring Conflict

Why did unification in 1990 happen? Much of the answer to this question turns on the fact that the two independent nation-states inaugurated in the 1960s were able neither to unify their respective populations nor to compel citizens to submit to their respective normative orders. Although available idioms of national belonging to a unified Yemen provided the conditions of possibility for unification, unity must also be understood against the backdrop of continuing political instability within each country and the ways in which leaders attempted to handle it. In keeping with a dialectical understanding of politics, however, this very instability should itself be seen as a product of the organizational efforts and political discourses that made alternative imaginings of national solidarity so persistent.

The revolution in the North of September 26, 1962, brought an end to the imamate and ushered in an Egyptian-trained military government. But the following years were wracked by civil war in the newly founded Yemen Arab Republic. Forces loyal to the imamate found support from the monarchies of Saudi Arabia and Jordan, while the "republican" officers who staged the coup were bolstered by Egyptian supplies and military personnel. Egyptian troops, numbering in the tens of thousands, occupied areas of the North from the early days of the revolution until 1967, when their defeat in the Arab-Israeli war forced an Egyptian withdrawal. The royalist "siege of Ṣan'ā'" followed, a seventy-day battle that in subsequent narrations has taken on epic proportions. Though royalists remained active in some parts of northern Yemen until 1970, the war was effectively won by the republican side when the capital was ceded to republican control three years earlier. The "national reconciliation" effected between some supporters of the imamate and republicans actually registered the triumph of more conservative forces within the republican camp. But turmoil did not end with reconciliation. The YAR was embroiled in two wars with South Yemen (in 1972 and 1979) and endured two dramatic presidential assassinations that were filled with plot twists. The first involved the populist military officer, President Ibrāhīm al-Ḥamdī, whose body was discovered along with the corpses of his brother and two unnamed French women (widely believed to be prostitutes) in 1977. His successor, Aḥmad al-Ghashmī (suspected of being implicated in al-Ḥamdī's death), died six months later when an envoy from Aden exploded a briefcase in his office.

'Alī 'Abd Allāh Ṣāliḥ, an army officer and confederate of al-Ghashmī, came to power in 1978 following this second assassination. He has constructed a regime based on alliances among self-identified tribal and military personnel. The North under his direction has pursued a free market economy and has avoided far-reaching social reforms. Ṣāliḥ is one of the world's longest ruling leaders. But his regime has not been able to exercise sovereignty over the entire territory of the nation-state, and as we shall see in the following chapters, the divide-and-rule policies he has adopted as an alternative have themselves created spaces of disorder that may, paradoxically, help enable his rule.

The South was also bedeviled by violence and chronic instability. The British withdrawal on November 29, 1967, left Aden to a divided leadership. From 1966 to 1967, the Front for the Liberation of Occupied South Yemen (FLOSY), an Egyptian-backed coalition of nationalists in South Yemen, looked for a time as if it might establish itself as the successor to the British, but, as it happened, it was the rival and more radical, leftist National Liberation Front, another anticolonial movement also initially supported by Egypt, that took over in November 1967.[65] Splits within the NLF, however, prompted a "corrective movement" in June 1968 and the exile of the then-president Qaḥṭān al-Sha'bī to Egypt. Further power struggles ensued, leading to the execution by firing squad of the Maoist-inspired President Sālim Rubayyi' 'Alī ("Sālmayn") in 1978. Unresolved issues within the ruling Yemeni Socialist Party in the South forced the retirement "for health reasons" of Sālmayn's successor, the Marxist-Leninist figure 'Abd al-Fattāḥ Ismā'īl, in 1980, and culminated in the notorious *aḥdāth yanāyir*, or "January events," of 1986. The latter began when 'Abd al-Fattāḥ returned from exile. His successor, 'Alī Nāṣir Muḥammad, instructed his bodyguards to open fire on 'Abd al-Fattāḥ's faction in politburo headquarters on January 13. The bloody coup d'état that followed was of civil-war proportions; at least five thousand people were killed in the thirteen days of violence.[66]

In other words, in both Yemens, political divisiveness, exemplified by the North's civil war (1962–70) and by the South's January events of 1986, compromised whatever loyalty might have existed for either fledgling nation-state. Such conflicts were themselves linked to aspirations for unity between the two Yemens: northerners (primarily from Lower Yemen) came to the South and occupied government posts while also fighting to overthrow the North's regime; southerners were exiled to the North as the anticolonial movement in the South took on a Marxist-Leninist cast. One key source of disagreement among leaders in the South was over the level of commitment to and strategies for promoting unity. Some placed a premium on supporting resistance movements in the North, while others were willing to find some accommodation with the YAR leadership. Some claimed that unification could only proceed once the North had abandoned its "feudal" or "capitalist" ways, while a minority argued that the South's small population and history of colonial rule explained why it had yet to establish a viable system of socialism, and therefore unity should take precedence over social struggle (Halliday 1990, 100). Those within the PDRY leadership who were originally from the North or who were from areas bordering the North tended to favor a more militant strategy than leaders from the South (99).[67]

Support for the National Democratic Front (NDF, or al-Jabha al-Waṭaniyya al-Dimuqrāṭiyya) proved to be a case in point, linking aspirations for unity with the imperative for far-reaching social transformation. A primarily peasant-based force headed by pro-unity progressives from the North, some of whom had escaped to the South and directed military operations from PDRY territory, the NDF gained widespread, if clandestine, backing among sharecroppers in Lower Yemen and workers and students in the southern uplands of Aden's hinterland. It was no accident that under the PDRY's northern leader, 'Abd al-Fattāḥ Ismā'īl, the NDF enjoyed considerable assistance. This financial and political aid, in turn, ended up encouraging the border war of 1979, which required the diplomatic intervention of neighboring states. The Kuwait Pact, the product of this mediation, reiterated the two countries' commitment to unify.

It was in this context of tumult in and between both Yemens that a national "dialogue" concerning unity commenced in 1981, bringing to an end a year later the fighting in the North between government forces and the Yemeni Socialist Party-backed NDF. High-profile visits between the leaders of the two Yemens followed, but the energetic push for unity only came after the January events of 1986, when members of the politburo who won the war in the South began to make arguments for "political pluralism" (*ta'addudiyya siyāsiyya*) in the context, first, of facilitating more open debates within the party and, second, as a condition for successful unification with the North. In a memorandum submitted to the Yemeni Socialist Party's Central Committee in 1989, YSP politburo member Jār Allāh 'Umar (a northerner who ended up living in the South for seventeen years) put in writing some of the views suggestive of the strategic interests involved in promoting unification at that particular historical moment: The early enthusiasm for socialism had devolved into preoccupations with bureaucracy. And "religious groups have, within a decade and a half, been transformed into a major power center exercising extensive political and ideological influence and undertaking active propaganda work, while in the past they had neither existence nor even any historic roots in the area" ('Umar 1989, 14). 'Umar had been head of the NDF (often directing activities from Aden), and as a northerner he had always championed unification. He had also been a student of the famous nationalist poet, al-Baraddūnī, and like others in the guerrilla movement could recite poetic longings for Aden on cue. But recalling the January events, 'Umar claimed that his plea for "pluralism" in the aftermath of the bloodletting was also an attempt "to save the party from itself," while promoting the unity he held dear. Rescuing the party would entail a Yemeni version of "glasnost," as 'Umar was to put it later, borrowing the term for the Soviet experiment in political liberalization, so that "party members could air their grievances in public rather than plot secretly."[68] Party reform would also provide a way to reconnect with citizens, many of whom had been disgusted by the January killings. As one witness to the events, a teenager and aspiring YSP youth leader at the time, recalled, "The smell of corpses in the streets was awful. And they were bulldozing bodies into makeshift graves. I gave up on the party then."[69]

In retrospect, one might trace the beginnings of formal unification to YSP secretary general 'Alī Sālim al-Biḍ's visit to the YAR in 1987. This meeting, according to al-Bīḍ, served to surmount "the obstacles that were set up in the period after the events of the January 13th conspiracy," when the vanquished leader ʿAlī Nāṣir and his supporters had fled north to establish a base in the YAR from which to foment rebellion against the PDRY's regime in the South.[70] Al-Bīḍ made clear that no rapprochement with his former comrades was possible, but that there was interest in resuming conversations about unification. The visit, and the statements espousing unification, did not immediately yield concrete plans. But subsequent meetings between delegates from each country, and considerable urgings for immediate unification by some, eventuated in the merger of May 22, 1990. Earlier, in November 1989, in the same month that the Berlin wall fell, the North's ʿAlī ʿAbd Allāh Ṣāliḥ and the South's ʿAlī Sālim al-Bīḍ announced in Aden that a draft unity agreement dating back to 1981 would be the subject of a referendum in 1990. No referendum was actually held, however, and the entire process sped forward; unification was announced abruptly six months later.

The YSP's precarious hold on power was a key precipitating reason for unification in 1990. Indeed, it has been argued that the rulers of the South might otherwise have lost power completely (Dresch 2000, 182). There were, however, options other than unification available to the Yemeni Socialist Party. Politburo members might have made the party more open or even allowed for multiparty competition rather than unify with the North. But they chose unification. Why? Some argue that South Yemen's economic troubles played a key role in the move toward union. With the demise of the Eastern bloc, there was simply "nowhere to turn" (Dresch 1995, 33) other than toward unity. But oil exploration had yielded results, the South had belonged to the IMF and had sought advice from the World Bank in the past, and it was possible that further liberalization measures would have enhanced the country's fiscal options in ways that union did not. From the point of view of YSP leaders who participated in negotiations, however, it was the end of Soviet support to the PDRY in the late 1980s and the internal problems within the YSP that had left the southern regime particularly vulnerable. The discovery of oil on the border between North and South (between Ma'rib and Shabwa), rather than representing an opportunity, made some leaders in the South worry that the North would attempt an invasion while the YSP was weak.[71]

In the more decentralized Yemen Arab Republic in the North, President ʿAlī ʿAbd Allāh Ṣāliḥ may also have had good strategic reasons to promote the merger in 1990. The regime was encountering general resistance to its rule in the northeast, and it could be argued that unification offered a way both to distract attention from efforts to squelch protests there and to secure the help of the more disciplined southern army. Relations with Saudi Arabia, moreover, were especially tense, and Ṣāliḥ might have hoped to use unification to fortify his regional power. It was also in the northern regime's interests to eliminate the historically contentious rivalries with the supporters of the NDF. The NDF could be (and was) permanently defanged as part of the agreement between the leaders of the two nation-states.

These identifiable political interests are nevertheless inextricable from a semiotic world in which expressions of (if not actual beliefs in) national commitment were authoritatively grounded in visions of and even concrete plans for a unified Yemen. The call for unity had long been an identifiable feature of the PDRY's foreign policy. And official state and party documents continued to reiterate those commitments in language that came to describe the two Yemeni states as "halves" (*shaṭrayn*) of a single Yemeni nation or homeland (*waṭan*).[72] So too did the YAR's leadership emphasize unity. As early as 1970, in the aftermath of the civil war, Article 6 of the YAR's constitution states that "Yemeni unity is a legitimate right of all sons of natural Yemen, and it is their shared duty to attain it by legitimate means."[73] In short, the concept of national unity did not *cause* unification to happen, but it did help structure official as well as informal ideas about the political future. Institutions, in turn, such as political parties, insurgent organizations, and official state bodies, were not only inspired by but also shaped the contours of nationalist thinking. As a result of the mutual implication of ideas and institutions, unity became thinkable. Historical circumstances and clever strategizing made it practical.

The Social Construction of Interest

In other words, unification cannot be understood without considering the ongoing context of specific organizational dynamics and nationalist categories of thought, ones that promoted the idea of Yemen as a unified territory and committed various organizations, particularly within the YSP, to the realization of that unity. Or to put it differently, ongoing strategic concerns operate under broader meaning-making conditions, which help determine what counts as a strategy or concern. Realpolitik may be analytically distinct from the ideologies of nationalism and socialism, but strategic actions undertaken by organizations operate dialectically with ideology, generating what gets understood as natural, taken-for-granted, desirable, and possible. The YSP had already spent considerable resources the party could ill afford supporting the NDF's civil war in the North in the late 1970s, with the stated hope of creating a unified Yemen on its own terms. In the aftermath of the January bloodbath in 1986, unification under conditions of political pluralism made historical, strategic sense for party members, raising the possibility of relativizing the party's position in order to preserve its existence.[74]

The interplay of political interests and semiotic circumstances makes attempts to isolate instrumental (or purportedly "material") motives from identity-derived or identity-aspirational ("ideational") ones as problematic as the dichotomy between institutions and discourses (Somers 1994, 627–28).[75] Or to put it differently, interests are no less historical or "constructed" than are nationalist ideas, and they are constructed in a critical sense in tandem with ideas. What counts as an interest will be mediated through the worlds of meaning making within which people act—in this case, circumstances that allowed Yemenis to take the unit of the nation-state increasingly for granted.

Nevertheless, such an approach does not really tell us why northern and southern politicians opted for such a quick unification process. Many YSP members claim to have had a more cautious image of unity, one that would proceed as a series of transitional (*intiqāliyya*) phases, in preference to the hasty unification that actually transpired.[76] There are reasons to believe as well that northerners within the YSP were particularly eager for unification and may have unwittingly or deliberately misled their southern counterparts by glossing over what seem in retrospect to be obvious problems.[77] General Secretary al-Bīḍ and others in the YSP also acknowledged feeling pressure from ordinary citizens; they claimed that once unification became a real possibility, events were driven by the momentum of Yemenis whose expectations were for a comprehensive and rapid unification. Citizen enthusiasm may be exaggerated, however. Certainly not all citizens were supportive of unification, despite widespread nationalist narratives to the contrary. There is evidence from the North's eastern province of Ma'rib, for example, that leaders there were wary; exiled southerners in the North did not want a YSP-led government; and many northerners considered the socialist party members of the South apostates (*kuffār*).[78]

The point here is not to provide a detailed history—there are a number of fine books on the history of the Yemens, as references in the previous sections attest.[79] Rather, my aim is to suggest why unification took place and why it happened in the way it did, and to relate this empirical question to our theoretical concerns with nationalism. In doing so, I am arguing that Yemen's novel experiment in unification was a blend of immediate political exigencies and the authoritative (but not undisputed) political narratives of nationalism. Unity was not the only available outcome; but it was a conceivable resolution predicated on a plausible, iterative vision of a specifically national collectivity—implied in previous plans, understood through policies (of both conflict and negotiation), and articulated in formulations of Yemeni political personhood in both North and South.

No more in Yemen than anywhere else are people born nationalists, and generating and sustaining nationalist principles always requires ongoing work. As we have seen, this work was done by various organizations (such as the short-lived Free Yemeni Movement or the PDRY-supported guerrilla movement in the North, the NDF), but also through the efforts of historians who generated chronologies of a territorially specific Yemeni history, relating an ancient Arabian past to the promise of Greater Yemen. Nationalist work was also performed, as the previous section noted, by poets and by radio broadcasts, oral forms of transmission that made affective connections to Yemen comprehensible to unlettered audiences. But such nationalist discourses were complicated by contending views of what the nation was, by Arab nationalist aspirations keyed to larger territorial imaginaries, and by local commitments to place. Moreover, although formal unification could not have happened if elites, at the very least, had not been able to imagine a unified Yemen, such imaginings did not suffice to accomplish it. Analyzing how nationalist sentiments are generated thus requires taking into account how the affirmative efforts of elites represent an intervention into, even a variation on, aspects of popular discourse such as poetry that were already vibrant.

Unification and War

Not surprisingly, the mechanics of unification in Yemen were more difficult than the convergence of discourses on a common national identity might suggest. Differences over how political power would be shared between the North's ruling General People's Congress (GPC) and the South's Yemeni Socialist Party (YSP) and over the content of the constitution quickly overwhelmed consensual projections of a unified Yemen. One of the major conflicts in the aftermath of unification took the form of heated debates about the role *sharīʿa* was to play in formal political life: the constitutional referendum of 1991 made *sharīʿa a* source, rather than *the* source of legislation, much to the dissatisfaction of Islamic activists. The YSP's defeat in the civil war in 1994, to be discussed below, prompted revisions to the constitution, which then declared Islamic law to be the *exclusive* source of legislation.

On the institutional plane, unification entailed the merger of two ideologically and structurally distinct political systems whose respective leaderships had historically been at odds. For the South, the state had been the addressee for people's moral and material grievances. During the twenty-odd years of its existence, the regime had pursued ambitious initiatives for eradicating illiteracy, encouraging women's education in particular, and developing cooperative farms. In contrast to the North, where local nonstate development projects often competed with fledgling state institutions as mechanisms for channeling resources, the South's government structure was organized on the basis of the Soviet model, with the familiar party central committee and the smaller, more powerful politburo ruling within it. A Marxist-Leninist reform program demanded not only the redistribution of property and ambitious land reform programs but also thoroughgoing secularization, including social policies that prohibited polygamy and also promoted less modest dress codes than those in the North. Like secularizing projects in other contexts, the South's attempts did more than simply relegate religion to the private domain. These efforts also helped to reconfigure how the category of religion was to be understood, deployed, and institutionalized (Mahmood 2005; Asad 2003). Secularism in South Yemen was thus a political project reliant not simply on legal codes but on everyday practices and new regulatory institutions.

In contrast to the Marxist PDRY, the North's YAR was not committed to state building or secularization in the same way as the PDRY. This does not mean that the North was unchanging or static, however. The public sector in the YAR grew markedly in the late 1970s and 1980s, fueled by aid and labor remittance income. In terms of secularization too, as the anthropologist Brinkley Messick (1993) documents, a *sharī'a* politics was gradually relativized by the introduction of new authoritative texts such as the legislated code. The project of secularization was nevertheless much more far-reaching and ambitious in the South, where an overtly anticlerical regime compelled religious organizations to operate clandestinely, if at all.

It is tempting to argue that the differences between North and South caused the problems of unification, but such a view, although partially true, would be too facile. As Sheila Carapico (1993, 1998, 2006), Paul Dresch

(2000), and others have pointed out, there were also important similarities in the ways that the regimes in North and South ruled. Both North and South depended heavily on aid and loans, and in the 1970s the South's major donors differed surprisingly little from the North's, despite the PDRY's Soviet support.[80] Moreover, both North and South by the mid-1970s had come to depend on labor and entrepreneurial remittances, although the South absorbed remittance wealth for state expenditure more efficiently than did the North (Dresch 2000, 134). Politically, too, both North and South shared underlying similarities, operating as dictatorships in which alternation in office was achieved only through violence. Although the South's mechanisms of social control were more totalizing—directed toward building state institutions to provide goods and services in return for some compliance—the inner workings of the regimes in both North and South tended to be shielded from public view. In other words, although Yemenis contrast the PDRY's "law and order" (*al-niẓām wa al-qānūn*) with the North's predisposition for "chaos" or "anarchy" (*fawḍā*), the two regimes both took advantage of extrajudicial forms of military control and special security courts, relying on security forces trained in Iraq and East Germany, in particular, to monitor and control their citizens (Carapico 1998, 39).

Moreover, the question of differences between North and South is no more (or less) critical than other forms of difference *within* North and South. Among the residents of the Tihāma in North Yemen, who generally trace their genealogical roots to Ethiopia, dress codes and norms of gendered propriety (to invoke two ways in which similarity and difference are signified) looked a lot like those otherwise typical of parts of the South. Zaydī men in the North tended to wear the *thawb* (or white robe), but the conventional dress for many male Shāfiʿīs in the North, like their southern counterparts, was the *fūṭa*, or sarong-like wrap. Many people in the North's Lower Yemen and in the Tihāma region identified politically with the South's YSP, while expropriated property owners from the South often moved to the North. And Islamic movements, like those in evidence during this period more generally in the region, were making headway in both countries (despite the PDRY's efforts to forestall them). In other words, just as there was no *necessary* connection between the regional differences of North and South and the difficulties of unification, nor was there any necessary relationship between regional similarities and the likelihood of successful unity. Authors who argue that political unity correlates with the greater homogeneity of some populations than others (e.g., Tilly 1990) may be reinterpreting historical events from the retrospective success of institutionalized nationhood. What counts as a politically salient difference changes over time, sometimes quite precipitously.

Celebrated as the realization of a natural, ancient unity, in fact the unification of 1990, in which Ṣāliḥ retained the presidency and al-Bīḍ became vice president, required reinforcement in the form of a violent two-month civil war in 1994. There were multiple reasons for the war. Power struggles between the two ruling parties combined with perduring ideological disagreements. Socialist leaders claimed that their people were being assassinated by Islamic activists and Ṣāliḥ's security forces. The ruling party and Islamic activists argued that the killings of YSP personnel were a result of historical conflicts within the party itself. In the 1993 parliamentary elections, moreover, the YSP gained few seats in the North and lost some in the South, winning only fifty-six out of 301 overall. YSP demands for an equal share of administrative appointments were therefore feeble. Falling aid receipts, depressed oil prices, and the related plummeting of hard currency reserves also forced the riyal downward in the early 1990s, and these economic conditions may have also intensified "the zero-sum reasoning" that led to war (Carapico 2006, 195). The Gulf's monarchies operated behind the scenes, encouraging southern separatist aspirations with secret payments. Personal animosities between Ṣāliḥ and al-Bīḍ were also at an all-time high. Al-Bīḍ accused Ṣāliḥ of placing cameras in his home; Ṣāliḥ worried that al-Bīḍ's trip to the United States was motivated by reasons other than the stated medical ones.[81] As early as March 1992 there were troop movements by forces loyal to the North. By the end of 1993, Ṣāliḥ had redeployed key army units in patterns that would considerably favor the North. A video of a meeting held in Jordan between YSP and GPC leaders in February 1994 showed the two leaders shaking hands.[82] Fighting began shortly thereafter on April 27, 1994, in the northern region of ʿAmrān, and the North's army subsequently conquered Aden, plundering the city's public infrastructure and destroying the files of the former PDRY ministries. Later the central banks, airlines, and other companies were merged, privatizing previously public enterprises at an accelerated rate. The northern army even blew up Aden's beer factory, an act whose symbolic importance was not lost on secular southerners.

Many YSP figures, labeled "secessionists" (*infiṣāliyyīn*) by newly victorious northerners, fled into exile;[83] others left politics altogether, while still others attempted to work for democratic reforms in the context of the North's predominance. In particular, despite the political eclipse of the YSP as a formidable political party, clashes between northern military and security forces, on the one hand, and the YSP's local constituencies, on the other, persist to this day in some areas. Residents of al-Dāliʿ, 150 kilometers north of Aden on the border with the North have staged periodic protests throughout the unification period, forming in 2000 a popular committee (*lajna shaʿbiyya*) to counteract overweening northern control. Similar committees were formed in other southern governorates, despite strong objections from the regime, which denounced the committees as "separatist" (*infiṣālī*) and "socialist" (*ishtirākī*). By the end of 2001 these committees merged into the Forum of the Sons of the South (*multaqā abnāʾ al-janūb*). Members of the Forum included almost a dozen members of parliament and several high-ranking military officers and former ministers. The Forum expressed grievances common to many citizens of the former PDRY governorates, where structural adjustment measures enacted in 1995 (to be discussed in chapter 5) caused some Yemenis to lose civil service jobs. Accustomed to subsidies and to a state that was, at least in principle, committed to (if not in fact up to the task of) delivering goods and services, many southerners depicted themselves as particularly disadvantaged by northern rule. Moreover, inhabitants complained that the South's oil and gas resources were being pilfered by northerners, with little benefit accruing to local residents. As politicians, members of the Forum also protested threats to their own positions, and even the vice president of Yemen, ʿAbd Rabbih Manṣūr Hādī, a southern military officer who was an important backer of the North during the civil war, purportedly supported the demands of the Forum.

The critical point, however, is that even though these grievances indicated divisions between North and South, such demands are also made *among* northerners in disadvantaged parts of the North. More important still, by and large the demands made on behalf of the Forum assumed unification as an established fact. In other words, in the context of ongoing tensions between southerners and northerners, unification, however incomplete and tenuous, has nevertheless become a primary if not incontestable basis on which appeals to the regime are made. Although calls for an end to the regime and even for outright secession were voiced during demonstrations and sit-ins in September 2007, organized initially by military and police pensioners' syndicates, the demand of most of the demonstrators was for the full reinstatement of personnel compelled to retire after the 1994 war, which is to say the reincorporation of police and army personnel into the apparatus of the unified nation-state.[84]

In response to enduring political pressure from southern elites and ordinary citizens, the regime has made some concessions and attempted to purchase the loyalty of politicians. President Ṣāliḥ has established several development projects in the South, offered bribes to would-be opponents, and replaced some key northern figures in government with southerners (substituting the northern prime minister ʿAbd al-Karīm al-Iryānī with the South's Bā Jammāl, for instance). At the same time, however, Ṣāliḥ has proved adept at playing southern politicians against one another, for example, in bringing former YSP leader Sālim Ṣāliḥ back from exile to dilute the vice president's support. Moreover, the South's significantly smaller population and the regime's ready use of security and military forces to quell resistance in areas of protest (albeit not always successfully) keep the region at a disadvantage. Whereas unification has paradoxically politicized the South's residents to identify *as southerners*, the ability of an entrenched regime to maneuver politically by co-opting key politicians and weakening rivals—combined with the heavy reliance on security and military forces—may make the North-South conflict less dangerous now to the regime's dominance than it was in the immediate aftermath of unification. The events of September 2007 nevertheless suggest that even now political discontent can be expressed in terms of division, of the threat by regime opponents to attempt to undo unification. Whether opponents have the power to make good on the threats is a question, and there remains evidence to suggest that even opposition to the results of unification tends to further consolidate the reality of unity. This is a point we shall explore more fully in subsequent chapters.

The North-South divide waxes and wanes, and violence continues to punctuate political life in Yemen. Yet all the while, the norms and practices of national unification are also continuously being created and carried diffusely by ordinary citizens in their informal everyday activities, quite apart from the judgment actors may hold at one or another moment of crisis about national unity as such. An anecdote nicely illustrates the point, and it may be assumed that equivalent scenes take place with some regularity: During a taxi ride I shared with strangers in 2000, heading from the former southern capital Aden to Ṣanʿāʾ, the capital of unified Yemen, two men in the front seat of the vehicle used the occasion of a brief rest stop to slip out of their southern attire and don the *thawb*, or white robe typical of the North. Passengers in the back seat giggled aloud at the public switch in costume. Teasing the men for opportunistically cross-dressing as northerners once they had left the South, one man said, "So now you are Zaydīs, eh? You have no more use for the South." The example of the two cross-dressers suggests a desire for "passing"—indeed a felt pressure to blend in—at the same time that it shows how such desires become the source of shared parody and an invitation to reiterate a consensual understanding of distinctions rather than to effect assimilation. The consensually understood distinction and the resistance to conformity both operate to reproduce the discursive and institutional effects of unification, albeit ambivalently.

Concluding Remarks

Recent scholars of nationalism have devoted a great deal of attention to practices expressive of claims to national community. Examples include pledging allegiance to the flag and classifying data for the census (Anderson 1991; Foucault 1991), enforcing citizenship laws and inculcating a sense of shared history through schools (Eley and Suny 1996), drawing maps (Sahlins 1991; Anderson 1991; Goswami 2004), using archaeological data to assert common origins (Abu El-Haj 2001), appealing to an abstract sovereign people in preparing for and waging war, and portraying styles of furniture, dress, dance, and food as explicitly national (Handler 1988). Taken as a whole, the scholarship (primarily outside of political science) makes a persuasive case for viewing national solidarities, like other forms of local or regional attachment, as the product of the ongoing activities of political and intellectual elites *in combination and interaction with* the acephalous transmission of identifications through people's ordinary activities.

As of yet, however, little research has been done to move beyond the assertion of a relationship between the representation and constitution of national citizens. The connection between official categories and their "reception" or assessment by ordinary citizens is seldom demonstrated in detail, leaving many important questions in this regard to be addressed, a selection of which will arise in the following chapters. Part of the problem has to do with the ambiguity in the notion of *constituting* selves or "subjects." Does the process involved in constituting subjects mean creating (legal, official, civic, or folk) categories? Or does constituting subjects refer to citizens' heartfelt identifications? What is the connection between, say, a state classification and any individual's substantive experience of belonging? Such questions are often difficult to answer in historical accounts, which tend to privilege written documents and therefore the discursive artifacts of intellectuals and officials. Yet, as I have pointed out in this chapter, elites who write nationalist tracts or are represented in them do not somehow exist outside of the conditions that have enabled their emergence as elites. Rather, elites and ordinary citizens are coformed in a discursive context, in which the language and symbols involved are continually being both absorbed and created anew. Whether a particular discourse is believable, or even intended to produce emotional commitment or political conviction, is another matter, however.

In this chapter, I have suggested two interrelated senses in which we might think about constituting selves. First, there is the way in which nationalist discourses work to constitute the *individual* through his or her performance as an explicitly national person. Here the emphasis is on individuals and their performative abilities—the ways in which they enact (self-consciously or unconsciously, fervently or mildly) their roles as citizens, patriots, or simply members of a nation-state collectivity who can imagine themselves existing simultaneously with anonymous like-minded others, speaking, reading, and listening to similar discourses, the content of which may or may not be specifically national. Second, nationalists, by invoking groups, help summon them into being. Here the emphasis is on categories of groupness and their potential performative qualities. In this view, a group's existence (e.g., the existence of Yemenis) is dependent on, and inseparable from, the category's invocations and institutional entrenchments. The political efficacy of a category resides in the ways in which its repetition helps bring into being the reality it ostensibly only describes.

Nationalist rhetoric has achieved its recognizable, distinct attributes through iterations around the world. But appeals to "the nation" as the source of sovereignty in the post-colonial world have not been replicable without important reconceptualizations in the context of colonial liberation movements and their discrepant experiences of secularism, piety, capitalism, and state formation (Chatterjee 1993; Goswami 1998, 2004). In Yemen, as we have seen, the existence of "the nation" was made possible somewhere between the 1920s and the 1940s as a result of a complex of developments, including changes in the imamate's administration in the North and because of the global circulation of anticolonial, modernizing ideas of "national" liberation. Innovations in technology not only provided a means to disseminate ideas of national solidarity but also created the assemblage of readers and listeners who, through their discursive routines, could imagine others having similar experiences simultaneously across space and over time. The effects of technological advances, moreover, were augmented and at times even supplanted in importance by local semiotic practices such as poetry. It was through these mechanisms and experiences that the nation became thinkable as a practical proposition, and in the context of Yemen so did the idea of unification. Proposed in language that initially rendered the idea of a unified Yemen plausible, institutional changes surrounding formal unification made a unified Yemen increasingly unavoidable: even resistance to the effects of unification has come to foster a subjectivity or presentation of self as *Yamanī*, which operates along with other presentations of self, for example, as pious or leftist or rural. It is in the aftermath of the 1994 war that we can witness anew the discursive, practical, and organizational dynamics that comprise Yemen's experiment in nation-state formation, an experiment that fosters not only new civic institutions but also such laments as this one from a poet in Lower (North) Yemen:

> This is me and my name is *Yamānī*
> I declare, and my history is my testimony (*bayānī*),
> The nation and the union are all that I need
> I don't want to be marginalized.
> I'm against extremism and selfish ones (*al-anānī*).
> Loving Yemen is my first and second priority
> And whoever leaves me or neglects me does not represent me.

This poem, declaimed after the civil war, exemplifies an understanding of Yemen that is much less inflected with regional references than earlier poetry tended to be. At the very moment when the union was most in danger of falling apart, this poet, a declared opponent of 'Alī 'Abd Allāh Ṣāliḥ, nevertheless reasserted his commitment to the idea of a unified Yemeni nation, whose task is to be present in order to "represent" him. Political differences between North and South are subsumed here under the assumption of unity, which also makes the regime subject to (even if not able to fulfill) distinctly "national" responsibilities.

On the whole, then, the creation of a united Yemeni nation-state has had contradictory effects on the possibilities for substantive experiences of national belonging. On the one hand, the communication of official rhetoric and the blending of previously distinctive northern and southern everyday practices (such as dress codes and moral policing activities) have generated some unprecedented bases for similarity among regions in the North and the South.[85] On the other, predatory regime practices and international pressures have combined to produce resistance in the form of specifically regional and denominational identities, as well as conflicting views about the importance of piety and what is taken to represent it.

These contradictory effects suggest an additional theoretically motivated point. Asserting an affirmative national identity does not of itself imply promoting order or shoring up an existing regime. Indeed, there is no necessary connection between claims of national solidarity and the likelihood of political stability, as such national imaginings can be used to criticize or undermine current regimes as well as to authorize them. In the next chapter, I use three exemplary events to analyze these matters, focusing on how sentiments of national attachment need not develop over time but can happen intermittently, congealing suddenly as a basis for individual and collective action.

CHAPTER TWO

SEEING LIKE A CITIZEN, ACTING LIKE A STATE

How are we to understand the relationship, in the aftermath of unification, between state power and the experience of citizenship? Providing an answer to this question presupposes an understanding of citizen participation in the workings of national identification, which is best revealed through a detailed examination of signal events in the processes of state formation and nationhood. Of the three events I have selected for analysis in this chapter, the first is a "direct," purportedly competitive presidential election that took place on September 23, 1999, the first since unification and unprecedented in the histories of the former countries of North and South Yemen. The second is the celebration of the tenth anniversary of national unification on May 22, 2000, including the extraordinary preparations leading up to the event. The third event differs from the other two in that it seems not to involve either the substance or the explicit trappings of national politics per se. The event concerns the public sensation created by the arrest and prosecution of a man touted as Yemen's first bona fide "serial killer," which occurred during the lead-up to the decennial celebration. As we shall see in the following, however, the mechanisms and experience of national identification, while keyed to occasions of official nation-ness, are especially apparent in events that reach well beyond them.

As a period in the short history of unified Yemen, these years can be characterized as ones of renewed political jockeying between a durable regime with meager institutional capacities and a mobilized citizenry. The events I explore are exemplary in the sense that each exposes aspects of lived political experience in Yemen—a country where critical public discussion, a weak but multiparty system, a free press relative to other parts of the Arab world, and active civic associations indicate vibrant, participatory political practices in the absence of fair and free elections (Carapico 1998; see also Habermas 1996 [1962]).[1] As I shall argue, viewing these episodes together makes it possible to draw more general comparative lessons about the anatomy of citizen contestation and regime control in newly forming nation-states.

Each of the events betrays a note of irony. The election was widely heralded as "the first free direct presidential election" ever held in Yemen, and there was never any doubt about the ability of the incumbent to capture a majority of the vote. Yet the ruling party, on dubious legal grounds, barred the opposition's jointly chosen challenger from the race and then appointed its own opponent. President 'Alī 'Abd Allāh Ṣāliḥ had a chance to win what the world would have regarded as a fair and free election, but chose instead to undermine the process, using the apparently democratic form to foreclose democratic possibilities. In the case of the unification anniversary, both the preparations and the event itself required the regime to introduce statelike interventions in domains where they had never been seen before. In areas of everyday practice, such as garbage collection and street cleaning, the state made itself apparent to citizens in ways that could only serve to remind them of how absent it usually was. Finally, the revelation that a shocking series of murders had taken place inside the state-run university produced communities of criticism in which people found themselves sharing a sense of belonging to a nation the existence of which was imputed by the failure of the state to exercise its expected role of protecting its citizens.

The first two events pose a puzzle. In the case of the presidential election, why would a regime that was guaranteed to win a real election choose to undermine its credibility unnecessarily? The case of the unification ceremonies repeats the puzzle in a different form (one common to many dictatorships in poor countries). Why spend a reported $180 million on a celebration in a country with a per capita annual income of less than $300 when state coffers are drained and the IMF is pressing for austerity? The third event differs from the first two in that it occurred independently of state officials' intentions, if not, as critics were quick to point out, of state practices. Like the other two, however, the publicity surrounding the arrest and the discussion that animated public life in the aftermath of the grisly revelations exemplified the ways in which a political community is formed by the shared experience of events, or in this case the shared experience of talking about a well-known event. Unlike the other two cases, the publicity attending the arrest, rather than exaggerating the presence of state institutions, advertised their absence. Registered in reactions to this event is the "moral panic" of citizens longing for a state capable of protecting them.[2] By being aware of the simultaneous and common character of their anxieties, moral entitlements, and desires, even in the absence of state institutions, inhabitants of a common territory were able to experience a shared sense of connection to it.

In this chapter I explore three counterintuitive understandings of the relationships among state sovereignty, democracy, and nationalism. First, whereas contested elections may require "strong" states and national coherence (see, for example, Rustow 1970; Linz and Stepan 1996; Marx 2003), other forms of democratic activity, such as widespread political activism and lively public debates, may exist because state institutions are fragile and affective connection to nation-ness, where evident, is not necessarily cohesive or supportive of regime practices. As we shall see, the fragility of the state and the vibrancy of civic life mean that the regime's exercise of power is both blatant and intermittent. Second, common experiences of moral panic may be just as effective as state spectacles, if not more so, in generating a sense of passionate belonging to the imagined community of the nation. Third and relatedly, experiences of national belonging may actually be shared in the breach of state authority—in the moments when large numbers of people, unknown to each other, long for its protection. Or put differently, Yemen demonstrates how events of collective vulnerability can bring about *episodic* expressions of national identification. This chapter is devoted to elaborating these arguments while narrating the events that bring them to the fore.

THE FIRST PRESIDENTIAL ELECTIONS: ACTING LIKE A STATE, PART ONE

As the introduction noted, unification between North and South occurred with the understanding that a "transition to democracy" would take place.

And in the early 1990s openly contested elections for parliament, a broad range of critical newspapers, and the emergence of over forty political parties made Yemen one of the only Middle Eastern countries to sanction a lively, oppositional politics. The war in May 1994 changed the conditions of democratic possibility, producing a political situation that reinforced the northern regime's dominance. The parliamentary elections of April 1997, which the Yemeni Socialist Party and two other small, southern-based opposition parties boycotted, were widely understood to be less democratic than the ones in 1993 (Glosemeyer 1993). Voter turnout in the South was low, the ruling party won a clear majority of seats (187 out of 301), and the seats of the main Islamic party, al-Tajammu' al-Yamanī lil-Iṣlāḥ, decreased from 62 to 53 (Detalle 1993a, 1993b; Baaklini, Denoeux, and Springborg 1999, 213; Schwedler 2002, 51). Indeed, although the ruling General People's Congress party and the main Islamic party had forged an informal coalition for the 1997 elections, thereby agreeing not to oppose each other in specific districts, many "independents" in those districts turned out to be identified with the ruling GPC. As a consequence, the ruling party's control of the parliament was overwhelming in 1997, with close to 266 seats, or 75 percent of the assembly (Schwedler 2002, 51; Dresch 2000, 209). In some districts outcomes were decided in advance, failing to fulfill even a "minimalist" view of a democracy, in which electoral outcomes are uncertain (Schumpeter 1962 [1950]; Przeworski 1991). The 1999 presidential "election" both demonstrated and contributed to the assertion of northern control and the corresponding constriction of permitted, institutionalized political contestation.

Although the regime represented itself to foreign donors and citizens alike as an "emerging democracy,"[3] the staged elections could not possibly have been intended to reassure Yemeni democrats or foreign observers of the regime's commitment to institutionalizing competitive, free elections. Opposition leaders wondered aloud when an "ornamental democracy" (*dimuqrāṭiyya shakliyya*) might become a genuine one. In newspaper articles and other public venues, people identified with the opposition denounced the elections as mere "trappings" (*libās*), another example of a "theatrical comedy" on the part of the regime, which was gradually narrowing the prospects for democratic politics in Yemen (al-Mutawakkil 1999; al-Saqqāf 1999; Muthannā 1999). The political scientist Muḥammad 'Abd al-Malik al-Mutawakkil even likened the event to "a Hindi film, long, boring, and exorbitantly expensive" (al-Mutawakkil 1999).

Two months before the election, a unified opposition had chosen its candidate for president, ʿAlī Ṣāliḥ ʿUbād, or "Muqbil," the secretary general of the Yemeni Socialist Party. Muqbil was a southerner whom everyone (even Muqbil) acknowledged had no chance of winning, but who could put forth an alternative agenda, increase people's awareness of democratic practices by competing, and enhance possibilities for future electoral successes. In order to begin his campaign, however, Muqbil had to be approved by 10 percent of the members of parliament. This system, borrowed from Tunisian judicial codes, enabled the regime to weed out undesirable nominees, and Muqbil's candidacy was thereby rejected. Thus the regime, rather than sailing to victory in an openly contested election, chose to disqualify the opposition candidate, turning the event into the phony referendum familiar to many postrevolutionary and postcolonial polities. Nor did the ruling party stop there. To replace the opposition's candidate, the regime nominated one of its own southern members, Najīb Qaḥṭān al-Shaʿbī. The son of its first president, who was deposed and imprisoned in 1969 during a coup d'état carried out by socialists, Najīb and his family had fled to Cairo where they had received support and protection for years from the antisocialist North. Election day, then, offered people the choice between two candidates from the same party, the ruling president from the North and the puppetlike contender whose origins were identifiably southern. One published cartoon depicted Najīb as a windup toy. A joke echoed this sentiment: "Najīb is elected and is then asked, 'What is the first thing you are going to do?'" He replies: "Make ʿAlī ʿAbd Allāh Ṣāliḥ president."

Yet even by producing a bogus alternative candidate, the regime enabled some form of limited choice. A few people voted for Najīb Qaḥṭān despite his compromised candidacy. As a taxi driver from Taʿizz argued: "Even though I don't know Najīb, he's got to be better than ʿAlī ʿAbd Allāh. The president steals and he allows others to steal. And when a good prime minister like Faraj Bin Ghānim tries to intervene, he is sacked."[4] People were broadly aware that they could register their protest in at least four ways: they could boycott the election; they could vote for Najīb; they could cross out both candidates' pictures; or they could write in a candidate, as some people claim to have done. For instance, several state employees and opposition politicians reported people writing in the name of Saʿd Zaghlūl, a famous Egyptian nationalist who died in 1927. Rumors circulated that another voter wrote "stupid" (*ahbal*) below Najīb's picture and "robber" (*sāriq*) under the president's.

According to official reports, more than 66 percent of the electorate took part in the presidential election, with President ʿAlī ʿAbd Allāh Ṣāliḥ garnering 96.3 percent of the vote. Independent observers and opposition party members alike, however, estimated that only 30 percent of registered voters bothered to go to the polls. In the aftermath of the election, stories abounded about poor voter turnout, three thousand stuffed ballot boxes hidden in reserve, army personnel dressed in civilian clothing casting additional ballots, and minors voting, some more than once.[5] The act of voting required people to put their thumbprint on the computer-generated list of registered voters, and afterward regime supporters and fearful citizens were eager to signal loyalty by displaying their inked thumbs in public. Stories were told of people who had failed to vote purchasing inkpads from local stores in order to dissemble having participated. People reported being visited by friends checking to see whether they had voted. The inked thumb became a particularly fraught signifier registering either participation in the elections or the fear of having not done so. Or to put it differently, an inked thumb could mean that a person had participated out of duty, love, or fear, or that a person had not participated but could act "as if" he had (Wedeen 1999). The following joke speaks to the latter condition: "A guy goes to a qāt chew and shakes hands with his thumb up to prove that he has voted [a practice many adopted the day after the elections]. His friend says, 'Why is your thumb red?' He replies, 'They ran out of blue inkpads at the store.'"

The ballot sheets themselves, however, signaled the solemnity of official state practice. Colored photographs and the names of the two candidates appeared on each ballot. ʿAlī ʿAbd Allāh Ṣāliḥ was pictured in suit and tie. Below him were the hallmarks of his campaign, three encircled images, the logos of the three main groups that had ostensibly supported the president: *al-majlis al-waṭanī* (a loosely knit group of parties, including Baʿthists and some Nāṣirists) depicts three hands clasping a torch to symbolize unity; the main Islamic party, al-Tajammuʿ al-Yamanī lil-Iṣlāḥ, portrays the sun shining brilliantly on the horizon to connote a "bright future"; and the ruling General People's Congress party's insignia is the horse—symbol of power and bravery (*shumūkh*) or of a shared Arabian genealogy (depending on whom one asks). Qaḥṭān's portrait was set against the backdrop of a sky, the scales of justice to the right, a rather innocuous reference to (both candidates') declared commitments to procedural justice and judicial reform.

Political posters of the president also covered the walls of buildings and the windows of shops.[6] The Delacroix-like portrait of ʿAlī ʿAbd Allāh Ṣāliḥ astride a stallion and draped in a billowing Yemeni flag conjured up for some Yemenis images of ʿAlī ibn Abī Ṭālib, the son-in-law of the Prophet and a symbol for Zaydī Islam of legitimate rule. The original poster, which towers over a main commercial thoroughfare, allegedly cost the regime $13,000, an exorbitant sum.[7] Other posters combined ʿAlī ʿAbd Allāh Ṣāliḥ's portrait with advertisements for companies such as Canada Dry and Daewoo, blending domestic kitsch with global capitalism in ways that probably saved the regime some money. Corporate endorsements signified that the president enjoyed the backing of capital, and that investor confidence was indifferent to, if not supportive of, phony electoral processes.

No one disputed that the Yemeni president would have won an openly contested election against Muqbil, if not by the margin by which he allegedly actually won. As the political scientist François Burgat points out, had leaders of the Islamic party, al-Iṣlāḥ, decided to put forward their own nominee, there might have been some cause for concern among regime officials, but the party's decision to support the president eliminated any prospects for competition, even before the regime's denial of Muqbil's candidacy (Burgat 2000, 70). Ṣāliḥ's assured victory raises the question of why the regime would bar the opposition's candidate, guaranteed to lose a fair and free election, from running. Members of the opposition and the ruling party speculated that Muqbil's personality was to blame; he was difficult and refused to ingratiate himself with members of parliament who might have voted to allow his candidacy. In the words of one opposition politician, "Muqbil doesn't hold his tongue—he'll say anything, and the impact on public opinion of criticizing the president's personality directly inclined the president to make that decision." Politicians close to the president and in the opposition argued that ʿAlī ʿAbd Allāh Ṣāliḥ had personally ordered parliament's members to deny Muqbil's nomination. The president was worried, in this view, that a Yemeni Socialist Party candidate would polarize North and South, thereby solidifying deep regional divisions that had emerged after union and had worsened in the aftermath of the civil war. "Victory" required more than winning the elections; it demanded a vision of unity in which ʿAlī ʿAbd Allāh Ṣāliḥ could represent both regions. Being a "tactician" rather than a "strategist" or statesman, argued one presidential adviser, meant that the president missed a historical opportunity, thereby revealing himself to be like other dictators who prefer garnering an unbelievable number of votes, rather than risk the political uncertainty that a less decisive but more credible victory would have entailed. One key opposition figure likened the president to "a guy who sells groceries at a road stand" (*ṣāḥib al-ṣandaqa*): "He's busy with the little things and can profit from the details, but he loses sight of the big picture. He has small ideas." Slogans congratulating the "father of Aḥmad" (Abū Aḥmad) also suggested the regime's dynastic ambitions, thereby implying that although the president knew that he would win, he did not want to set precedents that might endanger his son's succession. In contrast, some educated professionals who defended the regime justified 'Alī 'Abd Allāh's move by arguing that democracy must proceed gradually. This referendum was a first step in getting people used to the process, and future presidential elections would be fairer than this one. Within a roughly familiar "civilizing process" narrative, arguments about ill-prepared citizens suggested that some elites in Yemen viewed citizens as not yet ready to engage in the mature electoral processes of the developed world. No one, however, could answer why the regime would put forth another candidate from its own party in Muqbil's stead—a variation on the sham election that, to my knowledge, has no historical precedent.

I want to argue that the orchestrated event not only ensured an electoral outcome that was already obvious, but also provided an occasion for the regime to announce and enact its political power—that is, to establish "popularity" by suspending the means of its measure. This political power, in turn, resides and was made manifest in the regime's use of electoral procedures to empty democracy of what many liberals take to be its content: fair, competitive elections. The elections signaled that "support" for the president, by those who admire, fear, and loathe him, could be tied to public performances of democratic openness *and* to the sense of lost opportunities such public performances made apparent. For example: in response to a questionnaire asking whether she "supported the government's policies," a housekeeper from the remote northern mountainous region of Ḥarāz said that she did. When I asked her later how she could give this response when she complained constantly about government actions, she explained, "I'm with them because what's the point of being against them, right? They're the ones in power." The elections communicated this absence of actual alternatives by presenting a bogus one.

This excessive bogusness operated as both a signaling device and a mechanism for reproducing the quasi-autocratic political power it signaled.

On the one hand, the "elections" conveyed to politicians in the opposition and to disaffected ordinary citizens that the regime could actively intervene to foreclose certain democratic possibilities. The elections provided the occasions through which the regime could exercise this authoritarian impulse toward citizens, at least temporarily. On the other hand, although no Yemeni doubted the ruling party's ability to win a fair and free election, in a quasi-autocratic state such as Yemen's, rigging the elections also betrayed official insecurities about the level of victory and what a less than overwhelming majority would mean—reproducing for some a sense of the tenuousness of the regime's political power, as evidenced by stories about poor voter turnout and leaders' anxieties, as well as through public critiques of the electoral process. Yet even when the regime's disciplinary strategies reveal insecurities and are contested by citizens, they are still partially effective—organizing men and women to participate and consume the regime's idealized version of the real. Men and women worked to register voters and to ensure that polls functioned in an orderly fashion. Soldiers were bussed in to vote and ensure stability. Official institutions, including foreign donor organizations (Burgat 2000, 72), devoted time and money to organizing and orchestrating an event everyone knew to be fraudulent. People gathered together in crowds to hear both candidates avow their commitments to institutional reform, stability, security, the material well-being of ordinary citizens, and to democracy itself. The event had the effect of exercising power by announcing it publicly, thereby forefending against the deleterious effects of weak state institutions and IMF pressures by reminding citizens that even regimes without a monopoly over violence have some measure of control.

The control exercised by a regime derives in part from its efforts to act like a state. These efforts summon the state into being—staging occasions in which state power is made actual to both ordinary citizens and regime members. Such enactments always rely on preexisting mechanisms of coercive, utilitarian, and normative compliance. As this chapter shows, in the case of Yemen, where the preexisting forms are especially meager, the way the regime of ʿAlī ʿAbd Allāh Ṣāliḥ attempts to bring itself into being as a state can be seen especially clearly. Of course if crime statistics are any indication, no regime enjoys an undisputed monopoly over force. But the Yemeni regime's coercive control is exceptionally limited, especially outside of the capital. Nevertheless, Yemen's army has been used to quell resistance in the far northern town of Ṣaʿda near Saudi Arabia, in the northeastern areas of Ma'rib and al-Jawf, as well as in the southern areas, such as Kud Qarw village (near Aden), in Aden itself, and in al-Dāli'. Human Rights Watch reports the detention of political prisoners, torture, and death sentences (Human Rights Watch 2000, 420). In the past, the regime has also threatened to dissolve the already weakened Yemeni Socialist Party, and has harassed the independent press on a number of occasions. Security officials infiltrate opposition organizations in order to intimidate and divide would-be dissidents while also providing information about subversive activity to the president.

Even so, a key aspect of the Yemeni example is that such forms of social control do not generate the sorts of fear characteristic of many dictatorships. The government's deployment of military and paramilitary units has usually been a response to an overt challenge to the regime's authority, rather than a prophylactic, protective form of preempting dissent. Yemen, moreover, possesses a dense network of associations and a degree of local civic political participation unparalleled in other parts of the Arab world (Carapico 1998, 1996). As we shall see in the next chapter, in the public spheres of opposition-oriented conferences, political party rallies and meetings, Friday sermons, newspaper debates, and qāt chew conversations, even in the daily television broadcasts of parliamentary sessions, Yemenis from a variety of regional and class backgrounds routinely criticize the regime without the fear of repercussions usually found in regimes classified as "authoritarian."

The regime also exploits its utilitarian mechanisms of social control by purchasing the loyalty of would-be subversives. Automobiles, homes, vacations, and foreign bank accounts are the perquisites of allegiance. Politicians who do not support the regime may also periodically benefit from its largesse. Influential opposition figures sometimes have to make difficult choices about whether to accept such amenities as a bodyguard or a car for the family or money for medical treatment abroad—decisions that may ease life's burdens but may require compromises or generate unsettling questions from colleagues about political commitments. In the absence of state institutions that deliver public goods and services through common administrative institutions, the regime can use its command over resources to strike bargains and punish dissident political figures.

Finally, the northern Sanḥān-dominated regime seems to enjoy some genuine popularity in key areas of the North and in isolated parts of the South. (Sanḥān refers to a self-identified tribe within the larger confederation of Ḥāshid and also designates a region abutting the south side of

Ṣan'ā'.) The North is not a unified region, but many inhabitants—especially in the capital and the northern highlands—actively support the president even when they do not have to do so. The working-class area of Ḥudayda in the Tihāma, the city of Ta'izz and much of *al-minṭaqa al-wusṭā* (the "middle region"), as well as parts of the northeastern desert regions of al-Jawf and Ma'rib, do not overwhelmingly support the regime—if riots and organized, armed resistance are any indication. Even in these areas, however, some would have voted for the president (and did in the subsequent 2006 elections to be discussed briefly below). Although the minority of Yemenis living in the South would probably have voted for a southern candidate had a genuine representative of the region run for the presidency, the South's small population (of anywhere from 2.5 to 4.5 million inhabitants) would not have significantly affected the president's electoral majority.[8] Moreover, dissatisfaction with the former rule of the socialist party among people who self-identify as "tribal" in the interior or *wādī* region of Ḥaḍramawt would have given the president some support there. The ruling GPC has enjoyed backing among southerners whose organizations were prohibited during the socialists' rule there. Despite electoral infractions during the parliamentary elections of 2003, the Yemeni Socialist Party's poor performance—the party won seven seats out of 301—further supports the claim that the president would have won a fair and free election. The common assumption that nondemocratic regimes have no popular support is belied by the president's observable popularity in many areas. Even ambivalent voters argued on more than one occasion that "the devil you know is better than the human you don't."[9] Given the president's ability to win a credible election (or, for that matter, to rig one covertly), the regime's decision to produce an overtly phony one implies that the event did more than exemplify political power; it was also doing the work of creating power by demonstrating to regime officials and citizens alike that the regime could get away with the charade.

This power differs in important ways from the sort apparent in more repressive authoritarian regimes, such as Syria's (Wedeen 1999). In Yemen, this symbolic display gives the regime a power that citizens in many other instances doubt, and it demonstrates that the regime can behave in an authoritarian manner *temporarily*, if not consistently. The Yemeni regime cannot force citizens to *routinely* act "as if" (ibid.). And a vibrant oppositional politics results from the very actions of this weak authoritarian state, thereby requiring new modes of containment.

This difference between quasi-autocratic and more repressive authoritarian regimes is made apparent in the contestation over postelection politics, producing contradictory prospects for institutionalizing contested elections.[10] On the one hand, there are indications that possibilities for fair and free competition have become increasingly constrained. In an August 2000 letter to the speaker and members of Parliament, President ʿAlī ʿAbd Allāh Ṣāliḥ and 144 members of Parliament recommended constitutional amendments that would lengthen parliamentary members' tenure in office from four to six years, thereby postponing the elections scheduled for April 2001. A nationwide referendum in February 2001 approved this extension and also lengthened the presidential term from five to seven years, thereby enabling Ṣāliḥ to remain in office for two terms until 2013, when opposition leaders anticipate that Ṣāliḥ's son, Aḥmad, will make a bid to take over. The referendum also authorized the president to appoint a 111-member "Consultative Council," which activists charged allows Ṣāliḥ to offset the role of the elected parliament and to promote indirect executive control over legislation. Moreover, elections for local councils, held at the same time as the referendum, were marred by opposition charges that voter registration lists had been rigged. Violence also undermined these elections. Forty persons reportedly died and more than a hundred were injured in clashes between supporters of different parties and security forces; official sources claimed that eleven died and twenty-three were injured while people were voting. Disputes over irregularities in at least 20 percent of the polling centers meant that final results in those areas were never announced. The ruling General People's Congress celebrated a comfortable majority in the councils, but opposition leaders charged that results were fraudulent. Even were outcomes to be fair, the local councils' resources and decision-making powers remain circumscribed by the fact that the president appoints the heads of the councils (*al-Ayyām*, August 21, 2000; Human Rights Watch 2000, 420–24). Preparations for the parliamentary elections of April 27, 2003, were similarly tainted with charges of irregularities in registration, and postelection conflicts also raised doubts about the process (although parliamentary elections tend not to be flagrantly phony in the way that the 1999 presidential one was).[11] Parliamentary powers are likewise highly circumscribed even assuming fair elections. The unresolved assassination on December 28, 2002, of a key spokesman for liberal democracy, Jār Allāh ʿUmar, moreover, may have been intended, as many Yemenis claim, to undercut a united opposition.

On the other hand, 'Umar's attempts to forge an opposition alliance between the liberal wing of the main Islamic party al-Iṣlāḥ and the Yemeni Socialist Party have borne fruit in the form of an empowered "joint committee" (*al-liqā' al-mushtarak*) or JMP ("Joint Meeting Parties"). The presence of the JMP, an eclectic mix of five political parties, whose main source of political power comes from the alliance between YSP and Islamic activists, helped make it possible for a bona fide opposition candidate to run in what was framed (in some respects correctly) as Yemen's first genuinely contested presidential election in September 2006. Fayṣal Bin Shamlān, the JMP's chosen candidate and a southerner from Ḥaḍramawt, ran as an independent with the support of both the Muslim Brotherhood wing and the YSP.[12] (Ṣāliḥ was the first-ever incumbent president of an Arab country to find himself in electoral competition with opposition parties rallied behind a single candidate.) Yemenis were able to see speeches of the opposition candidate broadcast on state television and witness Ṣāliḥ being criticized in public in a way rarely experienced before in the region. According to one source, this circumstance arose both because members of al-Iṣlāḥ had allied with the YSP and because the United States "forced" Ṣāliḥ to "accept the challenge of the opposition." (Judging from Yemeni newspaper reports, Bin Shamlān was credited for not being beholden to the West, and the United States received some rare praise for its willingness to stay out of the election.) Particularly noteworthy for some Yemenis was the split among members of the ruling elite identified with the president's tribal confederation of Ḥāshid. For the first time, members of the regime's al-Aḥmar family opposed "a Ḥāshidī" (Ṣāliḥ) seeking reaffirmation of his power. Speaker of Parliament and Ṣāliḥ ally Shaykh 'Abd Allāh Bin Ḥusayn al-Aḥmar published a statement criticizing his sons Ḥamīd and Ḥusayn for siding with the opposition. His reaction came after hundreds of thousands gathered in his region of 'Amrān in support of Bin Shamlān. Most Yemeni analysts echoed the views of a diplomat and former presidential adviser who in an e-mail to me argued: "Ṣāliḥ will win, and will never surrender power. But the next elections in 2013 won't be the same."[13]

The presidential election of 2006 did indeed present in many ways a more sophisticated political drama than its predecessor, but it nevertheless underscored the regime's willingness and ability to assert its political power in the face of an independent, recently unified opposition. Ṣāliḥ issued a surprise announcement in July 2005 that he would not seek "re-election" in the next presidential election, but this was widely regarded from the outset, including by prominent members of the ruling party, as a bogus statement.[14] As predicted, Ṣāliḥ ultimately reversed himself, agreeing to stand for election only after the ruling party extended its two-day conference of June 2006 to an extraordinary third day, imploring their leader to remain at the helm. During the first day of the conference, the president had repeated his refusal to run, with the result that schools and government offices were closed for the next two days, as citizens took to the streets in what official newspapers called "spontaneous" demonstrations of support for Ṣāliḥ's candidacy. Various media reports around Yemen depicted throngs of supporters demanding that he run. When Ṣāliḥ finally did announce his decision to accept his party's nomination to a crowd of thousands at midmorning on the third day, civil servants were required to attend the announcement and residents of remote governorates were bussed to the capital to celebrate. Although, according to witnesses, the demonstrations of adulation were "rather poorly stage-managed," if credibility or discipline was the goal, they nevertheless brought to the fore "the dissonance" between two fundamentally different expectations—that there would be a genuinely competitive election and that the election would serve to reaffirm Ṣāliḥ's mandate (Johnsen 2006, 1–3). On September 20, poll returns registered a resounding victory for the incumbent. Official results, announced on September 23, gave Ṣāliḥ 77.17 percent of the estimated six million votes cast, while his main challenger, Fayṣal Bin Shamlān, received 21.82 percent.[15] Although the opposition alleged voter manipulation and fraud, it ultimately conceded Ṣāliḥ's victory, and Bin Shamlān accepted the results, he said, "as a reality" (Johnsen 2006, 2).

The regime was thus able to win a victory on numerous fronts: Ṣāliḥ's reelection was never in doubt; he could demonstrate to European observers and Yemeni citizens alike that he had permitted an independent opposition to run and lose; and Yemenis invested in electoral outcomes could hope that the unprecedented competition would pave the way for subsequent elections, in which outcomes really would be uncertain and alternation in office a possibility. The spectacles accompanying the election and the outcome itself provided an occasion for an opposition to vent its desires and conjure up alternative political visions. The event also staged public enactments of the regime's dominance, a dominance that resided in the interstices of that dissonance between institutionalized electoral contestation and the certainty of a known outcome, a dominance that is made possible, but also severely limited, by the fact of citizen activism. That this citizenry is armed to the teeth, as the introduction noted, also provides a check on the regime's power, and is a symptom of its weakness.

In summary, the extent to which the regime has been able to foreclose alternative possibilities is in part a result of "theatrical" occasions such as the 1999 and 2006 elections, which the regime puts on to reproduce its political power.[16] It is also the product of a balancing act, entailing the meting out punishments and distributing payoffs, as well as cultivating some belief in the regime's appropriateness, as perhaps the 2006 elections were intended to do. But the 1999 elections also suggest a "muddling through" approach to anxieties about citizen disorder and regional polarization. Subsequent events, including the unprecedented contestation in advance of the September 2006 polling, reinforce this picture in a context in which civil society and the agonistic public conversations it generates continue to be backed by the violent potentialities that an armed population makes apparent.

THE DECENNIAL CELEBRATION: ACTING LIKE A STATE, PART TWO

Preparations for the decennial celebration, like the first presidential election, exemplify the ways in which the regime has attempted to redefine the terms of electoral politics and national unity, orchestrating performances that specify the regime's dominance while simultaneously testing the limits of its political control. The posters of the president hoisting the Yemeni flag, distributed in the weeks before the spectacle celebrating the tenth anniversary of unification, summarized the regime's approach to the founding of the nation-state. The same picture had originally depicted the president of the North and the secretary general of the YSP in the South together in 1990; the northern president raised the flag while his southern counterpart stood behind him. In an effort to obscure the history of partnership that had initially animated union, the southern leader's image was deleted from the photograph in 2000.[17]

The festivities around the tenth anniversary of unification, culminating in celebrations on May 22, 2000, illustrated the regime's idealized representation of national belonging. They also registered a paradox at the heart of the regime's state- and nation-building projects, a project that in the Yemeni case has been ambivalently and sporadically pursued. On the one hand, unified Yemen was founded on what anthropologists Jean and

John Comaroff have termed "the modernist ideal of the nation-state," a "polity held together by the rule of law, by the claim of government to exercise a monopoly over legitimate force, by a sense of horizontal connection, and by universal citizenship which transcends difference" (Comaroff and Comaroff 1998, iii; see also 2004). The celebrations around unification were an attempt to project this image of the nation-state. On the other hand, the production of this ideal required the violation of some of its principles and the concealment of countertendencies, which included the sometimes regime-sanctioned appeals to local justice, or other assertions by regional communities—often termed "tribal"—against the jurisdiction of the state.[18]

In other words, in order to generate a modernist image of the nation-state, the regime had to do *whatever* was necessary to make the projection happen, or seem to happen, in actuality. For example, the unification festivities burdened the regime with a host of security concerns that, in turn, generated new forms of intervention and new efforts to monopolize force. The regime set up roadblocks, multiplied checkpoints, and ordered all mobile phones and pagers shut off at midnight on May 16. The regime also barred tourists from entering the country until June 1 to prevent the public relations fiasco that a kidnapping might cause. Ironically, unification celebrations made travel from one region to another particularly difficult. Rumors of curfews and of not being allowed to leave Ṣan'ā' kept many people off the roads and in their homes.

The regime also made an extraordinary effort to be an effective state by delivering public services. The main streets sparkled with decorative lights and were unusually clean. Garbage was collected more regularly than usual. Rumors suggested that workers actually moved refuse from areas of the city where the foreign delegations were visiting to areas of the city off the beaten path. Blue paint was distributed so that shop doors could be freshly coated.[19] Residents of spacious homes in the posh area of Ḥadda were given money to vacate them, and furniture was specially imported, so that visiting dignitaries could be comfortably housed. One educated woman in Ṣan'ā' noted that the occasion demonstrated the regime's ability to provide state services, at least temporarily. In this light, her sisters raised questions about the regime's seeming lack of "political will" (*irāda siyāsiyya*) to build durable state institutions capable of ensuring citizens' protection and stability, and of providing the services for everyday life on a more regular basis than an official occasion demands.

Preparations also generated considerable ire among ordinary citizens. The celebrations cost anywhere from twenty to fifty billion riyals (in the vicinity of $200 million at current exchange rates). In fact, teachers did not receive their paltry salaries and civil servants had their salaries halved in April so that the regime could pay for the festivities. Regime officials were so concerned that the sixteen hundred youths mobilized to participate in the festival would fail to show up that they postponed the announcement of examination results to induce participation.[20] Students who did not attend would automatically receive a failing grade. Air force planes had been flying in formation above the capital every morning for weeks, the deafening sounds from low-flying aircraft a consistent reminder, and indeed an instance, of the excess and militarism associated with the ceremonies. Rumors that prices would rise once the celebrations were over also made people nervous and angry. In the working-class neighborhood of Ḥaṣaba, people hoarded food in preparation for imagined disasters. Even families identified with the ruling GPC were anxious. One woman whose husband worked as a policeman asked why the regime would put on such a spectacle at a time when people had no money and the government was giving civil servants a smaller part of their salaries, or withholding salaries altogether, in order to pay for the event. Another lower middle-class woman said, "Many of my friends are stocking up on food because they are worried about a coup or something" during the ceremony. Another woman laughed, "We were afraid of the solar eclipse, and now we are afraid of the holiday." Another worried that the ceremony might result in an assassination, "like Sādāt's." Apprehension around the event spoke to the regime's inability to ensure order routinely. As the above statements indicate, that the regime could perform like a state raised questions about why it failed to do so regularly. People also reminded each other of the state's fragilities, so that activities in which the regime was required to be a state were fraught with anxiety.

The actual event began with 'Alī 'Abd Allāh Ṣāliḥ's arrival in a motorcade to the official parade grounds where foreign dignitaries and Yemeni politicians were already seated. Only invited guests were permitted to view the festivities from the parade grounds, and invitations specified that would-be spectators had to gather at six in the morning at the Police College in order to be bussed to the stands where they would watch the festivities. For those viewing the event on television, the beginning of the broadcast showed an edited sequence of clips of the president in a variety of official contexts: crowds cheer him, he responds to questions at a press conference, and planes fly overhead in a display of Yemen's military might.[21]

The president took his seat next to Saudi Arabia's crown prince 'Abd Allāh, perhaps the most important foreign official to attend the ceremony. A panegyric to 'Alī 'Abd Allāh Ṣāliḥ and the union could be heard over the loudspeaker extolling the leader as the "symbol of the nation" (*ramz al-waṭan*) and the "creator of the glorious union" (*ṣāni' al-waḥda al-majīda*).[22] Like the posters omitting the cofounder of the union, 'Alī Sālim al-Bīḍ, the speeches, poems, and visual displays of the unification's anniversary attributed the union to a single founder. The former ruling party of the South proved a specter that haunted the proceedings for those whose memories of history or whose political commitments made them want some acknowledgment of the original founding. When the camera mistakenly aimed its lens at rows of empty seats, knowing viewers could see the visible absence of the socialist members who had decided not to attend.[23]

The Yemeni Socialist Party members were divided as to whether to accept invitations to the gala event. Some members argued that the holiday commemorated unification and therefore was every citizen's holiday. The victory of the North in the war was a separate event and should be treated as such. Other members argued that although they were for the union, the 1994 war was a big loss. Attending the celebration would endorse the regime's version of unity and lend unwitting support to northern dominance. In one qāt chew conversation held at this time, Jār Allāh 'Umar, the assistant secretary general of the party, argued that "the absence of equality between North and South made the initial hopes of unification seem hollow, and its democratic possibilities elusive." For him, even the word *infiṣāl* (secession) had lost its dangerously titillating charge: "People are likely to use the word or to threaten its invocation as a way of policing public space, but it has lost some of its meaning. Words like 'revolution' have also been emptied of their political significance, subject to the banalities of repetition." Some members favored a separate YSP celebration in Aden, while others maintained that the capital of Yemen was Ṣan'ā' and any national event should be held there. After multiple discussions, leaders decided to let individual party members decide for themselves whether to accept the regime's invitation. Some went to the event and others did not.

In terms of the modernist ideal of the nation-state, the celebration represented the image of universal citizenship that is part of that ideal, but in the Yemeni context the image required a hybrid of particular regional practices subsumed under an assertion of northern dominance that seemed designed to unify but proved divisive. This hybridity was most evident during the folklore sequences, when a clunky float of terraced mountains and the façade of Bāb al-Yaman (the main entrance to the capital's traditional market) with ten candles on top and a big number 22 (for the original founding, May 22) on the front appeared on the grounds like a gigantic, mobile birthday or wedding cake. As the float moved to the center of the parade grounds, the names of the different regions of Yemen were recited over a loudspeaker system. Men on horseback and others with rifles dressed in northern highlands' tribal dress and brandishing the conventional daggers filled the parade grounds. At times, the television zeroed in on participants who looked confused or whose horses were misbehaving, but as the spectacle progressed television cameramen filmed an impressive array of men combining dance steps from the northern highlands with those from the northeastern desert.[24] As the dancers moved in unison, the event began to take on the regimented character of a Busby Berkley extravaganza, with the synchronized moves and geometric shapes common to most mass spectacles. The choreographed folk dance part of the spectacle was the regime's effort to make Yemeni "culture" into an explicitly national object—one that hybridized North and South, as well as the coastal and interior regions of the country (see Handler 1988, 14). In one recognizably coastal dance, for example, a northern highlands dagger was used rather than the typical stick. In another dance, men performed stunning southern sword work while dressed in identifiably northern highlands clothing.

These spectacles undoubtedly put forth *images* of unity (Adra 1993, 166; Anderson 1991, 22, 145), but there is little evidence to suggest that they either signaled existing unity or worked to create it. As is common to spectacles everywhere, on the level of visual representation such displays are open to multiple interpretations and invite re-signification. In this case, for some self-identified northern and southern spectators, despite the projection of an explicitly unified national culture, each region's practices were both referenced and relativized in relation to northern, and more particularly highlands, visual dominance. Others, particularly southerners, interpreted the spectacle neither as expressive of unity nor as an instance of northern dominance, but rather as the failure of an explicitly northern imagination to produce dances that did not borrow from the creative movements of the South.[25] Thus the significance of such public exhibitions is not their ability to weld an inchoate national community together, although the festival may have generated feelings of communal pride for some. Rather, the event defined national community in ways that required and advertised a substantial array of regulatory and intrusive capabilities associated with a state.

Although the spectacle's preparations required the careful consideration of the foreign delegates' comforts and distractions, the spectacle's images seemed primarily intended for domestic consumption. Few foreign spectators would be able to distinguish among various regional practices, but most Yemenis could. Similarly, the regimented military parade that followed the folkloric sequences implied the importance of the spectacle's domestic messages: ordered lines of soldiers in a modified goosestep and varying colors of camouflage fatigues represented troops' respective institutional affiliations. The occasion also entailed displaying the latest addition to the Yemeni army's military technology with an air show and presentation of an "all-terrain armoured vehicle built exclusively in Yemen" (*Yemen Observer*, May 31, 2000, 1). Although such displays of military power are typical of most national spectacles, it is inconceivable that Yemen's military hardware would frighten spectators from countries such as Saudi Arabia or the United States. Indeed, as two firsthand Yemeni observers with experience in military affairs told me after the spectacle, the purpose of the display of weapons was probably not to impress foreign viewers, but was intended for domestic consumption. The description of the tank manufactured in Yemen suggests that Yemen's defense forces might have domestic uses for the tank: "The vehicle has bullet-proof armour plating and a high-velocity machine gun with the ability to turn 360 degrees mounted on top. With Yemen's varied landscape a key factor in its design, the vehicle has been adapted to perform in all conditions, particularly in mountain regions. Its flexibility and ability to operate at high speeds have impressed military observers, who expect it to be a vital part of Yemen's defence forces" (*Yemen Observer*, May 31, 2000).

The ordered, mass-mobilization event was the largest and most regimented of its kind in Yemen's history of spectacular displays. Yet the representations of consensual unity could not mask the underlying tensions that preparations for the event had made public. Even members of the ruling party disagreed on how the nation should be represented. Not unusually for any polity, gender was one site of contestation. Among the 100,000 participants, about sixteen hundred were ten-year-old boys and girls representing the generation born after unification. Several Yemeni scholars, headed by Shaykh 'Umar Muḥammad Sayf, a member of the GPC, issued a religious opinion (*fatwā*) prohibiting the participation of females in the parades, but their efforts came to naught.[26]

Why would the regime spend scarce resources and risk alienating important domestic allies and ordinary citizens by producing such an event? In part, the answer rests on insights drawn from the first event discussed in this chapter. The example of the presidential "election" of 1999, in which the regime put forth an opposing candidate from its own party and converted what had promised to be the first free, competitive race into a flawed semblance of democratic politics, is an example of a regime acting to express political power for its own sake—to demonstrate its ability to induce modest participation in, and contain the disappointment of, bogus elections. Similarly, the unification ceremonies offered not only something of a preview image of a modernist nation-state, they also enacted the conditions of its possible emergence by giving the regime an opportunity to act like a state. State intervention entailed putting into practice mechanisms of enforcement that helped ensure the regime's temporary monopoly over violence, as well as producing public services to which most citizen-subjects remain unaccustomed.

In both events we see the regime attempting to reproduce power by developing competencies that allow the regime to monitor and control citizens, to act statelike. These attempts are all the more remarkable in the context of the regime's fragile institutional capacities. The regime's efforts to reproduce its power have therefore tended to rely not on generating durable institutions (although there are some), but rather on the sporadic, intermittent, uneven assertions of power that strategies like spectacular displays allow.[27] These spectacles may also be attempts to construct a national community in the absence of adequate state institutions, such as schools, that are generally entrusted with that role. (Many Yemenis do not attend school, school textbooks often fail to reach the countryside, and schools do not regularly follow the Ministry of Education's directives, instead focusing exclusively on elementary math and Qur'ānic studies while bypassing the courses on "national education" completely.) It remains unclear, however, how successful such festivities are at generating, as opposed to projecting abstractly, national belonging.

Images of national unity do not do away with the divisions that generate lively worlds of debate in Yemen. Both the elections and the unity celebration provided discursive contexts within which alternative forms of group identification and politics could take place. Indeed, in the absence of a repressive apparatus capable of controlling (let alone monopolizing) force, spectacles also inspire public communities of political argument that are often at odds with the regime's vision of political dominance, producing not only temporary and uneven examples of compliance but also unofficial visions of national belonging. The disclosure of serial killings on state property during preparations for the nation's anniversary celebration reinforced a disarticulation of state and nation while simultaneously affirming desires for a nation-state: citizens could make claims as a specifically national assemblage longing for a state capable of ensuring communal safety.

MURDERS IN THE MORGUE: SEEING LIKE A CITIZEN, PART THREE

The "murders in the morgue" case became public knowledge on May 10, 2000, when two mutilated female bodies were discovered at the state-run Ṣan'ā' University. Two days later, police arrested a Sudanese mortuary technician at the medical school, claiming that he had confessed to raping and killing five women. Muḥammad Ādam 'Umar Isḥāq (whose full name was rarely reported) was a forty-five-year-old Sudanese citizen who allegedly admitted to an increasing number of murders—sixteen in Yemen and at least twenty-four in Sudan, Kuwait, Chad, and the Central African Republic (*Observer*, June 11, 2000). The Nāṣirist newspaper reported stories that he had killed up to fifty women (*al-Waḥdawī*, May 16, 2000). It was said that Ādam also implicated members of the university's teaching staff who, he said, were involved in the sale of body parts.[28] According to Brian Whitaker's account in the *Observer* one month later, Ādam "had enticed women students to the mortuary with promises of help in their studies, then raped and killed them, videotaping all of his actions. He kept bones as mementos, disposed of some body parts in sewers and on the university grounds, and sold others together with his victims' belongings" (June 11, 2000).

A purported interview with Ādam published in the Yemeni armed forces newspaper, *26 September*, provided supposed details of the grisly killings. It registered the interviewer's fascination with the particulars and a desire for precision worthy of a detective, as in the following example:

> *Interviewer*: How did you kill and dispose of the corpse of your victim?
> *Ādam*: I strangled her or I banged her head on the ground of the tiled floor.

Interviewer: Immediately when she entered the morgue?
Ādam: As soon as the victim entered the morgue I hit her head on the wall or on the ground.
Interviewer: And why did you cut up or slice your victim after that?
Ādam: In order to obscure her features. I'd already started to cut up the victim and this cutting wasn't a process of slicing. . . . I would cut her in half and I cut her body in parts and then I would hide it for two days or three days, and then I'd skin it and chop the rest into small pieces, and I'd clean the bones and put them in the sink after dissolving the flesh in acid. (26 *September*, May 18, 2000, 4)

When asked why he had "chosen" these specific women to kill, he answered: "The impulse (*al-dāfiʿ*) is for some unknown reason (*huwa ḥājatun fī nafs Yaʿqūb*).[29] When I see girls, specifically beautiful ones, in my mind something happens. I can never resist it" (ibid.). Ādam claims to have begun killing early, before he married, when he was twenty-two or twenty-three years old. He was supposedly influenced by satanic books, especially those written by foreigners and translated into Arabic, such as an alleged book with the title *Qātil al-Nisā'* (The killer of women). He also acknowledged that he was pained by his actions, but could not explain what came over him. When pressed to clarify what his motivation or impulse for killing was, he replied, "I kill her in order to let her enter heaven without her realizing, and I go to hell." When asked why he had spared his wife, he replied laughingly, "Is she a woman?" (ibid.). He flatly denied marketing the organs, and refused to say how many women he had killed in Yemen and abroad.

In a broad spectrum of Yemeni newspapers, one of two pictures of the accused tended to appear. They showed either a wild-eyed man of color behind the bars of his cell, or an impish man in Sudanese dress, handcuffed. All newspapers uncovered the unfolding drama by reporting rumors, speculations, and questions that both reflected and generated anew a community of argument about the nature, causes, and disputed facts of the case. The progressive independent (then) triweekly *al-Ayyām* reported that the Council of the University of Ṣanʿāʾ had fired Ādam from his job in December 1999 after he was found guilty of bribery. The paper asked, "How was the killer reinstated in his job after being expelled for bribery?" (May 20, 2000). The independent weekly *al-Ḥaqq* said in a front-page story that the Sudanese serial killer had begun his life in Yemen as a gardener at the residence of the Ṣan'ā' Bank director, but was dismissed because he made the director feel "uneasy." The director's son was surprised to learn later that Ādam had become an anatomy technician at the Faculty of Medicine, because he knew that Ādam had no qualifications for the job (*al-Ḥaqq*, May 21, 2000). The English-language newspaper, *Yemen Times*, wondered whether the "mystery of the serial killer's accomplices" would be "revealed" (*Yemen Times*, May 29, 2000). The independent weekly *al-Shumū'* asked: "Who is responsible for these crimes of the murderer (*saffāḥ*) of the College of Medicine? The College of Medicine is lax (*sā'iba*) and its security administration doesn't fulfill its duties" (*al-Shumū'*, May 20, 2000, 2). The newspaper of the Sons of Yemen League, *Ra'y*, devoted its headlines to the "faculty butcher" who "kills 16 and sells their organs" (May 16, 2000). *Al-Umma*, the weekly paper of al-Ḥaqq (the Zaydī Islamic party) reported that "the luggage of the accused Sudanese was brought back from Kharṭūm Airport. Only the identity cards of the Iraqi student, Zaynab, and the Yemeni, Ḥusn, were found. No other documents were discovered except a videocassette that is said to contain recordings of two or three of the victims. A common feature among the corpses recovered is that they did not contain livers, hearts, or kidneys, which confirms suspicion that it involves a trade of human organs" (May 18, 2000). The Yemeni Socialist Party's *al-Thawrī* (May 18, 2000) cited police sources claiming that "several security men have been detained" in connection with the crimes at the Faculty of Medicine. *Al-Ṣaḥwa*, the major Islamic party's paper, covered the "demonstrations of anger" when over five thousand students took to the streets demanding broad investigations of the "butchery" (*majzara*) at the Faculty of Medicine (June 1, 2000, headlines). Literate people read newspaper reports aloud to others who could not read. Television and radio reports also informed illiterate Yemenis, and well-known mosque leaders such as 'Abd al-Majīd 'Azīz al-Zindānī recorded scathing condemnations of state impropriety and moral laxity that were then distributed on cassette tapes.[30] Children made extra money by selling photocopies of newspaper pages reporting details of the horror. Unprecedented stories of regime complicity and citizen vulnerability animated public discussions.

Debates in newspapers, in the streets, during Friday mosque sermons and qāt chews, and in government offices laid bare how easily civic terror can be generated by perceptions of ineffective state institutions, and how public appeals can be made on the basis of the moral and material entitlements that citizens of even the most nominal of nation-states felt were due them (see Comaroff and Comaroff 1999). People were outraged that the university had not done more to protect its students or to investigate the disappearances. Criticisms focused on the incapacities of the state, the corruption and potential complicity of the regime, and the need for the seemingly elusive but desirable "state institutions" (*mu'assasāt al-dawla*). In one qāt chew I attended someone went so far as to claim that serial killings could never happen in the developed United States (a point I hastened to correct).

Students of nationalism might be tempted to interpret the narratives about the Sudanese serial killer as an instance of "othering," in which understandings of the nation are brought into being by contrasting Yemenis with Sudanese. In a country with high unemployment, Ādam's status as a Sudanese immigrant with a job did bring to the fore prejudices rarely expressed in public (*Observer*, June 11, 2000, 3). A union leader, for example, charged that "the employment of a foreigner as a university technician contravened a presidential decree" (ibid.). The Sudanese community, which is several thousand strong, immediately condemned Ādam's crime and many said they feared a backlash. Yet, interestingly, although there were some expressions of anti-Sudanese sentiment, especially among the working-class poor, many Yemenis went to great lengths to disavow the chauvinist statements of others. Indeed, if homogeneity is a typical "national fantasy" (see Berlant 1991), Ādam's imprisonment and the subsequent talk about it suggested that not all national citizens shared this desire for homogeneity or thought that it required demonizing Sudanese others. In this vein, one Yemeni intellectual argued that within a broadly Arab nationalist framework Sudanese were not considered others at all, but were rather seen as a subgroup of Arabs whose "habits and ways of thinking were especially similar" to Yemeni ones.[31] What made a Yemeni a Yemeni *in this instance* was therefore the common moral panic that gripped citizens and enabled them to experience themselves as a community—as a group of people who shared a sense of belonging with anonymous others in "homogeneous, empty time" (Anderson 1991, 24; Benjamin 1973, 265). In this view, what gave these citizens a sense of their shared experience was not only the common practice of conversing about the crimes but the recognition that all over Yemen strangers were conducting similar conversations about this unparalleled event. Étienne Balibar argues that "a social formation only reproduces itself as a nation to the extent that through a network of apparatuses and daily practices, the individual is instituted as *homo nationalis* from cradle to grave, at the same time that he or she is instituted as *homo oeconomicus, politicus, religiosus*" (Balibar 1991, 93). In other words, as I argued in chapter 1, people are not born with feelings of national attachment; national citizens have to be made and remade. In the absence of state institutions capable of generating *homo nationalis*, the shared fascination with Yemen's purportedly first serial killings could nevertheless produce conditions in which a putative "nation" of Yemenis longed for a state capable of protecting them.

Admittedly, the existence of shared arguments and the knowledge that anonymous others are similarly engaged in conversation may be a necessary condition for national connectedness, but it is certainly not a sufficient one. For one, the debates were not confined to Yemenis. Non-Yemenis living in Yemen were also engaged in similar discussions. And the tabloid presses throughout the Arab world covered the event in all of its ghastly detail. Nevertheless, claims of moral and material entitlement, the outrage that attended the event, and the expressed hopes that a representative state could be made accountable and ensure safety—these were conversations in which Yemenis often appealed *as a people* (Berlant 2000, 45), wondering aloud too how such a crime could happen *in Yemen*. In other words, people often framed their complaints in terms of a territorially determinate group of Yemeni citizens, who, as "a people," could criticize the regime for failing to act as an effective political authority.

One might also argue that the murders in the morgue simply prompted people to gossip or to discuss a new topic, mostly with their familiar interlocutors and sometimes with strangers they were unlikely to see again. But technologies of communication, such as print media and tape recordings of Friday mosque sermons, worked in tandem with social practices, such as qāt chew conversations, to generate public knowledge both of the event itself and of anonymous others simultaneously engaged in discussions of it: people talked about the event *and* its circulation (about the boys selling photocopies on the streets; about relatives who telephoned to express concern for the well-being and safety of their kin; about the distribution of Friday mosque sermon cassettes; and about previous qāt chew conversations in which aspects of the event were probed with painstaking detail). To be sure, other events have generated lively discussion in public places, but the scope of debate about the murders in the morgue was by all accounts unprecedented. For example, one of the editors of *al-Ayyām* claimed that newspaper issues featuring stories about the murders in the morgue sold seventy-five thousand copies, more than double the number of copies usually circulated. The murders-in-the-morgue conversations constituted a self-organized "public sphere" (Habermas 1996 [1962]) in which citizens, many of whom were strangers to one another, deliberated on the radio, in newspapers, and in qāt chew conversations.[32] These debates represented the practice of "nationness" (Brubaker 1996)—not evidence of a real or enduring collectivity, but of a contingent event whose significance lies in its ability to reproduce the vocabularies of imagined community and popular sovereignty, occasioning the temporary manifestation of community in the warp and woof of everyday political experience.

In contrast to much of the mainstream literature on nationalism cited in previous chapters, the murders-in-the-morgue case suggests that experiences of national belonging can be generated by transient events of collective vulnerability rather than by state institutions (Hobsbawm 1990; Tilly 1975, 1990; Mann 1993, 1995; Weber 1976), industrialization (Gellner 1983), or even the continuous effects of print capitalism (Anderson 1991).[33] In this view, nation-ness need not develop; it can also happen, "suddenly crystallizing as a basis for individual and collective action" within a "political field" conducive to such consolidations (Brubaker 1996, 19–20; see also Sewell 1996; Calhoun 1991). In the broader political context in which nation-stateness is the privileged form of political organization, the "nation" then becomes the intelligible category through which people imagine political community. Doing so effectively may require a plausible rhetorical appeal to language, culture, and/or history, but it does not imply that those characteristics be historically correct and universally shared in the way imaginations represent them.[34] Rather, "protean" communities of argument, prompted by identifiable events, help generate conditions of possibility, idioms of affective connection, and practices of reproduction through which purportedly common experiences of belonging to a territory might be institutionalized or just made available as an organizing principle for making some demands and registering grievances (Brubaker 1996, 10). Nation-ness can wax and wane because the nation is not a "thing," but a set of dispositions inscribed in material practices. National solidarities (and other forms of local or regional attachment) exist through the ongoing work of political elites, but also, as in the case of Yemen's first serial killer, through the acephalous transmission of identifications in the ordinary activities of communication.

In the context of heightened and sustained public debate, the gender politics of the crime elicited multiple interpretations, which tended to coincide with the variety of prevailing attitudes about women's place in the putative nation. Yemen's medical school, established nearly twenty years earlier with thirty-five million dollars in donations from the emir of Kuwait, produced the first female doctors in the 1990s. Nearly half of the thirty-five hundred students enrolled in the college are women, and many women from other Arab countries without medical schools, or without medical schools that admit women, traveled to study at the $3,000-a-year institution (*New York Times*, December 3, 2000). When the killings were first disclosed, parents talked of pulling their daughters from the university. Some local bus (*dabbāb*) drivers and their fare collectors teased women who rode the bus to the university about their destination, often calling out ominously "the Sudanese, the Sudanese." Some members of the Islamic al-Iṣlāḥ party used the case to justify their position that educating women leads to trouble. Others within al-Iṣlāḥ suggested that appropriate safeguards had to be established so that women could be educated safely, and perhaps separately. Among socialists and their allies, discussions ensued about the normative attitudes that underpinned security police responses to reports of women missing. The mother of the twenty-four-year-old Iraqi woman, Zaynab Sa'ūd 'Azīz, whose remains were positively identified, had evidently been told to "search the dance floors" when she reported her daughter's disappearance (*Observer*, June 11, 2000). Other families did not report their daughters missing, supposedly because they worried that their daughters had engaged in illicit sex or run off with a lover.

In Arabic-language tabloids circulating in Yemen and elsewhere, Ādam was even referred to as "the Ṣan'ā' Ripper." The tabloids' analogy of the serial killer of Ṣan'ā' to the legendary Jack the Ripper of late Victorian London may be, in some respects, apt: both were what historian Judith Walkowitz calls "catalyzing" events in which the felt absence of law and order combined with fears of sexual danger to galvanize "a range of constituencies to take sides and to assert their presence in a heterogeneous public sphere" (Walkowitz 1992, 5). The narrative's potency—its ability to stimulate conversation outside the capital where the events took place—may also have to do with the ways in which the capital city is presumed to be the place where state power and services, including security, reside. Moreover, the seeming randomness of the crime helps give the event its nationalist form, inviting individuals to indulge anxieties about their interchangeability with anonymous others, so that despite the factual implausibilities, citizens could even come to imagine themselves or their loved ones in place of the victim, as some Yemenis overtly did.[35] One only has to read the letters in *People* magazine in the United States to get a sense of how this works: When the fashion designer Gianni Versace was murdered by a serial killer in Miami, for example, residents from small towns in rural states registered their worry that the killer in Miami was out to get them too.

The point is not that bad things happen in all countries. Rather, in the context of the dramatic events Yemenis from a variety of class and regional backgrounds, through divergent media, tended to coalesce as a community through the circulation of explanations that privileged state incompetence and linked it to both moral and political corruption. Citizens located themselves in relation to the implied threat and their sense of entitlement as a people in a fantasy of impersonal, effective state institutions and the consequent protection they might offer.

The regime's responses to the "murders in the morgue" were paradoxical. On the one hand, officials put forward the images of Ādam for public consumption. In the official view, Ādam was a depraved man who drank alcohol. In the unfolding of the official account, Ādam confessed to sixteen murders and provided explicit details of his crimes. In the first killing of 1995, according to his alleged statement to the police, he met Fāṭima, a Somali woman, in downtown Ṣan'ā'. He convinced her that he was a well-known professor at the medical school and he enticed her with money to visit him repeatedly at the morgue. There they would have sex; Ādam claimed to have had sex with her more than twelve times before killing her. Another woman came to the morgue to collect body parts for a medical experiment. As she entered he sprayed a chemical on her face, rendering her unconscious. It was at this point that he remembered that her friend was outside. He invited her in, sprayed her in the face as well, and disposed of both bodies in acid (*Observer*, June 11, 2000). The confessions continued, and the state, if slow to react at first, seemed to present an airtight case in which prosecution would be swift, justice enacted, and the rule of law upheld. True, some regime officials seemed incompetent or corrupt, but the state could operate to protect and unite its citizens in the aftermath of the tragedy. The prime minister suspended the dean of the medical school and his deputy, and he fired the university's head of security in attempts to respond to citizen unrest.

On the other hand, the regime's attempts to manage the Ādam affair seemed partial and ambivalent. Both police officers' slow response to initial inquiries by Zaynab's mother and the suspicion that regime officials were implicated in the killings were also part of the public discourses circulating vigorously in the aftermath of May 10, and the regime could do nothing to prevent criticisms from occupying much of public discussion. Moreover, when newspapers published the names of the victims in the beginning of June, several of the women Ādam had confessed to killing turned up alive and in court for the trial of June 3. A woman claiming to be Nadā Yāsīn, a twenty-one-year-old whose rape and mutilation Ādam had described in detail, apparently appeared in court with her sister, who verified her identity, although there was some disagreement about whether she was, in fact, Nadā. Indeed, as Ādam's confessions became obviously less reliable, stories began to spread about high-ranking government officials' complicity in an alleged prostitution ring. According to these accounts, Ādam was the "fall guy" for a great government conspiracy. None of the evidence at the trial supported these claims, but the fact that such rumors circulated revealed worries about a regime that not only failed to provide proper state institutions but also contributed to the nation's moral deterioration. As the school's founding dean said, "We have had to ask ourselves some hard questions, such as 'Is there a moral decay?' and 'What happened to our standards?'" (*New York Times*, December 3, 2000). The regime's decision to bring in a team of German forensic experts also proved embarrassing. They found pieces of more than one hundred bodies in the morgue, mostly from men, that had never been entered in the morgue records. Professors claimed, according to the *New York Times*, that "deliberately loose controls were adopted in the medical school's early years, when illicit importation of bodies and body parts was necessary to circumvent Islamic injunctions in Yemen against dissection." Certainly loose controls at the university were not merely the product of injunctions—Islamic or otherwise. The criticisms that circulated in public were simultaneously about the unusual horror of the event and the all-too-familiar experience of loose controls. The regime's attempts to manage moral panic, then, also registered its incompetence and laid bare the limits of state power. Legal scholars and ordinary citizens appealed to the constitution and bemoaned the absence of institutions that could make officials accountable and people safe. Even the sentence made evident some of the inadequacies of a regime and the vulnerabilities of supposed commitments to the rule of law. Ādam was eventually convicted of only two murders—Zaynab's and that of Ḥusn Aḥmad 'Aṭiyya, a twenty-three-year-old woman from Hamdān whose remains were found in the morgue's drains—and sentenced to death.

The sentence, too, exemplified the tensions between various aspects of a distinctly modernist ideal of the nation-state and actual regime practices.

The judge, Yaḥyā al-Islāmī, ruled that Ādam be taken to the "forecourt of the morgue" in plain view of students and faculty, where he would be "tied to a wooden board, lashed 80 times for his admitted use of alcohol, then executed, either by beheading with a sword or by lying face down and being shot three times through the heart" (*New York Times*, December 3, 2000). But the judge's insistence that the execution be carried out on university property drew criticism from students and faculty at the college, as well as from local human rights lawyers. Ādam's defense lawyer also complained that he had been permitted only one five-minute meeting with his client in the entire six months between arrest and conviction. Muḥammad Ādam 'Umar Isḥāq was finally executed, near but not on university grounds, in a public square in the neighborhood of al-Madhbaḥ, on June 20, 2001. With security forces cordoning off the square, in front of the victims' families and a crowd estimated to be in the thousands, a single policeman fired five bullets into Ādam's back.

The regime could mobilize its security apparatus and enforcement capabilities in retrospect. It could even exercise its "legitimate" or moral right to dispense violence by legally executing Ādam. But faith in constitutionality and desire for the rule of law, which were expressed in newspaper accounts, in ordinary conversations, and in the fact of the trial, were at odds with the prosecution's story, the judge's initial rush to judgment, and the choice of venue for the execution. The nation as an assemblage of anonymous citizens who share a sense of attachment by virtue of undergoing common experiences (not in the sense of having experienced the event itself, of course, but in the sense of experiencing the narrative and participating in its circulation) was being formed in the breach of state authority. The publicity around the serial killings demonstrated the fragility of state power at the same time that it made manifest a process of nation-ness predicated on moral panic and the desire for protection.

Protection, as Charles Tilly points out, has two contrasting connotations. The comforting sense of the term "calls up images of the shelter against danger provided by a powerful friend, a large insurance policy, or a sturdy roof" (1985, 170). The other sense connotes "the racket in which a local strong man forces merchants to pay tribute in order to avoid damage—damage the strong man himself threatens to deliver. The difference [between the two senses], to be sure, is a matter of degree" (ibid.). Tilly likens state making to organized crime in the sense that states tend to stimulate the very dangers against which protection is then required. Of course the analogy between a state and the Mafia has limits, as Diego Gambetta has pointed out (Gambetta 1993, 7). Plausible arguments can be advanced, moreover, that Yemen's regime does operate more like a mafia than like a state. The points to be made in the context of the three events analyzed above are simple: (1) Regimes that do not fulfill the conditions of a "minimal state" (Nozick 1974) by exercising enough control over violence that citizens feel protected "whether they like it or not" (Gambetta 1993, 7) *may* end up being more "democratic"—more encouraging of civic associations, vibrant political debate, and substantive thinking about politics—than regimes with efficacious state institutions and/or passionate attachments to a nation, a point we shall investigate in more detail in chapter 3. The fictitious elections dramatized the regime's power to foreclose democratic possibilities, but official power remains limited by the vigorous public sphere activities that coexist with, and offer public criticisms of, these phony rituals. (2) Public spectacles generate the sorts of security dangers that then prompt, and sometimes justify, state protection. The Yemeni regime can at times act like an effective state, and public spectacles such as the presidential election or the unification ceremonies place these acts on display for citizens' consumption. (3) Public criticisms of regime practices, however, reveal that many citizens want protection in Tilly's first, optimistic sense of that term. Incidents such as the serial-killing drama suggest that nation-ness might nevertheless be constituted in the absence of an effective sovereign state, through the shared experiences of belonging to a community whose members collectively long for an institutional authority they lack in common. In the example of the serial killer incident, nation-ness is evident in the content of discourses. This content consists of appeals to the corporate identity of "a people," uses the "we" to speak of fellow Yemenis, grounds that community in notions of territorial sovereignty, and consequently invokes the state as the addressee for citizens' material and moral grievances. Nation-ness is also apparent in the fact that these discourses circulate through a variety of media, including local newspapers, mosque sermons, and social gatherings, thereby generating multiple publics—audiences that can imagine anonymous others simultaneously having similar conversations within the boundaries of a nation-state called Yemen.

CONCLUDING REMARKS

Many scholars of political transitions have taken national unity and the existence of a sovereign state as prerequisites for the development of democracy. Dankwart Rustow, for example, views national unity as a necessary condition for a transition to democracy: "The vast majority of citizens in a democracy-to-be must have no doubt or mental reservations as to which political community they belong to" (Rustow 1970, 352).[36] Juan Linz and Alfred Stepan argue that a transition to democracy is exceedingly difficult in a country that has a "stateness problem." According to these authors, "modern democratic governance is inevitably linked to stateness. Without a state, there can be no citizenship, without citizenship, there can be no democracy" (1996, 27).

The Yemeni example, by contrast, suggests that lively political activity and experiences of citizenship may actually thrive under conditions in which, perhaps even because, the state is fragile and national identification limited. Admittedly, my account has not established a strong causal claim, but the evidence adduced here does support hypotheses to be "tested" or explored. First, state formation seems to entail modes of regimentation and pacification that may be antithetical to democratic activities, if by "democratic activities" we include the presence of civic associations and also the informal political practices of vigorously debating with others in public questions about action—about what should be done. In Western Europe, the birth of electoral forms of government occurred after "absolutizing" monarchies created unified institutions of power, controlled directly by the ruler, who gradually came to preside over the decentralized feudal aristocracy (Anderson 1991, 55). According to Norbert Elias's account, state formation also entailed the pacification of restive populations through the introduction of codes of conduct, manners, norms, prohibitions, and constraints that worked to co-opt elites and "civilize" the population—modes of "self-government" that conditioned the form that liberal democratic institutions assumed historically, and that may have helped to ensure their durability (Elias 1982). Similarly, in *Discipline and Punish*, Michel Foucault suggests that Western European states became increasingly capable of regulating their subjects, devising a "specific technology of power . . . called 'discipline,'" which replaced the external sovereign authority (Foucault 1979, 194). The disciplinary power of modern liberal states works by virtue of the internalization of patterns of authority previously experienced as external constraints. It operates by producing persons whose "subjectivity" or "individuality" is formed by a multitude of specialized institutions and disciplines (Mitchell 1991, 93, discussing Foucault; see also Althusser 1971). Disciplinary power produces "docile bodies," according to Foucault (1979), which both participate in and are the results of these new mechanisms of social control. The argument is by now familiar, and the coherence and unprecedented nature of these "technologies" may be exaggerated. The point to be registered here is that the institutions through which states generate power, such as armies, schools, and factories, may help to ensure the durability of electoral institutions while also destroying vigorous forms of public life that are participatory and discursively vibrant, but also inherently less stable and institutionalized than liberal democracy has come to be. Citizens in fragile states may thus enjoy lived experiences of participation and contestation that are eliminated when states regularize their monopoly over force and their control over populations. In the next chapter I explore this hypothesis in more detail, for the Yemeni case suggests not only that civic participation can exist under conditions of tenuous state control but also that it may be an effect of such conditions.[37] Similarly, the contested character of national unity may encourage civic participation rather than undermine it. A national politics that puts too much emphasis on unity and consensus often comes at the expense of not tolerating difference. When late centralizing regimes make efforts to be statelike or define the terms of national unity, they often narrow democratic possibilities rather than broaden them. In chapter 3 we shall see how the Yemeni case invites scholars to think of civic engagement not as an instrumental good leading to formal democratic institutions (Putnam 1993) but as the very activity of energetic political participation in its own right.

Second, if spectacles operate to teach or signal the reality of the regime's domination, they are also strikingly visible instances of that domination *and of its precariousness*. In Yemen, as opposed to an authoritarian context such as Syria, these spectacles can be occasions for temporarily dominating, without saturating, social or even political life. The regime has a monopoly over official pageantry, and it has some control over its self-representation as a nation-state. But the images a fragile state is able to convey are intermittent and transient—hints of political possibility rather than established facts. Some citizens were aware of the ways in which the elections and subsequent spectacles were simultaneously announcements, generators, and barometers of the regime's power. The regime had to mobilize people, channel goods and services, and produce the messages that would become the subject of newspaper reports, street and qāt chew conversations, and intellectuals' conferences. The regime could navigate various contestations in political life by ignoring most, co-opting some, punishing others—and doing it all publicly. By acting like a state, the regime was not dissimulating state-ness—it was being one. But this performance has unintended consequences, ones that are difficult for weak authoritarian states to control, opening up not only opportunities for compliance but also spaces of sustained and direct public critique. To put it in terms of performatives: the regime could summon into existence both the state and, at times, a national public; but producing a national public is not the same as generating unity; regime projections of unity do not in themselves foster it; ordinary citizens could also use idioms of national belonging to demand more than intermittent exercises of state protection, performing national attachment by voicing longings for security in the form of a state capable of ensuring it.

Third and relatedly, cases of early state formation in Western Europe suggest that the state evolved into a powerful set of institutions before nationalism developed as the articulated ideological expression of common political identification (Gellner 1983; Hobsbawm 1987, 1990; Mann 1993, 1995; Weber 1976; for a contrary account of nationalism in England, see Pincus 1999). National identity emerged from the state in the form of a legal framework for citizens as rights-bearing individuals (Shafir 1998). Scholarly accounts of a number of postcolonial states suggest a second, different relationship between state and nation "building." In these cases, regimes have had to construct an effective institutional apparatus while concomitantly cultivating national consciousness. The need to consolidate state power while generating national identification affects the kinds of institutions, practices, and loyalties these regimes can produce. In the examples of many postcolonial states, such exigencies have produced authoritarian regimes that deliver goods and services in return for a modicum of national allegiance and a lot of obedience.

The case of Yemen suggests a third model of political development, involving the emergence of vague, mildly constraining forms of national identification in the absence of an effective sovereign state. The serial-killing incident points to a possible grassroots source of national solidarity under such circumstances. It suggests that discursive practices, such as newspaper and television reports, mosque sermons, and some street and qāt chew conversations help to construct national persons by producing the shared conditions under which a community of anonymous fellow citizens can imagine itself into existence. This point already appeared prominently in chapter 1, in the discussion of the intellectual and popular history of nationalist ideas in Yemen, and it is one that we shall continue to explore in the next chapter. Violence, moreover, is generative in its own right, and the serial-killer melodrama reveals the limits of order while also providing the occasion for authorizing state control. The crime, rather than regime-initiated spectacles, thus summons into existence both state institutions and members of a national commonweal, citizens whose anxieties and entitlements are territorially specific and simultaneously experienced (see Comaroff and Comaroff 2004, 808, 813). In Anderson's terms, nationalism entails citizens becoming aware that their concerns are "being replicated by thousands (or millions) of others of whose existence [they are] confident, yet of whose identity [they have] not the slightest notion" (Anderson 1991, 35).[38] Yemen shows how the shared sense of entitlement to state protection can bring into being *episodic* instances of a national life.

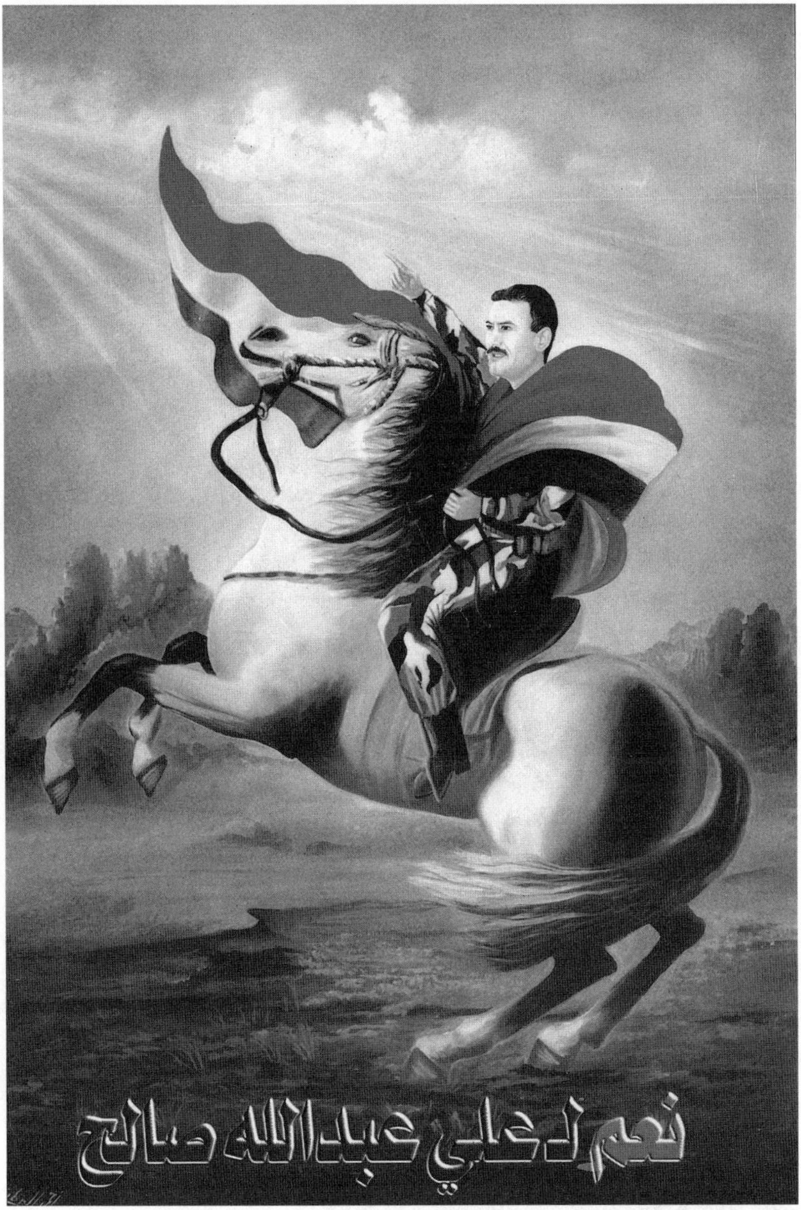

1. This Delacroix-like portrait of ʿAlī ʿAbd Allāh Ṣāliḥ astride a stallion and draped in a billowing Yemeni flag appeared during the first presidential "election" of 1999.

2. A bumper sticker in support of the president that circulated during the first presidential "election" of 1999. The caption reads "Yes to 'Alī 'Abd Allāh Ṣāliḥ."

3. President Ṣāliḥ raises the Yemeni flag in Aden on the occasion of unification, May 22, 1990. 'Alī Sālim al-Bīḍ, secretary general of the Yemeni Socialist Party and vice president of the new Republic of Yemen, stands behind him. After the 1994 war, in posters featuring this event, al-Bīḍ and other YSP members were airbrushed out of the picture. Photograph is the property of the author, from the original found in the Military Museum, Ṣan'ā'.

4. This illuminated map of Yemen on prominent display in the capital's Military Museum commemorates the North's "victory" in July 1994. Photograph property of the author.

5. Yemenis showing enthusiasm for the unification festivities of May 22, 2000.

6. A poster commemorating the tenth anniversary of unification, May 22, 2000. The caption reads: "Our armed and security forces . . . for defense and growth and peace." (The word for growth translates literally as building or construction.)

7. A photo from the actual spectacle celebrating the tenth anniversary of unification. Note the float with the façade of Bāb al-Yaman (the main entrance to the capital's historic market) with ten candles on top and a big number 22 (for the original founding, May 22), which looks like a mobile birthday or wedding cake.

8. A qāt chew gathering in the capital. Photograph courtesy of ʻAlī Sayf Ḥasan.

9. A young boy holding a bundle of qāt for the day's chew. Photograph courtesy of ʻAlī Sayf Ḥasan.

CHAPTER THREE

THE POLITICS OF DELIBERATION

Qāt Chews as Public Spheres

During a televised interview with the London-based Middle East Broadcast Corporation, President ʿAlī ʿAbd Allāh Ṣāliḥ rationalized his plans for his son Aḥmad's succession by claiming that another republic, the United States, had provided the example: George W. had "inherited" his position from his father, former president George Bush. President Ṣāliḥ was then asked whether he was aware of the U.S. electoral process by which President Bill Clinton had succeeded the elder Bush and then won a second four-year term. Ṣāliḥ laughed and said that Clinton was a "*muḥallil*," or legal facilitator. According to Islamic law, or *sharīʿa*, for a divorced woman to remarry her ex-husband, she must first marry a *muḥallil*, an interim husband who makes possible the return of the actual one. In this view, the Clinton presidency amounted to a mere formality, enabling junior's succession and putting the Bush family back in the White House (MBC interview, February 19, 2001; facsimile provided by ʿAlī Muḥsin Ḥamīd, private communication).

As analogies go, the comment was rather weak, casting Clinton as the stooge or dupe, a political facilitator whose own role amounted to getting "screwed" in the process of the Bush family's reascension to power. Yet to Yemenis, Ṣāliḥ's impertinence concealed a more serious matter. As one

Yemeni diplomat complained, "We fought hard to overthrow the monarchy. And now the republics are becoming monarchies. Worse, some of the monarchies are better than our republics!" The easy transition from father to son in Syria, from Ḥāfiẓ al-Asad to his son Bashshār, established the precedent, signaling to other aging fathers in the region that their sons too could assume power and "screw the people."[1]

Ṣāliḥ's sarcastic comment may have sparked ire or disapproval among some Yemenis, but it also cast aspersions on American democracy, reversing the conventional assumption according to which a country such as the United States is unquestionably democratic, while a country such as Yemen is not. The statement thus invites questioning anew what democracy means and how scholars recognize it in particular countries. In this chapter I take up that invitation, shifting from the previous preoccupation with nationalism to consider an alternative dimension of political identification. In doing so, I pick up on a proposition introduced in chapter 2, namely, that the very fragility of some authoritarian states may enhance opportunities for widespread activism and critical, deliberative discussion. Using the example of qāt chew gatherings, I argue that the deliberation so evident in these meetings represents an important aspect of democratic practice and personhood. These discussions are part of what it means to act democratically—to entertain lively disagreements about issues of mutual public concern, and to make worlds in common. They occur daily in public or semipublic places, in which qāt, a leafy stimulant with similarities in effect to caffeine, is chewed in the context of structured conversations that often last for four or five hours. In rooms set aside for this purpose in houses or a civic association's offices, as many as several dozen people, some of whom are strangers to one another, meet to debate literary matters, political life, and social problems. It is the political salience of such publics, specifically the significance of this type of activity for our understanding of democracy, that I want to investigate in the following pages. In addition, and in returning to this book's focus on nationalism, the chapter shows how the presence of an active public sphere can, although need not, coincide with an explicitly national one.

The chapter is divided into four parts. Part 1 examines an exemplary large-N, methodologically motivated analysis operationalizing a minimalist definition of democracy as contested elections.[2] I show how the minimalist definition, popularized by Joseph Schumpeter and now taken for granted in many areas of political science and policy-making circles, is deeply problematic and in need of revision. My claim is that the stripped-down notion of democracy as contested elections (represented here by the influential *Democracy and Development: Political Institutions and Well-Being in the World, 1950–1990* [Przeworski et al. 2000]) deflects attention from important forms of democratic practice taking place in authoritarian circumstances. In part 2, I enlist Habermasian public sphere theory as a possible way of redressing minimalism's lack of attention to the substance of democratic practices. By using the example of Yemeni qāt chews, I argue that everyday practices of vibrant political contestation, which exist in Yemen outside of electoral channels, confound aspects of both the minimalist and the Habermasian frameworks. I argue here that the very activity of deliberating in public contributes to the formation of democratic persons, but does so in conditions fundamentally different from the ones Habermas identified as seminal in Western Europe. Part 3 deepens the analysis by using ethnographic evidence to specify how qāt chews operate as performative, democratic practices, ones capable of conjuring up multiple publics, some of which are recursive and wide ranging enough to be national ones. (Although I sometimes use the word "performance" here because it is less cumbersome aesthetically, I am deploying the term to invoke the formal definition of the performative as bodily and speech acts that iterate norms in the context of everyday life.) Part 4 begins by suggesting why vibrant public sphere activities such as those found in Yemen do not necessarily lead to contested elections, and thus returns to the large-N work that best supplies a possible answer to the question of why not. But I do not stop there: I also explain how interpretive work adds value to our political analyses. I argue that close attention to the case of Yemen raises a crucial distinction between *democratic* practices and *liberal* values. By analyzing the effects of everyday democratic practices in the absence of genuinely contested elections, I specify the work public spheres *do*, in preference to the conventional focus on the values to which individuals subscribe.[3]

PART ONE: THE LIMITS OF A FORMALISTIC ACCOUNT

At least since Joseph Schumpeter, scholars have argued that in order for a government to be "democratic," political succession must be accomplished by competitive elections in which outcomes are uncertain and losing candidates agree to abide by the results in hopes of coming to power in subsequent elections (Schumpeter 1962 [1950]; Przeworski 1991).[4] This formalistic and minimalist understanding of democratic governance may represent a useful simplification for some purposes, but it also raises as many questions as it answers. What counts as uncertainty? When outcomes are all but certain because a candidate is obviously popular or the political machine proves particularly efficacious, such as in Chicago, does this mean the system is undemocratic? The minimalist definition also presupposes a meaningful choice among candidates. But what of cases in which the competing candidates seem uniformly terrible or their policy differences indiscernible? What if the choices do not seem like choices at all? Does it matter for democracy if people do not vote? Is a polity still "democratic" if its citizenry is characterized by apathy, resignation, despair, cynicism, and frustration, and therefore chooses not to participate in elections? The minimalist view has little to say about the sensibilities of voters or the conditions under which people might experience their elections as meaningful.

Democracy and Development attempts to address some of these questions by way of assessing the impact of regime type on "economic well-being." Yet, importantly, Przeworski et al.'s discussion of democracy not only reproduces a conventional Schumpeterian conceptualization of what democracy means but also contributes to a political project that has significant effects in the world. Przeworski et al.'s studies tend to be user friendly for international agencies, in a situation in which the labeling of a country as "democratic" or "authoritarian" can have far-reaching and sometimes devastating consequences for international funding or for relations among states. The authors' claims to value-free science also obscure important ideological commitments—ones that anchor democracy in a minimalist conception of electoral competition, disqualifying other understandings of the term and effectively rendering them impractical. My focus on Przeworski et al.'s text therefore takes that influence (both in policy-making circles and in political science) as a justification for analyzing the argument's key problems. In other words, I attend carefully to the specific logics of the discourse—the ways in which the arguments both reflect and instantiate distinct epistemological assumptions and convictions, ones that help to produce what Stuart Hall calls the "horizon of the taken for granted" (1988, 4). I show that Przeworski et al.'s definition is highly externalist; it presumes that democracy is framed in terms external to the ideological conditions of its emergence. Although the definition may provide a useful refraction, it also becomes a key point of reference, thereby displacing historical and philosophical uses of the term with a particularly narrow, incomplete (if seductive) scholarly one.

Przeworski et al. define democracy as "a regime in which those who govern are selected through contested elections" (Przeworski et al. 2000, 15). Contestation exists when there is an opposition that has "some chance of winning office as a consequence of elections" (16). The aim of their book is not strictly to analyze political regimes but to assess the impact of regime type on "economic well-being." They find that transitions to what they call democracy can occur in both poor and wealthy countries, but the probability that democracies will survive increases as per capita incomes get larger.

Operationalizing their definition of democracy entails the specification of classificatory rules that delimit the nature of a democratic regime: the chief executive and legislature must both be elected in a multiparty system in which alternation in office via elections is observable. Alternation in office is "prima facie evidence" of contestation, which requires "ex-ante uncertainty, ex-post irreversibility, and repeatability" (16). Uncertainty does not imply unpredictability, according to this view, because "the probability distribution of electoral chances is typically known. All that is necessary for outcomes to be uncertain is that it be possible for some incumbent party to lose" (17). Outcomes are uncertain because even though Chicago's Mayor Daley, for example, never loses, the rules and procedures are institutionalized so that he could. This clarification seems helpful and right, given the procedural notions underpinning a thin, formalistic position.

The formalistic, minimalist definition has much to recommend it, if the goal is to pursue a large-N, transhistorical study. Yet despite its attractions and value, the definition also has limitations for scholarly thinking about democracy. One problem is that the definition rules out substantive, as opposed to procedural, conceptions, which would allow for degree-oriented notions of democracy that better describe the dynamics of lived political experience in many cases, including Yemen. A related problem derives from the authors' reliance on a procedural notion of democracy that is itself derivative of the methods used to measure it, leading the authors to make troublesome claims that do not hold up under scrutiny. One such contention is that alternative definitions of democracy give rise to "almost identical classifications of the actual observations" (Przeworski et al. 2000, 10).

But that assertion *cannot* be true if those definitions are really different or "alternative." Rather, the authors' methods seem to *require* the minimalist conceptualization, which, in turn, generates particular kinds of classificatory rules that then necessitate a binary or nominal classification system. Or put differently, a binary classification system—in which a regime either is a democracy or is not—results from a shared reliance on a formalistic, procedural notion of what democracy *is*. Other definitions *could* conceivably yield different classification systems, but the authors' conceptualization forecloses such possibilities. The authors are thus able to analogize a ratio scale to the "proverbial pregnancy. . . . Democracy can be more or less advanced, [but] one cannot be half-democratic: There is no natural zero point" (Przeworski et al. 2000, 57). In their view, scholars who argue that democracy is a continuous feature over all regimes are simply wrong (e.g., Bollen and Jackman 1989, 612). Yet a binary classification system relies on a definition too narrow to capture democracy's substantive connotations—the intricacies of its grammar and the conventions of its use. Such a definition also works normatively to validate existing electoral arrangements in Western democracies, while allowing scholars to ignore a wide range of democratic practices in nonelectoral contexts.

There are, of course, definitions of democracy that might generate alternative systems of classification. As Ian Shapiro notes:

> Democracy means different things to different people. Sometimes it is identified with a particular decision rule; at other times it conjures up the spirit of an age. Democracy can be defined by reference to lists of criteria (such as regular elections, competitive parties, and a universal franchise), yet sometimes it is a comparative idea: the Athenian polis exemplified few characteristics on which most contemporary democrats would insist, but it was relatively democratic by comparison with other ancient Greek city-states. Many people conceive of democratic government in procedural terms; others insist that it requires substantive—usually egalitarian—distributive arrangements. In some circumstances democracy connotes little more than an oppositional ethic; in others it is taken to require robust republican self-government. And whereas some commentators insist that collective deliberation is the high point of democratic politics, for others deliberation is an occupational hazard of democracy. (Shapiro 1999, 17)

Imagine adopting a definition of democracy that emphasizes aspects of substantive representation, rather than simply the existence of contested elections. Substantive representation implies, among other things, that subjects have control over what a government does, and that governments are continually responsive and accountable to their subjects.[5] In this view, citizens might have more or less control over rulers, and governments might be more or less responsive to citizens—or responsive in some contexts but not in others. A definition predicated on citizen impact and regime responsiveness would presumably yield a system of classification based on a continuum rather than a dichotomy, with the effect of undermining the exclusive focus on elections that is central to the Przeworskian vision. A continuum allows us to produce more fine-grained, accurate accounts of politics, ones that do not commit the fallacy of confusing Yemen with states such as North Korea or Ba'thist Iraq.

Using a formalistic definition thus entails an additional limitation: it tends to obscure concerns of central importance to substantive representation, such as how democratic rulers should act once elected, or what their duties and obligations as rulers are or should be (Pitkin 1967). As Hanna Pitkin notes, a formalistic view of what she calls "representative government" operates like a "black box shaped by the initial giving of authority, within which the representative can do whatever he pleases" (Pitkin 1967, 39). This view—what Pitkin calls the "authorization" position—makes elections the key criterion of representative democracy; representation is "seen as a grant of authority by the voters to the elected officials" (Pitkin 1967, 43). The criterion of political success becomes the ability to capture elections, rather than governance as such. The problem with the formalistic approach from this perspective is that "if representing means merely acting with special rights, or acting with someone else bearing the consequences, then there can be no such thing as representing well or badly" (Pitkin 1967, 43). In other words, there can be no such thing as continual accountability or immediate responsiveness, no account of how those elected actually govern, and no standards for assessing whether their policies work for or against the citizens who have elected them.[6]

Substantive representation also implies citizen participation in political life. Surely the formal (and perhaps de facto) disenfranchisement of large numbers of people disqualifies a political regime from being democratic in most of our ordinary language uses of the word, but in the Przeworskian world, participation is not an issue. Avoiding participation as a factor may facilitate coding transhistorically, but it denies the context-specific ways in which we customarily understand democratic relations between rulers and ruled. Would a country in which contestation meant competition within a small, restricted elite circle be a democracy in any meaningful sense of the term today? If highly restricted suffrage can nevertheless count as democracy, then the reasons for insisting on a multiparty system seem arbitrary and unhelpful. It is unclear why a one-party system could not be democratic if divergent interests might be represented. As Boriana Nikolova points out, it is not even clear why, according to this minimalist view, elections should be held at all if divergent interests can be represented without citizens voting.[7] An account that privileges issues of substantive representation would allow us to distinguish between the United States before the Voting Rights Act, for example, and the United States in its aftermath. And as this section has been at pains to point out, citizen participation does not simply take place during elections. Participation also implies, as Hannah Arendt (among others) teaches us, discursively organized political action in which persons transform themselves through their words and deeds, fashioning themselves as citizens by forming agonistic publics and elaborating worlds in common.

As suggested above, Przeworski et al.'s adoption of a thin, or minimalist, definition is, in part, a way of facilitating coding in the interests of scientific testing. Yet this commitment to the scientific method comes at the cost of ignoring much of what is political and important about the practices of democracy. Moreover, ideological convictions trouble claims of impartiality, enabling the minimalist definition to coalesce with a defense of U.S. liberalism. For example, Przeworski et al. criticize Dahl's insistence on the importance of participation in his definition of democracy, justifying their own exclusion of it, because Dahl sets the threshold of participation "too high," thereby disqualifying the United States "as a democracy until the 1950s" (Przeworski et al. 2000, 34). It is unclear, however, why excluding the U.S. is a problem per se.

These troubles imply that Przeworski et al. (and others inspired by such an approach) might be better off avoiding the term "democracy" altogether. The overall objective of such studies would then be to explain the relationship between contested elections and economic development, without producing general accounts of democracy that would seem to foreclose thinking about political participation and accountability within and outside of electoral confines. By identifying the general relationship between regime type and economic well-being, *Democracy and Development* and projects similar to it evacuate politics of the messy stuff of contestation—of initiative, spontaneity, self-fashioning, revelation, ingenuity, action, and creativity—which often occurs *outside the domain of electoral outcomes.*

As I will show in this chapter, the example of Yemen demonstrates that any political analysis that fails to take into account participation and the formation of "public spheres" as activities of political expression in their own right falls short of capturing what a democratic politics might reasonably be taken to include.[8] I do not mean to suggest that because Yemen is more democratic in some ways than other countries in the Middle East, that it *is* a democracy in either the sense of holding fair, contested elections or occasioning adequate experiences of substantive representation. Rather, in this chapter I am interested in exposing the democratic deficits that the electoral definition conceals.[9] I also argue that there are different sites for enacting democracy, and a strong democracy needs to be using them all. Thus, a consideration of democracy also requires theorizing about *aspects* of substantive representation that *are* evident in Yemen, namely, the widespread, inclusive mobilization of critical, practical discourses in which people articulate and think through their moral and material demands in public. These critical discourses include demands for the very sorts of contested and free elections that Przeworski et al. see as central. Although these have yet to develop, they *are*, as we shall see in the description of qāt chew conversations, an important *part* of what some Yemenis understand democracy to entail. Relatedly, although the legislative branch remains a weak institution, hamstrung by the authority of the executive in both de facto and de jure terms, the electoral turnout in the last parliamentary elections suggests that the electorate is "keen to exercise the right to select lawmakers" (Carapico 2003), even when circumstances inhibit fair electoral competition.

Viewed from a perspective of citizen influence, impact, and participation, moreover, the fact of an armed population that can provide constraints on regime action, of a determined, if harassed press, and of civic associations operating independently of state control does make Yemen more democratic than most countries in the Middle East. Human rights associations and related groups pressing for women's rights, an unfettered press, fair treatment of prisoners, and a thorough and transparent judicial process hold conferences, sponsor debates, and publish articles in local newspapers. Mosque sermons, which are not effectively under state control, often address social inequalities and openly criticize the government, paying particular attention to political corruption and instances of moral laxity.[10] As noted in the previous chapter, no visitor to Yemen can help but notice the vigorous forms of nonelectoral contestation that animate daily life (Carapico 1998). Qāt chews are emblematic of this political activism, but they are by no means the only instance of it. They operate within a broader historical and semiotic context, one in which conferences coded as "tribal" (Carapico 1998; Dresch 1993, 2000; Caton 1990) have long been a means of resolving disputes and voicing grievances in parts of the North, and where citizens from various regions have drawn on local practices of deliberation to mobilize constituents and demand political change.[11]

The presence of political activism is not synonymous with democracy, however. The aim of this book is *not* to romanticize public sphere activities, but to deromanticize the ballot box. To provide such an account of politics, we need different studies and a reconsideration of our concepts. As Wittgenstein shows us, the point is not that a methodologically driven or ideologically motivated definition of a concept, such as democracy as contested elections, is wrong, but that the assumptions underlying such an analysis miss something important about what we mean by the term. As we have seen, the minimalist definition seems to go hand in hand with a binary classification system that neglects the presence of democratic practices in nation-states we might call authoritarian. Operationalizing democracy as contested elections also proves problematic because it obscures the multiple ways in which citizens might attempt to influence or hold accountable elected and appointed officials alike—and it forecloses possibilities for analyzing whether "democratic" regimes are adequately robust.[12]

The following section shifts attention away from formal considerations of electoral outcomes to the phenomenological dimensions of participatory politics by examining Yemeni qāt chews in the context of a Habermasian conceptualization of the public sphere. I show how qāt chews have become in many ways analogous to seventeenth- and eighteenth-century European salons and coffeehouses as depicted in *The Structural Transformation of the Public Sphere* (1996 [1962]), in which lively public sphere activities worked to produce important forms of political engagement and debate.[13] In Habermas's theory as in Yemen, moreover, sites of public sphere activity are themselves connected with one another through anonymous media, which produce reflexivity—discussions held in qāt chew gatherings are refracted through newspapers, intellectuals' conferences, and mosque sermons. Impersonal debates held in these mediated publics also influence the themes of qāt chew conversations. Participants are often aware that they are debating issues that others are discussing, thereby constituting a public in a broad, anonymous, non-face-to-face, often national sense. We saw this reflexivity at work in the previous chapter in the example of the political conversations circulating about the serial killings in Ṣan'ā', an event whose political implications not only became the subject of animated qāt chew conversations but also found expression in newspaper reports, protests at the university, and Friday sermons in the mosques. By investigating qāt chew conversations as instances of what Habermas calls the "public sphere" (1996 [1962]), we can specify the political role everyday practices of deliberation play in Yemen, as well as more generally.[14] The example of qāt chews in Yemen also draws our attention to some of the *problems* with Habermas's analysis, problems that have tended to be neglected by his critics and deliberative democrats alike.[15]

PART TWO: PUBLIC SPHERE ACTIVITIES AND POLITICAL PARTICIPATION

As the above discussion suggests, qāt chews fulfill the two requirements Habermas (1996 [1962]) sees as central to the public sphere, namely, citizens' engagement in critical discussion and the mediated, reflexive role that such minipublics, in tandem with other minipublics, play in helping to produce the impersonal, audience-oriented broader public of anonymous citizens, what Michael Warner calls "co-membership with indefinite persons" (Warner 2002, 76). As we shall see, Yemenis often speak and are heard in qāt chew conversations as participants oriented to strangers, in other words, as people who are able to recognize that even when they do know one another they are also speaking to an audience of imagined others (ibid., 74). The imagined communities that are established through these minipublics and their mediating effects, in contradistinction to national ones, may but need not rely on criteria of territory or on appeals to a "people." As Warner points out, whereas the concepts of religion, nation, and race have a "manifest positive content" because they specify criteria for group membership, publics unite "strangers through participation alone, at least in theory" (75). In practice, the content of discussions and the fact that afternoons are structured around deliberation—in other words, that these conversations take place simultaneously throughout the delimited territory of the nation-state—help to make these publics national, at least some of the time.[16]

In addition to their public qualities, qāt chews can be political in at least four senses. First, during some qāt chews, actual policy decisions get made:

government officials, opposition parties, and networks of activists meet separately and with one another to decide how to respond to a crisis or to determine how elections should be run. They debate which alliances will be forged, what political positions taken, statements drafted, and grievances voiced and heeded. Second, people make avid use of qāt chews to share information about political events and to discuss their significance in public. During my fieldwork, I witnessed opposition politicians using qāt chew conversations to ask how they should protest against constitutional amendments curtailing democracy (September 2000), as well as regime officials wondering aloud how to respond to U.S. foreign policy in the aftermath of September 11. Participants from a variety of political parties, ideological persuasions, and regional backgrounds raised critical questions, "Who will benefit from the September 11 attacks?" (September 2001); "Are ordinary Afghans better off under the Taliban or under American occupation?" (September 2002); "What sorts of positions should be taken on Iraq?" (September 2002). Third, these gatherings provide an occasion for negotiating power relationships between elites and constituencies in which elites are held responsible and are required to be responsive to the needs of participants by guaranteeing goods and services or by advocating on behalf of the village, electoral district, or local group. Fourth and relatedly, the "public" of the qāt chew is also a lived forum for political self-fashioning, an occasion for cultivating what Arendt (1958) called the "human capacity for action"—the ability to begin anew through words and deeds, to think in unanticipated ways about recent events, to make sense of their multiple meanings with others, and to take pleasure in the dynamism of specifically agonistic encounters.[17]

Policymaking, the first sense, may but need not be democratic, of course. The other three senses of the political have important democratic components. The sharing of information and the discussion of an event's significance publicly already begin to suggest the democratic dimensions of qāt chews, in the sense of an information-rich environment where people are able to discuss the meanings of current politics in conditions conducive to participants' temporary (albeit imperfect) equality. The third sense of the political also connotes "democratic": qāt chews are forums of accountability, contexts in which elites are held responsible and must be responsive to the needs of their constituencies. And fourth, insofar as "democratic" often means "agonistic," these gatherings are intrinsically democratic, occasioning the performance of a distinct form of personhood, one that revels in peaceful disagreement and is oriented toward an audience of deliberative strangers. These gatherings generate "loyal opposition"—not only because they provide opportunities for organized opposition groups to meet but because they make possible the performance of oppositional, critical publics in settings that are not formally regulated by the state (Moore 1989, cited in Shapiro 1999, 39).

Approaching qāt chew practices through Habermas encourages an understanding of them in terms of the structural-historical conditions under which such institutions arise, even while these conditions need not be identical for formal, everyday practices of deliberation to emerge. Or put differently, the experience of Yemen also tells us that there is no *one* path to critical, rational debate in public, or if there is, then Habermas misidentified the circumstances under which the "subjectivity"—or conscious presentation of self—that is conducive to such deliberation appears. Different historical conditions of possibility from the ones Habermas specified in Europe have allowed for the emergence of vibrant communities of argument in Yemen.

The Structural Transformation of the Public Sphere offers an historical account of the emergence and decline of the "bourgeois public sphere" in modern Europe. For Habermas, the term "public sphere" connotes a set of places (coffeehouses and salons) where bourgeois citizens of the time met to argue about literary and political matters, as well as the substantive activity of private persons coming together as a public for the purposes of rational-critical debate, *and* the mediated, reflexive ways in which these critical conversations in public places referred to, and actually influenced, events and arguments appearing in print. Public debate, according to Habermas "*was supposed to transform* voluntas *into a* ratio *that in the public competition of private arguments came into being as the consensus about what was practically necessary in the interest of all*" (emphasis in the original, 83). As substantive activity, the public sphere held out the promise of transcending the narrow confines of particular class interests because conversations allowed private bourgeois persons to come together as a public and to be "nothing more than human" in both their interactions with others and in their self-interpretations (48). Or put somewhat differently, the "fully developed public sphere" was a fiction, according to Habermas, that entailed the historical identification of "the public" of property owners with the more generalized notion of a public of "human beings pure and simple" (56). Thus, the specifically bourgeois character of the actual public sphere could *in principle* be broadened to include everyone by generating, in addition to an implicit attitude of equality, a vocabulary for and practice of critical debate conducive to the "freedom of the individual in general" (56).

Habermas's analysis of the public sphere explores the ways in which institutions produced specific "subjectivities" that then became crucial for everyday substantive participation in political life. The institution of the (increasingly nuclear) family in eighteenth-century Western Europe played a key role in the formation of individuals whose audience-oriented sense of themselves made a public sphere possible. The substantive activities of rational debate within the public sphere, in turn, seem to have provided the felicitous conditions for popular sovereignty and the rule of law to flourish. Habermas argues that "the public understanding of the public use of reason was guided specifically by such private experiences as grew out of the audience-oriented subjectivity of the conjugal family's intimate domain" (28). The family was thus the seat of the production of a distinctly bourgeois subjectivity that helped make the public sphere possible. Private persons sought rational-critical public debate, and the experiences that prompted people to seek agreement and enlightenment through deliberation "flowed from the wellspring of a specific subjectivity," whose "home" originated in the "sphere of the patriarchal conjugal family" (43).

Habermas concedes that this notion of the family as a private world was based on a denial of the economic relations supporting the family's very existence. But this denial was useful in establishing the conditions of subjectivity that would enable private individuals to join together in public rational debates, to become audience-oriented, empathic, self-knowing individuals, capable of what Arendt calls "representative" thinking—seeing the world from others' points of view (Arendt 1993 [1954], 241). The autonomy that property owners enjoyed in the relatively free liberal market "corresponded" to a "self-presentation of human beings in the family" (46). Individuals thus came to experiment with their subjectivities by writing letters, as well as diaries, autobiographies, and domestic novels. In short, the conditions of intimacy within "the patriarchal conjugal family" and of property-owning autonomy in the market permitted the individual to "unfold . . . himself in his subjectivity" (48), which was both an intensely private expression of an individual's interiority and also already oriented to an audience (*Publikum*) (49).

Critics of Habermas have pointed out that he conceives of the public sphere in the singular, thereby failing to consider the possibility of a multiplicity of public spheres, some of which are "subaltern" or "counter-" discursive spaces that challenge the prevailing ways of thinking in the critical mainstream one.[18] Many scholars have also argued that Habermas exaggerates the possibilities for equal treatment in public and neglects to theorize the ways in which each participant is enmeshed in particular power relationships affecting his or her ability to speak and to be heard.[19] Social and political inequalities, even among people from the same economic class, help determine who speaks when, and how convincing their arguments are.

More important for our purposes here, however, I take issue with Habermas's location of the source of the modern, public-oriented subjectivity in the bourgeois family. For public spheres to exist, in Habermas's sense, individuals need to have the reflexive capacity of critical thinking. Not everyone has such a capacity, in his view, and not all societies encourage it. Yet, to the extent that there exists in Yemen a recognizable public sphere in which critical discursive activities thrive and a significant number of Yemenis experience it, its source cannot be the bourgeois family. Indeed, if the argument I am developing is correct, it could also be that Habermas is wrong about the source of the public sphere for modern Europe.[20] Whereas he attributes the orientation toward an audience to circumstances within the conjugal family and to transformations within market relations that took centuries of capitalist development to unfold in Western Europe, expressions of subjectivity in Yemen operate in a context in which persons most often self-identify and are classified as members of a large extended family, or *bayt* (see Meneley 1996, chap. 3). The bourgeois individual is hardly the unit of analysis or identification for most Yemenis, nor are sources of agency and autonomy necessarily attributable to everyday practices associated with the commodity form. Approximately 75 percent of Yemenis live in the countryside and participate in some form of agriculture, and there exists no large or coherent middle class. In other words, this orientation toward an audience evident in rural and urban qāt chew conversations, as well as in intellectual gatherings, the press, "tribal" conferences, mosque sermons, and civic associations, exists independently of the developments in market and family relations that are central to Habermas's account.[21]

In short, Yemen is not a bourgeois society, and the Yemeni public sphere does not arise out of bourgeois notions of individuality or privacy in the intimate world of the family. Furthermore, Yemenis do not gather in the public sphere as a collection of property holders defending their private interests from state intervention in the market. They need not posit the possibility of an autonomous, abstracted universal subject who is a human being "pure and simple," but they do gather together as fully embodied, multipositioned, concrete persons whose diverse class locations and contentious political positions animate discussions, some of which are about the common good.[22]

In Habermas's idealized version, moreover, the European public sphere appeared against the backdrop of states that had achieved a more or less secure monopoly over violence, so that the "force" of social position was supplanted by the force of the better argument, rather than the force of weapons. By contrast, qāt chews are not predicated on the existence of robust state institutions, but actually thrive in their absence. Qāt chews defer political violence or replace it with discursive contestation (at least temporarily), producing expectations among participants that they will be seen and heard by others whose political positions are different from their own. In Yemen, this discursive contestation occurs *without* the institutional protections Habermas saw as central. As a consequence of these different conditions, participants often take considerable risks and are made vulnerable in ways that a Habermasian account does not anticipate.

Proponents of civil society arguments often make a different set of claims, suggesting that a lively associational life can produce effective governance or contested elections, or both.[23] Yemen arguably has both a rich associational life and spirited public sphere practices, and yet no one would claim that the regime either governs effectively or that its institutions generate alternation in office. Although public spheres may represent a condition of democratic possibility, they do not seem sufficient in themselves to prompt Przeworski et al.'s contested elections. Or put differently, although qāt chews and other public sphere activities in which people discuss their political worlds represent sites of important political vitality, the lively and obvious presence of such public arenas in the absence of fair and free contested elections suggests that such everyday practices may not be as instrumentally related to contestatory electoral arrangements as some political scientists would claim—at least not in the short run.[24]

One might argue in a different instrumentalist vein that qāt chews operate as a "safety valve," allowing people to vent frustrations and displace tensions that otherwise might find expression in more effective forms of political action. Some Yemenis describe qāt gatherings in just this way—as a mode of "*tanfīs*," a way of "letting out air." Scholars too assert that tolerated or authorized critical practices function to preserve a regime's dominance rather than undermine it (Guha 1983, 18–76; Adas 1992, 301; see also a discussion of "*tanfīs*" in Wedeen 1999). There are, however, at least three key problems with safety-valve arguments. First, it is impossible to demonstrate, were participants in qāt chews not engaged in such activities, that they would be organizing collectively against the regime. Second and more important, political rallies and other forms of collective resistance often *are* organized during qāt chews. The ideas and organization for oppositional political action frequently do arise out of discussions in which people cultivate shared concerns and resolve to act on them. Third, although qāt chews may either occasion subversive activity or re-signify dominant social norms, there is nothing about qāt chews that implies a necessary relationship between lively deliberation and resistance per se. Regime members also attend qāt chews and use the occasions for a variety of purposes—to try out new arguments, disseminate and collect information, interpret recent events, distribute patronage, and take account of the views of others. As Saba Mahmood, following Foucault, argues in a different context, there are "dimensions of human action" (and by extension, therefore, dimensions of qāt chew conversations) "whose ethical and political status does not map onto the logic of repression and resistance" (Mahmood 2005, 14). Performances of personhood in which animated, reasoned disagreements with others come to the fore may but need not be understood in relation to a framework privileging domination and subversion.

In short, instrumentalist explanations—whether they focus on the value of public sphere practices for elections or for compliance—fail to investigate qāt chews as sites of democratic practice in their own right. In this chapter I claim that the kinds of critical practices of deliberation taking place within public spheres can be intrinsically democratic. For Habermas, these activities perform the important political function of "legitimating" state authority, and indeed of abolishing the state as an instrument of domination altogether, transforming the *voluntas* of executive power into the *ratio* of law buttressed by reasoned public opinion (82–83).[25] By contrast, participants in the public sphere of the Yemeni qāt chew not only routinely fail to exercise this legitimating function but often offer pointed criticisms of the regime—lamenting the absence of state authority and the rule of law (*al-dawla wa al-qānūn*). I want to argue that qāt chews are democratic in substantive representational terms—less because they actually enable citizen control than because they facilitate a kind of political participation. They promote citizen awareness and produce subjects who critically debate political issues, allowing participants to build an agonistically inclined political world in which disagreements are entertained in common. They are the site for the performance of citizenship, for the critical self-assertion of citizens the existence of whom is made possible through these exercises of deliberation.

PART THREE: QĀT CHEWS

Qāt chews, like the salon and coffeehouse gatherings in Habermas's depiction, vary in the size and composition of their publics, the mode of their proceedings, and the topics open to debate. Like their historical Western European counterparts, they often entail formal, ongoing discussions, which might be prompted by international current events, by local domestic problems, or by a special guest in attendance. In addition, marriages are arranged and business deals solidified, village shaykhs (chiefs) chosen, and local troubles resolved over qāt. Qāt chews also enable the circulation of important information. The anthropologist Shelagh Weir likens these gatherings to a "kind of institutionalized grapevine" in which information about local and national affairs gets exchanged (1985, 125; see also Sheila Carapico, who analogizes qāt gatherings to focus groups, 1998, xi). Qāt chews also occasion the generation and verification of rumors (including ones about electoral results), the trading of knowledge by peasants about farming techniques and agricultural programs, the negotiation by religious experts of prevailing theological problems, and the bargaining among elites about policy, political positions, and alliances. Sometimes one issue is discussed in depth; at other times a number of issues animate the afternoon. Qāt is chewed at weddings and funerals, at intellectuals' workshops, political party conferences, poetry "jams," editorial meetings, and student study sessions. Shopkeepers may go back to work and chew there; physical laborers may chew on the job; physicians may attend a gathering for part of the time and then return to work. Most people, even those who do not chew, are organized in one way or another around the social world of afternoon qāt consumption.

Qāt chews are almost always segregated affairs: more men chew than women, and the latter's conversations tend to be about concrete relations among family members rather than about abstract political issues or current events.[26] Such conversations may be every bit as political—in the sense that marriage negotiations, for example, have consequences for power relationships among families. But they are not Habermasian public spheres: these chews are not open to a public; the women who gather to chew are almost always intimates of one another, not strangers. And their conversations do not generally operate as minipublics, forming in conjunction with other minipublics the impersonal, audience-oriented broader public of anonymous citizens. Women politicians complain that they are in many ways barred from an activity that is central to the work of male politicians and their constituencies, and that they do not have equal access to the processes of debate and decision making that qāt chews enable. For this reason, qāt chews can be considered a form of what Dipesh Chakrabarty calls a "flawed social practice" (2000, 181). Like the Bengali practice of *adda* (the long, informal conversations Chakrabarty describes), qāt chews are segregated and predominantly male activities that are also "oblivious of the materiality of labor" (ibid., 181). Unlike *adda*, however, qāt chewing is not a dying social practice, a vestige from a class-specific, urban modernist past, but rather an increasingly widespread contemporary activity.[27]

I have regularly attended male gatherings in which Yemeni identity, political culture, the nature of democracy, and the actual workings of Yemeni electoral politics have provided the themes of critical, vigorous debates.[28] Sometimes, in educated circles, an article from a newspaper might be read aloud and then discussed. At other times, a guest will be required to offer a summary of his political experience or research. A recently returned migrant may discuss his life abroad or his impressions of his former "host" country. A visiting poet may recite recent work and invite commentary from the audience. When no topic is immediately obvious, participants propose themes, and then engage in a brief discussion to decide which topic most merits further debate. Once a topic is chosen, individual speakers present their views in persuasive, politically relevant displays, which might be likened to what, in a different context, Gary Goodpaster terms "regulated storytelling" (1987, 120; cited in Matoesian 2001, 5). Often participants' social location is made salient in and through "the performance of knowledge" (Matoesian 2001, 4)—the emergent and often improvised discursive practices through which ideas about facts, people, and events are established.

Inevitably, some speakers are more persuasive than others, whether by virtue of their preexisting standing in the community, their particular expertise on an issue subject to debate, or their talents as an orator: qāt chew participants cite the importance of eye contact, the manner of dress, the ways in which a person organizes his thoughts and streamlines his views, and the use of concrete examples to bolster a claim as instances of what might make an argument ultimately compelling (March 2004). A man whose contribution is most eagerly anticipated because of his oratorical skills is termed a "*rajul al-ḥiwār*" (a man of discourse, or more idiomatically, an eloquent man). Going on too long may generate a spontaneous reaction from the listeners, who politely enjoin the speaker "to continue" (i.e., finish) so that others have the chance to deliver their brief monologues as well.[29]

The sociologist Erving Goffman introduced the concept of "footing" (1981) as a way of describing how speakers and recipients in conversational contexts signal who they are and what they are doing. Different kinds of qāt chews entail distinct interactional footings. For example, patronage networks are reproduced during some qāt chews, when villagers and self-identified tribesmen visit the home of a nationally powerful political leader or local notable to secure promises of goods and services. Politicians may use the qāt chew to meet with constituents, and legal experts may use it to promulgate legal judgments or to deliver *fatwās*—nonbinding but authoritative opinions. Important officials take part in qāt gatherings most afternoons, and "everyone knows or can easily discover where they can be found . . . , everyone has the right of access to officials" (Weir 1985, 125). Qāt chews, once an exclusive venue for aristocrats, have become a generalized, institutionalized form of social life, diminishing the importance of other ways of socializing or securing patronage, and also endowing the chew with a formality it did not previously possess (144). Although supplicants may attend chews for the sole purpose of securing a favor, many are nonetheless treated (or subjected) to a sustained conversation about prevailing political matters.

Ordinary, everyday qāt gatherings are public in the sense that they are "open to anyone who wants to take part. Men simply choose which party they want to attend, walk in and take a seat; no one questions their presence" (124). This openness stems partially from the fact that guests are not a financial burden on a host. Yemenis generally bring their own qāt to gatherings. During important ceremonies an affluent host might provide the qāt, but occasions when qāt is supplied in the absence of a ceremonial event are rare. When they do occur, they are an important way of influencing people by generating prestige for a host whose financial resources and generosity are thereby made manifest (123).[30] Everyday qāt chews, by contrast, are what Weir characterizes as "*free associations of people who have chosen to attend*, not because they are invited, but for a variety of personal reasons" (124)—and, as I show in this chapter, for *political* ones.

The accessibility of officials and the openness of everyday qāt sessions are qualities suggestive of the horizontal or equality-inducing aspects of Yemeni public life. Yet qāt chews do reproduce hierarchy and reaffirm differences in social status among participants (Weir 1985; Gerholm 1977).[31] The seating positions at a qāt chew roughly correspond to each person's status relative to others in the room. The most prestigious people sit near the head of the rectangular room (called a *dīwān* or a *mafraj*), and others of high status sit along adjacent walls near the head. From the head, the prestige of those seated declines with distance until one reaches the most humble positions, customarily occupied by those close to the door, where guests leave their shoes and exit to go to the bathroom (Weir 1985, 131; Gerholm 1977). As a new participant enters the room, those already seated make adjustments to the order, reflecting the newcomer's status in relation to those in attendance, as well as the timing of his entry. Paradoxically, it is the very equality-inducing openness of many qāt chews that also reproduces status distinctions by generating occasions in which social classes mix, although hierarchically. In public spaces accessible to intimates and strangers alike, policies and political practices can be challenged or reinforced through critical discussion, but people's seating positions nevertheless indicate their social position, as well, perhaps, as the seriousness with which their argument is likely to be received. Some chews are regularly held meetings; others are organized spontaneously—prompted by a political event or the lack of other scheduled gatherings. A formal gathering is generally termed a *maqīl* or *maqyal* (from the verb *qāla* which means "to speak"). Women's gatherings (sometimes referred to as *tafrīṭa*s, which connote relaxation or even laxity, negligence, and excess) are less formal.

The structure of the event corresponds in part to the effects of the drug. Participants first entering the room tend to interact primarily with others in the immediate vicinity, while beginning to chew the leaves, which are stored in the cheek. As the stimulant properties of qāt begin to take effect, a meeting is generally called to order and a topic chosen.

Individuals usually speak for five to twenty minutes, building their brief monologues on what others say, or raising questions directed to a guest speaker. At other times lively dialogic interchanges disrupt the more formal modes of communication. People report experiences of euphoria or feelings of deep commonality with other participants during the subsequent two or three hours of sustained debate. As the gathering wears on and the conversation begins to wind down, some claim to experience (and to note in others) a more philosophical, private sense of individual contemplation. People begin to depart; others stay, no longer chewing, as the consciousness of mundane demands and obligations returns (Weir 1985; Varisco 1986).[32]

One might argue that the proliferation of qāt chew gatherings as a particular instance of public sphere activity corresponds to identifiable economic and political factors. By all accounts, the percentage of men and women participating in qāt chews has increased over time.[33] In the former People's Democratic Republic of Yemen (PDRY), qāt chewing was prohibited on weekdays, which meant that gatherings were restricted in most places to Thursdays and Fridays.[34] In the former northern Yemen Arab Republic, the influx of labor remittance income in the 1970s resulted in a marked increase in the consumption of qāt, and of both men and women's qāt gatherings (Weir 1985, 85; see also Mundy 1981, 61).

The story of oil wealth and labor remittance is by now familiar: the significant rise in oil prices in 1973–74 caused a boom in the Saudi construction industry and prompted a sharp increase in the demand for migrant manual labor, which in turn generated a dramatic rise in financial prosperity and the greater circulation of cash in the Yemens. For example, in 1970 the daily wage for an unskilled laborer working in Saudi Arabia was about $1.40, while by 1975 it had risen to about $14 and by 1980 to $28 (Weir 1985, 88; see also Chaudhry 1997). Researchers reported the proliferation of formal and informal contexts in which a majority of men and a large minority of women spent their afternoons chewing qāt in sex-segregated public sessions, the increasing number of workers and small shopkeepers consuming qāt on the job, the expansion in the size and number of markets where qāt was sold, and the growing amount of land devoted to qāt cultivation (Gerholm 1977, 53; Carapico and Tutwiler 1981, 49–59; Weir 1985).[35]

Despite the dire straits of the bust economy of the 1980s and the subsequent return of an estimated eight hundred thousand to 1.5 million labor migrants from the Gulf states in 1991, qāt consumption has continued to rise—and thus so too have *occasions* for critical debates in public. This is not to argue that there is a one-to-one correspondence between the frequency of qāt chewing and the liveliness of political debate. As Carapico has argued, civic activism has been an enduring characteristic of recent Yemeni history. Identifiable periods of civic activism have punctuated Yemeni political life since before the broader generalization of the everyday practice of qāt consumption:

> The data show quite clearly that although modern Yemeni states have never guaranteed democratic rights and liberties . . . in the past couple of generations Yemenis have engaged in progressive labor militancy, strikes, and partisanship in late colonial Aden; in *al-ta'āwun al-ahlī* or "local cooperation" for basic services such as roads, education, and utilities from the 1940s through the 1980s; and throughout the century but most notably since unification in 1990, in intellectual production, partisanship, and events representing a wide array of political tendencies. . . . Passivity and violence are two possibilities; between these two extremes is a good deal of civilized activity. (1998, 10–11)

Carapico's chronology of vibrant political participation specifies three periods of "political opening" in Yemen: the 1950s and 1960s in Aden and the protectorates, when labor unions, an independent press, rural movements, and political parties emerged whose various ideological tendencies—from Marxists to Muslim Brothers—generated a wide array of political organizations and programs; the Yemen Arab Republic from the 1970s to the early 1980s, when civic activism was made manifest primarily in local development projects; and 1990–94, when the process of establishing the new Republic of Yemen allowed for vigorous multiparty competition, a free press, and multiple domains for pressing political and constitutional reforms (Carapico 1998, 16). As Carapico argues, "Civic participation quickly fills any space ceded to it by the state" (207). Or to put it somewhat differently, Yemeni citizens take advantage of opportunities presented by the regime and by the absence of effective state institutions, but they also create those opportunities through their activism.

Intriguing in this light is that even the regime's constriction of institutionalized electoral possibilities (from the brief 1994 civil war until the qualified relaxation in Yemen's first contested presidential election of 2006) seems not to have affected the relative ease with which Yemenis voice their critical opinions and put forth arguments about politicians and policies in public. A recent exile returning from the Gulf noted that the key difference among his friends between the early 1990s and 2002 was the ways in which participants in qāt chew conversations debated political issues more openly than they had in the past (September 2002). Others have echoed this impression.

Thus, qāt chew conversations have consistently flourished since unification as a key enclave of publicity through which frank discussions among politicians and ordinary citizens take place. Seating arrangements may underscore the hierarchical organization of society, but the public exchange that ensues also has the effect of equalizing participants in certain ways. Consider, for example, a September 2002 qāt chew where more than sixty men, ages eighteen to seventy, crowded into a large room to meet Jār Allāh 'Umar, the assistant secretary general of the Yemeni Socialist Party (YSP), also a former head of the National Democratic Front, the now defunct guerrilla organization in the North. The meeting was held in Murays, a northern border town before unification and a stronghold of guerrilla activity during the civil war years of 1972–82.[36] 'Umar arrived with an immediate political agenda, and to some extent he was merely performing the role of a political leader, as one might in any number of other settings. 'Umar's political commitments aside, however, it is important to note that he was not imposing a democratic form on the qāt chew so much as appreciating how well suited the institution itself is for work in this "season of politics," as he called it.

That the discursive content of the qāt chew was explicitly political in this case should not obscure the inherently political and public aspects of the chew's institutional form. The occasion provided a forum for renegotiating power relationships between party elites and would-be constituencies; for sharing information about political events and for discussing their significance in public; and for occasioning the kind of political self-fashioning central to democratic political activity. Speakers related to one another as "co-present strangers" (Warner 2002) in an encounter anticipated to be, and relished as, agonistic.

'Umar's self-proclaimed objective was to persuade those present to support the YSP, while making the case that electoral politics was the only way for the former ruling party of the PDRY to survive. His role as political leader was offset by an equalizing dynamic of the chew itself according to which leaders understand that it is necessary for political arguments to be won because they can also be lost (interview, September 29, 2002; see also Comaroff and Comaroff 1997). In this structured setting, 'Umar's task, then, was to cultivate a sense of active solidarity based on the persistence of the party and the shared political experience of its members:

> The party has championed the cause of women and realized a state of law and order in the South. When the war came in 1994, things changed, but the party wasn't eliminated. There were organizations that attempted to take its place and divide the party, but they failed. You don't hear about these organizations now, but the YSP, despite the closure of various headquarters and the intimidation of its members, persists. Even Muḥammad al-Yadūmī, the secretary general of al-Iṣlāḥ [the main Islamic Party and a former foe] told me that he couldn't believe that the YSP was still around.

'Umar's efforts involved providing this would-be constituency with information about the party, thereby making the YSP's historically opaque decision-making processes more transparent and accessible than they had been in the past. By making himself accountable he was also encouraging Yemenis to act politically, to "exercise their rights as citizens" by voting in the flawed, but available, upcoming elections:

> We now have to move to a new stage and also think critically. The fact that the Party has problems means that people are present. The first struggle was: Should we participate in the elections or not? In all honesty, to participate in democratic activities inside the party and not splinter has been a challenge. We were used to fighting with weapons. Now we have to talk. Both Muḥammad Ghālib [his fellow politburo member in the room] and I wanted to participate in the elections in 1997, but we were in the minority. We sat through that experience and now we've all decided to enter these elections. We know that the electoral battle requires money and power. . . . Yes, there is fraud. Yes, there's the regime and its coercive apparatus, but where there are people, a government cannot break their will. Fraud can make a 10 or 20 percent difference. Even money cannot buy everyone. We have to search for other means. . . . We don't have a lot of money, but we do have men and women. We must be proud of our participation in politics. Now we have to look for candidates. Yemeni Socialist Party people should run as Socialist Party candidates and not as independents.

Disclosing information is also a way of building community by generating common knowledge and forefending against anticipated criticism. On electoral problems, 'Umar concedes difficulties, but he also reports political victories:

> There are problems with the elections—problems with the list of registrars, with the registration of eligible voters. The opposition says that sixty to seventy thousand names are fraudulent. Lots of people who are sentenced to death, or are outside of the country, or are dead voted "yes" for the president [in 1999] and for the constitutional amendments [extending the terms of the president and of parliament in 2001]. But everything has its limits. Even power. We in the opposition proposed [when negotiating with the other political parties in 2002 for the parliamentary elections of 2003] that there would be no interference from the armed forces, that we would also have access to the media, that we would have a certain percentage of party people registering voters—and we got some of these concessions, but not all. Are these agreements going to be enforced? The problem with election laws is that there is the struggle to get the text we want and, second, to get the laws enforced.

The construction of a bona fide political opposition also entailed, in the Yemeni context, an alliance between the Islamic Party, al-Iṣlāḥ, and the YSP, according to 'Umar, and his comments are particularly directed toward those audience members he correctly imagines would reject such an alliance on historical and political grounds:

> It was possible for each party in the opposition to go its own way, but there were shared interests. This is not a question of love or hate.... Al-Iṣlāḥ used to be with the ruling party against the YSP, and it has not stopped its attacks on the party and in declaring us apostates *('amaliyyat al-takfīr)*. There is a big struggle among al-Zindānī and Daylamī [salafī extremists], on the one hand, and the Muslim Brothers, on the other, on this issue. But we are cooperating because there is shared political work. ['Umar then goes on to cite examples.]

Qāt chew gatherings may begin with a special guest's presentation, much like a university graduate workshop does. Subsequently, audience members are expected to respond, and disagreement and political debate animate the afternoon. In Murays, the usual complaints were heard—that the party leadership is out of touch or cannot deliver on its promises. One speaker even called into question the party's fundamental commitment to the current system:

> We suffer from the regime. You guys don't suffer like we do. We should be against parties that are not close to the YSP [such as al-Iṣlāḥ]. What's the victory we can get from the elections anyway? We used to be the ruling party with missiles. Now we are nothing.

The hierarchical seating arrangement aside, the qāt chew becomes the occasion in which basic features of a democratic order, in this case the virtue of forming a "loyal opposition," are put to debate in public.

At another less formal chew in the village of Kuhhāl in September 2000, this same key socialist politician spoke about amendments extending the tenure of president and parliament, arguing that they constrained "democracy" and gave more power to the ruling party. His statement inspired a security officer to endorse organized demonstrations against the amendments. One man explained that one problem with electoral politics in Yemen is that "before an election, the government distributes money and goods to people so that they'll vote the proper way." Another villager, who identifies with the Yemeni Socialist Party but ran as an independent candidate in the 1997 elections, recommended that people take the money and then vote for whomever they want. Another man argued that the "money doesn't go to everyone; it goes to a shaykh or someone in the village who then promises to distribute it after the elections. People vote in the hopes of getting the money, but they don't usually get it." The Socialist Party villager then argued, "Why not just promise to vote for the ruling party's candidate and then vote for the candidate you prefer—especially because you don't necessarily get the money anyway?" Someone else raised the question of whether such a practice was "ethical," while others dismissed such concerns as ludicrous, given the current regime. Many worried that regime members would find out and people would be punished. One person then said seriously: "If I had a choice between free elections and the money that elections cost, I'd rather have part of the money." The host replied: "People have three choices: first, they can complain and do nothing, in which case life gets worse; second, they can resort to violence, a practice we've employed in the past, but armed resistance can't win; third, we can work through peaceful means to establish democracy." A villager countered: "The biggest problem with establishing democracy—and with everything else—is corruption. How do we stop bribes?" The chew ended with this question—not one to be resolved in the moment, but a question posed and an acknowledgement of a shared set of problems. There was some consensual agreement about resisting the amendments and creating strategies to outsmart a system in which bribes were a necessary way of getting badly needed goods and services. Although there were participants who were more or less eloquent, or whose social positions were more or less prestigious, everyone could and did participate. Some left favoring the YSP member's suggestion that they take the money and vote for the candidate of their choice anyway; some claimed that they would vote against the amendments while figuring out ways to bring awareness to others about their effects.

In the capital, conversations about proposed amendments to the constitution were the subject of multiple qāt chews organized by the opposition and attended not only by political party members but also by lawyers, scholars, and former ministers—gatherings closer to the specifically bourgeois ones Habermas sees as central. During one meeting, a lawyer took out the proposed amendments and read them aloud. One politician spoke about how the country was becoming a "legal dictatorship." Most people agreed that the amendments were a symbol of the narrowing of democratic possibilities, another step backward. The upcoming referendum of April 2001, however, could offer "an opportunity to make citizens aware of this constriction, to embarrass the government, to mobilize political parties, and to reconnect the parties to ordinary people." The qāt chew evolved into a discussion of what sorts of slogans the opposition might use and where they could be posted. One scholar suggested that a simple slogan, such as "no to the amendments," might be affixed as a bumper sticker to cars. Some lawyers worried that "no to the amendments" would be understood by ordinary people to mean "no to all amendments" in principle. Others wanted slogans that criticized the government in greater detail, pointing out abiding problems, chief among them, corruption (all from September 14). The conversation was continued on the subsequent day with important questions coming to the fore: How would "public opinion" (*al-ra'y al-'āmm*) understand a referendum? How could lawyers and activists, as well as political parties, educate ordinary citizens? What would constitute winning the referendum anyway? If the majority said no, would such a victory be allowed to stand? Members of a small political party, al-Rābiṭa, argued that the opposition should offer a substitute for the amendments currently put forth, rather than simply reject these amendments. A lawyer recommended that those interested in defeating the amendments come up with reasons justifying a no vote to an electorate unlikely to understand the purpose of the referendum. A scholar summarized the meeting as follows and then added his own recommendation:

> We are all agreed that these reforms are wrong. We have three tasks before us: we can substitute other amendments or decide not to; we have to come up with justifications for why these particular amendments are bad; and we have to figure out ways to reach the people with this message. Why don't we start by trying to make the amendments fail from inside the parliament where the amendments have to be approved? Through our writing in the press we can help form public opinion and enjoin people to put pressure on their representatives. At present everyone basically seems passive. But we can organize demonstrations, send letters to representatives, and even wear armbands. (September 2000)

Those in attendance agreed to commence working on the Parliament, although few were hopeful that the regime's efforts could be blocked by a parliament with no independent political power. Still, such an attempt would begin educating a larger public, which might then defeat the amendments in the referendum. The quandaries and positions voiced in these gatherings found expression in broader public debates in newspapers, civic associations, in some villages, and through the mosques. Lawyers wrote about the constitutionality of the amendments and activist politicians about the constriction of democratic possibilities. The amendments did pass, approved first by parliament and then in a referendum. The government claimed that the amendments were approved by 75 percent of the electorate; the opposition contended that many voters chose to register their protest by not voting at all. The point, however, is not whether a qāt chew's conversations prove successful in influencing policy, although some do, but that creative forms of contestation are deliberated in qāt chews, which are part of a mediated process of producing public awareness in various parts of the country. What happens in the context of one gathering happens in another. People are made aware through communications media of the simultaneous character of multiple conversations about common concerns. The reflexivity that a person acquires is achieved by virtue of his ability to internalize information, some of which originates from strangers.

Qāt chew groups relate to each other and to other groups—to civic charitable associations, political party networks, journalists' syndicates, protest movements, and village cooperatives. Men may be members of a variety of networks at once, or be connected to others who are. In the previous chapter we saw how multiple public spheres generated politically relevant public opinion as a result of the unprecedented event in the serial killer case—and there are many similar examples. In that instance, I argued that events of collective vulnerability prompt experiences of nation-ness (Brubaker 1996), a sense of belonging in which citizens become aware that their concerns are shared by thousands (or millions) of anonymous others (Anderson 1991) who make appeals on the basis of their status as "a people." Qāt chew conversations may help to generate experiences of national attachment in the sense that they are an everyday, widespread minipublic practice that is related to, and mediated through, other less intimate and more impersonal publics. Information is spread through word of mouth by individuals connected to multiple gatherings, and chew conversations that include politicians often get reported in newspapers and mosque sermons, making them "public domain" in that sense. Some Yemenis (often jokingly) go further and suggest that what makes a Yemeni a Yemeni is the common practice of chewing qāt, that the activity, although found elsewhere, is a particular characteristic of the Yemeni people (qāt chew conversations July 1998; see also Varisco 1986).

I want to argue somewhat differently: qāt chewing is a particularly quotidian form of public sphere activity that enables people to learn about events and the views and interests of others. But, consonant with the Habermasian conception of the public sphere, we can also speak of a larger public that mediates among the various informal everyday practices and formal associations, creating a discursive arena in which people who are strangers to one another produce communities of argument, some of which are widespread and wide ranging enough to constitute instances of nation-ness. Qāt chews facilitate nation-ness to the extent that they create bounded assemblages (Anderson 1991) of fellow participants who have come to share the everyday experience of chewing within the limited, territorially demarcated space of Yemen. The content of these discussions does not necessarily presume a national identity or use vocabulary suggestive of one, although it may. And the public implied in these addresses can be both broader and more indeterminate than the nation-state, as Warner (2002) suggests the "public" connotes in principle, or narrower and more specifically local.

A further example will serve to illustrate the sense of a broad, impersonal public mediated by the minipublics of qāt chew gatherings and formal associations while also demonstrating how notions of Yemeni-ness find expression in these specifically reflexive, refractory contexts. Consider a particularly lively qāt chew with members of the Ḥaḍramawt Charitable Society in the summer of 1998 in which a discussion about Yemeni identities ensued. The conversation inspired political scientist Muḥammad 'Abd al-Malik al-Mutawakkil to write a series of articles for the Nāṣirist newspaper, *al-Waḥdawī*. (Members of the society tend to originate from the South's Ḥaḍramawt region; they meet every week in the capital on Fridays, but the gathering is open to the public and guests, such as al-Mutawakkil, are welcome.) Ḥaḍramawt, in al-Mutawakkil's view, was the most likely of all Yemeni regions to secede: it had been historically autonomous and has the physical resources to survive on its own. The chew conversation focused on the extent to which Ḥaḍramīs experienced themselves as regionally identified and on the degree to which members saw themselves as part of Yemen. In the articles (August 1998) prompted in large part by the chew, al-Mutawakkil violated a generally unspoken taboo and discussed the variety of collective identities that might override nationalist identifications with the Yemeni state.

In the fourth and probably most daring article of the series, al-Mutawakkil relayed a conversation he had had years before with a fellow Yemeni in Buffalo, New York, in which the man had taken him aside to say, "You've opened our eyes. . . . Those Zaydīs want to eat us." A man beside him exclaimed to the first speaker, "You've scandalized us; you are talking to one of the biggest Zaydīs of all." The gist of the conversation was reiterated, according to the article, twenty years later in Birmingham, England, during a meeting in which a Yemeni expatriate claimed that the main problem in Yemen was the dominance of "five Zaydī families. . . . If we get rid of them, then we get rid of all the problems in Yemen." Al-Mutawakkil claims in the article that the use of denominational identities to divide Yemenis from one another was a tactic employed by the British but also by subsequent Yemeni politicians. In addition, al-Mutawakkil argues, people's regional affiliations also continue to be politically salient, particularly the rift between North and South. Four years after the civil war of 1994, political sensitivities about unification and secession remained acute, and al-Mutawakkil's narrations of meetings over qāt lay bare these tensions. According to the article, while he was in Sheffield al-Mutawakkil met with members of an organization representing the "right of the southern provinces to decide their destiny." Their arguments implied that unification was "exceptional" and secession "authentic"; they advocated the fall of a "corrupt" regime and the departure of the "ruling family." Al-Mutawakkil is clear that he is a unionist, but his story centers on what he calls the problem of "identity, whether it be familial, sectarian, or regional," which he claims the regime has exacerbated rather than alleviated (*al-Waḥdawī*, August 18, 1998).

The qāt chew inspired the articles that then precipitated subsequent qāt chew conversations, which, in turn, prompted a telephone call from President Ṣāliḥ. The president registered his nervousness with the ways in which the qāt chew discussion had led to a broader public exploration in the newspaper and in qāt chew debates around the capital. According to al-Mutawakkil's own account, however, he was able to convince the president that airing such potentially incendiary topics in public would make them "less dangerous." Al-Mutawakkil's self-professed interest was not in offering the regime an opportunity to exercise its control, but rather in deliberating about matters of mutual concern in public. Several years later, al-'Afīf Cultural Center was able to sponsor openly a two-hour public colloquium on Yemeni identity in which views ranged from patriotic tributes to an indivisible Yemeni nation to one youthful audience member's comment that "there is no such thing as a Yemeni identity" (January 14, 2001).

Both formal and informal qāt chews can have this public-making effect, and sometimes the addressees are both Yemeni nationals and an international public. Because formal qāt chews emphasize speechmaking, a chew may end before every participant has had a chance to speak. In such instances, it is not uncommon for a conversation to find further elaboration in a subsequent chew or to generate written responses—especially when important guests are present and participation may have potential tangible collective benefits. For example, in a hastily organized but highly structured qāt meeting, approximately fifty Yemenis—representatives of civil society organizations, ordinary businessmen, and members of parliament from the three key parties—met with members of a United Nations mission team. The host asked the UN guests what they would like to know, and each guest specified an issue, including the status of local councils (first elected in February 2001), of democracy, of women's participation, and of civil society organizations. The respective heads of the GPC, al-Iṣlāḥ, and YSP blocs in parliament each delivered a brief monologue, highlighting, among other things, the problems of incompetence in the local councils, the fact that local council members are inexperienced and untrained, that local council members are unable to address problems or provide services to their constituents, and that the decision to retain appointed governors and district directors as heads of the local councils raises doubts about the regime's stated commitments to democracy, or "decentralization."[37] Because the room was crowded with people and because translating into English and Arabic takes time, not everyone had a chance to speak. Not unusually, however, a few people subsequently weighed in with letters diagnosing problems and recommending some solutions.

Consider this particularly eloquent example from an independent businessman from a distinguished, historically important, highly educated elite family from the North whose immediate relatives are strongly identified with the ruling party. The letter is comprehensive, reproducing the key themes of the qāt chew, while also identifying what he sees as the critical tensions in Yemeni politics (between "tribalists" and modernists). Here is his diagnosis of local councils:

> You [the UN team] asked about the local councils. Local councils were forced upon the regime by donor acclamation of YSP demands for decentralization. By now you probably have learned that the regime here does not employ Saddam's boxer strategy: you take the blows and wait for the opportunity to deliver a K.O. Our regime is aware of its weakness, so it endeavors to use its opponent's strength against it. That's judo. They allowed the election of local councils. They allowed it to go forward, and then tripped it by withholding funds and real authority. However, that is not their long-term plan for the councils. I think that the idea is to allow enough time to domesticate the local councils, get rid of troublemakers, understand the dynamics of the whole setup, and then allow it some authority when it is clear that it could dovetail nicely into the patronage system. Until that learning experience is achieved, local councils will remain under the whim of the Ministry of Finance.[38]

Although the letter did not offer a solution to this problem, the author did have general recommendations for how to further the "democratic experiment." He was "pessimistic," but nevertheless argued that the "weakest link" was the mass media and that efforts could be made to ensure that information would be supplied by a "free and impartial press." "To be free," he argued, meant that the press had to be "free from undue political *and* economic pressures. . . . The Libel Law and other terms of the Press Law must not be applied selectively." In this instance, one might argue that being democratic became a performance on two levels: first at the level of the qāt chew itself, and second at the level of who could mobilize the "correct" understanding of democracy for the UN representative. The fact that there was a need to follow up on the UN qāt chew (and in English) suggests that democratic meanings are also being contested and constituted in and through public-oriented qāt chew discussions (perhaps especially when that public is a judging eye from outside Yemen).[39] As in the United States or elsewhere, democracy (*al-dimuqrāṭiyya*) has multiple meanings in Yemen. It can be used to describe contested elections, to advocate for radical redistributions of income (as in democracy means fundamental equality), or to designate "rule of the people" (which, in turn, may imply an organic, corporate notion, as in the former People's Democratic Republic of Yemen, or a substantive representational view stressing accountability, fairness, and/or participation in politics). As should be evident, however, I am less interested in this chapter in democracy as a category of practice in Yemen, and more focused on its analytic utility for describing the work that qāt chews do while highlighting the limits certain scholarly definitions of the term have had for our understandings of politics.

Informal qāt chews often grapple with similar topics and have public-making effects but without the long speeches or letter writing follow-ups of some formal gatherings. Informal chews also tend to permit everyone to speak and be heard. Several topics are discussed during the course of the gathering, questions can be entertained spontaneously, and the host rarely intervenes to structure the conversation or mediate among participants. For example, during a qāt chew the day before the one UN guests attended, members of the Islamic party, al-Iṣlāḥ, gave an account of their own difficulties working as journalists (March 2004). A bit of background is necessary: Sa'īd Thābit had been detained for two days after filing a report about an alleged assassination attempt against President Ṣāliḥ's eldest son, Aḥmad. Thābit, 39, works for Quds News Agency, is a member of al-Iṣlāḥ, and is deputy secretary of the syndicate of Yemeni journalists. During the chew (March 2004), he recounted how he had been returning from mosque on Friday, March 12, with his three-year-old son when agents from the Political Security Organization (PSO) "kidnapped" him. He narrated how the intelligence officers refused to let him bring his son home, how numerous preeminent lawyers offered to defend him, and how over three hundred journalists came to court, some marching with tape across their mouths, as if gagged. (Images of gagged journalists protesting Thābit's incarceration got ample coverage in local newspapers and affirmed journalists' solidarity with the accused. The court proceedings were also reported in newspapers and became the subject of multiple qāt chew conversations.)[40] The prosecution charged that Thābit "published false information with the aim of destabilizing the safety and peace of the country," a charge Thābit has denied, of course.

By the time I arrived in Yemen, Thābit's arrest was old news, so the conversation about the event was short, motivated by my presence and by the informal conditions of the chew. The discussion then moved on to the recent elections in the Journalist Syndicate, by all accounts the most fair and free elections to be held in years.[41] According to one Islamic activist in the qāt chew:

> The younger reformers among both the ruling party and the opposition were able to work together to change the character of an organization that had previously been riddled with the regime's old guard. . . . First there was a heated debate at the conference. At the previous conference in 1999 delegates were sent; this time about nine hundred people attended, all of whom were journalists, many of whom had a stake in putting together a syndicate that could represent the concerns of journalists who care about upholding press freedoms and about having a syndicate that worked as a civil society organization should. People crossed party lines to vote for the people they felt were most qualified. During the conference there was an attempt to allot seven out of the twelve seats to GPC people, but this attempt was defeated.

I asked: "How could the government allow a fair and free election in the syndicate to happen?" And he responded: "The fact that many members of the GPC also wanted a more vibrant, independently minded syndicate mattered a lot." Another person from al-Iṣlāḥ added: "This event reflects our long thirst (*ta'aṭṭushanā al-ṭawīl*) to win elections. Half of the seats in the Central Council of the syndicate went to the opposition and three of the people from the GPC whom we wanted won as well." The conversation then moved on to the upcoming American elections and George W. Bush's chances of winning and finally, albeit tentatively, to the question of how difficult it was for political parties to acknowledge internal problems. "Now the YSP has an easier time doing that," remarked one member of al-Iṣlāḥ. "Sayf Ṣāyil and 'Abd al-Ghanī [two members of the YSP's politburo] can do that, but it's harder for al-Iṣlāḥ—maybe because we are more powerful. . . . We, too, are nevertheless constrained by propaganda. Whereas in the United States money limits what journalists can say, in Yemen it is the political parties."

Conversations range from the abstract to the concrete, from the meanings of Yemeni-ness to date palm cultivation problems in Ḥaḍramawt. As participants engage in dialogue with others, they sharpen some views and abandon others. In the course of a qāt chew on "culture and identity," for example, one educated male Nāṣirist began to change his mind about the ways in which people differed from one another. Whereas before he had thought about identities as ascriptive, or "vertical"—"imposed on people so that they do not have a choice, because they do not choose their families, tribes, or nationalities"—in the course of the conversation he began to consider some identities as more chosen, or "horizontal." He argued that the former vision was a "traditional" one, whereas a sense of horizontal identities was "modern." Contrary to a pan-nationalist vision held by his Nāṣirist colleagues in which Arab-ness is often construed in primordial or essentialist terms, he began to think aloud about the ways in which distinctions considered to be essential could be provisional and strategic rather than always already there: "Juxtaposed to distinctions that are vertical are those that are horizontal, whose bases are moral and cultural . . . and what importantly distinguishes them is that we choose them by our will and with awareness" (January 2002). The critical point here is not whether his statements were true or false, but rather that he experienced the insight as revelatory for his politics. As he reiterated in a subsequent letter to me:

> My words were an important announcement for me; they announced the liberation of my thinking. I had thought that the significance of such discussions about identity was symbolic for me, but I found that the conversation was extremely important as a basis for my discussions about a war against Iraq, about the issue of Palestine—that the example of a horizontal, humanitarian distinction offered more important and powerful support for my positions than an appeal to a vertical, given identity [such as Arab origins]. (March 8, 2003)

Qāt chews can occasion reflection and revelation. They provide a home for politicized debate, for entertaining competing perspectives, for discussing the question of "what shall we do," and for thinking collectively about issues of power and responsibility. They correspond, in some ways, to Arendt's notion of the political (1958), whereby people join together and cultivate their capacity for action. The "public" of the qāt chew is thus not simply a social category but also an existential one (Dietz 1995), a particular context for personhood through which participants stage scenes of "self-disclosure" and make worlds in common (Warner 2002, 59). Put differently, qāt chews in which politics come to the fore are also occasions for personal performances of courage and eloquence. They are moments of self-fashioning, interpretation, and revelation in which participants stake out and deliberate positions, define themselves for others, and take friends and foes, leaders and peers to task.

Whereas for Habermas the fiction of free and equal individuals defines the public sphere and distinguishes it from other spaces and forms of activity, in Yemen it is the multiclass, peaceful nature of political debate that distinguishes public spheres from other worlds where violence is the ultimate arbiter and force is privately held. Yemeni political subjectivity remains hierarchical in the sense that people are self-conscious about socially stratified familial relationships, occupations, and reputations—all of which may find expression in the seating arrangements at qāt chew gatherings. But political subjectivity within the qāt chew also entails an expectation of openness to a variety of political views and people. Political subjectivity in qāt chews emerges out of the commitment to verbal disagreement and the (temporary) foreswearing of the use of violence to accomplish political ends. Qāt chew gatherings thus foster personal accountability and at the same time provide a forum for challenging conventional wisdoms. If not a guarantee of consensus, they provide an awareness of the diverse ways in which any particular political problem might be seen and solved imaginatively.

To summarize thus far: In Yemen, qāt chews are sites of active political argument where issues of accountability, citizenship, and contemporary affairs can be negotiated.[42] Although the proliferation of such meetings can be historically situated in changes of capital accumulation in the oil boom period of the 1970s, neither the bust period of the 1980s nor the constriction of formal electoral politics after the civil war of 1994 has diminished the frequency or diluted the content of these gatherings. The persistence of qāt chew gatherings as sites for animated political debate suggests that they do not depend strictly on those historical conditions to exist; that people, having discovered such public sphere activities, find them valuable and therefore persist in reproducing them; and that tangible problems are handled by means of them.[43] In the North, there is a long-standing history of consultative, participatory politics in which public meetings were also occasions for the authority of "tribal" leaders to be evaluated (Carapico 1998; Dresch 1990, 1993, 2000; Caton 1990; see Comaroff and Comaroff 1997 for a similar phenomenon in Botswana).[44] The presence of cooperative local development projects in the 1970s similarly testified to the workings of "civil society" in the absence of state institutions capable of delivering goods and services (Carapico 1998). The conditions for substantive discourses about governance have existed both inside and outside of the regime for years. Unsatisfactory conditions encourage radical critiques, and qāt chews are one particularly widespread site where such criticisms are expressed, challenged, and refined.

These everyday practices of political participation operate in a context in which, since the civil war, the electoral process has come to be seen by many ordinary citizens, at least until recently, as a way of containing populist politics, rather than enabling its expression (Wedeen 2003). Yet qāt chews are also a key place where people are able to exchange conceptions of fair and free elections, while also deliberating about how to respond to the rigging. That exchange and deliberation are the very substance of both the development and practice of democracy. Debates may focus on registration infractions (September 2002), the trials and tribulations of running candidates (March 2001, September 2002), the efficacy of distributing goods to constituencies (March 2001, September 2002), the moral obligations of voters who receive goods in expected return for their support (September 2000), the current limitations of decentralization (March 2004, September 2004), and the nature of what counts as a compelling political message or a political program worth endorsing (September 1999, January 2001, September 2002). Przeworski et al., while recognizing such conversations as political, would regard them as irrelevant to how democracy gets defined. In contrast, a less minimalist understanding of democracy would think of these debates as themselves constitutive of democracy, as an instantiation of the "deliberative genesis and justification of public policy in political and civil public spaces" (Cohen 1998).

It may also be true that actors who are at odds avoid violence by taking part in qāt chew conversations: talking in qāt gatherings may function as diplomacy does in international relations, by helping people to work out disputes, keep aware of threats, and register changes in status.[45] In this view, qāt chews operate to alleviate uncertainty about intentions that might otherwise overwhelm good will and cause violence, especially in situations where the population is as armed as Yemen's is. This may be an important social function of qāt chewing, but it is not, strictly speaking, a democratic one. The democratic nature of qāt chews stems from the kind of political subject formation that takes place through the practice of discussion and deliberation in public. In other words, the political activity of discussing and deliberating is part of what a democrat does. Such conversations are themselves predicated on the expectation of argument and disagreement, on what Arendt called a politics of "unique distinctness" (Arendt 1958, 176), in which a person's speech can be a revelatory form of action in its own right. In the Yemeni context, qāt chews are an instantiation of this Arendtian politics of collective action and revelatory discussion in which Habermasian norms of "egalitarian reciprocity" (Benhabib 1992) find expression in each agent's ability to speak and be heard. At the same time, participants are aware of themselves and others as beings whose identities are assumed (by participants) to be coherent, related to others hierarchically, and "always already there." Or to put it differently, the possibilities for performative action and egalitarian reciprocity exist within socially constructed classifications and identifications, which are not natural states, qualities, or properties, but rather provisionally settled forms of categorization and affiliation—and themselves the subject of qāt chew debates.

The regime tolerates critical discursive activity generated through qāt chews if only because it is unable to suppress it, and meanwhile uses some aspects of the practice to its advantage. The regime, for example, may benefit from the information-rich environments that qāt chews afford. The practice makes it easy for the regime to keep tabs on who might be interested in challenging the regime violently. President 'Alī 'Abd Allāh Ṣāliḥ himself often calls members of the political elite from a variety of political tendencies after a qāt chew ends to find out what the topics of conversations were, who held which positions, and what, if anything, was potentially politically subversive. Indeed, members of the political opposition tend to interpret the president's subsequent speeches as testimonies both to his knowledge of current conversations and his relative approval or disapproval of positions taken by participants in a qāt chew gathering. For example, on the occasion commemorating the fortieth anniversary of the North's "revolution" of September 26, 1962, President Ṣāliḥ castigated some of the opposition's political parties for "loitering in front of foreign embassies."[46] Some members of the opposition interpreted this attack as a veiled reference to a well-attended qāt chew conversation the day before, September 25, 2002, in which several politicians had voiced their qualified support for American intervention in Iraq. Arguing on the grounds of Saddam Hussein's brutality and the possibilities for democratic transformations in the region, members of the opposition raised the question of whether Iraq would be better under American occupation or under Hussein. The point is not that Ṣāliḥ was, in fact, referring to this qāt chew, but that participants could plausibly expect him to, and could even name those who would potentially inform.

In general, qāt chews as an institutionalized everyday practice can serve both ruler and ruled, providing an authoritarian regime with crucial information, while giving ordinary individuals and an organized opposition more freedom than they would enjoy in other authoritarian circumstances. The "off-equilibrium" or destabilizing dimension of this information richness is that it should, and does, promote collective action against the regime under certain conditions. More important, collective action for or against a regime obviously requires prior discussions and deliberation. Qāt chews are sites where that discussion takes place, independent of more or less closed party councils. Most significant for our purposes here (and independent of issues concerning regime domination or citizen resistance), forms of political inclusiveness and temporary equality based on the commonality of shared concerns, disclosed in interaction with others, would seem to be part of what democracy means. Politically functional approximations of public spheres exist independently of Habermas's historical derivation of "the public sphere" from bourgeois private experience. Public sphere activities, moreover, exist without inventing a universal subject (brought about by expressing those private experiences in and to a public). But the debates and discourses of these gatherings (even the most formal and elite ones) are disseminated, through networks of acquaintances and visitation chains, to hundreds and thousands of additional chews, as well as to other minipublics. These publics thereby produce some of the conditions for nation-ness, circumstances in which embodied, concrete citizens are able to imagine that they are engaged in conversations that are simultaneously being discussed elsewhere in Yemen, and perhaps to conceive of their lives as shared with anonymous, specifically Yemeni, others.

PART FOUR: CONCLUSION

Although the classical Habermasian understanding of the public sphere may need to be shed of a distorting element of Eurocentrism to emerge in fully useful form, large-N studies such as Przeworski et al.'s leave out dimensions of lived experiences that are vital to any adequate concept of democracy. It nevertheless remains worthwhile to consider why everyday practices of political debate (and sometimes of an oppositional consciousness) do not seem to lead to contested elections in which outcomes are procedurally uncertain and the ruling party cedes power. Here large-N studies can help us explain why certain countries are less likely to experience enduring contested electoral arrangements.[47] In other words, large-N studies may identify constraints within which nonelectoral democratic practices are confined.

Przeworski and Limongi (1997), for example, find that although it is impossible to explain what triggers a transition to elections, wealthy countries are more likely than poor ones to maintain such a system once it is put in place. Carles Boix's *Democracy and Redistribution* (2003; see also 2001) provides a theory of why this is so. Following in the tradition of Barrington Moore and of rentier-state arguments, Boix considers variables such as initial levels of inequality, the distribution of assets and the demands for redistribution, and the types of capital (mobile or not-so-mobile) that help to determine whether political elites will or will not favor competitive elections.[48] Boix finds that in circumstances of low capital mobility the owners of capital are motivated to resist democratic control of the state. Immobile capital cannot be moved elsewhere, which gives voters an incentive to impose heavy taxes. In other words, holders of fixed capital, such as oil wells, agricultural products, and mines, will invest considerable effort in blocking contested elections, since the costs of not doing so are so high (Boix 2001, 16; see an elaboration of this argument in Boix 2003).

Thus, high per capita income is related to contested elections only to the extent that the former resides in mobile kinds of capital. High-income countries that base their prosperity on fixed natural resources, such as oil or diamonds or sugar, are liable to remain authoritarian (Boix 2001, 20; 2003). Lacking the ability to transfer their assets elsewhere, fixed asset-holding elites cannot cede political control (in the form of voting rights) to the poor without being left vulnerable to demands for redistribution and expropriation. In this view, dictatorships are the "direct consequence of a strong concentration of fixed natural resources" (Boix 2001, 21).[49] With regard to types of capital and to poverty indices, Yemen's chances of sustaining electoral arrangements prove low. Yemen is one of the poorest countries in the world, with a gross domestic product per capita of approximately US $537, ranking it 165th out of 177 countries, and a population growth rate of anywhere from 2.7 to 3.5 percent per year.[50] About 42 percent of all households live below the poverty line, and poor countries seem to be correlated with dictatorships (*World Bank Report* 2002).[51] As noted in chapter 1, illiteracy rates among men reach 50 percent and among women approximate 70 percent—among the highest globally. A modest level of oil production has been the most important contributor to GDP, economic growth, fiscal revenues, exports, and foreign exchange earnings in the 1990s and early 2000s (*World Bank Report* 2002; World Bank, *Yemen Economic Monitoring Update*, 2004). And although supplies are diminishing, oil remains the chief source of revenue for the regime.

Yemen did undergo a brief transition to fair and free elections upon unification in 1990. Before 1991, when labor migrants were expelled en masse from Saudi Arabia, Yemen's chief source of revenues derived from labor remittances (Chaudhry 1997). Although poverty was acute, the gap between rich and poor was not nearly as pronounced or as apparent as it has come to be since the civil war. It is possible, then, to suggest that the conditions of inequality and a reliance on fixed capital that obtain in Yemen today were not as characteristic of the immediate unification period. As discussed in the first chapter, an impetus for unification came from reform-minded politicians in the former socialist South who pressed for a unified democratic polity, in part as a way of saving the party from additional civil wars. The "transition" to contested elections might be explained by the combined influence of these immediate pactlike concerns and the structural conditions that made elections seem desirable. Boix's argument helps us understand why fair and free elections were difficult to sustain, given the prevalence of variables such as poverty, inequality, and a reliance on fixed capital that tends to undermine these prospects.

Yet if rentier-state-type arguments suggest why elections are hard to maintain in places such as Yemen, seemingly correctly between 1999 and 2006, then they are less able to explain qualified reversals such as the one represented by the 2006 presidential campaign. This historical variation is the product in large part of victories generated through ongoing skirmishes between a loyal opposition and an entrenched regime. Currently in Yemen, such renegotiations of political power are happening on a faster timescale than changes in the variables, such as oil revenues, that Boix tracks. In other words, democratic activism can turn into expectations on the levels both of average citizens and political elites, and these expectations, at least in a place where an armed populace limits state control, may encourage, and are certainly not inconsistent with, electoral concessions by an authoritarian regime. Large-N studies, then, may aid us in explaining the presence or absence of competitive elections over time, but they may be less helpful in thinking through why a regime like Yemen's is as democratic as it is in both electoral and substantive representational terms (Wedeen 2003b), or in identifying vibrant forms of debate and disagreement that produce creative, contestatory publics in the absence of fair and free elections.

An analysis of qāt chew conversations enriches our understandings of politics in at least two additional ways. First, the example of qāt gatherings raises important distinctions between *democratic* practices and *liberal* values. Second and relatedly, qāt chews invite theorizing the work performative practices *do* rather than focusing attention on the values to which individuals subscribe. Most Yemenis are not strictly speaking liberals, if "liberalism" means "religious indifference" (Krämer 1997, 80) or implies individual autonomy, to take two possible examples.[52] The content of conversations often betrays illiberal ideas—desires for a regime like Saudi Arabia's that delivers resources, the pining for a return of the socialist People's Democratic Republic of Yemen, the necessity of protecting *qiṣāṣ* (or the individual's right to avenge a family member's death by killing the murderer) independent of a court ruling. Some Yemenis are liberals in the sense that they champion pluralism, assume the centrality of individual autonomy, respect or believe in tolerating religious differences, and utilize moral vocabularies and expressions of entitlement that share important characteristics with liberal formulations of democratic institution building (such as the rule of law, the separation of powers, and respect for human rights). But others do not. It is possible to argue that qāt chews are the occasion for performing an explicitly democratic subjectivity—one that relishes deliberation—but it does not follow that such occasions necessarily produce explicitly liberal debates or forms of personhood.

These conceptual distinctions raise important theoretical questions, such as whether public sphere practices help to generate a regime in which procedures ensure fair and free elections. Here I have argued that there is a range of valuable scholarly activity to pursue without thinking about the instrumental value of qāt chews for contested elections. In the same way that political scientists such as John Waterbury (1994) or Stathis Kalyvas (1998) have argued that a democratic regime (by which they mean a regime committed to procedural, contested elections) does not need democrats, I want to argue that the existence of identifiably democratic practices does not necessarily imply the making of a democratic regime (however defined). The example of Yemen may show that there is no necessary relationship either historically or theoretically between agonistic disagreement, lively debate, rational-critical thinking, temporary equality, and revelatory politics, on the one hand, and either elections or liberal values, on the other. In short, democrats can exist without procedural democracy. Democracy (in substantive representational terms) may not even need the ballot box. And identifying democrats has less to do with specifying the values inhering in particular groups and more to do with recognizing the kind of work performances of democracy do.

Qāt chews may *ultimately* help to produce the kind of citizen or subject conducive to fair and free elections. Surely debates about elections—both abstract debates about the merits of such a system and concrete discussions about particular elections—are part of the content of conversations during election campaigns, even elections that are overtly rigged. Nevertheless, in this chapter I have been more intent on drawing attention to the practices of deliberation, the observable work the performance does rather than the inner values people hold. This is not to argue that values are not important or that electoral institutions do not matter. In the chapter I question what we might want to regard as democratic, while also focusing on the mechanisms by which such an expanded view of democracy gets instantiated in the everyday practice of qāt chew work. There are two implications for definitions of democracy. First, a suitable definition of democracy needs to include aspects of substantive representation ignored in the minimalist view, such as citizen participation, modes of continual accountability, and informed publics whose participants engage in lively deliberation and criticism. Second, and very differently: we may want to avoid thinking about democracy as a "thing" at all, or a label that we affix to a state, but rather focus instead on the existence or absence of democratic practices.

An interpretive approach need not romanticize these forms of political practice or imply their durability. Technological innovations such as the introduction and widespread accessibility of cell phones may end up unsettling the structure of qāt chews, making them less sustained and coherently deliberative than they have typically been. Television too has been gradually introduced into some qāt gatherings, with consequences for the kinds of interactions and depth of conversations pursued among people who used to gather in the absence of its seductions. The quality and intensity of political experience within a qāt chew also depends in part on the individuals who run them. To the extent that a generation of politicized (primarily) men saw it as their duty as citizens to address what René Char, in the context of the French Resistance, called the real "affairs of the country," the death of these men—by assassination, illness, and war—may make the imaginings of political action and the concerted deliberations about self-rule all the more elusive.[53] U.S. interventions in domestic Yemeni affairs, dramatized by the coordinated Yemeni-U.S. killing of an alleged al-Qā'ida leader, "Abū 'Alī" al-Ḥārithī, in November 2002, may also undermine the vibrancy of these gatherings—if not directly through the shoring up of state capacities to control populations, then indirectly through the short-term violence such interventions unleash. The state's inability to monopolize violence may have chilling effects as well, if its failure to protect citizens makes them particularly vulnerable for what they say.

As we have seen, qāt chew conversations are reiterated publicly in newspaper accounts and mosque sermons, as well as in private conversations among friends and government informants. Sometimes views expressed in intellectuals' conferences or through civil society organizations are initially "tried out" in qāt chew contexts; and often issues dealt with formally in a conference are pursued further in afternoon qāt sessions, thereby making citizens accountable (and vulnerable) to multiple publics. If political assassinations—of "loyal" opposition members (such as Jār Allāh 'Umar), of insurrectionary figures (such as al-Ḥārithī), and of regime officials (such as perhaps is the case in the 2003 car accident of the ruling party's Yaḥyā al-Mutawakkil)—become a preferred mode of political expression, then the instances of public sphere activity are likely to atrophy, as the openness and accessibility of deliberative political life retreats into the shadows of death and uncertainty. As of the time of this writing, such dark visions of silenced politicians and stifled discourse have, happily, not come to pass. On the contrary, there seems to be renewed political activism and novel forms of contestation at present, some of which find expression in legally sanctioned organizations and practices while others have led, as we shall see in the next chapter, to outright violence.

CHAPTER FOUR

PRACTICING PIETY, SUMMONING GROUPS

Disorder as Control

On June 18, 2004, the Yemeni police arrested and temporarily detained approximately 640 followers of the self-identified Zaydī (Shīʿī) cleric Ḥusayn Badr al-Dīn al-Ḥūthī in front of the Grand Mosque in Ṣanʿāʾ.[1] The regime's assault on al-Ḥūthī's organization, Believing Youth (*Shabāb al-Muʾminīn*), began in earnest several days later in Ṣaʿda, an arid, northwestern province on the border with Saudi Arabia. (Ṣaʿda was the original center of the imamate, an imamic holdout during North Yemen's first civil war [1967–70] after its "revolution" of 1962, and the current heartland of Zaydī activism.) Men blocked the governor of Ṣaʿda's passage into the Mārān region of the province, and the governor responded by returning to the area with military reinforcements. Over the next year alone, government officials claim that 525 soldiers and civilians were killed and 2,708 wounded.[2] Al-Ḥūthī's own death occurred in an on-the-spot execution in the mountains of Ṣaʿda. Having been bombed out of the cave where he and his family were hiding—a scene described by some as a "direct reference to Imām al-Ḥusayn's martyrdom" in 680 CE—al-Ḥūthī was reportedly shot at point-blank range by a Yemeni from the South. Whether the southerner in question pulled the trigger or not, the significance of the executioner's alleged regional identity was not lost on politicized Yemenis. Many saw the move as a way of simultaneously signifying the growing collaboration of southerners with the northern-dominated regime, the regime's purported commitment to the Shāfi'ī (Sunnī) majority in both North and South, and southern Shāfi'īs distrust of Zaydī (Shī'ī) "sayyids." (Recall that Zaydīs claim direct descent from the Prophet through his daughter Fāṭima and her husband 'Alī.) The image of al-Ḥūthī's blood-spattered head made front page news in the regime's daily newspaper, *al-Thawra*, and other newspapers followed suit. The fighting subsided in the aftermath of his death, only to resume when al-Ḥūthī's elderly father, Badr al-Dīn al-Ḥūthī (a well-respected scholar of Zaydism who took over the leadership of Believing Youth when his son was killed), returned to Ṣa'da from failed negotiations with President Ṣāliḥ in March 2005. Badr al-Dīn's followers, estimated at anywhere from one thousand to three thousand people,[3] claim that the government reneged on promises to release prisoners and to stop pursuing suspects; government officials argue that Badr al-Dīn was granted immunity. Whatever the case, fighting recommenced when a police station and a military vehicle were attacked on March 28, 2005. Neighboring areas of Ṣa'da then witnessed the spread of fighting, which extended even to isolated grenade attacks in the capital. As of this writing in 2008, clashes continue to occur, despite periodic cease-fire agreements.

As we shall see, the al-Ḥūthī conflict brings into bold relief how conventional scholarly categories of analysis differentiating Islamists from non-Islamists, Sunnīs from Shī'a, tribal fault lines from urban ones, and regional allegiances from one another and from transnational ties often fail to explain why political solidarities (and conflicts) take the forms they do. Using the example of Believing Youth, I consider how a range of cross-cutting issues—personal disputes, divergent scriptural interpretations of Islam, self-proclaimed "tribal" interests, incomplete state control of violence, and opposition to global issues such as the U.S. "war on terror"—combine to create and refresh political loyalties, thereby intensifying claims of "groupness," which themselves may be simultaneously national and pious. By focusing specifically on how heterogeneous Islamic social movements have evolved in the context of modern nation-state formation, moreover, in this chapter I reveal the diverse tangle of activities and concerns, movements, and debates underlying contemporary Islamic political practices.

My approach in this chapter in order to tackle these matters is "constructivist," by which I mean the following: First, understanding how political solidarities are constituted requires specifying the historical conditions permitting categories of group affiliation to make sense. In doing so, we need to be sensitive to the ways in which the meanings of categories and their importance change over time and according to circumstance. Second, the categories with which we are concerned here are relational. That is, group identifications exist in relation to other group identifications. In the U.S. context, for example, we may say that there is really no such thing as blackness independent of whiteness, just as the category Sunnī acquires meaning in relationship to the category Shīʿī. Third and relatedly, categories such as black and white or Sunnī and Shīʿī exist within distinct political orders. These orders are themselves reproduced and maintained, in part, through category-based knowledge. This knowledge is invoked and reiterated in the promulgation of laws; created and upheld through the classifications underlying the operation of specific state institutions or the strategies of particular regimes, or both; summoned into being and sustained through the work of intellectuals, clerics, and rhetoricians; and performed in the routine transmission of everyday norms and practices. The deployment of categories can be generative without being totalizing. Categories have the capacity to define aspects of selfhood while foreclosing others, even though no category exhausts the ways in which people view themselves or act politically.

Fourth, in political science most specifically, despite the lip service paid to the importance of constructivist arguments—to the recognition that "identities" are multiple, contextual, flexible, and strategically deployed—the demands of macro-level work often compel practitioners to abandon these constructivist commitments in the interests of scientific testing. Identity categories end up being fixed and static; they are often rendered ahistorical, transhistorical, monolithic, or primordial, whatever the pro forma assertions to the contrary.[4] Part of my aim in this chapter is to demonstrate the relationship between concepts of group affiliation, such as ethnicity or religion or tribe or nation, and the styles of social scientific reasoning that stabilize them.[5] As Wittgenstein (1958) teaches us, what we do is inextricably connected to our descriptions, to the concepts and other language available to us to describe our activity (see also Anscombe 2000; Hacking 1986). By showing how categories work in Yemen, I hope to offer both a persuasive critique of social scientific labeling and to suggest new possibilities for conceptualizing political identifications. I also intend to underscore the importance organizations, category-based knowledge, and regime strategies play in conditioning, even at times "making" (in Ian Hacking's phrase) people and groups.

An additional aim of this chapter is to use the case of Yemen to suggest that regimes can rely on spaces of disorder as a mode of reproducing their rule. Maintaining domains of disorder as a way of exercising control may not be a self-conscious or optimal strategy, but it has its own logic and efficacies for regime survival.[6] Whereas political science and policy-relevant literatures on "state failure" presuppose a regime's incentives to build state institutions, I argue that a regime's interests in survival can be at odds with processes of state formation—with the political will to monopolize violence and control territory.[7] Specific institutional weaknesses that scholars are quick to identify with "state failure" may, in fact, signal a regime's successful adaptation to circumstances, enabling it to endure. To study group formation in this context, I thus put Foucault's political theory into conversation with conventional political science approaches to governance. Foucault traces how power works in excess of the state, operating through discursive processes that suffuse all aspects of life. Power passes through institutional as well as micro spaces of health, education, science, theories of language, and ordinary communication. I use this perspective without asserting exaggerated coherence or epistemic integration, as some Foucauldians are wont to do.[8]

The phrase "divide and rule" generally refers to strategies that keep a regime's opponents from becoming united.[9] The problem with such well-established understandings, however, is that the groups to be divided and ruled are almost always portrayed as given. Descriptions of "divided societies" are rife in social science literatures, with the terms "divide and rule" presupposing the very affiliations that ought to be investigated. Categories may or may not originate with a particular regime, but they can be exploited by it, thereby helping to reproduce spaces of disorder that are a form of rule in their own right. In this vein, I am not making an argument based on notions of strategic calculation alone, although such strategizing is undoubtedly important. I am also suggesting that what regime actors see as viable political policies can have deeper consequences than regime leaders or those "divided" realize. How the regime recognizes whom to divide, and the extent to which those acts of recognition themselves invest divisions with political salience are crucial dimensions of political contestation and group making. The al-Ḥūthī story is thus about disagreement over what is going on, but also about who or what makes a viable group, with actors struggling to have their interpretation of events, people, and piety accepted as true.

I pursue the arguments above by splitting the chapter into two unequal parts. Part 1, on "categories and conflict," provides readers with background on the conflict; it then focuses on classifications of particular salience in Yemen, specifying how the debates and organizations associated with the terms Sunnī, Shī'ī, salafī, and "tribe" not only index important communities of argument but produce these communities anew. This section ends by discussing the role the regime plays in promoting both group solidarities and political disorder. Based on the empirical findings and theoretical arguments made in the first section, part 2 concludes with some additional, general lessons for social science. I concentrate here on the problems inherent in using notions such as "in-group" and "out-group," "social distance," or "cultural difference"; I underscore the difference between putative membership and actual belief or commitment; and I build on recent work to consider possible intersections between local cleavages and political-ethical claims.

POLITICAL IDENTIFICATIONS IN YEMEN: ON CATEGORIES AND CONFLICT

The reasons for the initial conflict and its escalation into a violent and persisting showdown between the regime and al-Ḥūthī's followers remain unclear. The various speculations by Yemeni citizens and Western scholars are themselves significant, however, in exemplifying how political projects and personal relationships are intertwined, how organizations and categories work together to summon groups into existence, and how affiliations shift over time. There were rumors that the initial confrontation was due to local acrimony between the governor of Ṣa'da and the men who prevented his passage, a confrontation that was exacerbated by a personal falling out between al-Ḥūthī and President Ṣāliḥ. Some Yemenis contend that the conflict escalated when al-Ḥūthī was able to galvanize support from the self-identified tribe of al-Razzāmī, which was allegedly being supported financially by Bakīl, the rival to the president's own tribal confederation of Ḥāshid. Some claimed that military personnel fighting on behalf of the government were actually shooting fellow soldiers and marking their allegiance to al-Ḥūthī with secret signs, thereby sustaining the conflict. Others saw the battles as a product of the historical tensions among Zaydīs supportive of the defunct imamate, republicans who had fought in the revolution or were committed to the regime, and self-identified "salafīs" (to be discussed below) within and outside of the regime whose scriptural interpretations of Islam differed markedly from those of Zaydī believers. In this view, the regime's reaction registered President Ṣāliḥ's political commitments to salafīs and amounted to an "assault on Zaydism." Still others noted that it was al-Ḥūthī's practice of encouraging his followers to engage in the Twelver Shī'ī practice of *al-hitāf*, or slogan chanting (popular in Iran and in parts of Lebanon, but not in Yemen), that had particularly irked members of the regime.[10] Some analysts of Yemeni politics attributed the regime's reaction to reports that Believing Youth had used the forum of a regularly televised Friday sermon from the Great Mosque in Ṣan'ā' to display a banner in the background calling for "Death to America, Death to Israel" (Phillips 2005). These latter accounts suggest that the war with al-Ḥūthī's followers should also be seen in the context of the regime's current, tenuous partnership with the United States and the local opposition this alliance generates.[11]

In its official statement on the events in Ṣa'da, the ruling party claimed that al-Ḥūthī was attempting to "turn the wheels of time backward," that he "lowered the flag of the republic and raised another particular to a party in a foreign country" (a clear reference, in the context of accusing al-Ḥūthī of Shī'ī sectarianism, to Ḥizb Allāh's flag), and that al-Ḥūthī and his group were guilty of "storming the mosques by force" and "acting brutally against the mosques' preachers."[12] In Manichean fashion, the statement portrayed the regime as the champion of the "national will" while painting al-Ḥūthī and his followers as sponsors of "denominational and sectarian dissension" (*fitna*).[13] 'Alī 'Abd Allāh Ṣāliḥ's regime depicted its actions as a defense of all Yemenis against the particular denominational and historical assertions of Zaydīs who claim direct descent from the Prophet.

Although the president is nominally Zaydī and the regime is sometimes accused of promoting explicitly Zaydī interests at the expense of Shāfi'ī (Sunnī) ones, the regime's rhetorical response lays claim to national generality, defining disorder in the narrowly national terms of sectarian difference. Such charges are not new, nor are they necessarily credible to everyone; but they do bespeak a long-standing hostility on the part of the ruling party toward Zaydī sayyids, who, as we saw in chapter 1, ruled (parts of) the territory associated with North Yemen for a thousand years before the revolution of 1962. As is typical of nationalist discourses everywhere, moreover, the regime's public justifications declared the nation-state to be under threat on two fronts: the fragmenting forces imperiling national unity from within combined with attempts to undermine the nation-state's sovereignty from without.

As the reference to Ḥizb Allāh's flag makes apparent, the regime's portrayal of disorderly conduct also, and perhaps paradoxically, broadened the category of sectarian dissension to encompass the more transnational category of "Twelver Shī'ism"[14] to which Iranians and Lebanese Shī'a also adhere. As fighting intensified, the category Shī'ī became ever more salient, with preeminent Shī'ī figures such as the Grand Ayatollah Ḥusayn 'Alī Montaẓerī of Iran coming to the defense of al-Ḥūthī's beleaguered supporters: "It is not acceptable that the Shī'a be persecuted for their faith in a country which defines itself as Islamic" (cited in Phillips 2005, 3). The Iraqi cleric 'Alī Sīstānī followed suit, accusing the Yemeni regime of waging a "politics of ethnic discrimination" (*siyāsat al-tamayyuz al-'unṣurī*) against the Shī'ī population.[15]

A historically entrenched discourse around oppression provided a basis not only for criticizing the current leadership but also for potentially justifying its overthrow. Al-Ḥūthī (as opposed to other Zaydī activists) propounded the principle of *khurūj*, or "coming out," against oppressors and the ungodly, a theme that was central to speculations about al-Ḥūthī's intent in challenging the president's policies.[16] The regime was thus able to charge Believing Youth with aspiring to reestablish the Zaydī imamate, an accusation that al-Ḥūthī's father, Badr al-Dīn al-Ḥūthī, denied. Stating instead that his son Ḥusayn was motivated by the need to "defend Islam,"[17] Badr al-Dīn nevertheless also conceded that the imamate was the "most preferable" system of government for Yemen if a "true and legitimate" imām could be found. As Sarah Phillips points out, the Ḥūthīs' public denials of plans to reinstate the imamate were thus ambiguous. Acknowledging, in an interview with the newspaper *al-Wasaṭ*, that "any just believer" can rule the country, Badr al-Dīn refused to answer when asked further whether he considered Ṣāliḥ a legitimate ruler. He responded instead: "Don't put me in a difficult position."[18]

The concept of khurūj evokes a moral dimension of political obligation rooted in the worthiness of the ruler, which the al-Ḥūthīs could use to galvanize support among some pious Zaydīs. But the ambiguity is also important, for documents such as Ḥusayn al-Ḥūthī's handwritten letter to President Ṣāliḥ, published in translation in the *Yemen Times*, avoided explicit references to Zaydī doctrine, stressing instead the worldly domain of current international policy:[19]

> I have met with Mr. Ghalid Al-Moaid, my brother Yahya Badr Al-Deen, and Shiekh Al-Dahman and we talked about many issues, including your displeasure with me. This has astonished me since I am certain that I have done nothing that would have led to such a feeling. I do not work against you, I appreciate you and what you do tremendously, but what I do is my solemn national duty against the enemy of Islam and the community . . . America and Israel. I am by your side, so do not listen to hypocrites and provocateurs, and trust that I am more sincere and honest to [*sic*] you than they are. When we meet, if God is willing, I will talk to you about matters that are of great concern to you all [*sic*]. The brothers will explain to you about the details of my meeting with them.

The letter reflects the personal relationship between the two men. It also suggests how the U.S. war on terror may have helped to exacerbate existing local tensions, placing Ṣāliḥ in a precarious position by forcing him to identify with unpopular U.S. policies. But perhaps most important, given the arguments of previous chapters, al-Ḥūthī also makes an appeal on behalf of "the nation" and of "Islam." The conflict between al-Ḥūthī's Believing Youth and the regime is itself a contest over the meaning of unjust authority, of one's political obligations in relation to it, and the ways in which piety and politics are enmeshed through claims of the sort that the al-Ḥūthī conflict both exemplifies and reproduces. These claims are mediated through explicitly nationalist imaginings of a Yemeni people, invoked as part of a larger community of pious believers or umma. Notably, in this instance the nation and the umma are not mutually exclusive but are differentiated from each other on the basis of scale.

In thinking about how nationalist and pious claims articulate, we need to keep in mind that stated commitments of national loyalty do not mean that people actually experience this allegiance, although they might. Feelings of national solidarity, moreover, in no way imply a consensual understanding of what "the nation" means or whose policies best represent the interests of an abstract national citizenry. Similarly, there are many different kinds of Islamic politics and practices, and whoever ventures to engage in or comment on them—whether politicians, scholars, or political activists—draws on concepts embedded in a historically evolving Islamic tradition (Asad 1986, 1993; Mahmood 2001, 2005; Hirschkind 2001, 2006). Tradition, in this sense, does not connote fixed or frozen elements, existing outside of deliberation and conflict. Tradition is instead constituted, often in excess of intended effects, by "communities of debate through which concepts are developed and challenged in historical context" (Tambar 2005; Mahmood 2005; Scott 1999; Asad 1986; MacIntyre 1981). This is why, as I argued in the introduction and in chapter 1, nationalism and piety can coalesce historically even if they presume different and even contradictory forms of collectivity.

Thinking about Islam as a historically evolving tradition has implications as well for the much-used label "Islamist." Although the term may be helpful as shorthand for an organized Islamic politics as such, we have to be careful not to assume that it implies a monolith or that it suffices to capture the wide variety of organizations, debates, and political commitments to which conflicts such as the al-Ḥūthī one refer. "Islamist" may be used to identify a political opposition against which the regime must defend itself. But this usage neglects the possibility of considerable overlap and crisscrossing alliances among members of the regime, political parties, and religious institutions of various sorts (see Mitchell 2002b; Agrama, n.d.). Parties on both sides of the struggle, to put it crudely, can reasonably be termed "Islamist." The term also gives the impression of a strict separation between politics and piety, and that Islamists are those who make piety political.[20] As Saba Mahmood points out, however, there are movements that serve to ground Islamic principles in the everyday practices of life, in which mosque lessons provide training in the strategies and skills that enable practitioners to comport themselves piously at all times. These movements are political in the sense that they aspire to render all aspects of Muslims' lives a means of realizing God's will (Mahmood 2005, 46–47). Islamic movements with various relationships to piety can also be viewed as political insofar as they renounce a privatized understanding of religion predicated on a separation between worldly and religious matters (47). Many of these movements do not seek to confront the political order directly (either through disruptive conduct or through party politics) but rather envision that transformations in ordinary life can bring about changes in the sociopolitical order. These changes require that ordinary activities be performed with a "regulative sensibility" (46) inspired by the Qur'ān and the Sunna.

The al-Ḥūthī conflict lays bare how the conventional scholarly and practical distinctions between Islamist and non-Islamist and Sunnī and Shī'a are actually misleading dichotomies.[21] In the case of Islamist and non-Islamist, both al-Ḥūthī's supporters and his salafī detractors engage in an explicitly Islamic politics, even while their doctrinal disagreements generate divergent communities of argument. As we shall see below, in the case of Sunnī and Shīʿa, the sectarian, "ethnic," or denominational distinction wrongly implies that the titular category indexes a political fault line, which it does not. President Ṣāliḥ and many of al-Ḥūthī's supporters are nominally Zaydīs, even while Ṣāliḥ does not claim descent from the Prophet and al-Ḥūthī did.

Conflating categories such as "Shāfiʿī" (Sunnī) and "Zaydī" (Shīʿī) with actual groups, "the Shāfiʿīs" and "the Zaydīs," obscures what Rogers Brubaker calls the "generally low, though fluctuating, degree of groupness" that comes to be meaningful under particular conditions (2004, 21). Treating categories as if they were substantial entities prompts scholars to take for granted, indeed to contribute to, the very phenomenon of group making in need of explanation. The questions raised here are: How does the al-Ḥūthī conflict make apparent the processes through which particular identifications get mobilized and groups made? And how does this case illuminate the conditions more generally under which particular categories of group affiliation become politically salient?

ON THE CATEGORIES OF SHĪʿĪ (ZAYDĪ) AND SUNNĪ (SHĀFIʿĪ AND SALAFĪ): DOCTRINES, DEBATES, AND ORGANIZATIONS

The terms "Zaydī" and "Shāfiʿī" designate juristic *madhhabs*, "interpretive communities," or schools of jurisprudence in which matters of Islamic practice and scriptural interpretation are debated and decided (Messick 2005b, 159). Madhhabs were historically rooted in the interpretive authority of specific interpreters and texts. "Shāfiʿī," for example, refers to the founding authority of the jurist, al-Shāfiʿī, whose interpretations continue to underwrite legal codes in countries reliant on that school of thought. But as the Yemeni case demonstrates vividly, it is important not to engage in what Brinkley Messick calls "*madhhab* essentialism" (161) by assuming that a group, the Shāfiʿīs or the Zaydīs, exists outside of the historical conditions and contexts that allow these categories to make sense—and that permit the interpretive communities they index to thrive. In other words, madhhab categories need to be historically contextualized: their meanings and importance change over time and according to situation, and they are "relational in nature, that is, individual madhhabs existed in interpretive worlds constituted of other such interpretive communities" (159). From the mid-twentieth century onward, denials of madhhab identities have become standard in ordinary conversations in Yemen, where modern legal codes are often drawn and mixed from various, established schools of thought or where arguments in the salafī tradition are made to suggest that madhhab teachings are no longer adequate to the modern era (ibid.).

In the Yemeni context the denominational term "Zaydī," so important in the al-Ḥūthī conflict, can refer to a doctrinal commitment, to an organized group, to disparate people who continue to believe that Zaydī sayyids are endowed with exceptional capacities to interpret divine knowledge, or to a category indexing nominal group membership. When analysts write, for example, that Zaydīs make up 20–25 percent of the population in North Yemen, they are offering an estimate of nominal groupness. That membership may be passionately felt and expressed among men and women, or it may be a mere titular classification. President 'Alī 'Abd Allāh Ṣāliḥ is Zaydī, but the regime, and republican regimes since the royalists' decisive defeat in 1970, have been only nominally Zaydī—at odds with intense Zaydī political identifications or doctrinal commitments. In fact, official ideology celebrates an explicitly "traditionist" (Haykel 1999, 2003) Sunnī-inspired legacy while denouncing some key Zaydī tenets.

Self-described Zaydī sayyids differ among themselves over issues of doctrine as well as the importance of Zaydism to their politics, of course. Before al-Ḥūthī's Believing Youth was formed in 1997 the main concerted effort to reclaim political influence on behalf of an explicitly Zaydī identity was through the political party Ḥizb al-Ḥaqq (Party of Truth).[22] Established after unification in 1990 (Ḥusayn al-Ḥūthī and his father were members from 1993 to 1997), Ḥizb al-Ḥaqq emerged for the express purpose of combating Saudi-style salafī practices, or what is sometimes termed derisively by Yemenis as "Wahhābism." Sayyid Aḥmad bin Muḥammad bin 'Alī al-Shāmī, al-Ḥaqq's secretary general, explicitly saw his party as a counterweight to Wahhābī-inspired Islam (Haykel 1995). In his words:[23]

> Wahhabism is a child of imperialism and is its spear-head in our country. Both are one and the same thing. How do we stand up to an enemy we don't see? We are seeing imperialism in our country in its Islamic guise. In reality, we are fighting something which is more dangerous than imperialism: its legitimate son. Wahhabism is readying conditions in order to colonize us indirectly for [the] imperialist [cause].

In an interview, Aḥmad al-Shāmī elaborated:[24]

> Look, Saudi Arabia is pouring lots and lots of money into Yemen to promote its own version of Wahhabi Islam. This is actually an irrational and uncompromising version of our religion, which we can do without. So, we need to counter those efforts . . . and to fight intellectual advances by Wahhabism into Yemen.

Despite this avowedly Zaydī political party's efforts to respond to the felt pressures of Saudi-inspired salafī influences in Yemen, the party has not even appealed successfully to all politically active Zaydīs. Nor has it been effective in parliamentary terms, winning only two seats in the genuinely contested parliamentary elections of 1993 and none in the more flawed polling of 1997. Decisions by al-Ḥaqq's leadership to collaborate with the regime and to renounce the doctrinal, potentially incendiary precept of khurūj have prompted some to leave the party and to operate outside its confines, as Ḥusayn al-Ḥūthī did. The latter's defection from Ḥizb al-Ḥaqq and his subsequent establishment of the clandestine Believing Youth in 1997 were accompanied by the proliferation of al-Ḥūthī-inspired centers of Zaydī piety in Ṣa'da and its mountainous environs.

Other organizations have been more significant in terms of membership numbers and widespread appeal than either Believing Youth or Ḥizb al-Ḥaqq, and this fact has implications for the meanings of the categories Sunnī and Shī'ī, and for the ways in which solidarities have been activated. Arguably, the most important is the mainstream Islamic political party, al-Tajammu' al-Yamanī lil-Iṣlāḥ, which has operated both as a counterweight to the Yemeni Socialist Party and, more recently, as a collaborator with it.[25] Al-Iṣlāḥ's views on the subject of interpretation, in contrast to those of al-Ḥaqq or Believing Youth, promote a typically nondenominational (or non–madhhab specific) Sunnī view of obedience to political authority, one that explicitly disavows the Zaydī doctrine of khurūj and other overtly sectarian premises:

> Every group must declare its adherence to the Book and Sunna as well as its obedience to the ruler (*walī al-amr*) in that which he orders in conformity to God's law. There is no obedience due to any man in that which involves disobedience to God. However, these groups must adhere to the principle of not rising [against an unjust ruler, i.e., of not

> endorsing khurūj]; . . . rather these groups must seek justice, adhere to it, and support it.[26]

Al-Iṣlāḥ's membership base further brings to the fore some of the problems with denominational or sectarian essentialism that would posit an Islamic world and divide it into Sunnī and Shīʿī without attention to historically distinctive and locally mediated circumstances. If one is counting the number of nominally Shīʿa and Sunnīs in the party—there are plenty of both. Moreover, many nominal Zaydīs in the party were republican combatants who maligned the imamate and the Zaydī school on which its authority rested (Haykel 1999).[27] These party members tend to self-classify as "tribal," a problematic term we shall discuss later in this chapter, and to treat that identification as more important than their denominational one. Many Iṣlāḥīs share the regime's republican line, attacking a variety of accepted Zaydī understandings of doctrine (including teachings that privileged sayyids), while also discriminating against sayyids when it comes to upward mobility within the party.

Titular denominational divisions, then, are not necessarily indicative of the political identifications Yemenis adopt. Party identifications may be more illustrative of political convictions, but even here the example of al-Iṣlāḥ underscores important qualifications. In matters of doctrine, al-Iṣlāḥ is an umbrella party,[28] accommodating a variety of opposing viewpoints that nevertheless share a common discursive terrain in being broadly traditionist, nondenominational Sunnī. In matters of political conviction, however, the party includes liberals and antiliberals, opponents of the regime, collaborators with the regime, and even members of the regime. With regard to region, in the northern highlands many of al-Iṣlāḥ's members are nominally Zaydī; the Iṣlāḥ party is nevertheless also made of constituents who are nominally Shāfiʿī. Their regional connections to Lower Yemen and to the former South can, in particular contexts, also prompt many of them to self-identify as specifically Shāfiʿī Sunnīs.[29]

But what are those particular contexts? Consider the following typical example as a way of exploring how political identifications might solidify. During the course of the al-Ḥūthī crisis, one high-ranking leader of al-Iṣlāḥ, who is viewed by his colleagues as representing the liberal wing of the party, admitted that the crisis had itself made him more attuned to his sense of being Shāfiʿī. To his mind, there are indications that members of the Iṣlāḥ party and regime leaders (some of whom are the same people) have themselves "become more Zaydī" over time, and that impression has generated in him "feelings of belonging to the Shāfiʿīs." As evidence of the regime's Zaydī tendencies, he pointed to a third-year law textbook invoking the phrase "*kāfir taʾwīl*" (unbeliever in interpretation), which in the context of the passage suggested to him "the Zaydī (Shīʿī) inclination not to respect all of the religious scholarly elite (*ʿulamāʾ*), but just the ones descended from the Prophet's daughter Fāṭima. According to the textbook, Shāfiʿīs are unbelievers in interpretation and their *ʿulamāʾ* don't count."[30] His reading of the passage and the sensitivities underlying such an interpretation help explain why some members of the Iṣlāḥ party, who were willing to go to Ṣaʿda and act as mediators to solve the crisis without bloodshed, were not willing to denounce officially the regime's military assault. Some party members worried about what they saw as "Zaydī intervention" in matters of elementary religious instruction, legal studies, and everyday rituals of piety.[31] The regime was able to exploit this ambivalence toward the conflict to create a broad coalition of acquiescent, if not fully supportive, Iṣlāḥīs and to divide party members. In this case, the history of political oppression against Shāfiʿīs by Zaydī sayyids under the imamate could be used to serve the regime's interests by fracturing a would-be opposition, making even those Yemenis who otherwise go out of their way to espouse inclusive nationalist, liberal human rights views attentive to their nominal affiliation. Perhaps ironically, the very fact that the regime had endorsed a textbook with specifically Zaydī arguments might also have shored up the regime's efforts to eliminate Believing Youth by tapping into fears about sectarian privilege and national disorder.

This example also hints at a broader set of claims. Because political identifications are a product of specifiable historical, political, and discursive circumstances, they are subject to modification as those circumstances change. Times of crisis may make people more aware of or invested in their own particular identifications, as part of actors' attempts to make sense of chaotic or confusing developments.[32] But political identifications generally imply some form of institutional intervention (whether by commission or omission) into the classificatory lives of ordinary citizens, positioning political organizations or networks to play a critical role in transforming a point of disagreement—about religious doctrine or ritual, for example—into a motivation for hostile self-differentiation and political or military action. By characterizing events in terms of preexisting categories of political identification, organizations often amplify mildly constraining forms of affiliation into a more vigorous and active sense of urgency and commitment. This is not to argue that elites are deliberately manipulating ordinary citizens with titular categories. It just means that organizations do crucial work in making some categories more salient than others, effectively prescribing available self-identifications, so that citizens even tangentially related to the designation have little choice but to engage in everyday political conversation and action using this category—whether they believe in the classification's merits or not. Divisive discourses do not *cause* violence, but they shape the conceptual space in which specific group solidarities become thinkable.

ON THE CATEGORY OF "SALAFĪ": DOCTRINE, DEBATES, AND ORGANIZATIONS

The term "salafī" designates those who believe in returning directly to the evidence of scripture, in preference to latter-day interpretation. According to the scholar of Islam Daniel Brown,

> The guiding principle of salafi reformism was the conviction that Muslims must emulate the first generation of Muslims, the *salaf al-salih*, and recapture the pure Islam of the Prophet. This could be done only by returning to the basic sources of authority, the Qur'ān and the Sunna, for only in these sources can the true essence of Islam be found. . . . It is in rejecting the way the Qur'ān and Sunna have traditionally been interpreted and in cutting through the interpretive accretions that classical scholarship had built up around these basic texts that the salafiyya set themselves apart. (Brown 1999, 31)[33]

Salafī scholars and activists therefore tend to deny the interpretive authority of traditional madhhabs, or schools of law, in favor of an unmediated relationship to the Qur'ān and the Sunna. As one exceptionally influential salafī activist in Yemen, Muqbil al-Wādi'ī, claimed:

> It isn't permitted for a Muslim to adhere to a school of law. These doctrines have divided Muslims. They have instilled hate and rancor. I don't permit adherence [to a madhhab] because there is no proof [in the Qur'ān and the Sunna] that it is necessary to adhere to one. It produces dissension between Shī'a and Sunnīs.[34]

Muqbil al-Wādi'ī inspired the establishment of several educational facilities in the Ṣa'da region and had at one point thousands, even tens of thousands, of followers. He identified as a "salafī," understanding the term to mean "all those who hold to the book of God and to the Sunna of the prophet." They "belong to the *ahl al-Sunna* (adherents of the Sunna), even if there exists no tie between us" (al-Wādi'ī, 20). The term "*ahl al-Sunna*" is typically juxtaposed to the term for the misguided, *ahl al-bida'* (adherents of innovation).

In a pamphlet widely circulated in Yemen, *Limādhā ikhtarnā al-manhaj al-salafī?* (Why have we chosen the salafī method?), and in its successor, *Limādhā ikhtartu al-manhaj al-salafī?* (Why have I chosen the salafī method?), worries about dissension and proper piety similar to the ones al-Wādi'ī voiced combine with a dialogic form of argument and counter-argument to produce the pedagogical space typical of written tracts and mosque lessons among salafīs. Consider the dialogue, reproduced in both versions, between a venerable shaykh and 'Abd al-Ḥalīm Abū Shaqqa (the Jordanian author of *Taḥrīr al-Mar'a fī 'Aṣr al-Risāla* [The liberation of women in the era of revelation]) on the term "salafī":[35]

The Shaykh: If somebody asks you to which school do you belong, what do you respond?

Abū Shaqqa: I am a Muslim. . . ."

The Shaykh: That doesn't suffice . . .

Abū Shaqqa: God calls us Muslims. . . . (*Sūrat al-Ḥajj* 78)

The Shaykh: That would be a fine response if we were still at the beginning, before the proliferation of sects (*firaq*). If we pose this question now—any Muslim from a group from which we differ substantially on matters of doctrine (*'aqīda*) wouldn't have a different answer from this word [he is going to respond as you did]. All of them would say—Shī'ī, Khārijī, Druze, 'Alawī—"I am Muslim!" Therefore, it doesn't suffice in our times [to say simply Muslim].

Abū Shaqqa: Then I would say: "I am a Muslim following the Book and the Sunna."

The Shaykh: That doesn't suffice either!

Abū Shaqqa: Why?

The Shaykh: Could you find anyone who would respond, "I am Muslim but not of the Book or the Sunna"? Who would say, "I don't follow the Qur'ān and the Sunna"?

[Then the Shaykh, God preserve him, made clear the importance of supplementing that which we'd adopted: the Book and the Sunna in the sense of our virtuous predecessors (*salafinā al-ṣāliḥ*).]

Abū Shaqqa: Then I am a "Muslim following the Qur'ān and the Sunna in the sense of our virtuous predecessors."

The Shaykh: If one asks you about your denomination you would respond like that?

Abū Shaqqa: Yes.

The Shaykh: What do you think of condensing the language? Because the best proposition is that which is brief and to the point (*mā qalla wa-dalla*). So we say: "salafī."

The worries about dissension and about proper pious behavior extend not simply to Muslims who are "adherents of innovation" and who therefore might follow conventional schools of jurisprudence. Purportedly Western influences, such as elections or political parties, also sow the seeds of disorder (*fitna*), and many self-identified salafīs reject such institutions on this basis. It is important to note, however, that even this avowed return to the founding texts and to the first generation of Muslims for guidance does not do away with difference. The category "salafī" designates a lively community of argument, one in which there are serious debates, political schisms, and multiple positions on the relationship between politics and piety. For example, whereas some salafīs oppose the main Islamic party, al-Iṣlāḥ, on the grounds that it is a political party and some are generally suspicious of all consciously organized political (especially statist) institutions, others make different choices. Some salafīs may vote or support al-Iṣlāḥ for pragmatic reasons, as the least objectionable option. Still others have actually joined the party, and salafī commitments inflect some of al-Iṣlāḥ's rhetoric. The prominent preacher and Iṣlāḥī leader ʿAbd al-Majīd al-Zindānī enjoys a large constituency that can reasonably be labeled salafī within the Iṣlāḥ party. Others call themselves part of an alternative movement (*ḥaraka*); they craft and distribute pamphlets, and engage in political work through mosque sermons, schools, and study groups, while avoiding party politics.

As we shall see in the next chapter, the salafī movement grew in Yemen, finding particularly fertile ground in Ṣaʿda, as residents who had gone to Saudi Arabia to work in the oil fields or to study or who had traveled to Afghanistan to participate in the jihād against the Soviets returned to their homes in the 1970s and 1980s and established lesson circles, institutes of learning, and mosques (see Weir 1997). Salafī activists (what Ḥizb al-Ḥaqq's secretary general referred to above as Wahhābī-inspired Islam) were primarily "young men from a wide range of 'tribal' (*qabīlī*) and low-status butcher families";[36] they were attracted to local salafī institutions as well as to the mainstream Iṣlāḥ party in part because of their respective social welfare programs (Weir 1997, 1). By the mid-1980s this growing minority of adherents calling for a return to the founding texts of Islam were increasingly confronting local Zaydī populations and defacing Zaydī grave sites, considered by salafīs to be un-Islamic. In contrast to the Zaydī religious elite of sayyids, moreover, salafīs preached a direct, unmediated relationship to God and valorized fraternal, egalitarian bonds among male coreligionists. Salafī doctrine could thus appeal to both "republican"-minded regime members who had fought against the imamate and to young men from lower occupational "castes," regardless of their denominational affiliation.

Such beliefs as these coincided with identifiable political interests. Take, for example, 'Alī Muḥsin al-Aḥmar, the president's elder kinsman,[37] a nominal Zaydī who has collaborated with salafī activists—presumably because they proved to be supportive combatants—against socialists in the South and against Zaydī sayyids in the heartland of Zaydī centers of piety such as Ṣa'da. 'Alī Muḥsin's connections to salafīs gave him an independent power base, one that he could use to demonstrate his indispensability within the regime's inner circle. Similarly, Muqbil al-Wādi'ī's connections to the regime and his explicit denunciations of khurūj enabled him to establish institutions that enhanced his local political power. And the influential al-Wādi'ī often took advantage of his considerable prominence to castigate other Islamic activists for their moral abuses and organizational corruption. He used the media of audiocassettes and pamphlets, as well as various educational centers in the province of Ṣa'da, to disseminate his message, involving the importance of literal readings of the Qur'ān and ḥadīth, a rejection of juridical schools, and perhaps most contentiously, an interdiction against evoking the dead, which included a prohibition against shrines.[38] Al-Wādi'ī's own politics, then, could jibe well with the regime's project of divide and rule. Al-Wādi'ī sanctioned the destruction of the tombs of the former Zaydī imāms and their domes in Ṣa'da, and his followers have, in fact, desecrated many grave stones in the cemeteries beyond the Ṣa'da city wall (Haykel 1995, 2). Some salafīs also headed south after the fighting between North and South in 1994, destroying the tombs of Shāfi'ī saints in Aden and later in the Ḥaḍramawt. The tombs of saints, be they Shāfi'ī or Zaydī, violated salafī notions of proper piety.

A history of longtime collaboration between the regime and some salafī radicals paradoxically shored up Ṣāliḥ's political power. By reproducing (if not always creating) spaces of ungovernability, the regime was able to exercise partial control over particular regions and thus limit the dominance of any one local organization. This collaboration has to be understood not only in the context of Ṣa'da's longstanding significance as the heartland of Zaydī institutions and beliefs, but also in terms of a cold war politics that lasted longer in Yemen than elsewhere—even while the goal was similar, namely, to eliminate leftist opposition. The followers of Muqbil al-Wādi'ī, for example, were actively engaged in denouncing the Yemeni Socialist Party and in declaring its members apostates. During the brief civil war of 1994 some self-proclaimed salafīs took active part in battling the South's military forces.

The regime has proven adept at using al-Wādi'ī and others to promote divide-and-rule policies, without becoming too dependent on any one organization. In fact, al-Wādi'ī's death in July 2001 coincided with the regime's efforts to curtail the activities of salafī activists, some of whom were overtly associated with Usāma bin Lādin's al-Qā'ida. Even before his death, al-Wādi'ī's "movement," or *da'wa* (literally, "summons"), had shown signs of fragmentation, with a number of his students taking issue with their teacher's views of doctrine and politics. And his absence as a key leader of the salafīs generated further turmoil, the result of which has been the emergence of at least three organizations competing over his legacy, an important political development that perhaps should be added to the factors explaining the regime's reaction to al-Ḥūthī's Believing Youth.[39] With al-Wādi'ī's organizations in disarray, the regime's need for a counterforce (in the form of Zaydī activists) to keep salafī militants in check may no longer have been as pressing as it had been previously.

To summarize thus far: The categories of Sunnī and Shī'a do not comfortably map onto the conflict between self-identified salafīs and Zaydī sayyids in Ṣa'da (or elsewhere for that matter). The categories of salafī and Zaydī, like those of Sunnī and Shī'a, refer to doctrinal distinctions. But these categories and the interpretive communities to which they refer are not always politically salient, are not necessarily unified, and are always relational. The tendency to take groups as the fundamental unit of analysis turns categories into substantial entities, and this has consequences for our theorizing about politics. Designating the regime as explicitly Zaydī, as some Yemenis and scholars are wont to do, makes it impossible to explain why the regime would crush an avowedly Zaydī political revolt, for example, and could never predict such an action. "*Madhhab* essentialism" rides roughshod over the contextual ways in which denominational categories matter, when they do.

More generally, conventional treatments of "religious groups" or "ethnicities" (and sometimes Sunnī and Shīʿī are understood to mean both) or "tribes" or "nations" tend to foreclose thinking historically, relationally, and dynamically about how categories of group membership work over time (Brubaker 2004). *Historically,* as we have seen, the terms salafī and Zaydī have taken on particular meanings from the 1970s onward, when an influx of Saudi-inspired preachers set up institutions in places such as Ṣaʿda and its rural environs. Such institutions coincided with republican state ideology, which has historically valorized a traditionalist Sunnī legacy and castigated aspects of Zaydī belief, particularly those associated with the "elitism" of the imamate. Regime members may therefore have been sympathetic ideologically, as well as open for strategic reasons, to the proliferation of such institutions and debates. In practical terms, this has meant that self-identified Zaydīs, especially members of the "caste" of sayyids, have been marginalized from official political life, and since 1962 Zaydī scholars have tended not to benefit from officially sanctioned administrative or political positions in the republic (Haykel 1999, 198; vom Bruck 1999, 2004).[40] *Relationally,* Zaydī political parties and schools, in particular, have been established as a defensive move on the part of activist Zaydīs, who are anxious about the proliferation of salafī-oriented scholarship and who are responding to the overtly hostile practices of some activists. These efforts have also received support from the regime. *Dynamically,* organizations devoted to mobilizing protagonists on the basis of these classifications have evolved over time, responding too to particular events, such as specific tomb desecrations or the death of key spiritual leaders, and to the changing calculations and fortunes of political actors in their associations with Ṣāliḥ's regime. As scholars have suggested, and as chapter 2 showed in relationship to national belonging, dramatic events can "galvanize group feeling, and ratchet up pre-existing levels of groupness" (Brubaker 2004, 14; Wedeen 2003b; Gelvin 1998; Laitin 1995).

The presence of organizations that can mobilize such categories as "Zaydī sayyid" or "salafī" is critical to how solidarities congeal. Categories are iterated in antagonistic relation to other categories. This iteration plays a role in the occurrence of conflicts. Organizations might take the form of political parties or be embodied in state institutions. But as the al-Ḥūthī conflict suggests, informal networks of activists, such as the followers of al-Wādi'ī or of al-Ḥūthī, are also central to generating category-based knowledge about selves and others. Organizations and informal networks are themselves motivated by conditions that have a history. This history can be seen, as chapter 1 enjoins us to do, in dialectical terms, so that categories of affiliation are suffused in institutional arrangements, even while institutions generate and reproduce knowledge about categories.

Knowledge about categories is also reflected in and created through everyday practices, just as we found in the case of nationalism; ideas about others are carried acephalously and anonymously through language cues like those contained in dialect distinctions and names, as well as in dress codes and other markers of group identification. For example, long beards and shortened robes for men generally signify salafī commitments. Women who wear a loose head scarf and do not cover their faces with the standard *lithma* are typically from Aden or identify with its former secularist politics. And these markers are themselves part of a lively discursive tradition in which commonly understood categories such as "*ahl al-sunna*" (adherents of the Sunna) and "*ahl al-bida'*" (adherents of innovation) signify virtue and defect, respectively—even by those who disagree with such assignations. On the one hand, quotidian practices such as whether one prays with arms crossed, as many Yemenis do, or with arms at one's side, as in strict Zaydī fashion, are likely to become politically contentious when organizations exist to mobilize people by making these more or less arbitrary distinctions the object of overt political signification. People come to view these differences as substantial, by virtue of their signification of other issues—such as the right relationship to God, a history of complicity with others who did wrong to one's own putative group, a sense of aesthetic or moral appeal—and organizations help with this process of meaning making. On the other hand, which practice is more likely to be mobilized at any given time is probably roughly predictable according to the context within which the organization has been established *and* the discursive tradition within which it is embedded. In the case of Ṣa'da, the heartland of Zaydī piety and the place where the imāms' shrines are located, a call to the return to foundational sources within the canon of Islam, combined with an organization capable of disseminating messages about the moral impropriety of shrines, found concrete expression in conflict over the everyday practice of shrine worship. Hostility towards shrine worship was imbricated in a broader political world in which Zaydī sayyids had long predominated, barring other Zaydī occupational "castes" from institutions of religious learning, for example. Attitudes toward shrine worship as superstitious and un-Islamic were also fueled by education abroad, particularly in Saudi Arabia, where calls to return to the wisdom of Islam's original, foundational texts were particularly prevalent.

Thus, everyday practices (such as prayer habits or shrine worship) represent key mechanisms through which the politicization of categories and the apparent essentialization of groups take place, and organizations are often critical to making some ordinary practices definitive while others are not. Language and everyday habits and rituals help secure the commitments of would-be and actual adherents. The overt politicization of a practice, which may or may not be deliberately strategic, has in any case the effect of fixing or intensifying the importance of that practice. A movement disseminating the message that praying with arms at the side is wrong, for example, creates the conditions under which those who do so knowingly are engaging in an act shot through with fraught meanings.[41] Depending on the context and the interpreter, a bodily comportment becomes a mode of defiance, an expression of group solidarity, and/or a sign of deviance. But it is not neutral. In this vein, those who pray with hands crossed in the way recognized as conventionally Sunnī are both performing piety and reproducing their affiliation with nondenominational and Sunnī-identified others. This enactment may register a desire to appear pious, adherence to a sect that represents piety, and/or a state of feeling pious. The significance of such practices in the Yemeni context of Ṣaʿda speaks to a history of prejudicial treatment (of non-sayyids) and to the expanded material and discursive possibilities opened up by the popularity of nondenominational notions of piety, some of which are currently inspired by organizations from abroad (particularly from Saudi Arabia), as well as by regime policies.

The al-Ḥūthī conflict highlights for us the historical processes and power relationships generating the "thin coherence" (Sewell 1999) that identifies a group, without our assuming that coherence a priori. As Rogers Brubaker has pointed out, "violence becomes 'ethnic' (or 'racial' or 'nationalist') through the meanings attributed to it by perpetrators, victims, politicians, . . . researchers, relief workers, and others. Such acts of framing and narrative encoding do not simply interpret the violence; they constitute it as ethnic" (Brubaker 2004, 16). Or to put the point somewhat differently, returning to a major theme of this book, categories of group membership have a performative quality. When scholars or on-the-ground protagonists invoke terms such as "the Zaydīs" they are also calling these groups into existence (Bourdieu 1991, 220; Brubaker 2004, 10). Categories are not groups, but they do make groups thinkable and legible, and indeed help constitute groups as objects available for self-identification. Such categories may have long, enduring histories or they may be of more recent origin. They are rarely fabricated out of thin air. Categories get institutionalized through organizations and the particular actions they encourage, as well as through everyday interactions among ordinary people and the institutional forms such interactions take under particular historical and strategic circumstances. Together, categories and the material practices instantiating them operate dialectically, separable ultimately neither from each other nor from group formation itself.

THE VEXED CATEGORY OF "TRIBE"

The conventional dichotomy between tribes and urban populations also misses the point in the al-Ḥūthī conflict in ways that are instructive for a general discussion of political identifications. Al-Ḥūthī himself could claim no tribal affiliation, but he was able to generate loyalty among populations who self-identify and are recognized as tribes, such as al-Razzāmī, many of whose members have fought on al-Ḥūthī's behalf—or at least have fought to oppose Ṣāliḥ's regime in the conflict. Ṣāliḥ himself self-identifies and is categorized by Yemenis as from "Sanḥān," a term that designates a region and a group within a very large confederation called Ḥāshid. Those identified with Ḥāshid have historically been at odds with those who identify with Bakīl, a term describing the largest, but politically less powerful, of the two confederations, even while there have also been organizations that have allied across this divide. Muqbil al-Wādi'ī, according to his own account, was born into the tribe of Wādi'a, part of the Bakīl confederation east of Ṣa'da. His efforts to continue studying after completing a traditional elementary school curriculum in the years before the revolution took him to the Great Mosque of al-Hādī Yaḥyā bin al-Ḥusayn in Ṣa'da, where he claims to have been thwarted by Zaydī sayyids, who discriminated against him due to his "tribal origins" (Haykel 2002, 28).[42] He subsequently went to Saudi Arabia, where trouble with authorities eventually propelled him back to Yemen. On his return, he sought and gained "tribal" (and regime) protection. Categories of tribal affiliation often refer to an organizational mechanism for political mobilization, particularly but not exclusively in North Yemen, and therefore it is unsurprising that in the context of this current conflict, networks indexed by the category "tribe" have been activated both on behalf of the regime and for al-Ḥūthī's Believing Youth.

But what exactly does the term "tribe" connote and how can we understand its political importance? An oft-repeated, widely circulated genealogy in Yemen—derived from written accounts in the early centuries of Islam—divides Arabian tribes into two separate lines, the Northern Arabs of the Ḥijāz (sons of ʿAdnān) and the Southern Arabs (sons of Qaḥṭān). In this narrative the origins of Yemen's two major tribal confederations stem from Qaḥṭān, "the father of Yemen" (Jirāfī 1951, 18; cited also in Dresch 1993). One of Qaḥṭān's key descendants was Sabaʾ, who had two sons, Ḥimyar and Kahlān. Whereas Ḥimyar's offspring are associated with the southern parts of Yemen, most Yemenis who identify as tribal from Ṣanʿāʾ northward are viewed (at least in early Islamic texts, in many contemporary histories and genealogies, and in popular lore) as descendants of Kahlān. According to this well-known genealogical account, Kahlān begat two sons, Zayd and ʿArīb. Zayd had Mālik, whose sons were Nabt and Awsala. Awsala begat Hamdān; Hamdān begat Nawf, who begat Ḥubrān, who had Jusham. Jusham's two sons, Ḥāshid and Bakīl, provide the eponym for the tribes of Ḥāshid and Bakīl, whose members are categorized as Hamdānī, the direct descendents of Hamdān (Abū Ghānim 1985, 61–62; Dresch 1993, 5). In the al-Ḥūthī conflict, those who claim membership in Razzāmāt belong neither to Ḥāshid nor to Bakīl, but they too are classified by Yemenis as Hamdānī because they purportedly stem from the same progenitor, Hamdān.

As the above genealogical narrative and its widespread dissemination suggest, tribal affiliation is one component of sociopolitical identification for many Yemenis, and this is especially true in areas where the state is institutionally weak, such as in Ṣaʿda. Mistaken impressions about what tribes are abound in the scholarly literature, however, including the common perception of tribes as pastoral nomads.[43] This is incorrect in Yemen, where tribes often denote territorial political arrangements made up of (grain and qāt) farmers or ranchers living in villages.[44] Tribes also do not invariably mean "large kin groups, organized and regulated according to ties of blood or family lineage" (Khoury and Kostiner 1991, 4), despite genealogical narratives to the contrary. Other organizing principles are also at work (Weir 2007, 3). Tribes often designate relationships centered on some form of legal jurisdiction and political obligation, in which *shaykhs* or leaders, usually chosen by a caucus of elders from contenders among particularly eloquent and wealthy elite families, have obligations to settle disputes and collect taxes (Weir 2007). Members, who may or may not be kin, are required to pay taxes and to abide by both religious and customary (*'urf*) law. "Tribal" in this sense of the term is often used as an occupational caste distinction and/or as a regional designation to characterize the 25 percent of the population living in the north-central plateau and the eastern desert. The inhabitants of this region are also noted for being suspicious of government, and appeals to tribalism tend to have a specific political valence, as populist, anti-sayyid, and egalitarian. These areas are also nominally Zaydī in the main, although residents have increasingly been won over to a version of Sunnī-oriented salafī piety, as Muqbil al-Wādi'ī's own life story suggests.

By contrast, in the more populous areas of the Tihāma and the southern uplands of the North, as well as in Aden's hinterland and the Ḥaḍramawt of the South, smallholding peasants, sharecroppers, landowners, and long-distance traders are the norm. People in the *minṭaqa al-wusṭā* or "middle region" (from Dhamār south to Murays), for example, do not identify as tribal, although, mirroring certain practices attributed to tribes, they do have important extended family relationships, carry arms, and settle disputes out of court. In these areas, where the leftist guerrilla movement was particularly strong, "tribal" often has pejorative connotations, designating lawlessness or backwardness, a hindrance to modernization.[45] Sometimes as well "tribal" is used to mean thinking instrumentally. In this view, tribesmen are driven by monetary concerns rather than by moral or political imperatives. The following poem, which can be invoked pejoratively by avowed modernists or humorously by self-identified tribesmen themselves, reflects such attitudes:[46]

I am nobody's tribesman
And no one is my state
My state is only that which fills
My palm with money (*qurūsh*).

In the southeastern region of the Ḥaḍramawt, the term's meanings vary (often in relationship to a person's political orientations). For leftists there, "tribal" signifies similarly to how it does in much of the country's "middle region." But the term can also be used to express communal pride and antagonism toward the former socialist regime of the South. City dwellers in a number of different regional areas, moreover, use "tribesman" (*qabīlī*) to mean "country bumpkin," and in this use it can refer to various types of rural people, many of whom would not themselves identify as tribal (Dresch 1993). In short, tribes do not necessarily denote particular unities of production or exchange, although they can, and the category's meanings and political significance vary markedly within Yemen. Most important perhaps, tribal identity is not fixed at birth; tribesmen can cease to be tribesmen when they move away from tribal territory, and people can switch tribes (*inqaṭaʿ min qabīla ukhrā*). As Dresch (1990, 255) notes:

> A man . . . who feels himself wronged but is denied support by his tribe may leave and take refuge with the neighboring tribe. His fellows are supposed to retrieve him and make amends. Sometimes, however, he will become permanently part of the set he joins, the moral redefinition being made by the slaughter of bulls. . . . Far from tribes cohering unthinkingly as wholes around men at odds, men are constantly being moved back and forth through the system and being "covered" for a time from the view of their antagonists.

As Shelagh Weir (2007) points out, defection is an institutionalized form of protest in the northern highlands, an option open not only to individuals but also to hamlets and wards whose members seek to transfer their political allegiance and obligations away from their former shaykh or leader to a new one, who is often described as "giving them sanctuary" (*awzāhim*) from political or legal oppression (113). In these instances, defection means that the houses and land of the defectors now also "belong" in political terms to the new tribe and that the receiving shaykh can legally enter them to enforce the law or conscript them during intertribal hostilities without violating the authority of the tribe in whose geographical domains they are situated (113). Religious taxes and subscriptions are paid to the shaykh receiving the defectors. Such defections are generally legalized through formal rituals and written contracts (114–15).

As the example of defection illustrates, "tribes" are not fixed, static groups with essences inhering in them. The term, moreover, denotes a conceptual category, in some ways not unlike religious denomination, subject to changing definition and used in different contexts for a variety of political purposes. This is not to argue that tribes and religious denominations operate in an identical manner, and the differences are also instructive. Although the invocation of Sunnī and Shīʿī can reflect a pragmatic political identification, religious denominations are discursive traditions. They therefore have a set of transnationally recognizable authorizing practices, forms of discipline and pedagogy, and a corpus of textual and practical knowledge borne out of conflict and accommodation over time. To invoke the terms Sunnī and Shīʿī is to index doctrinal disagreements, a history of contention over pedagogical practices and embodied forms of knowledge (Asad 1986; Mahmood 2005). Although tribal laws can be complex, including sophisticated modes of mediation and arbitration, as well as rituals to induct members (as in the case with defections), the term "tribe" itself does not imply practical and scholarly traditions of scriptural interpretation that connect practitioners to a set of foundational texts across past, present, and future. Although tribes can and do mobilize for collective action, the scale of that mobilization is therefore limited.

Conflicts coded as tribal by Western analysts and Yemenis alike, moreover, often obscure disputes over such issues as income disparities, resource allocation, or the benefits derived from development projects. According to the International Crisis Group,

> Yemenis living in the oil-rich governorates of Ma'rib, Shabwa, and Hadramawt, for example, believe they are not receiving a fair share of oil income derived from their territory. Residents of the governorates that formed the PDRY [the former People's Democratic Republic of Yemen in the South] similarly complain that they produce 60 percent of the national income but receive fewer benefits than the population of the "northern" governorates. Tribesmen from the northern governorate of Ma'rib have voiced similar complaints, albeit not on the basis of a North-South divide: they complain that the government tends to shower favors on those tribes that are in its good graces.[47]

It is therefore also a mistake to see "the tribes" as a group always at odds with the regime—a description that finds expression in some donor and media reports, as well as in scholarly publications. Although regional and tribal interests are sometimes invoked to undermine the government's ability to enforce law in particular areas,[48] self-identified tribesmen have interacted with the state on their own territory and served in state offices throughout Yemeni history (Dresch 1990, 2000). Take the example of the powerful Shaykh ʿAbd Allāh bin Ḥusayn al-Aḥmar. In his role as head of

Ḥāshid, his local interests (to keep his tribesmen armed, for example) may not always coincide with the interests of a central state (to monopolize violence, for instance). Yet as head of Ḥāshid (the tribal confederation to which the president also belongs) and as speaker of parliament, Shaykh ʿAbd Allāh is a recognized, active member of the regime. By contrast, as the leader of the main Islamic party, al-Iṣlāḥ, he sometimes allies with and sometimes is opposed to the ruling party, the General People's Congress.

In other words, actors are involved in multiple networks, many of which have been used by regimes in the North, at least since the founding of the Yemeni Arab Republic in 1962, to set up a wide-ranging patronage system. This system has tapped into tribal networks while also offering subsidies to "shaykhs" or local leaders in Lower Yemen. The latter were historically more like feudal landlords ruling over peasants than like the "tribal" shaykhs of the northern highlands (who do not control tribesmen's land), but both forms of organization were used to distribute payoffs and buy (albeit not always successfully) some loyalty. Since the 1994 civil war, the regime has also fostered new networks in the South and attempted to revive old ones. In the aftermath of unification, many southerners began to speak of "retribalization," juxtaposing the PDRY's stated commitments to a modern "state of law and order" with the purportedly primitive or traditional ways of the disorderly North. There is evidence to suggest that areas of the South have experienced the revitalization of structures that Yemenis call tribal, in parts of Yāfiʿ, Abyan, Shabwa, and the Ḥaḍramawt.[49] Appointments to high public office since the civil war of 1994 register the emergence of a new elite composed mainly of leaders who carry the title of tribal shaykhs. These men enjoy discretionary powers that are largely above the law. At the same time, the power of urban elites and peasants has diminished considerably in the South. Holders of high office who cannot rely on connections to maintain their standard of living or deliver resources to constituencies have established alternative patron-client relationships—becoming clients of those with access to key goods and services and patrons to their own constituencies, as was discussed in previous chapters.

In short, at times self-identification as tribal can be less salient politically than access through any of a number of social networks that have been harnessed to the regime through patron-client relationships. When that co-optation fails, the regime attempts to rely on its coercive power to eliminate challenges to its rule. In this light the conflict with Believing Youth appears as a political opportunity for the regime, an invitation to intervene and assert its power in an area of the country previously rife with a disorder that had outlived its political utility as a mechanism of control in its own right. The regime's intervention may also be an attempt to prepare Ṣāliḥ's son Aḥmad for rule, by eliminating political foes whose commitments to the idea of ousting an unjust leader (if not precisely the religious doctrine of khurūj) can inspire Zaydī sayyids, tribally oriented citizens, and oppositional politicians alike. To put the argument in more general terms, an account of political identifications should not only specify the events, debates, organizations, and everyday practices that disseminate category-based knowledge about people, places, and things. A persuasive discussion of political identity formation must move beyond these factors to consider the role that regimes in particular play in generating the distinctions that make groups seem quasi natural.[50]

THE ROLE OF THE REGIME

Michel Foucault and Pierre Bourdieu inspired a plethora of work on how the modern state classifies its citizens, revealing how institutions underwrite the ways in which people understand themselves and each other. Categories of all sorts, whether of citizenship, race, religion, ethnicity, occupation, income bracket, property rights, sexuality, or criminality become salient, in part, through the state's ability to impose classifications on the world. States use documents of identification, such as driver's licenses and passports, as well as methods of sorting people across categories, such as censuses, to do significant "organizational work" (Tilly 1998). The claim is not that the state creates these categories from scratch. But states do have the means to make these categories important by controlling how classificatory schemes and modes of social counting are put to practical use. State officials, judges, teachers, NGO workers, and local medical professionals, as well as others, make use of these categories in understanding their respective object worlds, in reaching decisions, ordering and apportioning populations, and reproducing the social conditions of their own expertise (Brubaker 2004, 43; Brubaker and Cooper 2000; Mitchell 2002b; Povinelli 2002; Dominguez 1997). Postcolonial countries, in particular, have also inherited the antecedent patterns of administrative classification devised under colonial rule, ones that may be undermined only partially by subsequent state-building processes or that may even be enhanced by the ways in which categories such as ethnicity or race or tribe are inscribed in a country's postindependence institutions (Posner 2005). Such classificatory systems help determine the contours of group membership, the self-understandings of actors, the mobilization strategies of leaders, and the political claims of citizens.[51] And citizen participation in embodying and disseminating these categories is critical to their success.

Given the insights generated by this extensive literature, the Yemeni case is notable in two ways: state institutions are exceptionally fragile and the North was never colonized, although, as discussed in chapter 1, the North was subjected to two periods of Ottoman occupation, the later one resembling aspects of colonial rule evident elsewhere. As the previous chapters make clear, the Yemeni regime, first, does not generate the forms of "governmentality" or mechanisms of social control that the literature often describes, nor do citizens regularly experience them.[52] In local disputes, courts and arbitrators (such as community leaders or local strongmen) typically have access to the same means of enforcing their rulings as the regime. Many local leaders command soldiers and run prisons of their own, and instead of relying on the state, they regularly use these coercive means to intervene in local events (Würth 2005; Messick 2005a). Nor does the Yemeni state tend to take advantage of its potential "educative and formative role," the ways in which public schooling, in particular, might play an important institutional part in producing national citizens whose consent is self-evident to them (Lloyd and Thomas 1998, 21; Gramsci 1971; Willis 1981; Kaplan 2006). As suggested in chapter 2, the schools that do exist are overcrowded; textbooks are not always supplied; the curriculum, especially in the countryside, is not enforced; and the regime has little control over what gets taught. Moreover, many children do not attend school and illiteracy rates remain exceptionally high.

My fieldwork in schools in the fall of 1999 provided a detailed picture. In a working-class area of the capital, I attended national education and Qur'ānic classes. The neighborhood streets remained unpaved and garbage accumulated on a makeshift soccer field abutting newly built houses funded with labor remittances from the Gulf. In an informal arrangement, I was able to attend class in exchange for teaching students English. Students crowded into small classrooms, many of which were dark and without electricity. In the eighth-grade class on national education, there were 184 students, but less than half that many chairs. Students would stand by desks or lean against the back walls. Many said that they could not afford the textbooks. The teacher, who was animated and knowledgeable, asked his pupils to distinguish between a royalist regime and a republican one; students could not do so. But in response to the teacher's narration of life under the imamate, pupils did ask lively probing questions, particularly about why people had not revolted against the imām before they did. One female student even drew parallels between the current regime and the imām's despotic one. If the state's educative role is weak in the city, it is more so in rural areas. In circumstances of profound poverty, rural schools often have only one or two rooms, without electricity, adequate bathroom facilities, or supplies. Overcrowding prompts teachers to bring students outside where classes are held under the hot sun. There is no sense of a national or organized curriculum in many rural areas, and the main classes taught are what local teachers, unaccountable to the state, deem appropriate.

The regime may at times act like a state by inducing compliance, staging scenes of domination, and by co-opting and punishing would-be dissidents. State institutions may also participate in evoking groups by naming them (e.g., through laws or censuses or household surveys or textbook references), but in the Yemeni case they do not seem to be producing the modes of systematic intervention attributable to "strong" states. Instead, it is primarily the regime's divide-and-rule strategies that have created the conditions under which passionate, contentious group-based solidarities thrive, and claims to group belonging in turn have contributed to the regime's durability. Identities do not by themselves generate action. They have to be mobilized by organizations, reiterated through everyday practices that convey meanings acephelously, and triggered or exacerbated by particular events. A politics of disorder yields a measure of order, while helping to structure the imaginative and organizational possibilities available to citizens. No regime produces these identifications out of whole cloth, and certainly not the one in Yemen. But the latter does take advantage of what resources it does possess, including, for example, funneling money selectively into organizations as it acts to pit one against the other.

Second, North Yemen was never colonized, although some significant current-day institutions were introduced in mediated form by the Ottomans, and later, in the 1960s, by the Egyptians. Previous chapters demonstrated that categories such as "the nation" and efforts aimed at building state institutions led to novel hybrid or composite forms, first under the imamate and later in a more far-reaching way through the institutional changes ushered in by North Yemen's leaders after the 1962 revolution. As Brinkley Messick rightly notes, "In a world influenced in different ways by the imperial and colonial West, highland Yemen represents a situation at one extreme of the continuum of possibilities, in which change occurred at a pace marked by an unusual absence of outside intervention" (Messick 1993, 254). Arguably, it was the Egyptian occupation of North Yemen between 1962 and 1967, with Egypt's backing of republican officers in their battles against Saudi-financed royalists, that had the most far-reaching consequences for models and expectations, if not the actual fulfillment, of state institutional development (Wenner 1967; Burrowes 1987). But that intervention was short, and although the Egyptians established bureaucracies, banned political parties, developed a state security system, and contributed as many as sixty thousand troops to the fight on behalf of the republicans (Schmidt 1968, 234–35; Aḥmad 1992, 286, 290, 591–97; Dresch 2000, 102), they failed to control much territory beyond the capital (Dresch 2000, 102, 106). Even in the South, colonial rule was not as totalizing or as effective as it was in other places such as India or, arguably, Algeria. One of the key challenges for scholars of postcolonial politics, then, is to comprehend the divergent conditions under which regimes have sought to build institutions, manage populations, and reproduce categories of identification intelligible to a country's citizens.

In this spirit, the case of Yemen invites us to consider that the logics of state building may be at odds with the strategies of regime survival. Political rulers may not have incentives to build durable state institutions that can project power across territory in uniform, standard ways.[53] Rather, regimes might enhance their durability not only by creating state institutions (a project that requires a lot of resources and implies significant risks) but by encouraging disorder in certain areas, or at least not intervening to end it. In this context it is important to note that although violence had erupted periodically in Ṣa'da before al-Ḥūthī's recent challenge, President Ṣāliḥ had previously been successful at managing conflicts between Zaydī clerics and salafī adherents, a strategy that may not have made Ṣāliḥ an effective state builder but that seemed to secure his rule. However, by the late 1990s and early 2000s, Ṣa'da in particular resembled the lawless frontier towns depicted in some American Westerns. If the regime's inability to control violence is evident in various parts of the country, it was particularly apparent here. The regime's reaction to al-Ḥūthī, so curiously disproportionate to al-Ḥūthī's apparent threat, must therefore be read as an effort and an opportunity to reassert—indeed, I want to suggest perhaps even *to establish* for the first time—the regime's territorial sovereignty in this area.

But why would it do so, given my argument that the regime not only tolerates disorder but often cultivates it? The answer to this question lies in changed conditions that made this move practical at the time that it occurred. Since September 11, the United States had been pressuring Ṣāliḥ's regime to collaborate in the "war on terror" with the effect, in part, of distancing the regime from its salafī allies in Ṣa'da. Because Muqbil al-Wādi'ī's death had already fragmented the salafī movement in that region, there was no longer a need for a strong Zaydī countermovement. The regime could use salafī militants against Zaydī activists without fearing a united salafī reaction. Importantly as well, negotiations with Saudi Arabia had recently concluded, delimiting for the first time a border in an area previously vulnerable to Saudi intervention. A boost in the state's military capabilities stimulated by oil revenues and foreign aid also explains why the regime could take the risk it did. Both the United States and Great Britain gave support to the regime in its battles, with the British allegedly providing bulletproof vests to Yemeni troops. Moreover, a key mediator between the regime and Zaydī sayyids, the ruling party's assistant secretary general, Yaḥyā al-Mutawakkil (himself a well-known Zaydī sayyid), was killed in a suspicious car accident in January 2003. Many Yemenis believe that the regime assassinated al-Mutawakkil for his outspoken views and his connections to the opposition, particularly to the Yemeni Socialist Party. When the al-Ḥūthī events began in 2004, regime critics wondered whether al-Mutawakkil's assassination was also designed to facilitate what was to become an all-out assault on Zaydism's regional heartland of Ṣa'da.

In short, although Yemeni state institutions are too fragile to regulate populations in the way that much of the literature on knowledge production asserts is necessary, the regime has been able to engage in divide-and-rule strategies that themselves reproduce and lend political salience to, if not create, categories of group membership—experiences of affiliation and possibilities for organization that have helped structure the current fault lines of Yemeni political life. Those categories are bolstered by the material, emotional, and spiritual incentives such group identifications afford. The regime's reaction to al-Ḥūthī's protest must also be understood in terms of the opportunities it gave the regime to assert its territorial sovereignty, to redefine the rules of the game in an area that had previously been controlled (to the extent that it was) through a politics of fragmentation alone.

IDENTIFYING "IDENTITY": THEORETICAL CONTRIBUTIONS AND CONCLUDING REMARKS

The approach to identity formation I am pursuing here has implications for the ways in which we study the politics of group solidarity. We need to understand how categories such as Sunnī and Shīʿī or salafī and Zaydī work in specific contexts, while also identifying how organizations and the debates they summon generate category-based knowledge. This injunction does not require eschewing generalizations, nor does it mean neglecting the ways in which categories exist and change through time. But it should discourage writing about an "in-group" or an "out-group" or about "social distance" between groups as if these things exist a priori. Such terminology often gets in the way of examining how experiences of group identity came to be, and why particular organizations find encouragement or are created, while others do not enjoy such advantages or are even punished (Smith 2004).

Judgments of similarity and contrast are methodologically and theoretically tricky: what counts as a similarity or a contrast must be situated historically, must be based on transparent criteria of comparison, must be sensitive to local meanings of sameness and difference, and must be attentive to the power relationships—the institutions and everyday practices—that make some politically relevant standards of similarity and difference more authoritative than others (Smith 2004). This issue is fudged in many texts in which conceptual categories—once again "social distance" or "group traits" are good examples—are treated as objective criteria. Social scientists invoking categories in this way naturalize a set of identifiable attributes, reproducing the very classifications they claim to interrogate. Ethnicity or social distance is not an objective thing, but a category whose political salience has a history and a range of meanings (including what counts as a sign of visible ethnicity), and whose importance is variable and should not be assumed.[54]

This critique reaches all the way back to shape what questions we should pose. Instead of simply asserting social construction or overlooking the ways in which social scientists contribute to the very phenomena they seek to describe, we need to ask what the definitions of identity in a given context are, what forms they take, how they are perceived, and under what conditions they change.[55] Moreover, how are solidarities created and maintained, when they are? Identities can be about choice (Laitin 1998; Posner 2005; Chandra 2004; Barth 1969), but they are also about the desire to be recognized (Povinelli 2002; Markell 2003), and they concern the sociohistorical contexts in which certain choices and desires seem possible or necessary, while others are foreclosed even to the imaginations of those making decisions. As the anthropologist Virginia Dominguez (1997) rightly notes, there are "epistemological and institutional systems" that stand in people's way, and mechanisms through which actors come to affiliate with a particular group or get classified over time. How people conceive of themselves and how they act in the world are results of microprocesses of social interaction (such as the ways in which self-conceptions of being Muslim may be bound up with daily imprecations to God) and formal institutional routines (such as state classifications), requiring theories that would explain the formation of selves to shed light as well on the social processes that generate those selves.

Following the social theorist George Herbert Mead (1967 [1934]), as well as many other more recent scholars, I want to argue that there is no such thing as a self prior to social interaction: selves are produced and continually reproduced in relation to others. In the case of the al-Ḥūthī conflict, "Zaydī sayyids" is an ascriptive designation, but those who embrace the label may choose to become politically active or not; as activists they are defined in relation to salafī militants, as well as through their dealings with regime representatives, and in the context of performing their duties as pious Muslims with one another. Not all Zaydī sayyids identify as such, nor does such a designation mean that the label actually indexes a substantial group. Carrying through on social constructivist insights means not mistaking a contingent category of "ethnopolitical" or national practice for social scientific categories of analysis (Brubaker 2004, 9–10). As Stathis Kalyvas points out, when scholars label actors as "Shīʿī" or "Sunnī" or "Kurds," they are not engaging in "neutral" description. Rather, "they typically imply a theory of causation" (Kalyvas 2003, 481; see also 2006, chap. 11). For example, in the case of analyzing civil wars, such labels are often understood to designate unitary groups that are causing the violence—or rather, that religious, ethnic, or class cleavages *cause* violence to happen (Kalyvas 2003, 481; 2006, chap. 11). But this is rarely the case.

Actors may construct a conflict as specifically ethnic or sectarian in line with their own understanding of the predicament they confront or in an effort to generate political support, or both. Al-Ḥūthī and his opponents were both able to draw on a repertoire of images familiar to (and contested through) the discursive tradition of Islam in order to make claims about authentic Muslim (as opposed to sectarian—*ṭā'ifī*) practice. Al-Ḥūthī and his followers invoked the martyrdom of Ḥusayn, the possibilities of khurūj, and the ethical-political superiority of descendants of the Prophet. Some social scientists argue that discourses matter because they can be used by elites to dupe constituencies into following ventures of interest primarily to the elites themselves.[56] Brass (1997), for example, argues that riots in India are institutionalized and systematic, and that ethnically oriented politicians use them to frame violence in ethnic terms, thus manipulating citizens to win their support. However, what is left inadequately explained in accounts of this kind is *why* elites are able to successfully attract followers by couching political matters in identity terms. Of course, individuals might also fall into an identity category and even be available for political action without feeling that affiliation deeply. In this regard, we need to pay attention to how people who can be classified or who self-identify with a particular category (such as Zaydīs or Ḥāshid or al-Ḥūthī's followers) might be mobilizing for reasons other than deep-seated emotion (while also recognizing that deep-seated emotion need not be counterpoised to strategic interest so that the two can work in mutually reinforcing ways). We may have to acknowledge that we cannot know how profoundly most actors believe or feel, although we can offer grounded speculation about their political motivations. We can also make intelligent guesses about the intensity of affect, if not its nature, at least on issues about which people are prepared to die.

Such accounts also assume a distance between elites and followers that may not exist on the ground, for leaders and followers share a semiotic world in which epochal events such as al-Ḥusayn's martyrdom make sense. As I argued in chapter 1, many analyses make leaders too distinct from the social setting in which they are situated, as if leaders and ordinary citizens are not implicated in the same discursive, sociopolitical worlds. In this light, many studies also regard discourses as epiphenomenal, as somehow outside of the material interests that actually determine solidarities and conflict. But material interests might be fruitfully viewed not as objective criteria but as being discursively produced: in other words, what counts as a material interest is mediated through our language about what "interest" means and what the material is. This is not to argue that personal animosities or solidarities are irrelevant. Kalyvas has shown how personal grudges and local cleavages often explain why civilian participation in what he calls "selective violence" takes the form it does (see esp. chap. 11, 2006; also 2003). Personal animosities are undoubtedly part of the explanation of how the targets of violence are chosen, hiding at times under the umbrella of political rhetoric.

I do want to suggest, however, that private, local antipathies are often themselves political and general—stimulated by conditions that make such enmities possible. Indeed, what counts as a "private" matter is itself discursively designated and often contested. Protagonists' choices and experiences, including their solidarities and aversions, both shape and are formed by a regional territory's relationship to the nation-state, by actors' relationships to resources, by individuals' connections (both personal and political) to one another, and by actors' projections of themselves into a future without the enemies or obstacles they act to eliminate. In the semiotic-historical context of Yemen, local organizations and issues often have broader political implications and consequences. Some personal grudges are themselves created and mediated through informal political organizations, such as mosque study groups, which might be funded by the regime, through the everyday but contentious practices of piety (including divergent notions of the proper way to pray or the permissibility of shrines), through patterns of transnational networking with people and institutions in Afghanistan and Saudi Arabia (to name two examples), and through the mobilization of specific ethical-political discourses. Discourses matter to the production of groups, not as monocausal explanations for solidarity or conflict or war (as is suggested by some accounts),[57] but because language and other symbolic systems both organize and exemplify the conceptual universe through which action (including violence) takes place.

What I want to emphasize here are three interrelated points, ones that to my mind pursue and clarify some of the promising aspects of recent literature (e.g., Kalyvas 2006). First, it is impossible to understand whatever local animosities or solidarities exist among actors without a proper grasp of the political environment in which those enmities and affiliations have continued to flourish. Many disputes in Yemen revolve around issues of resources, for example, and competition for resources is never strictly personal or local. Land disputes involve the political questions of access, of distribution, of property rights and historical entitlements, of modes of sociability and mechanisms for sharing, and of regime intervention. Second, the dichotomies of public and private, political and personal, national and local, ideological and instrumental may not adequately capture how political master narratives intersect, not only with personal enmities and solidarities but also, as we see in the al-Ḥūthī and salafī examples, with issues of moral reform. In other words, in our theories of social action we ought to pay attention to local dynamics while resisting the impulse to isolate instrumental or strictly material motives from wider political-moral discourses.[58] Third, these moral issues are not epiphenomenal, acting as smokescreens or instances of false consciousness that veil the substantive material concerns of actors. Rather, the current political efficacy of these movements of piety (al-Ḥūthī's and salafī ones) have to do with the ways in which they can appeal to both material and ethical concerns, grounding Islamic principles in the practices of everyday living.[59]

This is not to argue that actors simply act in accordance with master narratives or that these narratives are always significant for analyses. Local factionalism and alliances may be particularly good for explaining the forms violence takes, why certain people get involved, and how actors take advantage of situations to settle prior disputes. I am not attempting to explain violence per se, although the ratcheting up of the political solidarities I do discuss here may produce conditions conducive to violent conflict. And insofar as one of the most robust predictors of "civil war onset" is low levels of per capita gross domestic product (Fearon and Laitin 2003; Collier and Hoeffler 2004), Yemen, as a poor country whose state institutions do not always exercise sovereignty over peripheral territories, may be particularly prone to violence.[60]

For students of violence, the al-Ḥūthī conflict *does* have important lessons. The example suggests that the regime's ability to reproduce spaces of disorder, whether intentional or not, can have the effect of sustaining a tenuous but enduring political order. Violence occurring within the nation-state's borders, or "civil war onset," may be prompted by an overreaction on the part of a regime to demands made by organizations whose members were previously subject to a divide-and-rule system. A regime's efforts to bring the state into being by "monopolizing" violence may actually generate more violence. That strategy, in the case of Yemen, represents a shift. Pace Fearon and Laitin (2003), who argue common-sensically that "weak central governments render insurgency more feasible and attractive" (76), violence in the al-Ḥūthī example is arguably prompted by enhanced state capacities, by an intensified recourse to military and police resources as a result of foreign aid and Yemen's role in the war on terror. In this case, it is the boon to "state capacity" that seems to foster felicitous conditions for the regime's new policy and the subsequent violence that ensues.

CHAPTER FIVE

PIETY IN TIME

Contemporary Islamic Movements in National and Transnational Contexts

The details (if not the lessons) of the al-Ḥūthī conflict may be specific to Yemen, but a renewed interest in piety is evident across the Middle East in the proliferation of Islamic welfare associations, modes of dress emphasizing modesty, and increased mosque attendance (see Hirschkind 2006, 6). Cassette-recorded sermons of popular Muslim preachers have become a pervasive part of contemporary political social life in many towns and cities, pamphlets grounding Islamic principles in practices of everyday living circulate among literate citizens, and mosques are the center of neighborhood experience in both rural and urban areas (ibid.). Televisions broadcast popular call-in and talk-show programs, invoking the Qur'ān and the Sunna to resolve moral, practical, and political problems.[1] Politicians and ordinary citizens alike combine issues of ethical comportment with critiques of prevailing political conditions.

In this chapter I begin by departing from the ethnographic and textual foci of the previous chapters to explore in more macropolitical terms the reasons for the global emergence of contemporary Islamic movements. In contrast to studies arguing that religious movements undermine national solidarities, this book has already investigated how pious and national claims (as well as the commitments they index) have coexisted historically.

In the previous chapter we began to examine their coalescence in new forms of political self-identification and collective action. In this chapter I interrogate arguments linking global processes of neoliberal reform to a worldwide resurgence of faith, drawing on the case of Yemen to gauge the validity of this familiar claim. My aim is not to introduce complications for their own sake, but rather to show how by attending to the Yemeni example we can refine our general theorizations about the politics of piety.[2] Arguments focused too narrowly on the impact of neoliberal policy reforms are not up to the task of explaining the resurgence. And contemporary theory more generally has not kept pace with historical events, which requires us to rethink established concepts in light of local experience and to simultaneously capture what I want to call a transnational moral imaginary. This moral imaginary, independent of neoliberal reforms but also exacerbated by them, can be transported and shared across national boundaries, creating new forms of solidarity and conflict in the global present.

The term "neoliberalism" makes some scholars uneasy. As Taylor C. Boas and Jordan Gans-Morse (2007) argue, the term is not only capacious, it is often ill-defined, or used inconsistently and "adopted unevenly across ideological and disciplinary divides" (2). Whereas it was first used as a positive label by economists of the German Freiberg school to mean a renewal of classical liberalism, the word is now often deployed pejoratively by critics of "free market" ideology and of reforms promoting thoroughgoing economic deregulation and privatization. More strictly and closer to how the term is understood here, neoliberalism is used to refer to four different political-economy phenomena: (1) macroeconomic stabilization (policies that encourage low inflation and low public debt, and discourage Keynesian countercyclical tendencies); (2) trade liberalization and financial deregulation; (3) the privatization of publicly owned assets and firms; and (4) welfare state retrenchment. Sometimes these four aspects work in concert but often they do not, and their impact on population welfare varies.[3] In this chapter, I shall primarily be concerned with the latter three dimensions of reform.

One caveat at the outset: my attempts to historicize Islamic movements and to relate them to changing circumstances in a global economy should not be read as an "invented tradition" argument (see Hobsbawm and Ranger 1983; Kepel 1993; and Hirschkind's critique, 2001a and 2001b). Drawing on Talal Asad's work (1986, 1993, 2003), I underscored in the previous chapter that Islamic political practices exist within a dynamic and evolving discursive tradition, one that is constructed in and through deliberation. What I am trying to explain is how and why that tradition has come to be expressed in the form of an organized, vibrant Islamic "awakening" (*al-ṣaḥwa al-islāmiyya*). Or to put it differently, in noting that organizations and movements lay claim to a millennium-old tradition, I am not arguing that there exists somewhere a real authenticity to which these claims can be juxtaposed as false or misguided, as "invented tradition" arguments often seem to imply. Rather, I am interested in contributing to scholarly debates about the reasons for the current invigoration, widespread reach, and resonance of piety movements.

CONTEMPORARY ISLAMIC MOVEMENTS AND THEORIES OF NEOLIBERALISM

The story of neoliberal reforms may be a familiar one by now: in the late 1970s through the 1980s, under pressure from international institutions of economic reform such as the International Monetary Fund or the World Bank, states around the world began withdrawing economically, privatizing public assets, reducing or eliminating subsidies, deregulating prices, and ceasing to provide social services to which people had become accustomed, felt entitled to—and needed. As the welfare state has retreated in the Middle East, so the narrative goes, Islamic movements have often stepped forward to fill in the gaps, providing goods and services such as housing, textbooks, and health care that are not available from the state.[4] Egypt was one of the first Middle Eastern countries to initiate economic liberalization measures. In 1973–74 the government announced an "open door" economic policy (*infitāḥ*) after almost two decades of close regulation of foreign investment and imports. Private sector initiatives were to combine with government ownership, funding, and management of large industry, often in mixed partnership arrangements. Although such measures could be deemed successful during the oil boom years when oil wealth boosted household consumption and government revenues, they were disastrous in the bust period of the mid-1980s.[5]

Liberalization measures across the Middle East introduced citizens to a range of imported goods and luxury items to which they were unaccustomed, at the same time that oil revenues and privatization policies generated a new, Western-oriented "parvenu" class to consume them (Sadowski 1987; Mitchell 2002a).[6] This new class enjoyed a conspicuous lifestyle that, according to proponents of a political economy causal story, stimulated widespread resentment among the urban poor and middle classes. Such programs created markets, but they also enhanced perceptions of (as well as opportunities for) corruption. By the late 1980s, the IMF and USAID's successful imposition of structural adjustment policies in many Middle Eastern countries had removed safety nets, which combined with an oil bust to produce considerable economic suffering. Rising unemployment, decreases in subsidies, and housing problems all contributed to a glaring gap between rich and poor. In the late 1980s in Egypt, where reforms occurred early, strikes grew more common, food riots became "a frequent worry" among government officials, and middle- and lower-class citizens reported economic anxieties (Sadowski 1987, 44). As economic conditions became dire, Islamic organizations offered approaches to questions of social justice, based on mechanisms of redistribution such as the Islamic *zakāt* taxes, that were able to avoid the radical land reform language of old while lending approval to private property and entrepreneurial profit (Sadowski 1987; Kepel 2002).

The economic reforms of the last three decades of the twentieth century are an important part of explaining why Islamic movements have flourished, but their causal import is easily exaggerated. We need to take into account as well an increasing elective affinity between regime rhetoric and aspects of Islamic discourse, their close interaction and mutual historical constitution. The available idioms through which experiences of common belonging to a people became institutionalized in this post-1970s world are a product of what regimes will tolerate and what Islamic movements have won. In some cases, this discursive latitude has enabled pointed attacks on corrupt leaders. But in almost all cases, expressions of Muslim piety go along with consensual understandings of anti-American and pro-Palestinian solidarities, and these are evident in both officials' speeches and in the voices raised in mass demonstrations. Islamic discourses put forth a coherent anti-imperialist doctrine and suggest ways of reestablishing community, offering visions of an equitable, just, socially responsible way of life, much as the now-discredited Arab nationalist regimes of the 1950s and 1960s had done. Combining anti-imperialist and socioeconomic sentiments with concerns for family values, conventional sexual norms, and the desire to renew or "awaken" a specifically Muslim "culture" or "community," the Islamic revival has generated a broad range of adherents whose motivations—indexed in this chapter under the rubric of a transnational moral imaginary—cannot be reduced to economic determinations.[7] These discourses not only reflect contemporary political conditions that go beyond economic causes but are also themselves generative of novel political possibilities. An alliance between regimes and some Islamic movements both institutionally *and discursively* has helped to define the shifting parameters of political expression in the Middle East.

The popularity and institutional efficacies of Islamic political organizations must also be understood in the context of U.S. political projects and the "blowback" they have caused (Johnson 2000; Mamdani 2004). Long before empire became a fashionable (if apt) term to describe U.S. intervention, U.S. policies, both overt and covert, were stimulating widespread critique and providing reasons for action. Possible sources of blowback in the Middle East in particular include the following: the widely shared view that the United States serves as a proxy for Israel, that it has defiled the holy lands of Saudi Arabia by stationing troops there, that the United States is responsible for the decade of sanctions against Iraqis and for an ill-conceived war there now, that it continues to shore up corrupt dictators, and that it routinely upholds double standards between official commitments to democracy and equality, on the one hand, and its own political activities as well as those of its local allies, on the other. Current global economic arrangements are also viewed by many inhabitants of the Middle East, judging from ethnographic and survey work, as bringing wealth to the United States and its perceived institutional surrogates, the IMF and the World Bank, while rendering many parts of the world miserable and destitute.[8] And this critique suggests that neoliberal reforms are an important part of a broader concern, which encompasses not only worries about developments in global capitalism and the generalized commodification of social life but also about territorial sovereignty, about the ways in which the United States, in particular, projects its political power.

To some extent, the success of Islamic movements also has to be attributed to the state's elimination of leftist opposition by means of incarceration, torture, and co-optation. As we have seen in Yemen, unification between North and South in 1990 was followed by the northern ruling party's persistent assault on its southern socialist partners. In 1992–93, there were approximately 150 assassination attempts against members of the Yemeni Socialist Party—most of them carried out by self-identified radical Islamic activists who were encouraged financially and politically by the regime.[9] Even as other Arab regimes (and the United States) were cutting ties to Islamic groups in the 1990s, the Ṣāliḥ regime actively cultivated mainstream Islamic activists as a way to counteract the influence of the Yemeni Socialist Party in unified Yemen. In addition, the regime simultaneously lent encouragement to nonmainstream militants.[10] Some radicals rejected both the regime's overtures and the mainstream Islamic political party, while others were integrated into the regime and joined the ruling party. Various adherents also created independent militant organizations, such as the Islamic Jihād Movement and the Aden-Abyan Islamic Army. Organizational and financial relations have been alleged to exist between these organizations and al-Qāʿida, and personal ties between Usāma bin Lādin and members of the Islamic Jihād Movement are acknowledged publicly.[11] In this context, some organizations justify violence in spiritual and ethical terms, highlighting the regime's moral laxity, its toleration of socialist apostates, and the paramount importance of cultivating a pious, virtuous citizenry. Other regimes parallel Yemen's experience. In Egypt, the governments of Nāṣir and Anwar Sādāt worked actively to demobilize the working class and to attack leftist organizations.[12] In Jordan, Morocco, Tunisia, and Pakistan similar strategies of repression were the norm. U.S. support of the *mujāhidīn* as a way of combating a Soviet-backed leftist government in Afghanistan dramatizes a global process that was being pursued locally at least from the 1970s onward.[13]

Regime support of Islamic organizations and discourses, the fact of persistent U.S. intervention, and policies aimed at eliminating leftist opposition make it difficult to isolate economic reforms as the key variable or to establish a direct causal relationship between reforms and/or suffering, on the one hand, and Islamic political movements, on the other. We might nevertheless acknowledge that a politics of piety is "intimately connected with material conditions" without arguing that such conditions fully explain the appeal of ideas about piety (Euben 1999, 89). An economically deterministic argument also fails to explain why so many of the reforms demanded by Islamic activists are about everyday social practices rather than about establishing an economic balance between a rich minority and an impoverished majority (Abdo 2000, 4–5). Organizations and practices associated with Islamic revivals are often discussed in terms of realizing a virtuous life; they are an invitation to "retrain" one's ethical sensibilities in an effort to generate a novel, more satisfying moral, political order (Mahmood 2005, 193). As the above discussion suggests, consideration of economic motivations must thus be complemented by an analysis that takes seriously the discursive content and political-affective impulses underpinning Islamic projects.

In this vein, it is tempting to locate Islamic movements in the context of another recent global phenomenon, one characterized by proliferating appeals to ethnicity, culture, and identity. Scholars have even linked such demands for group recognition to projects of neoliberal reform and to what anthropologists specifically term "the mediations of the market." In some instances, these appeals find expression in attempts to commodify the exotic, to market cultural authenticity, and/or to underscore ethnic or cultural distinctiveness (Povinelli 2001, 2002; West and Carrier 2004; Comaroff and Comaroff 2001a, forthcoming).[14] Some Islamic movements operate with similar frames of reference in which practices of piety are viewed by activists as expressions of a distinctively Muslim or Arab identity (*al-hawiyya al-islāmiyya* or *al-hawiyya al-'arabiyya*). But as Saba Mahmood (2005) shows, based on an ethnographic study in Cairo, others do not. The mosque participants with whom she interacted are "quite ambivalent about the question of identity and are, in fact, emphatically critical of those Muslims who understand their religious practices as an expression of their Muslim or Arab identity rather than as a means of realizing a certain kind of virtuous life" (193). In other words, not all Islamic social movements, or for that matter contemporary social movements more generally, structure their claims through an identity politics or frame their grievances in terms of legal vocabularies stressing "rights, recognition, or distributive justice" (193).

Nevertheless, pious movements in general, movements organized around Islam in particular, and recent multicultural claims emphasizing ethnic difference or communal authenticity share two key commonalities. First, they all tend to insist on the historical integrity and continuity of the group, be it transnational, national, or subnational. This continuity in the case of religious movements is itself often anchored in calls for a "return to a foundational order of meaning and law—of life, family, ethics, marriage, the sacraments—free of . . . deviations and corruption" (Comaroff 2005, 22). Second, these claims tend to be politically important whether they are couched in terms of retraining ethical sensibilities, overriding nation-state divisions, or appealing to a specific "culture." Because modern institutions of governance help constitute and transform how piety gets cultivated even in fragile states such as Yemen (e.g., through laws or through strategies of divide and rule, or both), efforts to live a pious life in the context of other people making similar efforts may have transformative effects on the political order, even when seizing state power is not the aim (Hirschkind 1997). Pious Muslims have pressed for changes in public school curricula while also developing private institutions to educate students, for instance (Starrett 1998).[15] Attempts to restructure key aspects of ordinary life, such as commercial transactions, familial relationships, and welfare provisioning, all have potential political ramifications, and all reach beyond the sphere of the strictly material to generate and sustain the distinctly transnational moral imaginary that has emerged as a hallmark of the present age.

THE CASE OF YEMEN

Global trends associated with neoliberal reforms *have* found expression in Yemen mainly since unification in 1990. After the civil war of 1994, and with assistance from international organizations, the recently born Republic of Yemen launched a substantial program of economic and administrative reforms. In return for embarking on an IMF-supported structural adjustment program, entailing the lifting of subsidies, revaluing the local currency to coincide with the global market, and promising to streamline the bureaucracy, unified Yemen received considerable foreign debt relief in the mid-1990s (Detalle 1997). This relief has not translated into economic well-being for a large proportion of Yemeni citizens. The World Bank acknowledges that poverty seems to be increasing in Yemen and that the gap between rich and poor appears to be growing.[16] Yet the Yemeni case also lays bare how neoliberal reforms cannot be doing all of the work often attributed to them, and it does so in ways that shed further light on how and why a transnational moral imaginary has found expression in areas peripheral to, but affected by, global capitalism.

The points I want to make here are three: (1) Neoliberal reforms had a differentiated effect in Yemen depending, in part, on a particular region's prior economic and political experiences of state intervention. In other words, Yemen brings to the fore how attending to differences between North and South, as well as to variation *within* each region, undercuts assumptions about the context in which neoliberal policies worked their effects. (2) Islamic movements emerged in the 1970s and 1980s, before the structural adjustment reforms associated with neoliberalism got under way in Yemen. Yemen's relationship to Saudi Arabia (particularly through labor migration and the dissemination of audiocassettes of mosque sermons) and the subsequent politics of unification must be taken into account in order to understand the proliferation of pious political movements. Although the transnational circulation of religious ideas and practices bears a relationship to neoliberalism, these ideas and practices should not be misunderstood as immediate responses to the local implementation of policy if only because they predate it. (3) Contemporary Islamic political movements demonstrate how pious practices and national solidarities have coalesced into new hybrid forms of political self-identification and collective action, with implications for scholarly understandings of political allegiances more generally. It is often assumed that cultivating religious sensibilities (typically glossed in the literature as "sectarian allegiances") through, say, Islamic welfare provisioning, takes away from nation-state commitments. But as I have argued elsewhere in this book, this zero-sum reasoning is overly beholden to a secularization paradigm in which the religious is juxtaposed to, and is seen as in competition with, broader national identifications. Returning to a textual approach to illustrate the third point, I use the example of Yemen to demonstrate how this either/or formulation fundamentally misapprehends the ways in which nationalism and piety can and do work together in the present.

1. The Importance of Differentiation and Variation

Critics of neoliberal capitalism often presume a dramatic shift from a state that effectively channeled resources to its population to a market that does not. These images of working Keynesian welfare states or of postcolonial state-centric projects for redistribution just as often prove misleading, however. Not only in Yemen, but also in many other areas of the Middle East, Africa, and Asia, large swathes of territory have always been beyond the welfare state's reach and remain peripheral to global capitalism. The lessons to be learned here, in other words, should have some general applicability to similar circumstances in other parts of the world, toward which scholarly claims about state withdrawal erroneously presume a previously robust state presence and exaggerate the extent of global economic integration. Contemporary Yemen also demonstrates that populations both between and within nation-states experience neoliberalism variously, depending on a particular regime's projects and capacities, as well as on citizens' imaginings in relationship to them.

Recall from chapter 1 that the North's YAR (1962–90) and the South's PDRY (1967–90)[17] were ideologically and historically distinct polities, important economic and political similarities notwithstanding. Despite the considerable expansion in the North's public sector in the late 1970s and

1980s, including the regime's efforts to establish modes of repression similar to those of the South, the state in the YAR was never the addressee of people's moral and material entitlements to the extent that it was in the PDRY. State institutions in the YAR competed with local development associations as sponsors of economic change. Remitted earnings were difficult to tax, with the result that as much as two-thirds of the Yemeni currency in circulation in the North was outside the formal banking system. North Yemen was also a "no doors economy," an enclave of "peripheral capitalism" with "few legal barriers to imports, domestic trade, investments, speculation, transportation, or construction" (Carapico 1998, 34). In these circumstances state withdrawal cannot be a key mechanism for pious activism in the North, simply because the state was not delivering welfare state provisions before the worldwide retrenchment.

The PDRY presents what would seem at first glance a stark contrast to conditions in the North, as the regime nationalized and redistributed land under ambitious agrarian reform programs that expropriated feudal estates, seized religious endowments, and later even appropriated some family-sized holdings. The South's Marxist-Leninist state epitomized ambitions common to what was called in the 1960s "third-world socialism." Private property was confined to small enterprises; legal institutions supported a one-party state; and the regime embarked on ambitious educational and social reform programs. Many southerners have complained in the aftermath of unification, and especially since the civil war of 1994, that the state has ceased to be the guarantor of citizens' welfare. Even though, as we have seen, the PDRY was certainly beset by its own violence, citizens today cite increasing instances of lawlessness and disorder; the "retribalization" of regions; and the dispossession of lands formerly managed by peasants as reasons for anger, nostalgia, panic, and despair.

But this picture of a radically different South Yemen also has its problems for proponents of a theory linking neoliberal reforms to modern movements of piety. As chapter 1 noted, contrasts between the two states should not be invoked at the cost of neglecting convergences. That story has already been told, but the point of invoking commonality here is to underscore how variations between North and South were also matched by uneven developments within each nation-state, ones that are relevant for evaluating the differentiated experiences of state presence and retreat, and the role such factors might play in generating conditions conducive to piety in the present. There are areas in the former PDRY where inhabitants have never enjoyed electricity or running water, despite the state's ambitious plans to the contrary. The government of Aden may have attempted to extend education, medical care, and other goods and services to its population, but in much of the country, such as in parts of Abyan, Laḥj, and Shabwa, that promise remained unfulfilled. After the rise in oil prices in 1973, worker remittances tended to contribute more to consumption than to productive investments in industry or agriculture. Levels of education and health services were slightly higher in the South, particularly for women, but both countries remained among the world's "least developed," according to a United Nations Human Development report (Carapico 1993).[18] Despite an avowedly developmentalist state discourse in the South, problems with state capacity (for lack of a better term) in both countries thus bring to the fore variations in the provision of resources within each nation-state, and this too matters for our theorizations about the impact of neoliberal reforms on piety movements.[19]

This variation between nation-states and within them has important implications. One might argue that because the prevailing discourse in the South presupposed a state responsible for the welfare of its citizens, inhabitants of the PDRY—even those who did not actually experience the benefits of redistribution—nevertheless could imagine and hope for a world in which the state provided adequately for its citizens. In this view, neoliberal reforms also entailed the recalibration of the state's role in the national imaginary—in the ways in which official discourses broadcast commitments to state institutions and inhabitants of the South could make claims to the commons. The story would go something like this: as the promise of welfare provisioning became even less plausible to citizens, many of whom had never actually experienced its benefits, people turned to new forms of collective action and found political, emotional, and material redress in practices of piety. The state ceased to be the moral and political source of reparatory claims and religion took its place. There may be some truth to this argument, even in this crude formulation. Variation within the nation-state should imply, however, that areas of the South that had reaped the benefits of state presence would be particularly vulnerable to a politics of piety as the state retreated. Aden, the capital of the Marxist-Leninist polity and an emblem of its secular, state-oriented developmentalist ideal, did become increasingly a site for radical Islamic preachers and institutions to flourish. But this was by no means simply a result of Adenis themselves becoming more pious as state services diminished. Indeed, many native inhabitants of Aden spoke of feeling "imperiled" by the concerted efforts of Islamic activists who hailed from the North. In the immediate aftermath of the civil war in 1994, a group of militants descended on Aden and desecrated the tombs of saints there, and women who had never covered their hair were increasingly compelled to do so for their own safety as attacks on immodestly dressed women became more common. Islamic charities also grew markedly as increased poverty (caused by a number of factors) encouraged people to donate (Dresch 2000, 200). Areas of the South such as Aden have become more ostensibly pious over time, but it is unclear whether neoliberal reforms are doing the work. If state retreat is the mechanism, then inhabitants of Aden should be particularly susceptible to the enticements of piety. To the extent that Aden has become a site of struggle between avowed secularists and Islamic militants, the proliferation of pious practices seems to be more a result of northern militants' activities than about a shift among Adenis per se. Moreover, as the September 2007 protests in Aden indicate, critiques of regime corruption and institutional inadequacies need not take an explicitly Islamic form.

2. *The Issue of Timing: Labor Migration, Unification, and the Transnational Dissemination of Ideas*

Importantly too, the proliferation of overt signs of faith, of new communities of interpretation, and of active organizations actually *preceded* the particularly prominent reforms initiated after unification. The Islamic revival has to be understood in the context of the traffic in labor migrants and the lively publics such circulation of people and ideas enabled. It is this flow of workers that was critical in entrenching salafī forms of piety in Yemen (Weir 1997). During the oil booms of the 1970s and early 1980s, it was not uncommon in both North and South for migrant laborers to return periodically, from Saudi Arabia in particular, with an invigorated sense of public virtue. Saudi proselytizing (primarily through schools—*ma'āhid 'ilmiyya*) inside parts of the North reinforced this demographic influence, even as the North's decentralized power structure left the regime vulnerable to Saudi pressures, permitting Saudi officials and dissident clergy alike multiple avenues of access both to official decision-making processes and to informal institutions and practices of piety (Gause 1990).[20] As early as the 1970s, even when the public sector in the North was expanding dramatically, mosque schools and lesson circles not only provided training in the everyday strategies for pious living but also served as a recruiting ground for militants. Many of these newly energized stalwarts of radical Islam went to Afghanistan to join the struggle against the Soviet occupation, some of them returning subsequently to attack Yemen's own "infidels," particularly socialists in the South. These organizations enjoyed the support throughout the 1980s of the northern government of 'Alī 'Abd Allāh Ṣāliḥ, who doubtless saw in them a means of fortifying his rule.

Structural adjustment reforms seem to have strengthened piety movements already under way, but it is important to note that other historical factors were also in play. The influx of returnees from abroad in the 1990s, including Yemeni *mujāhidīn* coming home in significant numbers from the conflict in Afghanistan, is one such factor. At around the same time, anywhere from eight hundred thousand to 1.5 million labor migrants were repatriated from the oil-producing Gulf countries, especially Saudi Arabia, as a result of Yemen's vote in the UN Security Council against the U.S.-backed resolution authorizing force to expel Iraq from Kuwait. Of these returnees, 75 percent owned no land or housing in Yemen. Although many were hosted by their fellow villagers, others were able to find accommodation only in camps constructed for that purpose, or in shantytowns, where they continue to live in poor conditions.[21] In areas of the Tihāma, where people returned after living abroad with their families on a long-term basis and where about 30 percent of those repatriated were forty-five years old and over (Republic of Yemen Ministry of Planning 1991; cited in Van Hear 1994, 24), life was particularly dismal. Many of these returnees had a particularly difficult time reintegrating into Yemeni society (Van Hear 1994; Stevenson 1993). They had not planned to return to Yemen—commonly tracing their genealogical roots back to Africa—and had tended to sever their Yemeni connections. Some were also subject to racial discrimination because of their darker skin color.[22] Shantytowns in Aden, where approximately 5 percent of returnees settled (Van Hear 1994, 26), were similarly abysmal, and rendered increasingly so as refugees, many of whom could claim Yemeni origins, fled the conflict in Somalia (Van Hear 1994, 26). In the northern highlands of Ṣan'ā', al-Maḥwīt, and Ṣa'da, and in the North's southern highlands of Ta'izz, Ibb, Dhamār, and al-Bayḍā', returnees had lived in Saudi Arabia, as a rule, for shorter periods than those in the Tihāma, usually between five to seven years. These residents remitted money and made periodic visits to their relatives; they thus had an easier time reintegrating, finding some means of livelihood in rural and urban settings—farming, driving taxis, and pursuing construction work. In the Ḥaḍramawt, returnees tended to come from Kuwait and to be wealthier than their counterparts in other parts of Yemen. They had maintained relationships with fellow Ḥaḍramīs, and many had invested in property and construction. Some had even returned before the expulsion to take advantage of potential investment opportunities provided by modest oil discoveries within Yemen.

Repatriation had consequences for modes of piety and collective action in the present. Many of those repatriated from the Gulf brought back practices associated with the Saudi intellectual tradition of *tawḥīd,* advocating the oneness of God, embracing as well salafī ethical commitments to cut through the interpretive accretions of classical scholarship and return to the foundational texts of the Qur'ān and the Sunna.[23] In addition to people returning home with new beliefs, styles of dress, and sociality, religious associations took on a new prominence, providing important social services to those in need. The predominantly landless returnees of the shantytowns could not qualify for soft loans, and local and national governmental assistance in the form of small welfare payments and bread distribution were largely discontinued by 1992 (Van Hear 1994, 30). In this context, international aid provided some welfare.[24] But more important were the charitable organizations sponsored by al-Iṣlāḥ, which stepped into the breach, offering water, bread, clothing, and education in impoverished areas. In what were arguably Yemen's fairest, certainly most highly contested parliamentary elections, in 1993, residents of shantytowns returned the favor, voting heavily for the main Islamic party. Shantytown residents also participated in large numbers in the cost-of-living riots that convulsed most major towns in Yemen in December 1992.

Initiating structural adjustment policies at a time when remittance income had been severely curtailed[25] and foreign aid withdrawn (also largely as a consequence of Yemen's support for Iraq) worsened already harsh conditions, and there is little reason to doubt that these reforms in the 1990s intensified the shift in religious attitudes and political preferences. Yet it is possible to name other key events even in the 1990s—including Yemeni unification—that likewise fueled the growth in pietistic practices. Unification prompted the Ṣāliḥ regime to offer renewed encouragement to Islamic activists, deploying them as a counterweight to the Yemeni Socialist Party, much as Islamic activists in the 1970s had been used to offset the influence of leftist guerrillas in the North. The mainstream Islamic al-Iṣlāḥ took advantage of the regime's overtures to expand social services, providing significant assistance on the community level, including school supplies (such as uniforms and textbooks), health clinics, wedding-day clothes, and even a place for celebrations, not only in areas where repatriated refugees lived but also in former areas of socialist party control.[26] Other organizations such as salafī ones in Ṣaʿda produced pamphlets and mosque sermons that castigated both socialists and advocates of Zaydī piety, shoring up the regime's political power by ratcheting up expressions of group affiliation, solidifying some organizations while dividing others.

These developments, in part a response to neoliberal reforms, but in a crucial sense *in addition* to them, lie behind the visible changes in dress codes, mosque sermons, and everyday rituals of prayer indicative of an expansion of a politics of piety, producing a broad-based, diverse Islamic public that is at once territorially situated in Yemen and spiritually beholden to a transnational political world. There are two additional lessons to be gleaned here. First, although the Islamic political party's outreach capabilities may have helped to garner support from impoverished communities, the wide range of participants in mosque activities, organized protests, or in electoral politics by no means suggests that these residents, in particular, are opting for an increasingly faith-based orientation toward politics. The proliferation of Islamic practices seems both a response to increasing poverty and a mark of spiritual dissatisfaction extending beyond the particular needs or experiences of any one economic class. In other words, elections and political parties are an inadequate measure of resurgent piety and should not be used as proxies for it. Although support for the Islamic party, al-Iṣlāḥ, may register a constituent's piety, it may not. Support for the ruling party (in the form of votes or political complacency), moreover, does not signify a lack of religious conviction, and many former Iṣlāḥīs have joined the ruling party or routinely cooperate with it. The regime's successful use of pork-barrel politics before the 2006 elections helped the ruling party win a stunning 70 percent majority in local elections. This victory does not mean that Yemenis are becoming less pious. What it does suggest is that scholars should examine piety in ways that account for but also move beyond political parties and the welfare services they provide. In this light it is important to note that many salafīs do not vote at all, arguing that electoral contestation contravenes Islamic principles.

Second, attending to the specific circumstances of resurgent piety in Yemen requires considering factors we might be missing by concentrating too narrowly on neoliberalism's impact or by using the category capaciously. What looks like the flow of capital, labor, and goods from the point of view of analysts may look like internal moral decay and an assault on public virtue from the angle of Islamic activists. This view of the Western world as a moral problem has to be understood, not as a cultural essence inhering in Muslims, nor simply in terms of economic determinations, but in a broad historical context of perduring global interventions and vigorous debates disseminated about them. This means too that the forms of moral reasoning and critique characteristic of the Islamic revival are highly exportable, by way of labor migrants and via mosque sermons circulated on audiocassette, for example. And this dissemination of ideas is independent, to an extent, of the political and economic reforms associated with neoliberalism.

3. *Piety and Nationalism Revisited*

As I have argued in previous chapters, the example of Yemen further illuminates how members of contemporary religious movements do not necessarily understand their pious solidarities as undermining their national ones. Rather, it is their very commitment to both national unity and a pious ethics that obliges actors to rebellion or critical comment. These movements essentially take for granted the territory of the nation-state at the same time that they appeal to and are inspired by transnational, nonterritorial experiences of belonging. In Yemen and elsewhere in the Middle East, most of these movements do not share much affinity with neoliberal orthodoxy, in contrast with Pentecostalism in Latin America, for example (see Comaroff 2005). Rather, they ardently criticize the process of IMF and World Bank intervention, and they do so mainly by tying regime corruption to a far-reaching moral decay, one that threatens both the Islamic community *and* the citizens of the nation-state. Although neoliberalism cannot be said to have *caused* movements of piety to develop, the ideas and consequences of neoliberal reform have become important subjects for debate and criticism within Islamic communities.

Consider a particularly dramatic example, a sermon by the self-appointed preacher ʿAlī Jārallāh al-Saʿwānī, who gained notoriety by assassinating YSP leader Jār Allāh ʿUmar in December 2002. The sermon on audiocassette had caught the attention of regime authorities in early 2001, and al-Saʿwānī was subsequently imprisoned briefly for the tape's incendiary content.[27] The sermon shows how nationalist and Islamic appeals work in tandem—how they can coalesce into a critique of reforms associated with the general phenomenon of neoliberalism, as well as of specific regime practices. It reveals how images of Yemen's national crisis blend with the moral authority of the Islamic community's foundational texts. But what is particularly surprising given al-Saʿwānī's outlier status is the way in which even he appeals to the impersonal legal apparatus of the state as an arbiter of the regime's own excesses. The tape demonstrates how idioms of affective address are both territorial and extraterritorial, operating in a context where the nation-state nevertheless remains an important presumed legal addressee (even in "weak" states and in an era of neoliberal reforms) over and against the acknowledged corruption of the ruling regime.

The audiocassette begins as such tapes typically do, by praising God and invoking key passages from the Qur'ān.[28] It then proceeds to voice concern for two distinct but overlapping collectivities, the national and the Islamic. I am not arguing that Islamic concerns can be reduced to nationalist ones. Rather, the tape demonstrates that for al-Saʿwānī (and I would contend for many others in Yemen), Yemeni nationalism continues to be compatible with Islamic allegiances, despite the different understandings of subjectivity and sovereignty that nationalism and Islam presume. Al-Saʿwānī's sermon brings to the fore how the connections between nationalism and piety are more historically contingent than narratives insisting on nationalism's exclusively secular dimensions allow.

> Based upon the words of the truthful and trusted one [i.e., the Prophet Muḥammad], I say, dear brethren, that those who call the people and the public to participate in usurious interest (*ribā*) are in reality calling upon the nation and the people to participate in what is more grievous than thirty-six crimes of adultery (*zinā*). They are in reality calling upon the nation and the people to participate in what is more grievous than having intercourse with their own mothers.

What makes the crime of usurious interest worse than even incest is the complicity it requires from ordinary citizens, according to the sermon. And the crime, it turns out, is a direct product of the regime's policies—particularly of the regime's relationship to the IMF and the World Bank, as the following passage asserts:

> And hear, hear! God has forbidden us to obey and follow the Jews, the Christians, and the rest of the infidels and to take them as advisers. God

> has forbidden us to do this in the Qur'ān clearly and adamantly. But despite this we disobey the texts with projected fangs and removed veils [rhyming words], as it is evident and apparent with the Poverty Fund (*jur'at al-ifqār*) through which the World Bank and the International Monetary Fund advises and directs, and whose leaders are Jews and Christians. Our Lord said: {O believers, if you obey the infidels they will turn you upon your heels, and you will return headlong to perdition}. (Sūrat Āl 'Imrān 3:149)

Al-Sa'wānī then goes on to give an account of a legal matter involving the Prophet's son-in-law, 'Alī ibn Abī Ṭālib, a story in which 'Alī accuses a Jewish person of stealing his shield and a certain judge Shurayḥ finds the accused Jewish person not guilty because of the lack of evidence against him. This story finds widespread circulation in mosque sermons in Yemen, serving generally to underscore the rectitude of Islam—the fair and just implementation of justice within a legal system whose public virtue in the Islamic past is demonstrated by the judge's finding in favor of a non-Muslim. It is often invoked to dramatize the contrast between a righteous past and a morally compromised present. The story prepares the ground for 'Alī Jārallāh al-Sa'wānī's own legal claims, ones that allow a public rhetoric of ethical propriety to confront the troubled practices of the nation-state.

> On the basis of this ['Alī's experience with the judge Shurayḥ], tomorrow I will, God willing, present a legal suit to put on trial two big figures. The first figure: the president of the republic, for going against the book of God and the Sunna of His Messenger, may God's prayers and peace be upon him and his family, and against the constitution which emanates from them. . . . In my accusation, I am not reckless, nor am I slandering the president. Rather I have built it upon the most elevated rational foundations, and upon equations and logical proofs. For the first half of the equation says that these abominable acts are being committed in the land of Yemen. And the second half of the equation says that the president of Yemen is 'Alī ibn 'Abd Allāh ibn Ṣāliḥ. Therefore, the outcome of this equation states that he is the prime culprit. My brother, do you see in this equation any faults? Turn with your sight and mind twice, sight, mind, hypocrisy, and adulation will turn back to you mean and weary. [Based on Sūrat al-Mulk 67:4]

Al-Sa'wānī uses the jurisdictional authority of the state, which he says he hopes will be "neutral," to indict its leader on behalf of a nation of Yemenis, and he grounds this critique in the widely understood discursive tradition of Islam. There are two important points to be made about these passages. First, al-Saʿwānī's appeal to the "law of God" is complemented by an understanding of his rights as a citizen, rights that enable him to bring his case in front of a court and to try the president on behalf of the imagined community of "the nation." Second, in al-Saʿwānī's diagnosis, Yemen is threatened specifically by foreign pressures such as those of the IMF and World Bank, by the elites in power who allow such interventions in Yemeni affairs, and by domestic infidels, who as "secularists" and "socialists" do not belong to the community of righteous believers because they are "against Islam."[29] These themes of foreign threat and domestic decay find expression throughout the tape.[30]

Al-Saʿwānī's hostility toward the regime is much more prominent than his disdain for the Yemeni Socialist Party, but his ideological disagreements with the latter are clear and seemingly irreconcilable. The socialists are secularists and not respectful of or constrained by Islamic law. The kind of state they envision is fundamentally different from the ethically proper one al-Saʿwānī believes to be sanctioned by God. The democracy these Yemeni socialists have come to advocate finds no basis in the Qur'ān or the Sunna. But nevertheless, al-Saʿwānī's criticisms register a longing for a state that is impartial and inured from a corruption that can be both territorially located in regime politics and globally carried through World Bank and IMF interventions.

Al-Saʿwānī's criticisms of the regime extend to Shaykh ʿAbd Allāh, who, in his capacity as speaker of parliament, is the second person against whom al-Saʿwānī intends to bring suit. He, like the president, has permitted the World Bank and IMF to interfere in Yemeni affairs, has supported the Poverty Fund specifically, and has participated in "democracy." In spite of his heroic past as a republican fighter against the imamate, moreover, Shaykh ʿAbd Allāh has contravened the Qur'ān by promoting usurious interest or *ribā*. The monologue against the shaykh repeats, almost verbatim, many of the accusations al-Saʿwānī levels against the president. His singling out of Shaykh ʿAbd Allāh, however, exposes the entangled relationships among members of the Yemeni regime, raises questions about what "opposition" means in this setting, and highlights dissension among Islamic activists. It underscores how divergent organizations of piety in Yemen are, and it makes apparent some of the classical fault lines in Yemeni politics, ones, as we saw in chapter 4, that challenge conventional distinctions between

Islamists and non-Islamists and between regime members and an Islamic opposition. Instead of a unified, monological understanding of the meanings of Islam or of piety, al-Sa'wānī's tape evokes the contested field often concealed by the category "Islamist."

This is the tape of an uncompromising militant, but perhaps for that reason it also dramatizes how divine authority and human law can be imagined to interact and generate justice. A study by Charles Hirschkind, *The Ethical Soundscape* (2006), argues that such tapes provide a way for Islamic ethical traditions to be refashioned for modern political and technological orders, offering sensory pleasure to audiences while also putting forth calls for ethical living and political participation.[31] Hirschkind rightly argues that these tapes are not generally a source of militant indoctrination, but rather center on self-improvement, on cultivating the sensibilities and affects necessary for a pious life. These tapes operate in the context of an expanding "Islamic counterpublic" (Hirschkind 2001, 2006), vibrant communities of argument and deliberation that connect Islamic practices of ethical discipline (*al-dīn*) to the challenges diverse Muslim communities confront around the world.[32] A sermon might focus on the obligations of Muslims, enumerating the duties incumbent on the faithful. In *al-'Ashr al-Wājibāt lil-Fard al-Muslim* (Ten duties of the Muslim individual), for example, the fulfillment of obligations such as believing and relying on God (duty no. 1), studying the Qur'ān and the Sunna (duty no. 5), and loving one another (duty no. 7) is predicated on a politics in which "when Muslims perform their duties" they are acting in ways "tantamount to fighting injustice and their enemies." According to this tape, "Bullets are not the answer to the challenges faced by Muslims today."

More generally, although the term "neoliberalism" is a scholarly category of analysis rather than a Yemeni category of practice,[33] some of the problems scholars identify as emanating from market reforms are crucial concerns in mosque sermons. In particular, injustice is a focal point in many contemporary sermons in Yemen. Injustice is a product of domestic corruption, as well as the result of United States policies (e.g., the sermons of 'Alī; Ṣa'tar; al-Zindānī). These policies have allowed "hypocrites" to take "advantage of the situation," using "opportunities to attack Islamic groups and get closer to the United States" (Ṣa'tar). The United States has worked "to destroy the foundations of Arab countries" including the economy: "The Gulf countries have started borrowing money after the arrival of American troops. The hunger that has spread in Yemen for five years is due to the rise in prices that has been described as economic reforms. Who is behind this? The World Bank. . . . The aim is to leave 90 percent of Yemenis poor and begging from the remaining 10 percent who hold old wealth" (al-Zindānī).[34] Such sermons invite Yemeni Muslims to identify with the broader umma of Arabs and Muslims across the world while also grappling with issues specific to Yemeni sovereignty, such as anxieties about a U.S. invasion there (al-Miswarī) or worries about foreign infiltration into Yemeni politics (Ṣaʿtar; al-Zindānī). In foregrounding injustice, sometimes the appeal is to the state against the regime, as in the case of al-Saʿwānī, while at other times it is the president himself who is addressed (e.g., al-Miswarī, al-Ānisī, al-Zindānī). Even in an epoch of market reforms, imposed unevenly on large swathes of territory, political imaginings among Islamic activists in Yemen, far from renouncing the state, can fuse moral prescriptions with legal entitlements, blending faith in God with desires for a nation-state capable of securing the law.

To recap thus far: Neoliberal reforms are important to our understanding of the Islamic revival, in part because they have incited various appeals to a community of believers, who are enjoined to live ethically within a context that often presumes the moral and legal obligations of the state. Those appeals actually predate market reforms, but have proliferated in the wake of neoliberalism's impact. This impact is not uniform in all places, because the historical conditions under which the reforms were initiated differed. In places where the state had not been the primary addressee for people's moral and material entitlements, its contraction cannot be having the same effect it might in settings where citizens were accustomed to welfare provision. And these provisions themselves have been unevenly withdrawn and, in some cases, actually expanded, despite the claims of neoliberal orthodoxy and the expectations of scholars studying it.

FOCUSING ON SPECIFICITY FOR THEORETICAL REASONS: CONCLUDING REMARKS

My arguments about Yemen have implications for our general and practical understanding of pious solidarities by inviting analysis of the diversity of current Islamic movements. This diversity is made manifest in discursive and institutional forms that can be liberal or illiberal, violent or nonviolent, focused primarily on everyday practices or on official governance, democratic or authoritarian, supportive of or in tension with nationalist imaginings. This variation matters for our generalizations and theories because the fact of variation bears directly on the question of what it is we are trying to explain. Can a study geared to explain the reasons for peaceful grassroots movements organized to create a pious order also help us understand religious militancy? To what extent can insights about social piety movements in, say, Egypt, be used to explain the Islamic Salvation Front (FIS) in Algeria or the making of al-Qāʿida? If not, then why not? Or if so, then in what ways? And what of countries like Yemen (among others), where pious practices may signify one's commitment to an organized movement, one's labor history in Saudi Arabia, or antagonism toward leftists, a private choice to be more pious, a belief in violent transformation, or a commitment to peaceful contestation from the bottom up?

This emphasis on variation not only allows us to stress the diversity of Islamic practices and political projects, it also requires us to investigate divergences in neoliberal reforms. The political scientist Isabella Mares (2005), for example, has argued that there has been a significant expansion in social service provision worldwide, that the welfare state has been remarkably resilient, despite reforms.[35] She makes a compelling case for disaggregating social reforms in order to look for variation within states. There have been major divergences across policy areas (so that Mexico introduces universal health care but privatizes other dimensions of social service provision, for example).[36] Mares also argues that there has been a change in financing risk, with some countries' reforms tending toward privatization (as we would expect) while others remain or become public. East Asia is an example of the latter, with universal social policies being enacted during the period when the welfare state has supposedly been shrinking globally. Jean Comaroff has pointed out that African countries with means are also expanding aspects of welfare provision—Botswana, for instance; and South Africa is financing public housing as it encourages privatization in health.[37] Even Yemen has resisted pressures to overhaul completely its civil service, and the paltry paychecks do provide a safety net to some citizens, albeit an inadequate one. In considering why particular neoliberal reforms get initiated while others do not, or why in certain areas state activities expand while in others they contract, one might point to factors such as the size and historical organization of the workforce or levels of education among the citizenry (Mares 2005), or the strategies available for inducing compliance and the level of state capacity (to deliver goods and services, to fend off IMF demands, and so forth), to name just a few possibilities.

Appreciating specificity does not prevent us from thinking generally, theoretically, or globally. What it does require is a historical examination of the present, one that is attentive to the emergence of pious sensibilities and a finer specification of how neoliberal reforms work. Paying attention to variation requires us to account for the ways in which the state can simultaneously be withdrawing from and intervening more actively in people's everyday lives. And it demands that we consider the diverse activities, movements, and communities of argument that have characterized Islamic political practices worldwide. These comments are intended as invitations for further research. They suggest a scholarly strategy of systematically tacking back and forth from the general to the particular in ways that allow us to produce nuanced theoretical generalizations while doing justice to the facts on the ground. Such attention should make us wary of pronouncements that neoliberal reforms are in and of themselves the agent of novel modes of piety, or that these forms of piety necessarily indicate denationalizing tendencies or that they threaten the nation-state. As some evidence from the Yemeni case suggests, they may not even imperil regime politics as usual. More generally, many movements of piety, even violent ones that seek to overthrow a particular regime, take the nation-state for granted and make their appeals in reference to its enduring importance.

In summary, it is clear that neoliberal capitalism is not the only factor in fostering the peaceful movements of piety and the violence (not necessarily inspired by piety) currently affecting Yemen. Neoliberalism is certainly part of the story—of rising poverty, the increasing perception (and fact) of inequality, and the expressions of moral anxiety and collective vulnerability such experiences occasion. Registrations of discontent find expression in mosque sermons and in political protests. But other historical factors are also at work in the Islamic revival, such as the localized way in which a post–cold war politics played out between North and South Yemen, the renewed efforts to eliminate leftists in the aftermath of unification, Yemenis' specific relationships as unskilled migrants to Saudi Arabia (and Afghanistan), and the new modes of communication and forms of sociality enabled by this traffic of workers, including the interregional circulation of ideas, people, and objects (such as audiocassettes) giving voice to spiritual and material dissatisfactions that preceded these reforms. Wide-reaching circuits make possible the dissemination of political critiques and solidarities in the language of both national sovereignty and transnational moral revelation.[38]

This book has focused primarily on the performance of nation-ness, on the ways in which national political identifications articulate with deliberative publics and with piety. This chapter has extended those concerns to consider transnational or "globalization" processes and their relationship to religious revivals. Much scholarly debate revolves around the imprecision of the term "globalization," the historical newness of the processes to which the concept refers, and globalization's impact. Frederick Cooper, for example, laments the vocabulary of globalization because it fails to specify how "commodity circuits are constituted, how connections across space are extended and bounded, and how large-scale, longer-term processes, such as capitalist development, can be analyzed with due attention to their power, limitations, and the mechanisms that shape them" (2005, 110–11). For him, the term flattens out the geographical unevenness of these processes (see also Hirst and Thompson 1996), and it ignores important historical continuities between past and present (discussed in Eley 2007). Others, such as the social theorist Anthony Giddens, identify globalization's novelty in a new "time-space differentiation," which has displaced a "classical emphasis on the analysis of [discretely demarcated and sovereign] 'societies' or 'social systems.'"[39] In this vein, David Held and Anthony McGrew (2000, 3–4) argue that globalization "denotes the expanding scale, growing magnitude, speeding up, and deepening impact of interregional flows and patterns of interaction. It refers to a shift or transformation in the scale of human organization that links distant communities and expands the reach of power relations across the world's major regions and continents." (See also Hobsbawm 1994; Halliday 2001.) At times, such definitions are used to argue that globalization undermines the sovereignty of nation-states (Held 1996); at other times, globalization sustains or generates novel means of embedding nation-state sovereignty in interregional relations (Sassen 1998; Held and McGrew 2000).

On the one hand, my own critical analysis has attempted to focus on a dimension of globalization central to its historical novelty, neoliberal reforms. These reforms seem to upset the bounded regulation of national economies, but they do so unevenly and without necessarily entailing the state's withdrawal from other domains. State sovereignty may be undermined economically while being bolstered by new opportunities for and aggressive modes of policing borders and managing populations, for example. But even here, some states continue to perform a more vigorous redistributive role than others, and most postcolonial states never had the resources or capacities to operate as Keynesian welfare ones could. The variation within and between nation-states suggests that there have always been large swathes of territory inaccessible to state institutions.[40] In order to consider the impact of neoliberalism and its connections to a politics of piety, however, we have to identify how state institutions operated before neoliberal reforms, taking into consideration how territorial control was exercised (when it was), and how citizens were governed (to the extent that they were).

On the other hand, my analysis invites considering those aspects of globalization captured by the term's references to the accelerated circulation of "people and money, images and ideas, through . . . networks of almost planetary scope" (Foster 2002, 1). Experiences of solidarity and transnational identification are continually being produced at the periphery of global capitalism, spread through processes of labor migration, pamphlet circulation, and audiocassettes of mosque sermons—enactments of moral self-fashioning that affix far-reaching ethical certainties to local, practical problems. We can thus begin to understand how pious movements operate variously within this global, unevenly instituted current context: as a response to forms of economic injustice and political foreclosure, as an ideology that shares (at least in Latin American contexts) important affinities with the very world it seeks to criticize, as a novel recasting of affective attachments in the idioms of both national and religious solidarity, and as a regulative sensibility that reorders the sociopolitical world through everyday practices of ethical comportment and moral action.

In short, there may be a connection between neoliberal reforms and piety movements, but this relationship is not one of lockstep cause and effect. Neoliberal reforms occurred in the global context of unfulfilled state-centric aspirations and ongoing great power interventions, which have helped to advantage some organizations and weaken or destroy others. I am suggesting that we expand our perspective to explore not only the combined factors that produced the "why" of contemporary piety but also the "how": how the economic and political frustrations of certain audiences become channeled through pious discourses that enjoin the remaking of ethical sensibilities, and how demographic traffic and developments in communication technologies are important mechanisms for piety's traction over time. This circulation of people and ideas has facilitated a far-reaching territorially indeterminate public, one whose collective imaginings anchor everyday challenges in a specifically moral commonweal while also sustaining (rather than undermining) territorially rooted commitments to the nation-state.

CONCLUSION

Politics as Performative

This book began with a specific question, "What makes a Yemeni a Yemeni?" as a vehicle for exploring the dynamics of political identification in general. One response would have been to rehearse the current legal regulation of Yemeni citizenship. According to Law No. 6, article 2: "the Yemenis" are "inhabitants whose regular domicile has been Yemen . . . for at least fifty Gregorian years prior to the promulgation of this law [1990], and the domicile of the originals will be deemed to apply to those branches [of the family tree] and the spouse whenever they [family or spouse] have the intent of being such inhabitants."[1] This passage and the detailed legal stipulations that follow point up some of the key themes of this book, detailing how nationalism as an ideology presupposes distinct notions of space, time, and collectivity. Yemenis as national citizens are members of a demarcated territory. They are genealogically linked to one another. They live in calendrical time and are subject to the force of the state's citizenship laws. The law constitutes a unity according to which every person either is or is not a Yemeni. Covering all contingencies (patrilineal, matrilineal, born in or outside of Yemen, and so forth), the law allows for considerable variation, registering the transnational contexts within which contemporary national identifications are formed, barring from potential inclusion only those who lack all temporally determined ties to a place called Yemen.[2]

Peripheral Visions has not been concerned with the specific legalities of citizenship because, although citizenship requirements do fall definitively within the state's powers, the Yemeni state remains weak, with limited means of enforcement. The burden of this book has been to explore the range of ideas, practices, institutions, and events—some of which are experienced in the breach of state authority—through which the categories of Yemeni or Shīʿī or salafī become thinkable, desirable, and for some, even natural. While Yemenis, as well as other national groups, may be defined in legal terms, they are actually summoned into being through the quotidian discourses used—through poetic invocations of a "nation" called *Yaman* or in acts of deliberating with others in public. Sometimes these activities make specific claims on behalf of a Yemeni people. At other times, cross-fertilization, not only of nationalist ideas but of knowledge about a region, mountain, or custom, generates the conditions for a territorially circumscribed assemblage of addressees, a national public. Put somewhat differently, *Peripheral Visions* emphasizes the performative dimensions of political life, how persons are established as national through iterative performances of particular national acts, just as pious or democratic persons are produced through everyday enactments of piety and agonistic deliberation respectively. Such a framework accounts for the fragility and contingency of solidarities in a way that many explanations do not. Claims of attachment can and often do shift precipitously. A theory of politics as performative adds value to our political analyses because it denaturalizes political identifications, thus drawing attention to the mechanisms that make identity categories seem fixed.

Understanding the performative dimensions of politics also allows us to maintain the importance of category-based knowledge without assuming that categories of belonging presuppose belief or emotional sincerity, although they may be part of cultivating such convictions. Rather, classifications are part of a process of interpellation (Althusser 1971), a way of "hailing" citizens—in our case bringing Yemenis into being as national subjects. In Althusser's well-known allegory, the policeman hails the passerby with the statement, "hey, you there." The one who recognizes him/herself in the call turns around to answer. For Althusser, the passerby becomes a "subject" (the person who acquires an "identity") by virtue of being recognized (see also Butler 1997).

For our purposes, two key points should be made in reference to this allegory. First, the allegory of the policeman hailing the passerby presumes reciprocity between two agents. For interpellation to take place, the passerby must not only be called out by the law, but must also turn around and recognize it. Similarly, if new state classifications, to take one example, can generate "new ways for people to be" (Hacking 1986), the effectiveness of these categories requires the addressee's participation in these new ways of being. As we have seen in the Yemeni case, the state's weakness means that the law is not doing the work of "hailing" citizens in ways that obtain routine compliance, and classifications around group identities do not produce the sort of coherence that studies of category-based knowledge often assert. Instead, these processes of iteration can create the conditions for public critique and oppositional politics. We saw this dynamic at work in the spectacles surrounding the presidential elections and the decennial celebration of unification, but also in the mundane activities of qāt chewing and in reactions to the regime's routinized strategies of divide and rule.

Second, interpellation does not require that an individual believe in the ideology of the law, but only that he/she enter into the ideology's routine rituals, perhaps dissimulating, perhaps not. For example, I do not have to believe that what makes an American an American is knowledge of the territory's history or an oath of loyalty to its stated principles, although I may. But noncitizens who want to become citizens must pass the required exam, engaging in at least a ritual invocation of the practices that summon them into being as Americans. And in going through the routine they become legal citizens, whether they believe in the iterative performance or not. Similarly, those seeking Yemeni citizenship will have to go through the legal procedures of establishing their relationship to place and family. Prospective Yemenis enter into the ritual of ideology regardless of whether or not there is a "prior and authenticating belief in that ideology" (Butler 1997, 24). In parallel terms, as Austin (1965) notes in discussing performatives, phrases such as "I promise" do not require the speaker to keep the promise or even intend to keep it in order for the promise to be made. Rather, the conventions of speech around promising are what make the act a promise (Butler 1997; Pitkin 1993).

Althusser's allegory and efforts to draw parallels between it and Austin's performatives raise a host of thorny issues I cannot do justice to here. My point is to invoke the logic of performatives to get at ways in which discourses not only reflect political processes of community-making, but also establish or reinstate visions of group affiliation (e.g., as Yemeni or Shīʿī or Muslim or American). "We hold these truths to be self evident" is a classic example of the community-constituting power of speech (Honig 1991 on Arendt 1963). This constitutive power also depends on the ensuing action—on the practices of a "we" that, in effect, continually restate the "truths" and insist on their self-evidence. The point of thinking about politics as performative is not to underscore the peculiar quality of specific verbs that in being uttered perform the action they name, but to explore the insight that "most or perhaps all of language is performative in a looser sense" (Pitkin 1993, 39).

The efficacy of language, as Butler rightly notes (1993, 32-33), relies on the "historicity of convention," the ways in which discourses are iterated over time. Austin distinguishes helpfully between types of performatives. Illocutionary statements such as "I hereby pronounce you" are themselves forms of doing in which the enunciation and the effects are temporally simultaneous. Perlocutionary acts are those utterances that initiate a set of consequences. They too are a form of action, but the saying and the consequences are temporally separate. They are "what we bring about by saying something" (Austin 1965, 109; Butler 1997, 17). Or to put it plainly, though speech may not always be performing the action named, it is always performing an action.

This understanding of politics as performative allows me to recapitulate three points that have been of critical importance to this book. First, performatives are context dependent in the sense that they are a product of iterative social conventions that both presuppose and conjure anew distinct visions of community (e.g., in the case of a "national" community, one that presumes a collectivity of strangers who are aware of sharing a territory in homogeneous empty time). Second, while it is often difficult to identify the origins of social conventions or categories, their circulation and reproduction are observable in a variety of organizational and discursive practices. In chapter 1, for example, we saw how oral poetry carried understandings of the nation form acephelously from village to village, how the acquisition of transistor radios reproduced such ideas on a larger scale, introducing lettered and unlettered alike to nationalism as a novel form of collective representation. The first chapter demonstrated how processes of circulation helped to create citizens who understood a shared set of references within the demarcated territory of Yemen. And in chapter 5 we began investigating how interregional circuits could bring into being a distinct transnational moral imaginary. Third, claims to and experiences of group solidarity can both change over time and come and go suddenly. In chapter 2, for example, we saw how Yemen's first serial killing brought into being a national community temporarily, generating appeals to the nation in a moment when state institutions were incapable of ensuring the safety of citizens. In chapter 4 the meanings of Sunnī and Shī'ī indexed a vibrant discursive tradition that nonetheless was contextually specific, subject to important shifts in salience, and enmeshed in a broader political system that relied on spaces of disorder in order to rule.

Recognizing context and specificity does not require eschewing generalization. On the contrary, chapter 3's analysis of qāt chews demonstrates that practices of deliberating critically with others in public are constitutive of democratic personhood insofar as "democracy" connotes agonistic debate, accountability, and temporary (albeit imperfect) equality. Rather than treat democracy as the singular outcome of a given (bourgeois European) history, as Habermas would argue, we learn from the Yemeni example that democracy is always there, a possibility available to human beings in their capacity as actors who make political worlds in common.

Some discourses have causal effects, or in the language of political science, can operate as independent variables. My first book, *Ambiguities of Domination* (1999), examined the "cult of personality" around Syrian President Ḥāfiẓ al-Asad (1970-2000)—the rhetorical practices and imagery that worked to displace the possible discussion of substantive political issues in public. I argued that this official rhetoric functioned to enforce obedience, induce complicity, and structure the terms within which transgressions could take place. The "cult" generated the guidelines for public speech and action, while atomizing people from one another; it tired people out, rendering absurd language that could once seem politically inspiring. *Peripheral Visions* also registers the effects of discourse, but the emphasis on practices as performative does not fit comfortably into an approach that privileges independent and dependent variables. Qāt chews are enactments of democratic personhood, for example, but they do not cause a democratic regime (in the procedural sense) to happen; nor do they require or necessarily promote liberal values. Phrases highlighting how the circulation of discourses or the administrative routines of institutions "make possible" or "thinkable" new modes of political imagining (which may or may not be deeply felt) do not provide us with a strong causal story. This is not to argue that the social science convention of isolating variables is always wrong-headed. Such exercises can be helpful analytically. It is simply to suggest that this book tends not to be concerned with the kinds of claims conducive to such shorthand, even while insisting that the claims it does make are critical to any reasonably comprehensive understanding of politics.

In addition, rather than make monocausal arguments that privilege institutions or separate them from discourses, this book contends that institutions and discourses are mutually coforming. Discourses saturate and shape institutions as well as being promoted by them. Far from being epiphenomenal, discourses are critical to the production of groups, because language and other symbolic systems both structure and reflect the conceptual universe through which political action takes place, and because language is a form of action in its own right. Discourses make possible certain understandings of group affiliation while foreclosing others; they also specify the conditions of "otherness"; they suffuse institutions, can summon and resummon groups into existence, and in all of these ways are inseparable from political action.

IDENTITY

The "work" discourses do must be investigated along two axes: (1) examining a text's or ideology's logics—the assumptions the discourse implies, its context-dependent uses, and the possibilities it forecloses; and (2) investigating the rhetoric's effects—the ways in which that discourse is mediated, reiterated, and transmitted, and how it is assessed and resignified over time through political organizations, extraordinary events, and everyday practices. Studies of "subjectivity" and "identity" often assume a connection between consciousness and distinct discourses, according to which the latter both exemplify and generate fundamental changes in a person's cognitive and affective being. I have no doubt that some discursive practices can do just that, especially over time and through iteration, but this book endorses a notion of "subjectivity" as only indeterminately about conditions of interiority and explicitly about observable practices of self—be they national, democratic, or pious.

The semantically opposed usages of "identity" to mean both what is constant and what is changing, what is essential and what is "constructed" have caused some to reject the term as too confusing for continued scholarly usage.[3] As Rogers Brubaker and Frederick Cooper argue in their essay

"Beyond Identity," alternative vocabulary—words such as "identification," "allegiance," "self-understanding," and "groupness"—may evoke less conceptual turmoil than "identity" and allow us to designate the contingent and variable relationships existing between institutional formulations of group affiliation and people's substantive experiences of belonging. In fact, this book has tended to avoid the word "identity," for precisely such reasons. But I also want to suggest that the tensions in the word register an important part of actual, messy political life. Recognizing people's contradictory experiences of both essentialist solidarity and fluid identifications while remaining analytically sovereign over these tensions is an important challenge for social constructivist thinking. Moreover, arguments claiming that solidarities derive their raw material from latent attachments that must be historically deep and widespread, and arguments that emphasize how identifications are constructed, even for strategic reasons over short periods of time, need not be mutually exclusive. Vague, historically situated, differentially experienced, long-standing visions of community can be invoked by political ideologues for strategic purposes in the short run, but they are not all equally resonant or generative of politically efficacious emotional commitments. Ideologues, moreover, exist in a semiotic universe in which some categories of group affiliation make more sense politically than others, both to potential constituents and, just as importantly, to themselves. Ordinary men and women might reproduce forms of group membership more or less unknowingly. Experiences of solidarity might serve strategic purposes, but they need not. And identification can serve strategic purposes without being a product of conscious calculation.

It is impossible to get into people's heads, to discern what a "strongly binding" allegiance is and how it differs from a "loosely structured," mildly constraining example of "affinity and affiliation" (Brubaker and Cooper 2000, 21)—except insofar as such sensibilities relate to observable action. In thinking about studying solidarities, then, consider the following template: we need to examine the political environment, including the sorts of *organizations* (both state institutions and informal networks) that stimulate category-based knowledge about selves and others and, in turn, cultivate group affiliations. *Dramatic events*, as we have seen, can intensify solidarities, transforming an action such as chanting anti-American slogans into a national crisis. *Discourses* make these events intelligible, and they also can act as performatives, helping to call into existence the very groups being invoked.[4] And *everyday practices* are often the means through which such notions of group identity are carried from one person to the next, grounding ideas of moral rectitude and political promise in the activities of ordinary life.[5]

This approach to political identifications could be used to analyze the proliferation of sectarian claims in Iraq or Lebanon, or for that matter anywhere. An interpretive perspective allows us to understand how contemporary claims to group affiliation are beholden to the institutional and discursive legacies that shape possibilities for political action. Rather than delve into the inner processes or psychological lives of individuals, interpretation in this sense focuses on the observable conventions of personhood and collectivity, attending to the historical conditions of continuity and change, while also questioning some established social scientific categories used to describe such patterns. This approach requires tacking back and forth between the specific and the general, wedding empirical concerns to philosophical ones, and registering the forms of political domination, solidarity, and moral reasoning that organize people's lives.

QUASI-NATIONALISM?

In its focus on social scientific concepts, this book has been especially keen on questioning the minimalist notions of "democracy" so prevalent in political science. Although one possibility is to abandon the activity of labeling regimes altogether and focus on various forms of democratic activity, some of which will take place in the absence of electoral contestation, another is to have a more expansive, less formalistic notion of what a democratic regime is. Still another possibility is to invent new terms for regimes that do not seem to fit into the authoritarian/democracy binary of old. As political scientists become increasingly interested in explaining why established dictators bother to hold elections, the term "quasi-autocracy" has emerged as a useful shorthand for a set of family resemblances among regimes that share at least some of the following features in common: state institutions unable to inculcate national values or control violence; vibrant democratic practices in the absence of alternation in executive office or "fair and free" elections; a legislature that has some independent power but is nevertheless hamstrung by the executive; an armed, politicized population that constrains state tyranny and limits repression; and a sense of political possibility that emerges from conditions of perennial uncertainty and periodic efforts to contain it. Yemen, a durable but perennially unstable regime, with a weak state incapable of monopolizing violence or delivering goods and services within a delimited territory, is an exemplary instance of this type of rule. Other examples, whether as consistently as Yemen or more situationally, might include Lebanon, Pakistan, and a number of countries in Africa.

In the particular circumstances of quasi-autocracy we should expect a regime to act like a state intermittently, bringing the state into being by performing various executive functions associated with it. This occasional appearance of the state makes apparent its usual absence, an absence that can itself trigger experiences of nation-ness and generate idioms of affective national connection. Quasi-autocracy thus suggests a corresponding form of "quasi-nationalism," with the critical proviso that the extension lays bare a *general* aspect of nationalism that tends to be undertheorized in scholarly accounts. As we have seen, national solidarities are rarely as all-encompassing as students of nationalism presume. Like the coming and going of the quasi-autocratic state, they can occur episodically, are often transmitted diffusely, and congeal suddenly, only to dissolve once again in apathy or discord.

Such discord can be violent, but it need not be. As chapter 2 underscored, scholars committed to the idea that national unity and a strong state are required for democracy to thrive run the danger of confusing order with democracy. Democracy may presuppose a commitment to a certain degree of stability, but equally to ongoing disagreement, debate, and oppositional political action. Such commitments are all but ignored in minimalist formulations privileging what Susan Marks (2000) calls "low-intensity" democracy—theories that justify current power-sharing arrangements in Western liberal polities and reaffirm an image of the citizen as an atomistic, passive consumer of politics (see also Scott, n.d.). Indeed, the literature in comparative politics on democratic transitions, to borrow the anthropologist David Scott's words, "comports almost seamlessly with the contemporary self-image of American liberal democracy, the rights-oriented public philosophy of what Michael Sandel aptly calls the 'procedural republic'" (Scott, n.d., 19; Sandel 1996). The Yemeni example offers a corrective to this vision and the self-satisfactions it engenders, returning us to an understanding of democratic power as that which is "generated when people gather together and 'act in concert'" (Arendt 1958, 244). To a current sensibility it may seem that Arendt's formulation smacks of voluntarism, and that it conjures up the specter of the crowd, of masses enlivened by tyrannical forms of solidarity-building and exclusion, an image Arendt would have clearly disavowed. The statement thus requires supplementing: the "concert" of democratic power, both in people coming together and producing a course of action and in engaging in the collective project of action itself, is necessarily contingent, provisional, and transient, forged of internal differences that are never negated but only temporarily suspended.[6]

Arendt recognized the unpredictability and open-endedness of action and saw social scientific efforts to divide communities into rulers and ruled as an "escape from the frailty of human affairs into the solidity of quiet and order" (ibid., 222; discussed in Zerilli 2005, 21). Such a critique need not be restricted to accounts of democracy, but is also applicable to understandings of identity more generally. By adopting a notion of politics as performative and by looking at the details of the Yemeni case, we can begin to address the problems Arendt identified, seeing with finer resolution the dynamism apparent in the ways people form and maintain, shed and take on, are constrained by, or seek emancipation through, new political identifications. This approach should not be confused with a view that depicts identities as preference-ordering systems in which actors make choices about which identities to adopt (e.g., Posner 2005; Laitin 1998). There is value in this literature, despite the unempirical voluntarism it can imply. But the Yemeni case shows that many identifications are not subject to rank orderings, nor are they at odds with one another, but rather articulate together in complex ways. Yemen is a place where meaningful coalescences (of, say, nationalism and piety) happen, where political subjectivities come and go and return again, and where actors are clearly not in control of their own political life stories. This unpredictability is not unique to Yemen, and it need not be lamentable, for it is part of what political action means. Accepting the dynamism, rather than attempting to confine it to a predictive schema, allows us to understand identity *not* ontologically as what people are, but politically in terms of what they do.[7]

NOTES

INTRODUCTION

1. See http://www.irinnews.org/report.asp?ReportID=55607&SelectRegion=Middle_East; last accessed November 29, 2006. In a country of 21.5 million people, widely varying estimates put the number of privately held weapons at anywhere from six to sixty million. The oft-cited figure of sixty million is the Ministry of Interior's estimate (*Yemen Times*, January 28, 2002). *The World Fact Book*, published by the CIA, estimates 2006 population at 21,456,188; https://www.cia.gov/cia/publications/factbook/geos/ym.html; last accessed November 29, 2006.

2. This characterization of the contemporary world is taken from Beiner (1995).

3. I tend to prefer the terms "pious" and "piety" to "religion" and "religious." Talal Asad (1993) has written influentially about the problems with "religion" as an anthropological category beholden to a specifically Christian history and to social science debates that posit the concept as a transhistorical essence. (See also Keane [2007], esp. chap. 3.) The English word "piety," according to the *Oxford English Dictionary*, originates in the fifteenth century and means devotion to God or divine worship. A "pious person" is one who has or shows reverence and obedience to God. My use of the term is expressly not intended to conjure up seventeenth-century Christian pietism, whose crucial ambition was to eliminate the mediating authority of the clergy. Piety in the context I use the term here embraces both those who seek to strip away the interpretive accretions of classical scholarship and return to foundational texts, as those in the *salafī* movement do, and others who do not abjure clerical mediation. Of course, even here the concept of "piety" is the historical product of discursive processes arguably no less problematic than those highlighted by Asad. In the end, though,

one has to communicate, and so I have made the somewhat arbitrary, but nevertheless considered, choice specified above. I am grateful to Nadia Abu El-Haj, Rosalind C. Morris, and Kabir Tambar for their thoughts on this issue.

4. Abū Bakr al-Saqqāf (1996) terms this annexationist politics "internal colonialism"; see also al-Saqqāf (1999). For a brief but helpful discussion of the war, see Carapico (1994), and the essays in al-Suwaidi (1995).

5. Here I understand deliberation in Arendtian terms as a form of action, since action involves speech.

6. This formulation is adapted from Geertz (1980).

7. Kelly and Kaplan are referring to the emergence of an internationally sanctioned system of "self-determining" nation-states with the establishment of the United Nations. Scholars who focus on the importance of state formation for the emergence of nationalism differ on issues of timing, with Hobsbawm locating nationalism in the late eighteenth century while Marx argues for greater attention to the "earlier foundations of the process" (2003, 10).

8. Kelly and Kaplan are an exception insofar as they are against the analytic use of the category of the modern because they claim that it and alternative ideas (such as "alternative modernities") are ideologically tenacious abstractions that allow analysts to ignore the specificities of post–World War II structural reorderings. Whatever one thinks of the category's analytic utility, there is nothing about the word that prevents scholars from looking at the post–World War II era. I use ideology as Raymond Williams (1977, 109) does, to mean "an articulated system of meanings, values, and beliefs of a kind that can be abstracted as [a] worldview." See also Jean and John L. Comaroff, *Of Revelation and Revolution*, vol. 1, chap. 1.

9. For a discussion of the theoretical contradictions, see Asad (2003) and my discussion below.

10. Lebanon's Ḥizb Allāh is a religious party, but its goal of getting Israel to withdraw from Lebanese territory was a nationalist one. Similarly, although the political commitments of Ḥamās exceed the nation-state, Ḥamās also has explicitly nationalist objectives: to create a Palestinian, Muslim state in all (or parts) of former Palestine. The Muslim Brotherhood in Egypt shares a certain critique of Arab regimes with other Arab nationalist and Muslim Brotherhood parties, but its agenda to affect change has become explicitly Egypt oriented. The same can be said for the main Islamic political parties in Yemen and Jordan.

11. Anderson (1991) takes the phrase "homogeneous empty time" from Walter Benjamin's "Theses on the Philosophy of History," in *Illuminations* (1973, 263); see also Rutherford (2003) and Kelly and Kaplan (2001). Anderson writes: "What has come to take the place of the mediaeval conception of simultaneity-along-time is, to borrow again from Benjamin, an idea of 'homogeneous, empty time,' in which simultaneity is, as it were, transverse, cross-time, marked not by prefiguring and fulfillment, but by temporal coincidence and measured by clock and calendar" (24). It is possible to argue that Anderson's use of Benjamin is to some extent a misappropriation, but my interest here is rather in the way Anderson uses this notion of time as he understands it to think about the specificities of national imaginings.

12. According to the anthropologist Talal Asad, for example, the medieval Christian worldview entailed interconnected temporalities of "eternity and its moving image: Creation, the Fall, Christ's life and death, Judgment Day." The medieval Christian world also had a distinct "hierarchy of spaces (the heavens, the earth, purgatory, hell)." Modern secularism, by

contrast, operates in terms of linear, progressive, historical time; it also divides the world spatially in two: "a world of self-authenticating things in which we really live as social beings and a religious world that exists only in our imagination" (Asad 2003, 194). See also Reinhart Koselleck's *Futures Past: On the Semantics of Historical Time* (2004 [1979]) in which he contrasts the eschatological understandings of time or "timelessness" exemplified in Albrecht Altdorfer's painting *Alexanderschlacht* (1529) with Friedrich Schlegel's praise of the work in "critical-historical" terms three hundred years later. Koselleck argues that in these three centuries "there occurs a temporalization [*Verzeitlichung*] of history, at the end of which there is the peculiar form of acceleration which characterizes modernity" (11). See also Koselleck's example contrasting Maximilien Robespierre's formulations of time as linear and Martin Luther's time compression (12–13). Important antecedents to modern notions of temporality can be seen in the Renaissance (see part one, 3–80, of the *Machiavellian Moment* by J. G. A. Pocock [1975]), although, as Koselleck contends, the differences are just as instructive as the fact of precursors. In *The Nature of Time* (1975) G. J. Whitrow contends that time as a linear progression measured by clock and calendar superseded cyclical conceptions of time only in the past few centuries. This argument is probably overstated and too beholden to modernization theory, however. Cyclical conceptions are not superseded exactly, and notions of linear time (which are not *abstract* in the sense discussed in the text) are evident before the modern era, as Postone rightly notes (1993).

13. Postone concentrates on the new social relationship between the level of wages and labor output, measured temporally in terms of invariable, constant, commensurable hours. According to him, this radically new relationship may have first arisen in the cloth-producing urban communes of Western Europe (211).

14. Dohrn-van Rossum (1996) extends this analysis, describing the change in time consciousness that was brought about when clocks were introduced in European cities starting at the end of the fourteenth century; by the seventeenth century, the equal hour had become self-evident; from the eighteenth century onward, ordinary citizens had private timepieces, ones that they could use to contest how many hours they had worked and to press for hourly wage increases; public discussion over standardizing time was widespread in the nineteenth century and was tied not only to operating railroads but to other nationalist projects of unification as well. (On the latter, see esp. 349.) See also Thompson (1967); Landes (1983); Mumford (1934).

15. This is what Gellner (1983, 1) means when he writes, rather vaguely, that nationalism is a political principle that maintains that the political (read, state institutions) and the national unit (the imagined community of "the people") should be congruent.

16. The Sunna describes the practices of the Prophet and his companions. In Islamic jurisprudence, the Sunna is generally understood to be the second most important source for deriving Islamic laws after the Qur'ān. This issue is nevertheless subject to debate, as Daniel Brown documents (1999).

17. The political philosopher Charles Taylor similarly posits modern simultaneity as an understanding of time that is "exclusively secular" and tied to the nation form (Taylor 2004, 157). Taylor mistakes here the contingent for the constitutive. It is by no means clear that such notions of simultaneity are "exclusively secular" or that nationalism has to be so. The logical relation is clear but the assertion of historical necessity is ungrounded.

18. Chatterjee's (1993) is the most prominent. Pace Chatterjee's contentions, however, I see no evidence that Anderson actually rejects the argument that anticolonial movements were "posited on a difference" against the West. Nor does he deny that anticolonial nationalism was understood in terms of "cultural difference," as Chatterjee suggests. What Anderson means by "modular" is only that decolonization movements took a nationalistic form—that is, they adopted the same nationalistic frame of reference as the colonizers. I am grateful to João Gonçalves for his insights on Anderson's notion of modularity. See also Foster (2002). For a critique of the notion of "modularity" more generally, see Rutherford (forthcoming).

19. For a discussion of the administration of *ḥudūd*, see Messick (1993, 51); Obermeyer (1981, 181–82); and Willis (2007), esp. chap. 4, "Disorder and the Domain of Obedience."

20. Cited in Willis (2007, 51). From IOR R/20/a/2922, Imām Yaḥyā to al-Wāsiʿī, 9 Jumādā al-Ākhira 1347/Nov. 20, 1928.

21. Arguably too, denominational or *madhhab* affiliations had already been undermined by al-Shawkānī's jurisprudential innovations in the eighteenth century, as well as by some of Imām Yaḥyā's practices of rule in the early twentieth.

22. This is a problem that Postone's analysis (1993) happily avoids because abstract time does not obviate other experiences of time, and abstract, concrete, and secular time can all be linear. I would like to thank Jim Chandler for this formulation of "pure succession," which emerges out of his comments in response to Harry Haroutinian at the Chicago Center for Contemporary Theory inaugural event, April 8, 2005.

23. Thanks are owed to Kabir Tambar for his helpful formulations here.

24. See, for example, Lomnitz (2001), who argues that this view of nationalism as succeeding religious solidarities is historically incorrect: "The first moment of Spanish national construction was, then, quite different in spirit and content from that posited by Anderson; Spanishness was built out of an idea of a privileged connection to the church" (18).

25. A variety of scholars have noted that practices are subjected to risk because their very iteration creates possibilities for intervention, action, innovation, and subversion. On subversion, see, for example, Butler (1993, 1997); for an account emphasizing improvisation, see esp. Bourdieu (1977, 1991). The anthropologist Marshall Sahlins shows how the reproduction of rituals, customs, and cosmological narratives places them at risk in *Islands of History* (1987). See also his *Historical Metaphors and Mythical Realities* (1981). Key studies in practice theory include Bourdieu (1977, 1990) and de Certeau (1984).

26. For a discussion of Austin's problems in distinguishing performatives from descriptive statements, see Hanna Pitkin (1993, 38). See also J. L. Austin's *Philosophical Papers* (1961) and his posthumously published *How to Do Things with Words* (1965).

27. Importantly, there are also critical differences among these theorists. Butler remains close to Austin in *Bodies That Matter* (1993) and *Excitable Speech* (1997), but Derrida's deconstructionist argument is specifically targeted at Austin's failure to understand that "the boundary between text and context is not so easily drawn," as Rosalind C. Morris has pointed out to me (2007, personal communication). Moreover, Derrida's notion of iterability, which Butler embraces, differs from Bourdieu's practice-oriented theory. The Derridean (and to some extent Austinian and Butlerian) notions get away from the simple logic of "reproductive enactment," to borrow Morris's (1995) term, and can thereby stress the creative gestures and multiple possibilities for innovation and subversion. This latter critique of Bourdieu may not

be fair, given his attention to improvisation, but the general point that theories of performativity tend to emphasize reproduction or to see iteration as an opportunity for fresh political possibility holds. For an approach to the text/context issue derived more from Mikhail Bakhtin and Valentin Vološinov than from Derrida or Butler, see Michael Silverstein and Greg Urban's helpful discussion in *Natural Histories of Discourse* (1996, 1–17).

28. See also Pierre Bourdieu's discussion of the performative in *Language and Symbolic Power* (1991), esp. 220–28; Morris (1995, 2007); Brubaker (2004).

29. For example, see Bauman, who works within and between folklore and anthropological linguistics (1974, 1978, 1986); also Turner (1969, 1982). There is a rich anthropological literature on Austin's notion of performativity, including the perhaps dated but well-known take on Austin by Tambiah (1985), Rosaldo's discussion of speech act theory (1982), and Silverstein's (1987) critique of Austin in Hickmann (ed.).

30. Thanks are owed to Rosalind C. Morris for this formulation.

31. Derrida is not operating in sociological terms; he is producing a quasi-structural or quasi-logical argument, but this does not mean that a Derridean argument need disavow context.

32. See Steven C. Caton's discussion in *Peaks of Yemen I Summon* (1990, esp. 263). Caton is inspired by the writings of Bakhtin, Vološinov, and Charles Sanders Peirce, among others, who allow him to show how ideology emerges in "poetic practice." See also chapter 1 of this book.

33. I am not presuming here that we have to share an understanding of what these democratic deeds are or who controls the terms of their definition; chapter 3 deals with these latter issues explicitly.

34. The Institute for Qualitative Research Methods has even changed its name and mission statement to capture this growing trend in political science, now calling itself the Institute for Qualitative and Multi-Method Research. For the former ethnographer David Laitin (2003), "narrative approaches" are by themselves inadequate. When combined with large-N statistical work and formal models, however, they can help generate robust findings (Pachirat 2006; Hopf 2006). Laitin advocates "productive complementarity" among these three different conceptual and methodological orientations (175). In practice, calls for productive complementarity tend to subordinate the epistemological concerns of narrative approaches to the aims of science. Ethnography is often deployed in the service of the very sorts of objectivist aims that current ethnographic approaches in anthropology undermine. And ethnography is seen as the least prestigious method, treated as the "summer intern" to the "senior partner" of formal methods (Hopf 2006).

35. For a description of what interpretivist social science means and entails, see Rabinow and Sullivan (1987); see also my "Concepts and Commitments in the Study of Democracy" (2004) and my "Ethnography as Interpretive Enterprise" (in preparation).

36. I have traveled to Ṣaʿda in the far northwest and to Maʾrib in the northeast, and to the area on the Red Sea known as the Tihāma, but I have spent the most extensive time in the capital of Ṣanʿāʾ, in the village of Kuhhāl and the surrounding regions of the *minṭaqa al-wusṭā* (or "middle region") in the North's Lower Yemen, and in both Aden and Ḥaḍramawt in the South. This book, although not a conventional ethnography in the anthropological sense, does have chapters that are primarily ethnographic. Ethnographic saturation entails,

as Bayard De Volo and Schatz note (2004, 267), distinct activities, such as the ones I list in the text. The book also shares with ethnographic methods a particular "sensibility" (Pader 2006; Yanow 2006; Pachirat 2006), a perspective that anthropologist Daniel Miller (1997, 16–17) argues entails a specifiable set of "commitments," including: (1) to be in the presence of the people one is studying, not just the texts or objects they produce; (2) to evaluate people in terms of what they actually do, i.e., "as material agents working in a material world, and not merely what they say they do"; (3) to engage in an analysis that understands actions within the broader framework of people's lives and cosmologies.

37. Footnotes are inserted for formal interviews only.

38. See Asad (1986, 1993); Agrama (2005); Hirschkind (2001, 2006); Mahmood (2001, 2005); Messick (1993).

39. Sometimes the nexus is triadic, with nationalism conjoined to both secularism and liberalism. But in addition to the points made in the text, and as should be obvious, there are also fascist and socialist versions of secularism that are not liberal.

40. Arguments assuming that the social services organizations such as Ḥizb Allāh provide necessarily detract from state building are common.

CHAPTER ONE

1. I use Étienne Balibar's term "nation form" to underscore that despite variations among liberal, ethnonational, or nationalisms founded on heterodoxy, nationalism is a distinct form of political imagining.

2. On the North, see especially Messick 1993; Kühn 2003; Willis 2004; on the South, see Willis 2004.

3. Foucault (1982) writes that modern power "applies itself to immediate everyday life . . . imposes a law of truth on [the individual] which he must recognize and which others have to recognize in him. It is a form of power which makes individuals subject" (212). Foucault was aware of the dual connotations of the word "subject": "There are two meanings of the word subject: subject to someone else by control and dependence, and tied to his own identity by a conscience or self-knowledge. Both meanings suggest a form of power which subjugates and makes subject to" ("The Subject and Power," 1982, 212).

4. "There emerged a world of perversion. . . . An entire sub-race was born. . . . In the course of the century [these perverts] successively bore the stamp of 'moral folly,' 'genital neurosis,' 'aberration of the generic instinct,' 'degenerescence' or 'physical imbalance'" (*History of Sexuality*, vol. 1, 40). Or consider too: "Our carving out of sexual behaviors into homo- and heterosexual is absolutely not relevant for the Greeks and Romans. This means two things: on the one hand, that they did not have the notion, the concept, of homo- and heterosexual; and, on the other hand, that they did not have experience of them" (*Dits and écrits*, 1954–88, vol. 3, 160).

5. For a discussion of the varying ways in which Yemen was understood, see, in addition to Dresch, Mermier (1999; also 1997a, 1997b) and Messick (1993, 1998). For a discussion of aspirations toward unity prior to unification, see Gause (1987, 1990). On unity in Arabic, see Ṣarrāf (1992), Jallūl (1999), al-Ghafārī (1997), and Abū Ṭālib (1994).

6. See the medieval geographers such as al-Hamdānī (d. 945 AD), *Ṣifat jazīrat al-'arab* (1989), and Yāqūt al-Ḥamawī (1179?–1229 AD), *Mu'jam al-buldān* (1955–57); for more mod-

ern Yemeni geographers see al-Ḥajrī's *Majmūʿ buldān al-Yaman wa qabā'ilihā* (1984) and the republican author al-Wīsī's *al-Yaman al-kubrā* (1962).

7. There is a voluminous literature on British colonial administrative practices. The ones concerning India are particularly relevant because Aden was initially administered through the Bombay presidency, and the India Office was the office of the secretary of state for India. See, for example, Dirks (1992, 2001) and Cohn (1996).

8. Talal Asad (2003) argues that "it is the power to make a strategic separation between law and morality that defines the colonial situation" (240). Although he acknowledges Timothy Mitchell's important point (in *Colonising Egypt,* 1988) that the European task of establishing order in Egypt required a new notion of what "order" was, Asad emphasizes how colonial rule demanded new conceptions of what the law "can do and how it should do it" (240). I am suggesting here that law was particularly important in the colonial construction of Aden, whereas preoccupations with "order" structured colonial policy in the hinterland. In fact, the laws in the Protectorate dealt mostly with the slave trade, the arms trade, and the status of British subjects within the Protectorate. The publication in the 1930s of the "Laws of the Aden Protectorate" runs about thirty pages, while the "Laws of the Aden Colony" published in the 1940s runs five or six volumes.

9. Willis (2004, 121). In Africa, see Mamdani (1996); Phillips (1989); Vail (1989). See also Comaroff and Comaroff (1991, 1997, chap. 8). One of the most precise statements of indirect rule in Africa is Lugard (1965).

10. This was especially true with the "Amīrī tribe," which was purely a creation of the British. Approximately two-thirds of this population of the northwest corner of what was later to be termed the Protectorate belonged to a number of independent, autonomous clans or "sections," some of which were seminomadic and many of which lived in small villages. See Gavin (1975, 201).

11. Zaydism is a branch of Shīʿī Islam named after a fourth-generation descendent of the Prophet, Zayd ibn ʿAlī, who died in 740. Zaydīs traditionally required that the ruler or imām be a *sayyid,* a descendent of the Prophet through Fāṭima, his daughter and the wife of ʿAlī ibn Abī Ṭālib. For further details, see chapter 4.

12. During his reign, Muḥammad ʿAlī took control of Ottoman provinces in Arabia, Palestine, and Syria.

13. The sequence of events runs something like this: Worried over Muḥammad ʿAlī's independent efforts to upset the imperial balance and pursue an autonomous course of action, the British forced him back under Ottoman suzerainty. As we have already noted, the British took Aden in 1839, expanding both the city and their influence over the coming decades, in particular with the opening of the Suez Canal in 1869. The Ottomans, who had already established a foothold on the Red Sea coast in the North by 1849, responded to increasing British involvement by seizing control of the central highlands, which were, at the time, in a considerable state of disorder. Yemeni historians refer to these years as the "time of corruption" (*ayyām al-fasād*).

14. Thanks are owed to John Willis here. In a series of e-mail exchanges, he has helped me to sort out the impact of Ottoman rule. See also "*kitāb al-siyar*" in al-Shawkānī (2000).

15. As John Willis points out, the Ottomans did not have the financial resources or manpower to support the institutional infrastructure associated with a modern state; wild

fluctuations in rainfall and poor road networks meant that there was no way North Yemen could provide a tax base conducive to such innovations.

16. This reliance on a leader's presence recalls too the processional rituals of Queen Elizabeth I's rule in England. See Strong (1977); Yates (1975); Geertz (1983).

17. Imām Yaḥyā's relationship with the Ottomans was complicated. Like that of all imāms, he could trace his lineage back to the Prophet Muḥammad, and his duty was to wage *jihād* against oppression. His father had also been imām, and like his father, Yaḥyā fought the Ottomans, charging them with moral and material corruption. Ongoing military skirmishes between the Ottomans and Imām Yaḥyā culminated in an agreement in 1911, allowing the imām to appoint judges for the Zaydī school of jurisprudence, understood as a distinct denomination or *madhhab*, and to control the *waqf*, or property endowed for pious ends. Zaydī populations, moreover, were to pay their taxes directly to the imām, and he was to submit a tithe to the Ottoman government. Neither side was to attack the other's "borders," although what "borders" meant at that time remains unclear (Dresch 2000, 7). The truce allowed the Ottoman administration to maintain control of much of Lower Yemen while Imām Yaḥyā attempted to rule the northern highlands. Ṣan'ā' was a mixture of Ottoman and imamic jurisdictions. After the Ottoman empire fell apart (1918–20), Imām Yaḥyā's troops took over Lower Yemen, wrested parts of the Tihāma on the Red Sea from the control of local dynasts (called the Idrīsīs, 1927–29), suppressed rebels from the self-identified "tribal" confederation of Ḥāshid (1928) in the highlands, and (by the 1930s) controlled the east around Ma'rib.

18. In Michael Cook's *Commanding Right and Forbidding Wrong in Islamic Thought* (2000) it becomes clear that this injunction is not specifically a Zaydī one.

19. I am not arguing that there were no earlier attempts to override *madhhab* distinctions, simply that earlier efforts were not reflections of nationalist aspirations (see Messick 1993, chap. 2). After the peace of Da'ān in which the imām gained nominal independence from the Ottomans, the imām's appeals to the inhabitants of the "*quṭr al-yamanī al-zaydī minhum wa al-shāfi'ī*" (the Yemeni region among which are Zaydīs and Shāfi'īs) reflects attempts to be inclusive, as do much earlier shifts in law (such as the move toward the "*ahl al-sunna*" or "people of the *sunna*").

20. The second edition of al-Wāsi'ī's book in 1948 (reprinted in 1991) is not simply a second printing, but a rearrangement of the material, one that registers the changed political climate between the two editions. The second edition adds new information, specifically including events from the year of the publication of the first edition (1346 AH) to the year of the second edition (1367 AH) and the author also deleted some material. The sections "On the tribes of *Yaman*," "On the cities of *Yaman*," "On Tihāma," "On the minerals and mines of *Yaman*," and "On Ḥaḍramawt" are greatly expanded. More interestingly, omitted from the newer edition are passages "On the people of Ṣan'ā' attacking the Muftī and the loyalty of the people of *Yaman* in their love of the imām"; "On the conflict between the Arabs and Turks in Syria in 1330 AH"; "On a Syrian's call for Arab unity"; "On Syrians' opinions concerning unity with the Ottomans"; and "On the Sa'ūd killing *Yamanī* pilgrims in the year 1340 AH." Even in the second edition, however, al-Wāsi'ī uses the term *ahl al-Yaman* to mean "people of *Yaman*" as opposed to the more nationalistic term, *al-sha'b*. For a discussion of the word *sha'b*, see Zolondek (1965) and *The Encyclopedia of Islam* (1995, 150–52).

21. See Peter Sahlins's discussion of the difference between jurisdictional and territorial sovereignty in the Cerdanya of France and Spain (Sahlins 1991, 28–29).

22. In addition to early-modern Europe, there are also parallels with Mughal India's ritual acts of "incorporation." See F. W. Buckler (1922, 1927–28); Cohn (1996).

23. In other words, disputes between Ottoman and British rulers were augmented by disagreements within the imperial administration. The secretary of state, according to one British diplomat's diary, was more interested in "securing an outer line which Turkey would respect" and believed that such a consideration "outweighed any advantage of any attempted tribal division." Therefore, His Majesty's Government, which had appealed to the line of 1891 in the past, was "pledged to follow it." But others in the government of India, which had jurisdiction locally in Aden and the hinterland, disagreed: they did not know whether the demarcation line referred to the survey of 1891–92 or to the approximate line in the tracing that accompanied the surveyor's note of March 1892; they appealed to the "consensus of local authority" (42); and they expressed anxiety about recent Turkish encroachments, ones that limited the protectorate to "a portion of the Amiri tribes" (42). See "Summary of Lord Curzon's Vice-Royalty: Aden 1899–1905." See also Gavin (1975, chap. 8).

24. Cadastral surveys usually record the quantity, value, and ownership of land for the purposes of taxation—but this one, according to its stated purpose, was initiated to draw a political boundary.

25. See Gavin (1975, 195). The Ottomans backed such claims with military incursions into territory occupied by the British, arguing that the whole peninsula formed part of the sultan-caliph's historic possession.

26. "Greater Yemen" did not always include Aden's port, although sometimes it did.

27. See, for example, Mitchell (1988) and Mamdani (1996).

28. For a fascinating discussion of the importance of modern maps (and the understandings of a national spatial reality modern maps both exemplify and foster), see Winichakul (1994). Other works that concentrate on the delineation of particular nation-state boundaries include Sahlins (1991), Weber (1976), and Kashani-Sabet (1999).

29. The South was initially called the People's Republic of South Yemen (from November 1967 until December 1970).

30. I have in mind al-Wāsi'ī, al-Jirāfī, and Zabāra; for a description of the importance of intellectuals to nationalism, see Suny and Kennedy (2001).

31. For an analysis of the ways in which the discipline of history has been implicated in constituting the imagined community of the nation, see Duara (1995). Duara shows how historians actively participate in creating the narratives that make up national histories. The extent to which historians in Yemen actually helped to generate national consciousness remains a topic for further research, however. Certainly by the 1950s it was not uncommon for nationalist intellectuals to refer to "recovering" or "awakening" a "national" past. By that time national categories often determined how history was written and the purposes it served.

32. Al-Wāsi'ī (1991 [1948], 294).

33. Ibid., 149, 150, 282.

34. Ibid., 139, 199.

35. Ibid., 55, 68, 80, 83.

36. Ibid. On Aden: 258–60 and 263–64 (fight against the British), 322–23 (description of the city), 358–63 (English occupation). On Ḥaḍramawt: see 291 on the "learned men of Ḥaḍramawt" and 335–36 for a general description.

37. Consider, for example, the famous poet and political commentator 'Abd Allāh al-Baraddūnī's oft-cited poetry collection *Min Arḍ Bilqīs* (*From the Land of Bilqis*—the Queen of Sheba).

38. The 'Abdalī Sultans of Laḥj broke away from Qāsimī rule in 1728 and claimed power in ministates or sultanates (roughly like principalities). The sultan of Laḥj used to own the Aden port, which is why the British opened negotiations with him in the 1830s, and the 'Abdalī used their connections with the British to affirm their political power. Aḥmad Faḍl al-'Abdalī's book is entitled *Hadiyyat al-zaman fī akhbār mulūk Laḥj wa-'Adan* (Beirut: Dār al-'Awda, 1931) or *Gift of the Age: Chronicles of the Kings of Laḥj and Aden.*

39. The importance of Java and Singapore in these narratives reflects long-standing trade and pilgrimage connections among Muslim communities in the Indian Ocean. Dresch notes how marginal the North is to Ḥaḍramī historical accounts (2000, 50). See Ṣalāḥ al-Bakrī's two-volume *Political History of Hadramawt* (1935–36) and Ḥaḍramī responses to it, as well as the work of Linda Boxberger (2002) and Engseng Ho (1997, 2006), especially the latter's discussion of Aḥmad ibn Muḥammad al-Miḥḍār's (d. 1304 AH/1887 AD) *Maqāmat āthām al-dunyā*. Al-Miḥḍār's writings give the reader a sense of an explicitly Ḥaḍramī identity, one that juxtaposes a morally safe Ḥaḍramawt to the corrupt "*dunyā*" or world outside. Ḥaḍramī accounts of collectivity and selfhood are also reproduced in Freitag (2003).

40. For a discussion of the importance of newspapers and periodicals for Arab intellectual life in the early twentieth century, see Khalidi (1997), esp. chaps. 3 and 6.

41. My understanding of *Fatāt al-jazīra* emerges from reading extensively from the newspapers in the library in Mukallā and in the British Library in 2000 and 2001. I am also grateful to Dr. Muḥammad 'Abd al-Malik al-Mutawakkil for allowing me to use his private library of newspapers during my many visits to Yemen from 1998 to 2004. His book, *al-Ṣaḥāfa al-yamaniyya: nash'atuhā wa taṭawwuruhā* (1983), analyzes Yemeni newspapers and chronicles the emergence of print media in Yemen.

42. Shelagh Weir (2007) points out that in her area of fieldwork, Jabal al-Rāziḥ in the province of Ṣa'da, men visiting the capital, Ṣan'ā', in the 1970s, "were said to be 'away in *al-yaman*,' and only gradually has *al-yaman* primarily come to mean the republican state" (12).

43. Anderson (1991, esp. chap. 7) writes of similar processes of increased physical mobility of populations, the effects of institutional expansion on the demand for educated bureaucrats, and the spread of modern-style education.

44. Intellectuals were what Suny and Kennedy term "active agents" in propagating national values, disciplining the population, and enforcing the rules and boundaries of the constituent people (2001, 1–51), but their influence should not be exaggerated.

45. Author's interview, July 2001.

46. Anderson may overstate the primacy of print in Western Europe and the New World; literacy rates were low, and it may have been oral media that did some of the work that Anderson attributes to "print capitalism."

47. For a discussion of radio in the Arab world, see Boyd (1999). For an excellent book on the ways in which Egyptian television serials helped to forge national selves, see Abu-Lughod (2005).

48. Radio Ṣanʿāʾ began broadcasting in 1947. According to J. Leigh Douglas, its programs were "restricted to those of a religious nature and to news about the Imam's family and officials" (1987, 12).

49. For a discussion of the "uneasy" relationship between Yemeni nationalism(s) and Arab nationalism, see Halliday (1997). Halliday points out that in the founding document of the southern NLF of 1965, Arabs are referred to as the *shaʿb* or "people," but by the 1970s Yemenis are "the people" and Arabs are part of a loosely connected umma (referring in this context to a pan-Arab community).

50. The Free Yemeni Movement refers to a series of short-lived groups comprised of intellectual reformers who actively participated in North Yemeni politics from 1935 to 1962; they tended to represent, to varying degrees, the key opposition to Imām Yaḥyā and his son Imām Aḥmad Ḥamīd al-Dīn (1948–62) before the revolution. For a description of the groups and their activities, see Douglas (1987). For a discussion of the political movements in Aden, see Bujra (1970). There were Adeni elites (almost exclusively wealthy, commercially oriented Adenis) who were willing to cooperate with the British, and others from Aden and from the Protectorate (primarily from the middle and lower middle classes) who opposed such collaboration.

51. SWB, Pt. 4, 435 (January 29, 1954, 55); this is an excerpt from Cairo Radio's Voice of the Arabs, cited in Douglas (1987, 65).

52. Both Anderson (1991) and Herbst (2000) stress the importance of colonial boundary making to postcolonial states, which is no doubt true. But in the Middle East, there is the Syrian effort to commit what might be thought of as "state suicide" when it surrendered sovereignty to Egypt in the short-lived United Arab Republic (1958–61) and the Yemen case of unification. These examples suggest that despite the resilience of colonial borders they are not without some flexibility.

53. Interview with nationalist leaders in London, July 2001.

54. The poem is cited in Renaud and Fayein (1979). It is discussed in Dresch (2000, 88) and the translation is his.

55. Poem recited to me in July 2001.

56. For a remarkable book on poetry and its political import in Yemen, see Caton (1990). Caton distinguishes between three different genres of poetry: the *bāla*, the *zāmil*, and the *qaṣīda*. The *bāla* (which he transcribes *bālah*) is "composed in a performance"; it is the most "collective and dramatic of all poetic genres. Always more than one poet compose the verse, and the poets enter into a competition, which is referred to in the poetry as a *laʿbah* (game)" (79). The *zāmil*, like the *bāla*, is composed in the course of a performance, but "only one poet composes the verse lines, not a group of poets in competition with each other. In addition, the roles of the chorus and the audience are greatly diminished. Since the utterance is brief—a complete *zāmil* poem comprises only two lines—there is no time pressure on the poets. The constraint rather becomes one of compression and terseness" (127). The *qaṣīda*, by contrast, is composed by specific individuals, some of whom have the reputation for being masters (chap. 8), and the moment of creation is spatially and temporally different from the moment of reception (185). Indeed, the poet often addresses a messenger whose task it is to deliver the poem to its receiver.

57. Poem recited to me, July 2001. Different versions of this poem and the response are noted in Caton (1990, 151–52) and Dresch (2000, 95).

58. The phrase "silver has become brass" is a reference to the Maria Teresa silver coins in circulation at the time. The Sharp is a British rifle; the M1 is an American rifle; "fighter jet" is my translation of the Arabic al-Sūd Khāṣṣ.

59. In the lower region of North Yemen, this well-known *zāmil* captured the political conflicts of the time in verse—in language that registered the hopes and disappointments of participants who had fought in the revolution of 1962 for a new political order (author's interview, September 2001):

Sabīʿ [the poet who initiates the exchange]:
The Day of Judgment has signs
The most conspicuous of which is when a crow becomes a pigeon [*ḥamāma*] in the eyes of the people
Some people are satisfied with inequity and with eating piled up garbage
They live deprived of dignity and without feelings.
The Reply:
Sabīʿ, whose stature is like those of seventy men [an invocation of hell]
You reminded us of the horrors of Judgment Day.
Your revolutionary volcano,
Like *ḥamāma* from a volcano [but the word *ḥamāma* for pigeon is a pun on *ḥimāma*, lava from a volcano] that shook the people.
We rebelled against the Imām's rule,
And freed the people from injustice.
And the beret [worn by the new president after the revolution] is just like the turban [the "*ʿimāma*" worn during the Imām's era]
Worn above the head.

60. See especially Caton's (1990, 205–15) discussion of Muḥammad al-Gharsī's self-proclaimed masterpiece for President Ibrāhīm al-Ḥamdī (1974–77).

61. Halliday (1997) lists these important external events and makes the point that the Palestine question, in particular, had an "impact on Yemen" because it entailed the departure of its large Jewish community (in 1949–50). More work would need to be done to chart the distinct effects that this issue had on Yemeni discourses of the late 1940s and early 1950s. For a detailed discussion of Jewish-Muslim relations in Lower Yemen prior to 1950, see Hollander (2005).

62. Andreas Glaeser points out to me that in sociology the dialectic would be between organizations and discourse, but I am using institutions and organizations interchangeably. In the discipline of political science, it is institutions or organizations and ideas or discourses that are seen as being in opposition.

63. This formulation is particularly popular in political science and economics.

64. For a critique of this bifurcation between state and society, see Mitchell (1991). See also Migdal (2001). In Hansen and Stepputat (2001), the contributors concentrate on the state's appearance in the quotidian lives of ordinary citizens.

65. NLF members were primarily drawn from the provincial lower middle classes; they connected Aden to areas of the rural protectorate and to parts of the North such as Ḥujariyya. They also had significant links in part through the Arab nationalist organization

Movement of Arab Nationalists (MAN) to Yemenis living abroad. Arguably, the British decision to federate Aden with the Protectorates and the Yemeni revolution in the North—both in the 1960s—played a crucial role in strengthening opposition to colonial rule in the South and to the rise of the NLF (Bujra 1970).

66. Splits within the party may have reflected ideological differences, but the 1986 war revealed that the opposing political factions also tended to map onto two key regions in the South: the area of Abyan supported President ʿAlī Nāṣir, and the area of Laḥj supported the recently returned ʿAbd al-Fattāḥ Ismāʿīl (who died in battle) and ʿAlī Sālim al-Bīḍ (who became secretary general of the YSP when the civil war was over).

67. PDRY leaders originally from the YAR included ʿAbd al-Fattāḥ Ismāʿīl, Muḥammad Saʿīd ʿAbd Allāh (known as Muḥsin), and Jār Allāh ʿUmar. ʿAlī ʿAntar, also a firm supporter of resistance movements in the North was from an area bordering the North, Shaʿīb. Sālim Rubayyiʿ ʿAlī and ʿAlī Nāṣir Muḥammad, by contrast, were from Abyan in the South and favored a more conciliatory position (Halliday 1990, 99–100). The latter faction lost the 1986 war and fled to the North.

68. Author's interview, September 2000.

69. Author's interview, May 2000.

70. Al-Bīḍ's statement is cited in Halliday (1990, 134).

71. Author's interviews September 2000, July 2001.

72. For an excellent discussion of the changes in terminology over time in the PDRY's documents, see Halliday (1990, esp. 106–10). Halliday registers the shift in emphasis over time from documents that situated Yemeni unity in an overall pan-Arab project to a notion of Yemeni unification as primary.

73. *Al-Dustūr al-Dāʾim lil-Jumhūriyya al-ʿArabiyya al-Yamaniyya.* The constitution is cited in both ʿAfīf (1982) and Halliday (1990).

74. This view was explicitly stated by "informants" during my fieldwork in 2000–2001. Also see Abū Ṭālib (1994).

75. I am grateful to David Newstone for this formulation.

76. Author's interviews, April–May 2000; September 2000; June 2001; July 2003. Some in the YSP argued that it was President Ṣāliḥ in the North who urged immediate unity and that the South's secretary general ʿAlī Sālim al-Bīḍ, over the opposition of his comrades favoring a gradual approach, was "very enthusiastic to actualize unification" (June 2001). According to al-Bīḍ, the impatience came from Ṣāliḥ, who feared Saudi intervention: "Saudi Arabia wouldn't have let it happen otherwise [i.e., more gradually]. That was the North's worry. It was a coup d'état—exactly like a coup d'état" (July 2003). Others in the YSP blamed al-Bīḍ himself for rushing into an arrangement that many in the party thought ill-advised, at least in hindsight. They claimed that al-Bīḍ threatened to destroy anyone who opposed immediate unification—that his impetuousness and impatience had accelerated the pace of unification and had caused the subsequent loss of political power for the YSP (April 2000).

77. Author's interviews, July 2003.

78. Indeed, in an interview with *al-Wasaṭ* in Jidda, subsequently summarized in the YSP's paper *al-Thawrī*, a leader of the main Islamic party in Yemen, ʿAbd al-Majīd al-Zindānī, allegedly said: "Yemeni unity was imposed on the people of both parts [i.e., North and South

Yemen] for colonialist ends." Moreover, al-Zindānī called on members of the YSP to "repent or their blood would flow copiously" (cited in Dresch and Haykel 1995, 410).

79. In addition to the books already referenced in the body of this text, there are many additional political histories of North and South Yemen, including al-Shamāḥī (1972), Sālim (1971), ʿAbd al-Fattāḥ (1974), Halliday (1975), Stookey (1978), ʿAfīf (1982), Peterson (1982), Ṭarābulsī (2000), Abū Ṭālib (1994), to name a few.

80. For fascinating research on this matter, see Carapico (1993); also Carapico (1998) and Dresch (2000, 134). Dresch notes that like the North, the South had joined the IMF and had solicited advice from the World Bank in 1969. Although the PDRY and the Soviet Union had a strategic relationship from 1969 onward, Moscow contributed no more than a quarter of the PDRY's aid, and even that aid was in the form of projects rather than budgetary support.

81. Author's interviews, August 2001, July 2003.

82. Al-Bīḍ did register his frustration in his speech. Much to the surprise of many colleagues in the party, however, he did not return to Yemen after the gathering but proceeded for meetings in the Gulf in encounters widely understood to be about preparing his side for war.

83. The label "secessionists" refers in large part to the ephemeral existence of the Democratic Republic of Yemen, declared by al-Bīḍ on May 21, 1994. The scholar Bernard Rougier claims that this announcement was made to generate international recognition for southern forces, which were losing the military battle. See Rougier (1999, 101).

84. Demonstrations were particularly fierce in the former South's areas of Aden, al-Dāliʿ, and the coastal area of the Ḥaḍramawt, where several people were killed, but they were not confined to these regions. In addition to demanding the reinstatement of military personnel dismissed after the 1994 war, protestors called for the consideration of petitions filed by pensioners whose property had been expropriated, as well as general demands for solutions to the unemployment problem. The protests, which seem to have been triggered by price hikes, continued to spread and to involve more citizens (including a significant number of women). Raising prices before the holy month of Ramadan puts a great burden on families already taxed by the pressures of holiday spending. Wheat prices doubled, for example. The regime's repressive reaction to the protests in this instance seems to have precipitated further unrest, including the blockade of the Aden-Ṣanʿāʾ highway. The protestors' blockading of the highway is a particularly eloquent reminder of how unification requires ongoing cooperation and communication. Also noteworthy was an open letter from the former secretary general of the YSP, ʿAlī Ṣāliḥ ʿUbād (or "Muqbil"), to the president chronicling the sufferings of southerners since the 1994 war and urging the president to take specific reparatory steps to prevent Yemen's "suicide" (published at http://www.al-ayyam.info/default.aspx?NewsID=2f686845-05ce-4b27-ad36-af5778d05fce; last accessed September 18, 2007). Muqbil is an advocate of union, but his letter caused consternation among some unionists because it praised former YSP colleagues associated with secession. It also referred to both the ʿAmmān agreement between the YSP and the GPC prior to the war of 1994 and to the United Nations Security Council resolution in the wake of the secessionists' defeat, signaling possible doubts about whether unity, in the form in which it has been achieved, remains desirable. Others familiar with internal politics within the Yemeni Socialist Party argued that rather than alarm, Muqbil's letter was an attempt to reduce tensions with the president in the wake of an incendiary press statement issued by the party's central committee.

85. Michael Billig (1995) has called these instances of everyday nationalism, such as weather reports or postage stamps, "banal nationalism." For a sophisticated discussion of nationalism's banality, see Foster (2002).

CHAPTER TWO

1. According to a deputy in the Ministry of Labor and Social Affairs, there are approximately twenty-five hundred active and inactive civil society organizations in Yemen today. The United Nations' Common Country Assessment document supplies the figure of twenty-four hundred for 1999. According to Aḥmad (2003), there are forty-five human rights organizations; forty-one women's organizations, eleven of them devoted to health; twenty-seven development and cultural organizations; twelve organizations dealing with agriculture and the environment; and forty-six unions or syndicates. For a history of trade unions in Yemen, see *al-'Amal al-niqābī al-' ummālī fī al-jumhuriyya al-yamaniyya: al-judhūr al-tārikhiyya, al-wāqi', āfāq al-mustaqbal* (2004).

The title of this chapter is beholden to James C. Scott's *Seeing Like a State* (1998). By "state" I mean a common set of institutions capable of distributing goods and services and controlling violence within a demarcated, internationally recognized territory. By "nation" I refer to a shared sense of belonging simultaneously with anonymous others to an imagined political community. By "regime" I mean the political order of a particular leader or administration.

2. See Jean Comaroff and John L. Comaroff (1999, 5) and their *Critical Inquiry* piece of 2004. According to Sonya O. Rose (1999, 218), the expression "moral panic" originated with Jock Young in "The Drugtakers: The Social Meanings of Drug Use" (1971); see also subsequent uses by Stanley Cohen, *Folk Devils and Moral Panics: The Creation of the Mods and Rockers* (1972), and Stuart Hall et al., *Policing the Crisis: Mugging, the State, and Law and Order* (1978). Thanks are owed to Jennifer Cole for bringing this literature to my attention.

3. The National Democratic Institute, an organization associated with the Democratic Party in the United States, helped the regime to host the "Emerging Democracies" conference, in which fifteen countries participated in June 1999.

4. Faraj Bin Ghānim served as prime minister of Yemen from May 17, 1997, until his resignation on April 29, 1998.

5. According to one source, there were 20,100 ballot boxes made, but only 17,148 distributed. The source took this to mean that the undistributed ones were to be used in an "emergency situation" so that the regime could show that it had not only amassed the required majority but also generated enthusiasm for the elections.

6. There were relatively few political posters of Najīb Qaḥṭān, and those that did exist were hand placed by party members on public walls. No such posters were available for purchase, nor could they be found in shop windows.

7. Estimates of the average per capita income for the period under consideration vary from about $270 to $347, depending on the source and year. See *World Bank Report* (1999) and the *Yemen Times*, November 13–19, 2000.

8. It is difficult to obtain population breakdowns by region in Yemen. *The World Gazetteer*'s estimates of approximately 4.5 million inhabitants in the South in 1994, and 4.2 million in 2003, strike me as inflated; the overall population figures cited are high by any other

source's standards (close to 16 million in 1994; close to 23 million in 2003). Officials in the ruling GPC and members of the opposition quoted me the figure of 2.5 million inhabitants of the South in 1999 out of a total population of close to seventeen million.

9. The idiomatic expression in English would be "the devil you know is better than the devil you don't."

10. Several scholars have recently examined authoritarian regimes in which at least one key political institution, usually the legislature, is selected through elections (Brownlee 2007; Lust-Okar 2006; Magaloni 2006; Boix and Svolik 2007).

11. For a discussion of how Yemen's ruling party managed to enjoy an electoral landslide in the April parliamentary elections, see Carapico (2003).

12. For a detailed interview (in Arabic) with Fayṣal Bin Shamlān in which he introduces himself to the electorate, putting forth his political platform and providing readers with his biography, see www.newsyemen.net, July 5, 2006; last accessed September 12, 2006. In that interview, Bin Shamlān makes a point of saying that he is a candidate for all of Yemen and not simply a representative of the South. For an important analysis of the events and alliances leading up to the 2006 elections, see Makram (2005).

13. E-mail correspondence, September 2006.

14. See the remarkable interview between Nabīl al-Ṣūfī and the head of the GPC's ruling bloc in Parliament, Sulṭān al-Barakānī, at www.newsyemen.net, August 24, 2005. My e-mail interviews in July 2005 and August 2005 confirm this view.

15. Interestingly, as Johnsen points out, al-Jazeera and al-'Arabiyya satellite channels initially projected Ṣāliḥ winning by 82 percent of the vote.

16. For a discussion of the ways in which rhetoric and symbols not only exemplify but also produce power for a regime, see my *Ambiguities of Domination: Politics, Rhetoric, and Symbols in Contemporary Syria* (1999). The contrasts with Yemen are instructive here.

17. Such an act was not without precedent, of course. Stalin deleted Trotsky from the historical record, for example. The fictional account from Milan Kundera's *The Book of Laughter and Forgetting* is also noteworthy. Importantly, several Yemeni Socialist Party members recall that the two leaders jointly raised the flag, but I could find no picture to substantiate that memory. Instead, in the capital's Military Museum a photograph taken in 1990 does depict al-Bīḍ, the former secretary general of the South's YSP, gazing up from behind as 'Alī 'Abd Allāh Ṣāliḥ raises the flag. Museum curators argued that although political posters had excised al-Bīḍ's image, they displayed the photo of the "traitors" because they were "protecting the historical record" (author's interview, September 2002).

18. The words "tribe" and "tribal" are deeply problematic, fraught terms, perhaps especially in the Middle East studies literature. My use of them here is not meant to disregard debates about usage, or to ride roughshod over the complex issues invocations of the concept bring to the fore. I address the term's scholarly and local connotations in depth in chapter 4.

19. Blue paint was an innovation of the northern regime in the mid-'80s. Before that, shop doors were metal gates throughout the Yemen Arab Republic and they were works of folk art, each unique and brightly colored. This executive decision to standardize shop doors by painting them blue is itself part of the political process I am describing. Thanks are owed to Sheila Carapico for this information.

20. Author's interview with the minister of education, May 2000.

21. State-run television is another vehicle for enacting state power, of course.

22. Interestingly, the former special advisor to the U.N. secretary general, Lakhdar Brahimi, notes that it was during the festivities surrounding unification that the two leaders resolved the border dispute between Yemen and Saudi Arabia—and largely in favor of Yemen (personal communication, March 2007). In addition to the event's domestic effects, then, the spectacle may have occasioned important diplomatic developments, although these probably would have happened anyway.

23. In the video version of the festival, the scene of empty seats is edited out.

24. Najwa Adra's work on "tribal dancing" links the *bara'* (a Yemeni group dance performed by men outdoors in the northern highlands) to the growth of Yemeni nationalism in her essay, "Tribal Dancing and Yemeni Nationalism: Steps to Unity" (1993). In "Dance and Glance: Visualizing Tribal Identity in Highland Yemen" (1998) she connects dancing to conceptions of tribal affiliation.

25. I watched this spectacle with northern and southern Yemenis on May 22, 2000. I thank W. Flagg Miller for bringing my attention to additional alternative readings.

26. Unease at women's participation was registered in a number of mosque sermons. Muḥammad al-Ānisī's *Saffāḥ Kulliyyat al-Ṭibb* sermon (2000) also wonders why the Russian minister of defense had been permitted to attend the festivities in the VIP section when the Russians were responsible for killing Chechen Muslims.

27. There are a plethora of works dealing with the political importance of spectacle. For a partial bibliography, see my *Ambiguities of Domination* (1999). Classics include Guy Debord's *Society of the Spectacle* (1994) and Clifford Geertz's *Negara: The Theater State in Nineteenth-Century Bali* (1980).

28. There is a growing literature on the sale of body parts that interprets actual marketing practices and the stories circulating about purported trafficking as products of "globalization" or neoliberal capitalist policies. See, for example, the provocative account by Comaroff and Comaroff (1999).

29. It is unclear whether this phrase means a reason unknown to all or a reason that the speaker knows but refuses to divulge. Both ordinary language uses have been noted. The phrase is originally from the Qur'ān, Sūrat Yūsuf 12:68. When the sons of Jacob were leaving for Egypt, Jacob advised them not to all enter the city from the same gate, but to use various gates. The reason for this suggestion was *ḥājatun fī nafs Ya'qūb*. According to the Qu'rānic scholar al-Ṭabarī (839–923 AD), Jacob advised his sons to use several gates because he feared for their safety. Even though Jacob knew that the fate of his sons would be in God's hands, he advised them so that he might feel less worried about them. In *Tafsīr al-Jalālayn* by Jalāl al-Dīn Muḥammad ibn Aḥmad al-Maḥallī (1389–1459 AD) and Jalāl al-Dīn 'Abd al-Raḥmān ibn Abū Bakr al-Suyūṭī (1445–1505 AD), the sentence is interpreted to mean "a desire within Jacob that he wished to be fulfilled." The sentence seems to suggest to these interpreters that there was a worry or fear within Jacob about what might happen to his sons during their trip to Egypt that was alleviated when he felt that his sons were going to follow his advice. I thank Aram Shahin for his research here.

30. See also al-Ānisī's sermon *Saffāḥ Kulliyyat al-Ṭibb* (2000), in which al-Ānisī argues that the "evils that have befallen society," exemplified by the serial killer, are due to the

"abandonment of the laws of God." He demands a public trial for the murderer so that "everyone *in Yemen* is made aware of the case and its details" (my emphasis). He also, as was common among Islamic *khaṭībs* (those who deliver sermons), attacks those in charge (*al-mas'ūlūn*) for allowing both sexes to mix at the university. He demands that those in positions of responsibility at the University of Ṣan'ā' also be put on trial for their responsibility in the case.

31. Author's interview, May 2000. This view was not only held by liberals. Indeed, the militant preacher al-Ānisī in his sermon *Saffāḥ Kulliyyat al-Ṭibb* also reprimands those Yemenis who attacked Sudanese individuals in Yemen in retaliation for the actions of the murderer.

32. I discuss the theme of public sphere practices in detail in chapter 3. See also my "Concepts and Commitments in the Study of Democracy" (2004).

33. The example of September 11 provides a case in point.

34. I am indebted to Patchen Markell and Craig Calhoun for this formulation.

35. I thank Rosalind C. Morris for pressing me on this point.

36. See also Anthony Marx's discussion in *Faith in Nation* (2003) in which he argues that the early-modern "impetus for national cohesion" was a "basis for democracy" (32, and chap. 6). Marx's argument is beholden to Rustow, but Marx is keen to underscore (correctly) that national cohesion (to the extent it exists) emerged out of conflict and deliberate exclusions, a point that Rustow does not acknowledge.

37. The history of the early United States suggests the same phenomenon, as do many prerevolutionary situations. Sheila Carapico makes a compatible but not identical argument; her emphasis is on the ways in which "Yemeni states, lacking major outside benefactors or domestic wealth, may be unique in the region in their need for civil society" (Carapico 1998, 17 [see also chap. 5]; and 1996). Her aim is to challenge prevailing stereotypes of conservatism and passivity often attributed to tribalism and to Islam by charting the history of activism within the context of local civic associations and self-help projects. My point here might also be likened to Joel Migdal's insights from *Strong Societies and Weak States* (1988), but it differs in two ways. First, I am not claiming that there is a zero-sum relationship between weak states and strong societies, or that we can even measure weakness and strength in ways that make consistent sense. I am suggesting that the Yemeni example—in which the state is "weak" *by anyone's definition* and political participation is vibrant and backed by significant coercive power—provides a corrective to some of the prevailing assumptions in the literature on democracy or "democratization." Some of these assumptions are dealt with at greater length in the next chapter. Second, my argument is concerned with the phenomenology of citizenship, the ways in which people talk about and practice their experiences of, and desires for, state authority and political community.

38. As discussed in the introduction, this simultaneity has specifiable qualities that make nationalism distinctive from other imaginings of collectivity.

CHAPTER THREE

1. A joke, told by an educated self-identified northern woman from a well-known conservative family to her northern and southern women friends, reiterates this understanding of the Yemeni president's rule: 'Alī 'Abd Allāh Ṣāliḥ, Bill Clinton, and his wife, Hillary, were going for a swim. They took off their clothes and went into the water. Afterward, Hillary turned to Bill and said: " 'Alī 'Abd Allāh's penis is so big. . . . I didn't expect that from such a short man." Bill said, "Well, he's been screwing twenty million people" (January 2002).

2. "Large-N" refers to sample size, bearing effectively in this context on the number of cases considered.

3. All quotes from *qāt* chews and from supplemental ethnographic work are from my field notes and are in Arabic; there is one exception in which the person addressed a letter to me in English. This is specified in the text.

4. The comparative politics literature on democracy, democratization, and transitions is simply too voluminous to be treated adequately here. Key texts include Lipset (1959); Diamond (1992, ed. with Marks; 1999); O'Donnell and Schmitter (1986); Huntington (1991); Putnam (1993); Powell (2000); Collier (1999); Linz and Stepan (1996); Boix (2003); and Boix and Stokes (2003). At the risk of riding roughshod over important differences, it is fair to say that few of these works spend much time problematizing the concept of democracy or investigating ordinary *practices* of political participation, which is to say performances of democratic subjectivity that exist outside of electoral confines. Most of these authors see themselves as exploring the causes of democracy or the relationship between economic development and democracy, some of them explicitly invoking a minimalist definition of democracy, and some suggesting that elections are an indicator or "instrument" of democracy but not the thing itself (e.g., Powell). Putnam's *Making Democracy Work* is one partial exception and is invoked in later parts of this chapter. To be clear, I am not claiming that there has been no work on the concept of democracy, but that this work, as Taylor Boas and Jordan Gans-Morse (2007) rightly note, has generated close to a consensus in favor of a "procedural minimum" definition (5). Boas and Gans-Morse have in mind, in addition to Schumpeter and Przeworski et al., discussed in the body of this chapter, also Dahl (1971), O'Donnell and Schmitter (1986), Huntington (1991), Schmitter and Karl (1991), and Collier and Levitsky (1997). David Collier is the comparativist most attentive to concept choice and its implications. See also Collier and Adcock (1999); Adcock and Collier (2001) and Collier, Hidalgo, and Maciuceanu (2006). Whereas many scholars studying democracy prefer a stable definition of the concept as bounded by rules, my own preference is for a Wittgensteinian understanding of democracy as a set of language games. See *Philosophical Investigations* (1958), par. 67. In this chapter, I am willing to think both in Wittgensteinian terms and, by bracketing reservations, in terms of a rule-bound but more expansive definition than the minimalist one. I am grateful to Linda Zerilli for discussions on this issue.

5. Iris Marion Young, for example, suggests a working definition of democracy in which citizens influence and have a direct political impact on the choices and actions of those who govern. For Young, there are regimes in which such connections are strong and those in which they are weak (Young 2000, 173; see also Cunningham 1987, 2002). I take the term "substantive representation" from Hanna Pitkin's extraordinary *The Concept of Representation* (1967). For a recent work, inspired in part by Pitkin's, see Nadia Urbinati's *Representative Democracy: Principles and Genealogy* (2006), which makes the argument that representation is not incompatible with democracy and should not be seen as a second-best solution to the ideal of direct democracy. For Urbinati, "representation can encourage political participation insofar as its deliberative and judgmental character *expands politics beyond the narrow limits of decision and voting*" (16, my emphasis).

6. In fact, the treatment of accountability in Przeworski et al. suffers from a telling confusion. In the first chapter, they state that "governmental responsibility either directly to voters

or to a parliament elected by them is a defining feature of democracy" (15). Yet subsequently they also make what could easily seem the opposite claim, that "accountability," "responsiveness," or "representation" should not be treated as definitional features of democracy (33). "Governmental responsibility," according to this understanding, exists in the absence of "accountability." The apparent contradiction reveals some of the tensions inherent in formalistic understandings. On the one hand, there are good reasons for not including accountability in a definition designed to facilitate large-N coding—the term accountability is itself muddled and may be hard to measure. On the other hand, formalists should have no difficulty accepting a view of accountability and responsiveness in which holding politicians accountable simply means reelecting them or removing them from office (Pitkin 1967). Both the authorization and the accountability view are "formalistic in the sense that their defining criterion for representation lies outside the activity of representing itself, before it begins or after it ends" (Pitkin 1967, 59).

7. Boriana Nikolova's essay exam was written for my class on Rethinking Democratic Practices.

8. For a review of anthropological treatments of democracy, see Paley (2001, 2002); Karlström (1996); and Comaroff and Comaroff (1997). Like anthropologists who employ ethnographic methods, I am interested in everyday practices outside of formal institutions, but my chapter is not about democracy's meanings in local contexts. For an ordinary-language-use analysis of "democracy" in Senegal, see Schaffer (1998). For a critique of the transition paradigm in political science, see Carothers (2002).

9. I am grateful to Linda Zerilli for this formulation.

10. Mosque sermons in Yemen offer a contrast to Turkey or Syria, to take two examples, where sermons are vetted routinely by state officials. Moreover, although the sermon can be argumentative and critical (and in that sense deliberative), it tends to be monologic, although even this is not always true. Some, if audiocassettes of sermons are any indication, do turn into a forum for discussion.

11. There is vigorous disagreement in Yemen about whether "tribal" conferences are a hindrance to democracy or a proper site for civil society expression.

12. This is a point made by Susan Marks as well in a recent and lucid overview of some problems with Schumpeterian notions of "low intensity democracy" (2000, chap. 3). Marks relies primarily on the work of Gills, Rocamora, and Wilson (1993) and Robinson (1996). I thank Jennifer Pitts for drawing my attention to some parallels between these arguments and my own.

13. Habermas locates these new institutions in Great Britain and France: coffeehouses emerged as popular gathering places in around 1680 and 1730, respectively, and the salons became important sites of critical debate in the period between regency and revolution. For a description of coffeehouses in Beirut from 1950 to 1990, see al-Duwayhī (2005). For a discussion of "public spheres" and "counterpublics" in the Middle East, see, for example, Hirschkind (2001, 2006); Asad (1993); Eickelman and Anderson, eds. (1999 and 1997); Lynch (2003, 2006); Tétreault (2000); Najmabadi (2005); al-Rasheed (2007); and Salvatore and Levine (2005).

14. Fearon (1998) in "Deliberation as Discussion" enjoins political scientists to employ the word "discussion" rather than deliberation because it is a "more concrete object of analysis," which can help scholars better ascertain why more deliberation might be a good thing. He supplies six reasons for discussing an issue rather than employing a decision rule that does

not involve discussion (44–68). Discussion discloses "private information"; diminishes or overrides "the impact of bounded rationality"; compels or encourages "a particular mode of justifying demands or claims"; helps render the final choice "legitimate," thereby contributing to group solidarity and making the implementation of decisions easier; improves "the moral or intellectual qualities of the participants"; and is a way of doing the " 'right thing' independent of the consequences of the discussion." The first five justifications are consequentialist; the sixth is not. I use the two terms, discussion and deliberation, interchangeably. My approach is less concerned with the relative merits or demerits of engaging in public discussion and more focused on how everyday practices of deliberation generate explicitly political subjectivities and are part of what democracy means.

15. Scholars of deliberative democracy argue that deliberation can transform "preferences" by allowing individuals or groups to understand the views of and to be persuaded by one another (Bohman 1996; Cohen 1989, 1996; Dryzek 1990, 2000; Fishkin 1991). Others have underscored the problems in privileging consensus as the definitive or desirable aim of democratic debate (Benhabib 1992; Mouffe 1996, 2000; Young 1990, 1996). Discussion may generate considerable disagreement rather than foster unity, both because individuals are unequally related to symbolic and material resources and because interests often diverge (Gutmann and Thompson 1996; Sunstein 2000, 2001). I am indebted to Yasmin Dawood for her insights here.

16. Thanks are owed to Iris Marion Young for pressing me to emphasize this aspect of Habermas's concept.

17. Importantly, Markell (1997) draws out some of the unappreciated similarities between Habermas's public sphere and Arendt's public. Many theorists claim that Habermas's public sphere is concerned with overcoming contestation and dissent. Markell argues that Habermas's account "commits him, albeit in ways that he does not consistently acknowledge, to the view that a legitimate democratic system is not only compatible with agonistic action but actually requires it" (391; see also 379). For the most explicit treatment of the roles contestatory speech and action play in constituting and sustaining "democratic legitimacy," see Habermas (1996).

18. See, for example, Nancy Fraser's oft-cited piece "Rethinking the Public Sphere: A Contribution to the Critique of Actually Existing Democracy" (1992, 123–25).

19. The idealized account of argumentative dialogue is especially apparent in Habermas's *Theory of Communicative Action* (1984, 1987). For criticism of this development, see Lee (1992, 402–20). See also Warner (2002). In addition, there are a number of essays that challenge the fiction of equal access to, and equal conditions within, the deliberative process. See, for example, Young (1996, 120–35); Mansbridge (1993), and Sanders (1997).

20. Indeed, recent scholarship on eighteenth- and nineteenth-century France seems to confirm these doubts. Sarah Maza's work (1993, 2003), in particular, suggests that the subjectivity supposedly generated in the bourgeois family may instead be a product of arguments in the public sphere itself. See also Dena Goodman's discussion of the salons (1996).

21. As Craig Calhoun points out, "Habermas does not mean to suggest that what made the public sphere bourgeois was simply the class composition of its members. Rather, it was *society* that was bourgeois and bourgeois society produced a certain form of public sphere" (Calhoun 1992, 7). Few public spheres are composed of "bourgeois individuals" in Yemen, but

more important, my point is that Yemeni *society* (however one construes it) can in no way be defined as bourgeois.

22. I am indebted to Anita Chari for pressing me to clarify this paragraph and for her substantive suggestions.

23. For a particularly influential discussion of civil society, see Putnam (1993).

24. For an important critique of Putnam's idea of civil society, see Jean L. Cohen's "American Civil Society Talk" (1998). In that paper, Cohen argues that Putnam's notion of civil society ignores the concept of the public sphere, thereby failing to "articulate the complex relation between social and political institutions." For Cohen, the concept of the public sphere is at the core of any conception of democracy. Modern constitutional democracies enjoy "legitimacy" to the extent that "action-orienting norms, practices, policies, and claims to authority can be contested by citizens and . . . affirmed or redeemed in public discourse" (2). See also Charles Taylor's extended discussion of civil society (1990, 95–118) and Partha Chatterjee's response (1990, 119–32).

25. Many thanks to Anita Chari for this point. See also Habermas (1996), esp. chaps. 7 and 8.

26. This is not to say that all women's qāt chews avoid current events or fail to engage with abstract political issues. I have attended educated women's chews in Ṣan'ā' in which issues such as electoral reforms, the importance of and problems with local councils, and the place of the novel in Yemeni literature were each the subject of some discussion. Current events may animate conversations for part of the time, but rarely in a structured or sustained way. Some women, like their male counterparts, chew with other members of their *shilla*, or clique, on a once-a-week basis; they use the occasion to unwind or to exchange information. Often women sing songs or dance to music with other women. In the teenage chews I attended, younger women brought food for a potluck preceding the qāt session. In the village, women catch up on the gossip in the neighborhood but they also use the occasion to make up poetic (often playful) songs and to assess the relative merits of potential wives for their respective sons.

27. See Chakrabarty's social history of *adda* in *Provincializing Europe* (2000).

28. I have attended more than 270 qāt chews. Approximately 175 of those have been with Yemen's elite—with male politicians and intellectuals (who are often at gatherings with less educated, but every bit as politicized, men from the countryside). In these situations I am often treated as a "third gender" or, in the villages, as a preadolescent, giving me the flexibility to travel between segregated worlds in a way that Yemenis and foreign male researchers cannot. As long as my father and husband do not object, it tends to be fine with Yemenis that I am there. Indeed, husbands use my attendance to convey messages to their wives in adjacent quarters, and women too see me as a conduit, a way to communicate with their menfolk.

29. See the essays in Bloch (1975). I am not making the argument that Yemen is a traditional society (whatever that means), however. Moreover, these face-to-face encounters still qualify in Habermasian public sphere terms because many chews are open to a public and even when strangers are not present, people's discourses are addressed to a broad, anonymous non-face-to-face audience.

30. Weir's book, the most comprehensive discussion of qāt and its social implications to date, makes observations about the "qāt parties" that largely jibe with my own fieldwork experiences. Weir also notes that the host of a large chew may invite some guests to lunch

beforehand, or lunch may be hosted independently before a qāt chew. Lunches are also ways to manifest generosity and enhance prestige, and they prompt reciprocal invitations or favors from beneficiaries, which an everyday qāt chew does not. Guests at lunch are present because of their relationship with the host, and they may not know (or have an interest in knowing) each other. Conversations during lunch are brief and interaction limited. Food is consumed quickly and without extended socializing, so that guests can move on to the day's central activity, the qāt conversation. Other studies on qāt include a survey by Rodinson (1977); Serjeant (1983); Varisco (1986), and Gerholm (1977). In Arabic, see the articles in *al-Qāt fī ḥayāt al-Yaman wa al-Yamaniyyīn* (1981–82), 'Abbās Fāḍil al-Sa'dī (1983), and al-Sayyid Ayyūb (1963). The latter book is a polemic arguing that qāt is largely responsible for Yemeni "backwardness." It seems sometimes that qāt, in tandem with a corrupt, oppressive government, accounts for Yemen's poverty and the population's passivity, according to the author, and sometimes that qāt is responsible for the corrupt, oppressive government as well. The book was published one year after the 1962 revolution and so the author, whose analysis reproduces an Arab nationalist, avowedly modernist, teleological perspective, suggests that qāt is the key remaining impediment to progress in Yemen. Having researched the book before the revolution, however, the author has no explanation for how a population so beholden to qāt could effect a revolutionary transformation in the first place.

31. To some extent, views about the ways in which seating arrangements reproduce status hierarchies—or fail to do so—may relate to the region in which the ethnographic research was conducted (see Varisco 1986, 9). Varisco claims that, in general, "greater emphasis on social distinctions" is evident in urban contexts, while "rural interaction is more egalitarian."

32. Skeptics might contend that the drug interferes with rational discourse, but I saw no evidence to support such a claim, and nonchewers attend and converse with those chewing without appearing frustrated or suffering from out-of-the-ordinary miscommunication. Interestingly, in an eighteenth-century French dictionary compiled by a prolific commentator of the time, coffee was described in ways similar to descriptions of qāt today: "Coffee animates conversation, it holds back the vapors that rise to the brain, it warms in winter, it refreshes in summer, and it always has excellent qualities, up to the moment when one begins to be disgusted by it." The entry for the coffeehouse mirrors in some respects what might be a vivid description of the *maqyal*: "It is the meeting place for those who wish to be found, the center of gossip, the news bureau, the refuge of the lazy and the indigent" (Caraccioli 1768). The translation is by William H. Sewell Jr, and I thank him for bringing this passage to my attention.

33. Men sometimes complain of the pressures to conform by attending qāt chews (Weir 1985, 147). There are specifiable groups of Yemeni men who do not chew, however. Self-identified salafīs (those who claim to follow the ancestral practices of the Prophet and his companions) tend not to chew, although there are those who do. Some Western-educated Yemenis also identify chewing with "backwardness" and do not chew; some have even organized campaigns to dissuade people from consuming qāt. See, for example, the pamphlets published by al-'Afīf Cultural Center or the government's unsuccessful and ambivalent campaign to limit qāt chewing in October 1999. In the regions of Ḥaḍramawt and al-Mahra chewing is still considered crass, although inhabitants are increasingly engaging in the activity. One educated Ḥaḍramī estimated that about 30 percent of men now chew in al-Mukallā, for example (October 2002).

34. For those devotees of qāt who wanted to chew on other days, areas of the country, such as Saylat 'Aqlān in the province of Laḥj, were designated as "free zones," but only the wealthy could afford the extravagance. In regions where qāt was grown, such as al-Dāli' (on the border with North Yemen) and Yāfi' (also close to the border with the North) qāt was consumed by men on weekdays and also transported for sale to the North's Yemen Arab Republic. In Ḥaḍramawt and al-Mahra, qāt was not consumed at all. The socialist regime regulated the cultivation of qāt, monitored its entry into Aden, Abyan, and other parts of Laḥj during the week, and punished violators through the courts.

35. Weir estimates that qāt production at least doubled during the 1970s (86). She cites the 1979 World Bank country report on the Yemen Arab Republic, which notes that there is "ample evidence that qāt growing has increased rapidly in recent years (93; Weir 1985, 176). A USAID report (10), also cited by Weir, estimated that qāt production increased "two- to threefold" during the period of the Yemen government's first Five Year Plan (1976/77–1980/81). According to the International Monetary Fund's 2001 Country Report (No. 02/61), qāt chewing is a "widespread practice" (104). This IMF report cites a study from the 1960s that "found that in the city of Taiz about 60 percent of males and 35 percent of females were 'habitual chewers.'" The report notes that there is insufficient quantified data on contemporary qāt production and use, in part because of "official uneasiness with the importance of qāt in Yemeni society," but according to available information "consumption is in fact widely thought to have increased in recent years"; qāt cultivation is estimated to have increased by 10 percent between 1990 and 1995, redistributing wealth from the urban areas to the countryside (104). Approximately 170,000 families (i.e., one million people) benefit directly from the sale of qāt. The IMF's information on qāt is derived from interviews with officials and from an unpublished World Bank paper, derived from a Yemini Ministry of Agriculture and Irrigation report (Ward et al. 1998). An updated World Bank report (2007), whose aim is to reduce demand for qāt, notes that chewing has become a "nationwide habit." Approximately 72 percent of males and 33 percent of females report that they chew, and "more than half of those who chew do so each day of the week."

36. Murays is ten minutes by car from Damt, which was the central headquarters of the insurgent National Democratic Front in the 1970s.

37. In another qāt chew, a lawyer noted that although the regime may have gained new capacities to collect local taxes, the local councils have come to "epitomize taxation without representation."

38. This is the only message or qāt chew citation in English and it was crafted with the express purpose that I pass the letter on to members of the UN. All other quotes in this chapter are in Arabic, as I noted at the beginning, and the translations are my own. I have changed nothing about this message except to correct a few spelling errors.

39. I am indebted to Jessica Greenberg for this formulation. I would also like to thank Samera Esmeir for pressing me on this point.

40. For descriptions of the initial arrest and the subsequent trial proceedings, see *al-Ṣaḥwa*, March 13, 2004 and April 15, 2004; *Yemen Times*, March 15, 2004; Al-Jazeera.net, April 14, 2004. Indeed, a heated debate in the courtroom erupted when defense lawyers demanded that the court hold the intelligence officers accountable for "kidnapping" a member of the Yemeni Journalist Syndicate and for incarcerating him for two days.

41. The subsequent harassment of journalists and the syndicate's inability to intervene have diminished the optimism registered in this chew, but these conditions have not curtailed journalistic activism.

42. The vast majority of the 270 qāt chews I attended entailed political discussion, and at no time did I have the impression that such discussion was exceptional for regular participants. Although I realize that these gatherings do not constitute a random sample, my fieldwork does suggest that political debate at chews, far from being a rare event, is an integral part of many gatherings, and a choice available to both urban and rural Yemeni men.

43. This latter function, as Rosalind C. Morris has pointed out to me, is empirically demonstrable but not logically necessary.

44. The anthropologist Steve Caton (1990) shows how Khawlānī "tribal" poetry works in North Yemen to mediate disputes, highlight debates, and persuade constituents. The genre of *bāla* poetry, for example, is a competitive game in which poets, chorus, and audience participate in what might be thought of as a rhetorical joust. Oratorical talents are displayed and political positions communicated through poems constructed in public interactions. See also my chapter 1.

45. Thanks are owed to Matthew Kocher for this point. There is a vast anthropological literature on dispute settlements. Especially in linguistic anthropology, this literature concentrates primarily on small-scale conflict resolution. See, for example, Alessandro Duranti's oft-cited *From Grammar to Politics* (1994), which focuses on settling disputes in the "fono," the West Samoan village council where titled members of the community discuss political and legal concerns; Susan Hirsch's discussion of Kenyan Islamic courts on marriage and domestic issues in *Pronouncing and Persevering* (1998); and Gregory Matoesian's *Law and the Language of Identity* (2001), which deals with the William Kennedy Smith rape trial. I am indebted to Susan Gal and Michael Silverstein for introducing me to this literature. Importantly, however, my own work is less concerned with dispute settlement per se and more interested in the ways in which qāt chews instantiate and enable contestatory publics.

46. *al-Thawra*, September 27, 2002; see also *al-Thawra*, last page, September 28, 2002, which featured various Arabic media sources' excerpts from and brief commentaries on the speech. The editors noted that media throughout the Arab world were particularly interested in Ṣāliḥ's statement about the opposition parties, which was reproduced in the following newspapers: *al-Ra'y* (Qatar), *al-Bayān* (Dubai), *al-Ittiḥād* (United Arab Emirates), *al-Ra'y al-'Āmm* (Kuwait).

47. It is important to keep in mind that because statistical studies are concerned with the median, they have little to say about variants or outliers, such as, say, India or Singapore.

48. There is a large literature on the "rentier state." For a recent analysis of how oil, in particular, affects regime type, see Ross (2001).

49. In response to questions I posed about Canada, Australia, and Norway, Boix underscored that he did not mean to be arguing that natural resources alone determine regime type. According to Boix, "the effect of natural resources may be 'neutralized' if there are political institutions in place at the time those resources are discovered or exploited. If those institutions make the resources 'public' (i.e., widely shared among the public), then no private faction should arise with the tools to impose/maintain a dictatorship. So, the effect of natural

resources is a conditional one: it depends on the institutions in place" (e-mail correspondence, May 14, 2007).

50. For details on per capita income, see Abdulkarim I. Arhabi, "Poverty and Social Risk Management in Yemen," cited in the International Crisis Group's report, "Yemen: Coping with Terrorism and Violence in a Fragile State" (January 2003, 7). The figures on gross domestic product are from the United Nations Development Programme's *Human Development Report* (2004). For this report, the UN relies on statistics drawn from a variety of international organizations. The resulting figures are nevertheless quite similar to those provided by the government of Yemen. The ICG estimates 2000 per capita income at less than US$300; UNICEF estimates 2000 per capita Gross National Income at US$490. On population growth rates, figures differ: the Yemeni government estimates growth rates at 3.5 percent; the World Bank estimates at 2.7 percent.

51. The World Bank's figure may come from the *Poverty Reduction Strategy Paper* (PRSP), Republic of Yemen, May 2002, which estimates that 41.8 percent of the population lives in poverty, with 17.6 percent of the population unable even to meet basic food requirements.

52. Krämer's use of "indifference" in this context may seem curious because it is not to be expected that liberalism entails indifference to religion, although it would seem to require a degree of tolerance. My point here is that Yemenis, as a rule, are by no means indifferent to religion, and neither are they necessarily committed in principle to toleration, if by toleration we mean an attitude according equal value to divergent or heterodox religious views.

53. Char is cited in Pitkin (1998, 283).

CHAPTER FOUR

1. The number is a crude estimate reported in the *Yemen Times*, June 24, 2004. Even the date may be off. The ruling party's statement suggests that the government went into the mountains of Mārān on June 19, 2004. See *Bayān al-mu'tamar al-sha'bī* from al-Ṣaḥwa net, June 28, 2004.

2. Sarah Phillips, "Cracks in the Yemeni System," http://www.Merip.org/mero/mero072805.html; last accessed December 18, 2005. As Phillips points out, the figure is likely to be significantly higher than this, and does not include the number of rebels killed. Amnesty International reports that civilian targets have been attacked by "security forces reportedly [using] heavy weaponry, including helicopter gunships" (Amnesty International, "Yemen, Report 2005, Covering Events from January-December 2004," http://web.amnesty.org/report2005/yem-summar-eng; cited in Phillips). When I was in Yemen in September 2004, opposition members from both the YSP and al-Iṣlāḥ estimated that about three thousand people were killed. Sambanis (2004) points to the problems with acquiring accurate death count figures for large-N (large sample size) coding purposes.

3. Not all of these adherents were "youth." The term signifies in Yemen, as it does elsewhere, self-sacrificing idealism, innocence, willpower, and the prospect of a bright future. To the best of my knowledge, demographic data on Believing Youth was not available at the time of this writing.

4. Fearon and Laitin (2000) claim that arguments based on the importance of discourse can also end up being primordialist. Although this is unquestionably true, there is nothing about an enterprise that takes into account the importance of discourse or pursues "interpre-

tivist" social science that requires categories of groupness to be fixed in the way that counting "ethnic groups," for example, does.

5. Here I am indebted to Michel Foucault and Ludwig Wittgenstein, as well as to an essay by Arnold Davidson (2001) that seeks to bring these two philosophers' thoughts about concepts into conversation.

6. This argument also differs from Appadurai's observation (1996, 146) that many "racial, religious, and cultural fundamentalisms are deliberately fostered by various nation-states, or parties within them, in their efforts to suppress internal dissent, to construct homogeneous subjects of the state." Leaving aside whether such policies are intentional or not, I want to argue that group identifications can be encouraged with the effect of promoting, rather than suppressing, internal dissent, thereby shoring up the regime, perhaps at the expense of state institutions.

7. One of the most sophisticated accounts in this genre is Robert Jackson's *Quasi-States* (1990) which constructs third world sovereignty as a "problem" for international relations theory. I am grateful to David Scott (n.d.) for bringing this book to my attention and for his thoughtful critique of it. *Foreign Policy* and the Fund for Peace's July–August 2005 issue established a "failed states index" (FSI). It has subsequently updated that index in 2006 and 2007. In *Foreign Policy* and in *Foreign Affairs*, as well as among journalists such as Robert Kaplan, "failed states" are understood in relation to the security threat they pose to the United States. Although Patrick Chabal and Jean Pascal-Daloz in *Africa Works* (1999) make an argument that is in some ways compatible with mine, their broad focus on the continent of Africa and the absence of ethnographic and textual evidence, to name two differences, do not comport with my approach.

8. Ussama Makdisi's (2000) study of how the categories of Druze and Maronite worked to make possible sectarian violence in nineteenth-century Ottoman Lebanon is instructive here. Makdisi, unlike others who work on colonial divide-and-rule policies or who are influenced by Foucault's work, does not assume that ordinary Druze and Maronites necessarily believed in the primacy of their communal identities over others or were permanently constituted as Druze and Maronites. But whereas he establishes that a conceptual transformation, prompted by Ottoman reforms (the Tanẓīmāt) were key to making intercommunal violence thinkable, he cannot explain why violence actually occurred. I thank Rohit Goel for reminding me of this argument.

9. See Ellen Lust-Okar's *Structuring Conflict in the Arab World* (2005) for a discussion of how leaders manage opposition in Egypt, Morocco, and Jordan.

10. All from author's interviews and ethnographic work, September 2004. See note 14 for a description of Twelver Shīʿism.

11. As various scholars point out, worshippers in Arab countries often leave mosques reciting anti-American and anti-Israeli slogans without prompting a regime reaction of the sort generated here (Glosemeyer 2004; Phillips 2005).

12. See *Bayān al-mu'tamar al-shaʿbī*, published on al-Ṣaḥwa net, June 6, 2004. In some accounts, Ḥizb Allāh was mentioned by name, but Ḥizb Allāh has denied a relationship with al-Ḥūthī claiming that no one in Lebanon had heard of him. See Glosemeyer (2004); *Yemen Times* (June 28, 2004).

13. *Bayān al-mu'tamar al-shaʿbī.*

14. Approximately 80 percent of those who are classified or self-identify as Shīʿī are "twelvers" or *ithnāʿashariyya*, which means that they believe that there were twelve infallible imāms, beginning with the Prophet's son-in-law, ʿAlī ibn Abī Ṭālib, and ending with the twelfth or current imām who has gone into hiding by order of God and will reappear when God commands. They are the largest Shīʿī school and predominate in Iran, Lebanon, Iraq, Bahrain, and Azerbaijan. Zaydīs are occasionally referred to by Westerners as "fivers"; they recognize the first four *ithnāʿashariyya* imāms but identify Zayd ibn ʿAlī as the fifth and final imām, in contradistinction to twelvers who recognize his brother, Muḥammad al-Bāqir, as the fifth and then acknowledge six more. This doctrinal difference between Zaydīs and twelvers did not seem to matter in the context of the regime's assault on Believing Youth.

15. Quoted at http://www.newsyemen.net, May 7, 2005, *Risāla min al-Ḥūthī lil-Sīstānī: ta'thīr ḥarb bayānāt bayn ʿulamā' Ṣanʿā' wa Najaf*; last accessed May 6, 2005. The term "ʿunṣurī" can be translated as ethnic or racial, and in this context seems to express that this politics is prejudicial against Shīʿī Muslims.

16. See also the small Zaydī political party Ḥizb al-Ḥaqq's former endorsement of al-khurūj in its *Barāmij siyāsiyya* (n.d.), article 3. Cited in Dresch and Haykel (1995, 413).

17. *Al-Wasaṭ*, March 9, 2005; last accessed December 18, 2005.

18. Ibid. Also cited in Phillips (2005).

19. Mohammad bin Sallam, *Yemen Times*, June 28–30, 2004, http://yementimes.com/article.shtml?i=750&p=front&a=1; last accessed September 14, 2007. I have kept the transliterations as is, since this is an English-language paper.

20. The assumption of a strict separation between piety and politics also characterizes the literature on "political Islam" (e.g., Kepel 1993; Roy 1996, 2004), which tends to treat Islamic activism as a problem to be addressed.

21. Analyses of Islamic activism *have* begun to retreat from the Islamist/non-Islamist or Islamist/Muslim distinction, favoring instead categories such as "jihādī," traditionalists, modernizers, and so forth. Despite weaknesses in some of these terminological alternatives, such efforts all point to the problematic implications of the Islamist/Muslim divide. See, for example, Salwa Ismail (2003); Sami Zubaida (2005); and the International Crisis Group report on Jordan (2005) in which the distinction drawn is not between Islamists and ordinary Muslims but between types of Islamic activists, traditionalists (*taqlīdī*), reformers (*iṣlāḥī*), and violent militants (*jihādī*): (http://www.crisigroup.org/home/index.cfm?id+3801&I=1, 5). The problem with all of these formulations is that they still take as self-evident clear membership in these groups or categories. Mobilized people do not necessarily equate to "members."

22. The other political party whose actual members are primarily Zaydī sayyids, Ittiḥād al-Quwwa al-Shaʿbiyya, while defending al-Ḥūthī's right to free expression, tends to be less interested in doctrinal issues and more intent on establishing a liberal, democratic republic and of protecting Zaydī sayyids from discrimination. I have chosen to refer to Believing Youth in English while using the Arabic names of the al-Ḥaqq and al-Iṣlāḥ because the latter are generally referred to by their Arabic names when speaking and writing in English, whereas Shabāb al-Mu'minīn is almost always translated.

23. ʿIzzān (1994, 89). Cited in Haykel (1999, 198).

24. *Yemen Times*, July 1, 1992, cited in Dresch and Haykel (1995, 412). Also cited in Haykel (1999, 198).

25. Jillian Schwedler documents al-Iṣlāḥ's changing relations with the regime after the defeat of the YSP in the civil war of 1994 in *Faith in Moderation* (2006).

26. Dresch and Haykel (1995, 413). They are quoting from *Mu'tamar al-waḥda wa al-salām: al-qarārāt wa al-tawṣiyāt* (1993, 4–5). I have changed the translation ever so slightly to conform to grammatical conventions.

27. Part of the reason for this hostility is historical, as the first chapter suggested. Since the eighteenth century Yemen has become, in many ways, more oriented toward Sunnī doctrinal teachings—no longer fulfilling the rigorous qualifications stipulated by Zaydī law and instead permitting sons to succeed their fathers regardless of aptitude (Haykel 1999, 2003). By the mid-eighteenth century, Zaydī leaders were actively patronizing Sunnī traditionist scholars who helped justify the imām's increasingly dynastic rule and to vilify those who supported rebellion against a ruler. The republican leadership of 1962, which was socially and intellectually varied, pursued aspects of this traditionist approach, condemning the imamate and criticizing sayyid practices that prohibit sayyid women from marrying nonsayyid men (Haykel 1999, 195).

28. In this sense, al-Iṣlāḥ is more like an American political party than like narrowly based European ones.

29. In regional terms, in the aftermath of unification al-Iṣlāḥ had a particularly "radical edge in the south insofar as it opposed the YSP and a conservative aspect in the North insofar as it differed little from the [ruling] GPC" (Dresch and Haykel 1995, 407). Its constituency continues to be largely from the North, but the party also enjoys some support particularly in poor areas of the former South Yemen.

30. Interview, September 18, 2004. The two passages he cited from the textbook are: (1) "The second category: involves issues like the matter of the dream vision (*al-ru'yā*), the creation of actions, the creation of the Qur'ān, intercession (*al-shafā'a*), and the coming out of Hell-fire or spending eternity in it. Judgment in these issues is similar to that of the first category, except that the perpetrator is a mistaken sinner and innovator (*mukhṭi' āthim mubtadi'*), while some call him an unbeliever in interpretation (*kāfir ta'wīl*). It has been narrated from Abū al-Ḥasan 'Abd Allāh al-Ghabrī that scholars (*al-mujtahidīn*) of *uṣūl* (of the foundations of Islamic Jurisprudence) from this *qibla* [in other words, those who pray toward the Ka'ba or are practicing Muslims] are all correct. But he has been criticized by many scholars (*'ulamā'*). It is reported from al-Jāḥiẓ the opinion that the scholar (*mujtahid*) does not incur any sin even if his opinion (*ijtihād*) leads to the negation of Islam (*nafy al-Islām*)" (75). (2) "Inquiry over his moral and religious rectitude (*'adāla*). For, if he is openly debauched (*fāsiq*)—such as having committed a grave sin (*al-kabā'ir*), or insisting on committing small sins (*al-ṣaghā'ir*), or similar things which slander rectitude (*qawādiḥ al-'adāla*)—or if he is unsound of doctrine (*mukhtall al-'aqīda*)—such as being a corporealist (*mujassim*), or anthropomorphist (*mushabbih*), or a transgressor against a just *imām*—then he is not suited to be followed (*lil-taqlīd*), and it is not permissible for the follower (*lil-muqallid*) to follow him (*an yuqallidah*)" (100). I thank Aram Shahin for help in translating these passages. Another party member later provided clarification (e-mail correspondence, January 2005): "'Unbelievers in interpretation' is a technical term among jurists—men of Islamic faith—to distinguish between unbelievers who disavow Islam in principle and those who oppose rules of jurists in some matters only." The latter group is less disparaged because they only differ

in matters of interpreting judgments or verses in the Qur'ān, for example, but usually such phrases are invoked by governments in order to "oppress the opposition." See also Bernard Haykel's *Revival and Reform* (2003).

31. Interviews, September 2004.

32. This finding jibes with those offered by scholars who study race in the U.S. context, beginning with St. Clair Drake (1966). See also Wilson (1980); Dawson (1994, 2001); Bobo et al. (1994, 103–33; 2001, 262–99), and Cohen (1999).

33. See also Ramadan (2003, 51–52).

34. al-Wādi'ī (1982, 75).

35. The text, *Limādhā ikhtarnā al-manhaj al-salafī* (Why have we chosen the salafī method?), was drawn to my attention by Burgat and Sbitli (2002), 128. But his name is misidentified as al-Shaqra rather than 'Abd al-Ḥalīm Abū Shaqqa. Both *Limādhā ikhtarnā al-manhaj al-salafī* and the subsequent *Limādhā ikhtartu al-manhaj al-salafī*? (Why have I chosen the salafī method?) are authored by Salīm bin 'Īd al-Hilālī (of Saudi origin). The translations of these passages are my own, not Burgat and Sbitli's, and I am relying on the later text (2001, 37).

36. The reference to low-status butcher families connotes an occupational caste within Yemen.

37. According to rumors, this relationship may be a fictive one. Whatever the case, the president has relied on 'Alī Muḥsin to squelch rebellions (as commander of the 1st Armored Brigade and as commander of the eastern region), and he does seem to be from the president's village.

38. For a comprehensive list, see Haykel (2002, 30).

39. The first key indication of dissension came when a former well-known student of Muqbil's, 'Aqīl al-Maqṭarī (based in the Lower Yemen city of Ta'izz) broke from his teacher. Maqṭarī thereby earned the unfortunate label of "surūrī," a deviant innovator who is worse than others because he knew the truth while still a participant in the movement (see Haykel 2002, 31). Muqbil also divided his leadership into two parts before he died, naming Muḥammad bin 'Abd al-Wahhāb al-Waṣābī to be "supreme leader of the movement," while the teacher center at Dammāj was to be run by another student, Yaḥyā bin 'Alī al-Ḥajūrī.

40. Zaydī sayyids, in particular, as the former ruling elite and the key target of the revolution in the North, report that they experience stigmatization (vom Bruck 2004), although there are some who are prominent politicians and intellectuals.

41. This signaling is especially true for men who pray in mosques. Women pray at home and their habits are not as open to public scrutiny, although they do transmit gendered and pious norms of propriety to their children.

42. See also Engseng Ho's account (2006) of an influential Ḥaḍramī teacher whom Ho describes as being of tribal origin. As a boy, the teacher was refused admittance to a class in a local mosque by a sayyid teacher who allegedly said, "No, why don't you just take some bullets and a gun and go shoot and kill? *Harām* [it is forbidden] for a tribal to study" (317). The rebuffed boy later studied abroad (in Singapore and Saudi Arabia) and returned to open up a successful school in 1960; he has worked there ever since. Ho notes the parallels between this teacher and the famous al-Wādi'ī: both encountered prejudice from the local religious establishment early on because of "social origin," and both stories involved "subsequent ac-

cess to education abroad, trouble with authorities, return and establishment of a permanent educational mission under tribal protection at home, gradual expansion of antiestablishment religious ideas, and social influence through students" (318).

43. See, for example, Crone (1986).

44. See esp. Shelagh Weir's impressive *A Tribal Order: Politics and Law in the Mountains of Yemen* (2007). I would also like to thank Sheila Carapico for her guidance in thinking through what "tribe" and "tribal" mean. In addition to the sources cited in the text, the following account of tribal politics comes from my field research as well as from the following sources: Carapico (1998); Dresch (2000); and Abū Ghānim (1985). For a discussion of tribal identifications relevant to this conflict, see Weir (1986, 225–39), and Weir (1991, 87–101). Whereas Dresch's fieldwork was primarily in the Khamir-'Amrān region, others focused on the mountains and discussed local specificities there. See Tutwiler (1987); Meissner (1987); Mundy (1995); Adra (1982); and Varisco and Adra (1984). Other informative works include Stevenson (1985) and Caton (1990).

45. Inhabitants of these areas (e.g., in the provinces of Ibb and Ta'izz) do have nontribal categories for sharecroppers, classifications that tend to be class defined (Carapico and Tutwiler 1981).

46. Mā anā qabīlī aḥad, wa lā aḥad dawlatī, mā dawlatī illā mā mala', kaffī qurūsh.

47. International Crisis Group (2003).

48. UNDP (2002).

49. This evidence is from my fieldwork but comports with Dresch (2000, 197).

50. For an explicit discussion of racial identifications in the American context, see Dawson (1994).

51. See Young (1976); Horowitz (1985); Abu El-Haj (2001); Anderson (1991); Comaroff and Comaroff (2001); Mamdani (1996); Appadurai (1996); Dirks (1992); Jackson (1999); Suny (1993); Stoler (2002); Povinelli (2002); Goswami (2004); Brubaker (2004).

52. The term "governmentality" is, of course, Michel Foucault's (1991). As he enumerates, "governmentality" means: (1) "The ensemble formed by the institutions, procedures, analyses, and reflections, the calculations and tactics that allow the exercise of this very specific albeit complex form of power, which has as its target population, as its principal form of knowledge political economy, and as its essential technical means apparatuses of security." (2) "The tendency which, over a long period and throughout the West, has steadily led towards the pre-eminence over all other forms (sovereignty, discipline, etc.) of this type of power which may be termed government, resulting, on the one hand, in the formation of a whole series of specific governmental apparatuses, and, on the other, in the development of a whole complex of *savoirs* [knowledge]." (3) "The process, or rather the result of the process, through which the state of justice of the Middle Ages, transformed into the administrative state during the fifteenth and sixteenth centuries, gradually becomes 'governmentalized.'" See pages 102–3. Discussions of governmentality in non-Western contexts include Chatterjee (1995); Hansen (1999); Mitchell (1991); Scott (1999).

53. I am grateful to Dan Slater for discussions on this issue. I have in mind the literature on "failed states," as well as the provocative book by Jeffrey Herbst, *States and Power in Africa* (2000), which presumes that regimes benefit from "projecting power" over "inhospitable areas."

54. In mainstream comparative politics, Daniel Posner's work (2005) jibes particularly well with constructivist impulses to the extent that he poses a critical question previously taken for granted by others. Drawing on his work in Zambia, he asks: Why do some ethnic identities become politically salient while others do not? Given that individuals operate within contexts that allow for potentially multiple ethnic group memberships, he also asks: "Which coalition should a political actor interested in gaining access to state resources seek to mobilize or join?" (4).

55. A telling example comes from those who maintain the Minorities At Risk (MAR) data set at the University of Maryland. According to Jillian Schwedler, MAR receives a handful of letters every year from "minorities" asking to be included, precisely because the recognition in such a prestigious and widely used data set lends credibility and gives authority to claims of group membership. Those who make such claims are not uniformly effective in mobilizing feelings of groupness or in convincing MAR scholars of a particular organization's claims. As Schwedler put it to me, some spokesmen have "greater resources in 'selling' their categories in the marketplace." For a discussion of the commodification of group affiliations, see John and Jean Comaroff's *Ethnicity, Inc.* (in preparation). This issue will receive further attention in chapter 5. I am not making the claim that the state necessarily has more resources to "market" its categories of groupness, or that one need appeal specifically to its institutions for "recognition" as some of the literature inspired by Hegel and by multicultural claims suggests. I am contending that in the absence of robust state institutions, regimes may animate existing categories in ways that serve its strategies of rule, and that divide-and-rule policies necessarily presuppose an understanding of and a willingness to cultivate experiences of group affiliation.

56. See also Brubaker and Laitin's review essay, "Ethnic and Nationalist Violence," in Brubaker (2004, 88–115).

57. See Fearon and Laitin (2000) for an insightful review of this literature.

58. Elisabeth Wood's (2003) discussion of support for insurgents in El Salvador jibes well with this account in the sense that it challenges conventional understandings of participation that privilege instrumental concerns at the expense of considering moral and emotional commitments. Wood argues that appreciation for the process of participation itself (240), defiance against a repressive state apparatus (234), and the "pleasure of agency" (236) explain civilian participation in El Salvador's risky insurgency. Wood's analysis, however, relies on a problematic notion of intention, which she interprets from the statements of her interviewees in the post–civil war period. As Hanna Pitkin notes in her critique of Peter Winch, who, like Wood, argues that action can only be explained in terms of the declared intention of the actor, social scientists must explain action through an analysis of an actor's stated intention for acting *and* the observable consequences of her action. This is what I mean, following Pitkin, in understanding practices as "dual," composed of what the observer can see and of the actors' understandings of what they are doing (Pitkin 1993, 261; Wedeen 2002 and the introduction to this book). For a particularly sophisticated critique of intention as a way of understanding action, see Elizabeth Anscombe's *Intention* (2000).

59. Please note that I use moral and ethical synonymously throughout this book.

60. Although per capita GDP seems to be a good predictor of violence, the explanations for this correlation diverge. Fearon and Laitin (2003) use GDP as a proxy for state capacity

(financial and bureaucratic strength), claiming that weak states are unable to police insurgent groups adequately. Weak states, according to this view, tend to employ less costly indiscriminate violence against civilians who, as a result, support insurgent groups. Weak states are unable to establish infrastructures (such as roads, transportation, and communication lines) that make it more difficult for insurgents to hide. Jacqueline Stevens (2007) points out that although the authors provide data demonstrating a correlation between GDP and lagged conflict, they do not provide evidence that GDP correlates with low levels of police and military spending. Nor do they show that low levels of police and military spending are good predictors of civil war (5). Stevens argues that expenditure of GDP on the military has different effects on recruitment in high- and low-income countries. Variation and lack of correlation mean that GDP is not a good proxy for military and police budgets. (High-income countries spend about 40 percent less of their GDP on the military than low-income countries do, but they have about 20 to 30 percent more military personnel, as a proportion of the labor force [2007, 15].) Fearon and Laitin's understanding of weak state capacity includes not only actual police and military spending, however, but also infrastructural spending crucial to preventing insurgency. In Yemen, according to the *CIA Factbook*'s last assessment of the matter in 2005, there are only 6,200 kilometers of paved road out of a total of 71,300 kilometers of road. See also Nicholas Sambanis's critique of current coding criteria in the political science civil wars literature (Sambanis 2004). Whereas Fearon and Laitin concentrate on a state's policing capacities, Collier and Hoeffler (2004) argue that poverty explains civil war because it creates opportunities for rebel recruitment. Given either story, Yemen would seem to be particularly vulnerable to such internal strife, and it has been historically. (Another robust predictor of civil wars is prior civil wars.) As I argue in the text, however, in poor states with weak infrastructural services and an inability to "monopolize" violence, it may be when states attempt to seize more complete control than they have previously enjoyed that violence intensifies, sometimes reaching "civil war" proportions.

CHAPTER FIVE

1. For a discussion of satellite television's impact on public debate in the Middle East, see Eickelman and Anderson (1999); Lynch (2006).

2. The phrase "politics of piety" is from Saba Mahmood's book of the same name.

3. For example, in Latin America, the imposition of macroeconomic stabilization policies seems to have benefited the poor, who had experienced a dramatic erosion of their meager salaries and savings during the hyperinflation crisis of the 1980s. The literature on neoliberalism and on the related phenomenon of globalization is simply too vast to do it justice here. What is intriguing, however, is that important work in history, anthropology, sociology, geography, and cultural studies, on the one hand, does not seem to converse with seminal studies in political science and economics, on the other. Most of the work in the former category tends to be critical, which may be one reason why there are so few conversations. For a summary of works about neoliberalism in anthropology, see Peet (2002, 62–66). Much of the literature on globalization and neoliberalism overlaps or discusses similar phenomena, such as the growth of international trade, the proliferation of financial flows and instruments (Sassen 2001), and the integration of nation-states previously understood as more autonomous or bounded. In sorting out these arguments, helpful studies include Gilpin (2000) and Harvey

(2005). On labor, see Golden and Wallerstein (2006). Eric Hobsbawm's *The Age of Extremes* (1994) permitted me to grasp the importance of the breakdown of Bretton Woods in the 1970s; for an impassioned account of the flaws in "Washington consensus" thinking from a World Bank insider, see Joseph E. Stiglitz's *Globalization and Its Discontents* (2002). Gérard Roland's discussion of privatization provides a helpful overview of the dramatic shift in institutions in eastern Europe and the former Soviet Union, describing the welfare consequences of public assets sales in *Transition and Economics: Politics, Markets, and Firms* (2000). Jonas Pontusson's *Inequality and Prosperity: Social Europe vs. Liberal America* (2005) provides a summary from a social democrat's perspective. I am grateful to Carles Boix for helping me navigate this rich literature.

4. See Al-Naqeeb (1991); Beinin and Stork (1997); Berman (2003); Chaudhry (1997); Hamzeh (2004); Henry and Springborg (2001); Kepel (2002); Medani (1997); Munson (2001); Sadowski (1987); Singerman (1995); Vitalis (1997); Wedeen (2003a); White (2002); Wickham (1997, 2002); Wiktorowicz (2004); Yamani (2002). For an alternative view, see Clark (2004). Clark argues that this claim about the provision of social services does not hold up under empirical scrutiny. In Cairo, many of the celebrated Islamic health clinics do not actually function (doctors do not show up) though the narrative is that the Muslim Brotherhood provides health services to poor Cairenes. Islamic groups do seem particularly good at providing emergency services, but it remains a question how well they operate on a more routine basis. For a discussion of services provided by the main Yemeni Islamic party, al-Iṣlāḥ, see the body of this text. As Melani Cammett has suggested in unpublished papers, it is important to begin considering whether different kinds of services might also generate varied levels of loyalty, or whether service provision is doing the work of cultivating allegiance at all. Poor people are likely to accept services from anyone offering them, but that does not mean that beneficiaries experience receipt of services uniformly. This first section is a fundamentally revised version of Wedeen (2003a).

5. During the brief oil boom from the late 1970s to the mid-1980s in Egypt, the income of the poor seems to have improved and the gap between low- and middle-income families may have narrowed, but the wealthiest 5 percent increased their income share between the years 1974–75 and 1981–82 from 22 percent to 25 percent in the case of rural households and to 29 percent in the case of urban ones (Mitchell 2002a, 214). Importantly, Mitchell's work does not make the sorts of causal claims I attribute to authors in note 4.

6. In *The Rule of Experts: Political Economies of Postcolonialism* (2002a), Timothy Mitchell demonstrates that grain imports were a result of an increased consumption of meat. Increasing wealth, together with growing numbers of resident foreigners and tourists, led to a large increase in the demand for meat and other products (214–15). A household survey in 1981–82 revealed that "the richest 25 percent consumed more than three times as much chicken and beef as the poorest 25 percent" (215). Greater demand for red meat required a large and costly diversion of staple food supplies from human to animal consumption. According to Mitchell, it was this switch to meat consumption, rather than a growth in population, that required the dramatic increase in imports of food, particularly grain. Between 1966 and 1988, the population of Egypt grew by 75 percent. In the same period, the domestic production of grains increased by 77 percent, but total grain consumption increased by 148 percent, or almost twice the rate of population increase (215). For Mitchell the point is that population growth actually lagged behind the growth of domestic grain production in Egypt

but that development agencies were so intent on reducing population that they neglected other political solutions.

7. Geneive Abdo (2000) suggests that what distinguishes the past from current revivals is the fact that "Islamic thought in the late 1880s, and again in the 1940s and 1950s, focused on anti-imperialist sentiment and socio-economic concerns while the contemporary Islamic fervor emphasizes family values, traditional sexual mores, and cultural authenticity" (8). But this distinction is overdrawn. Current movements also invoke anti-imperialist and socioeconomic concerns, and previous Islamic theorists also advocated conventional sexual values and championed cultural authenticity.

8. Such attitudes find expression in numerous fieldwork accounts, including my own, as well as in survey research. In Turkey, for example, Ziya Onis (2004) argues that key segments of the electorate identified a candidate "as an agent of the IMF" (117) because he had support from the transnational financial community and had previously worked at the World Bank; he was therefore unable to appeal to a broad-based constituency.

9. Interviews with Yemeni Socialist Party leaders, September and October 2001; see also the interview with Ṭāriq al-Faḍlī in *al-Quds al-'Arabī*, November 10, 2001, reprinted in the YSP's weekly *al-Thawrī*, January 3, 2002. Al-Faḍlī was a well-known Yemeni Islamic Jihād movement leader who joined the ruling General People's Congress party in the mid-1990s.

10. International Crisis Group (2003, 11).

11. Ṭāriq al-Faḍlī discusses his past ties to Usāma bin Lādin in *al-Quds al-'Arabī*, November 10, 2001, reprinted in the Yemeni Socialist Party's weekly, *al-Thawrī*, January 3, 2002.

12. Sādāt found tactical allies among the Muslim Brotherhood and among the newly growing radical Islamic movements in the universities. He released imprisoned Muslim Brothers in 1972–73, and encouraged them to attack leftists, whom he regarded as his major political adversary (Waterbury 1983; Sadowski 1987). As Timothy Mitchell points out (2002b), this alliance with the Muslim Brotherhood was indirectly supported by the U.S. government, and it was also used to repress at times more militant Islamic opposition.

13. As Timothy Mitchell notes (2002b), the shah drew on a CIA-funded clerical leadership to overthrow the nationalist government in Iran in 1953; in Saudi Arabia, the *muwaḥḥidīn* (those who insist on the oneness of God, or Unitarians, called "wahhābīs" by many Westerners) were a pivotal social force that helped build the Saudi state, and hence facilitated the running of the American oil industry (see Vitalis 2002). Mitchell notes, pace Barber (1996), that although U.S. foreign policy has indeed been hobbled by contradictions, inconsistencies, and shortsightedness, the crisis in Afghanistan (to take one powerful example) underscores specific weaknesses in this form of imperial capitalism: it "can only exist by drawing on social forces [such as the *mujāhidīn* or the *muwaḥḥidīn*] that embody other energies, methods, and goals" (4). On U.S. involvement in Afghanistan, see also Gates (1996); Cooley (2000); and Rubin (2002).The point to be made here too, as the Iranian and Saudi example bring to the fore, is that there are important antecedents for U.S. support of religious movements in the 1970s.

14. Such attempts have important antecedents in colonial administrations. In Elizabeth Povinelli's (2002) study of northwest aborigines of Australia, for example, she argues that multiculturalism is a legacy of the colonial period, which has helped to maintain unequal, hierarchical systems of power, requiring aboriginal subjects to identify with an impossible standard of "traditional" indigenous culture in order to be legally recognized.

15. See also Eickelman (1997).

16. See the statement of Christiaan Poortman, vice president for the Middle East and North Africa Region, December 12, 2005, discussed in the *Yemen Times* (December 12, 2003). The World Bank announced that it would decrease its subsidies by 34 percent, with the $420 million assistance reduced to $280 million in the next three years (last accessed December 18, 2005). The announcement registered the Bank's frustration with the regime's inability or unwillingness to fight corruption. Poortman argued "the poor should receive more subsidies in order to make progress." According to the *Yemen Times*, only 15 percent of oil derived subsidies go to the poor; 85 percent go to those "who are not poor." (Note: In Yemen, there is no local chapter of Transparency International, a global civil society organization that monitors corruption.) In a Bank document of 2004, the Bank's analysts were a bit more circumspect. The report states: "On the one hand, the literature points to deteriorating living standards over the 1990s due to the Gulf War of 1991, the return of labor migrants, the civil war of 1994, and the falling of real public sector wages. On the other hand, some evidence also suggests that capita incomes and human development indicators have risen over the past decade." Most of the literature suggests that Yemen is not only becoming more unequal but poorer, despite rises in GDP. Marta Colburn argues that poverty levels doubled between 1992 and 1998 in *The Republic of Yemen, Development Challenges in the 21st Century* (2002, 54). Paul Dresch also claims that Yemen has been getting steadily poorer over the last two decades in *A History of Modern Yemen* (2000, 186).

17. As noted in chapter 1, the South's PDRY was initially named the People's Republic of South Yemen, but the name was changed in 1970.

18. James Ferguson (1994) notes how reports generated by the World Bank help produce Lesotho as a least developed country or LDC, which then implies a certain set of characteristics, needs, and interventions (see also Mitchell 1991, 2002a).

19. According to the Republic of Yemen's *Poverty Reduction Strategy Paper* (2002), the proportion of the population defined as poor continues to vary significantly among governorates, with the highest incidences of poverty in the former North's Ta'izz (56 percent) and Ibb (55 percent), as well as in the former South's Abyan (53 percent) and Laḥj (52 percent). These statistics suggest that however important commitments to state-centered social reform and economic equality were in the PDRY, and however lax the state may have been in this regard in the North, citizens' experiences of state institutions varied markedly within the delimitations of both nation-states.

20. These *ma'āhid 'ilmiyya* or religious institutes received funding from the Yemeni regime as well, and by 1996 there were approximately four hundred at the secondary level with overall student enrollment estimated at 330,000. Of these pupils 12,600 were training to be teachers (Dresch 2000, 200). The regime has gradually made efforts to incorporate these schools into the state education system, but the effects remain uneven.

21. See UNDP (2002); Van Hear (1994).

22. For a discussion of racial discrimination in Yemen, see Seif (2003, 2005); or the earlier work of Delores Waters, "Perceptions of Social Inequality in Yemen" (1987). Engseng Ho's discussion of the category of the "muwalladīn" (1997, 2006) in the Ḥaḍramawt is also worth noting in this light.

23. The Saudi intellectual tradition of *tawḥīd* is sometimes called "Wahhābism," especially by foreigners or by Muslims (such as Ḥizb al-Ḥaqq's leader in Yemen) who use the

label as an insult. The term refers to the eighteenth-century thinker Muḥammad ibn ʿAbd al-Wahhāb.

24. In this case, Dutch government and nongovernmental British programs were involved.

25. The loss of remittances may amount to about $400 million annually, with consequences for local development projects previously funded by labor migrants. See Van Hear (1994). See also Colton (1991). For a discussion of the diminishing possibilities for labor migration in Yemen, see Ho (1999).

26. Women in the village of Kuhhāl, a former center of leftist guerrilla resistance, claimed that they had taken to wearing the *niqāb* (or cloth covering all but the eyes) and the black *bālṭū* (outer coat) because the Iṣlāḥ party provided this clothing for free; they could look fashionable and modest like their city counterparts, while also protecting their skin from the brutal effects of the sun (October 2002).

27. Allegations that his brief imprisonment was used by members of the security forces to "turn" al-Saʿwānī into the assassin of the late YSP leader Jār Allāh ʿUmar are widespread.

28. "Praise be to God! We praise Him, ask for His aid and for His forgiveness. We seek refuge in God from the evil of ourselves and the wickedness of our deeds. Whomever God guides, no one can lead him astray. Whoever goes astray, no one can guide him to the right path. I bear witness that there is no god but God, alone, who has no associate. And I bear witness that Muḥammad is His servant and messenger, may God's prayers and peace be upon him and upon his family, companions, wives, and descendants."

{Mankind, fear your Lord, who created you from a single soul, and from it created its mate, and through them He bestrewed the earth with countless men and women; and fear God, in whose name you plead with one another, and honor the mothers who bore you. God is ever watching over you} (Sūrat al-Nisāʾ 4:1).

{O believers, fear God as He should be feared, and do not die except as Muslims} (Sūrat Āl ʿImrān 3:102).

{O believers, fear God, and speak appropriate words. He will set right your deeds for you and will forgive your sins. Whosoever obeys God and His Messenger has won a mighty victory} (Sūrat al-Aḥzāb 33:70–71).

29. Al-Saʿwānī specifically cites a media whose commitments to sensationalist stories subvert its moral authority. And he worries too about women with "dyed hair" who undermine proper modes of gendered propriety.

30. The U.S. Baptist doctors at Jibla who were shot to death two days after Jār Allāh ʿUmar by ʿAlī al-Saʿwānī's confederate are accused here of putting Qurʾāns in the toilet, as are Christian missionaries in Ibb: "It is appropriate to mention to you that more than a year ago the people of Ibb entered the toilets belonging to some mosque and discovered copies of the Qurʾān in them, exactly in the same fashion as it occurred in Jibla a few years ago. The state definitely knows more than this, and knows greater matters than this. For who opened the path for the Christians other than the state?" The state encourages Christians' access to vulnerable Muslims. But Yemen is also imperiled by other enemies from within, particularly by secularists: "Religious scholars have asked the secularists to repent before God and to repudiate every thought that goes against Islam and contradicts it. And on a pulpit similar to this one I have heard the Shaykh al-Zindānī demanding this from the secularists, and

taking as reference the words of God: {If they repent, and perform the prayer, and pay the alms-tax, then they are your brothers in religion. Thus we make plain the signs for people of understanding}" (Sūrat al-Tawba 9:11). Al-Sa'wānī then connects secularism to members of the Yemeni Socialist Party in particular: "In the midst of these accusations and uttered criticisms against this noble shaykh and against other scholars, in the midst of these accusations and criticisms the current secretary general of the Yemeni Socialist Party, 'Alī Muqbil 'Ubād, declared at a press conference more than a year ago during the conference of the Socialist Party: 'We adhere to secularism.' And a colloquium was held during the party's fourth general conference at the Center for the Study of the Future with the title 'The Future of the Socialist Party.' And at this colloquium, the secretary of the central committee, Jār Allāh 'Umar, said openly and with insolence: 'We are not convinced by Islamic law, and we will not please people in this matter. We do not want a religious state. Our problem is with the earth and not with heaven.'" (All from al-Sa'wānī's audiocassette.)

31. There are a plethora of anthropological studies on audiocassettes, including Bull (2000); Greene (1999); Manuel (1993); Qureshi (1995); Rogers (1986). For other works dealing explicitly with Islamic sermons in the Middle East, see Gaffney (1991) and Antoun (1989). I am grateful to Charles Hirschkind for this list.

32. Most of these tapes concern the ethical obligations and proper behavior of Muslims. Some of the most popular ones in the early 2000s in Ṣan'ā' were the following: 'Alī, 'Abd Allāh Aḥmad, "al-'Ashr al-Wājibāt lil-Fard al-Muslim"; 'Alī, 'Abd Allāh Aḥmad, "al-Thabāt 'alā al-Mabādi'"; al-Ānisī, Muḥammad, "al-Tanṣīr fī al-Yaman"; al-Ānisī, Muḥammad, "Sakarāt al-Mawt"; al-Ānisī, Muḥammad, "al-Taskhīr wa al-Tadhlīl"; al-Duwaysh, Muḥammad, "Akhṭā'inā [*sic*] fī Mu'ālajat al-Akhṭā'"; al-Duwaysh, Muḥammad, "Kayfa Nata'āmal ma' Ma'āsī al-Muslimīn?"; al-Duwaysh, Muḥammad, "Fann al-Taharrub min al-Mas'ūliyya"; al-Ḥazmī, Muḥammad bin Nāṣir, "Layl al-Ẓālimīn"; al-Ḥazmī, Muḥammad bin Nāṣir, "al-Ṭūfān al-Mudammir"; Kishk, "Mumayyizāt al-'Ālam al-'Āmil"; Kishk, "al-Qulūb Thalāthat Aqsām"; Kishk, "al-Ṣidq wa al-Kidhb"; al-Miswarī, Hazzā', "Risāla 'Ājila ilā Ḥukkām al-'Arab al-Mutakhādhila"; al-Miswarī, Hazzā', "Inna lil-Muttaqīna Mafāzan"; al-Miswarī, Hazzā', "Lā Ḥayā bi-dūn Īmān"; al-Qaranī, 'Ā'iḍ, "Lā Taḥzan"; al-Qaranī, 'Ā'iḍ, "Man Yaṣna' Majd al-Umma"; al-Qaranī, 'Ā'iḍ, "al-Ṭarīq ilā Allāh"; al-Qaṭṭān, "Ahammiyyat al-Istighfār"; al-Qaṭṭān, "al-Farāgh al-Rūḥī"; al-Qaṭṭān, Aḥmad, "al-Mawt wa 'Adhāb al-Qabr"; Ṣa'tar, "An Urīd lā [*sic*] al-Iṣlāḥ"; Ṣa'tar, "al-'Aqliyya al-Jāhiliyya"; Ṣa'tar, "Quwwat al-'Adl lā 'Adl lil-Quwwa"; al-Zindānī, 'Abd al-Majīd, "al-'Asal wa Āthāruh 'alā al-Amrāḍ"; al-Zindānī, 'Abd al-Majīd, "Sharī'a li-Kull Zamān"; al-Zindānī, 'Abd al-Majīd, "al-Īmān bil-Yawm al-Ākhir." Note: most of these preachers are Yemenis, but Kishk is a well-known Egyptian preacher whose tapes circulate widely throughout the Middle East and al-Duwaysh is from Saudi Arabia. The tapes of the salafī preacher Ibn Bāz (from Saudi Arabia) also seem to be popular; his sermons can be heard in urban Yemeni households (in both the capital and in Aden). I am grateful to Aram Shahin for his help in translating these tapes.

33. As noted earlier, this is Brubaker and Cooper's distinction (2000), one inspired by Bourdieu.

34. The sermon, "Khuṭbat 'Īd al-Aḍḥā," then goes on to blame the Americans and "the Jews," which in the context of the tape sometimes refers to a religious group (as opposed to Christians or Muslims), sometimes to global financiers, and sometimes to the state of

Israel's efforts to establish a "Greater Israel." Al-Zindānī may be a popular preacher especially among the urban poor, but he tends to be an embarrassment to leaders of the mainstream Islamic party, al-Iṣlāḥ. He is particularly well known for his sermons on science that focus on science's compatibilities with Islam.

35. On the one hand, leftist intellectuals generally depict systematic welfare retrenchment. On the other hand, some scholars argue that empirical evidence suggests otherwise, with considerable expansion until the 1980s, followed by stability.

36. The Mexican case may demonstrate some of the problems with Mares's willingness to take official rhetoric at face value, however. It is unclear whether stated policy translates into actual welfare provision, as many Mexicans have pointed out to me. In the Yemeni case, new clinic buildings funded by international donors are often left empty, for example; without medical staff or electricity, even a proliferation of clinics does not necessarily mean access to health care.

37. Personal communication, September 2006.

38. Pan-Arab movements in the 1950s and 1960s and the earlier pan-Islamic movements in the 1920s and 1930s may have created the precedent for some of today's transnational circuits, and the circuits themselves also need to be examined through ethnographic work and network analyses. Salafī trends in the Arab world have a profound impact on movements in South Asia and Turkey, for example. What are the mechanisms through which this influence has been effected?

39. This phrase is cited from Geoff Eley's "Historicizing the Global" and it is taken from Justin Rosenberg's critique of Giddens, *The Follies of Globalization Theory: Polemical Essays* (2000, 89). Rosenberg is referring to Anthony Giddens, *The Consequences of Modernity* (1990). See also Giddens, *Runaway World: How Globalization Is Reshaping Our Lives* (2003).

40. Ankie Hoogvelt (2001) asks whether the shift from what she calls Fordist production to a post-Fordist world of flexible production means that the geographical understanding of core-periphery polarization (to use her Wallersteinian vocabulary) is being supplanted by social core-periphery polarizations that cut across territorial boundaries and geographical regions. She invites us to consider how money is increasingly being made out of the circulation of money, so that capital is being disconnected from the social relationships in which money and wealth were previously embedded. This has meant the intensification of linkages within areas of core wealthy countries of the global system while peripheralization becomes a process of marginalization and expulsion cutting across territories and national boundaries. Parts of the traditional core are vulnerable to the same sorts of marginalization as large areas in Africa, Latin America, and Asia. But I would argue, as the Yemeni example suggests, that there have always been large swathes of nation-state territory, particularly in poor places, that have been outside the domain of welfare provisioning and redistribution. Indeed, the terms Fordism and post-Fordism do not seem to accurately portray worlds where industries have been scarce or inefficient.

CONCLUSION

1. *Qānūn raqm 6, bi-sha'n al-jinsiyya al-yamaniyya*, Law No. 6, Article 2, 1990. Translation modified by the author.

2. Not surprisingly, in the Yemeni example the genealogical connections are least problematic when established through patrilineal descent: Yemeni nationality can be "enjoyed" by those who are born to a father with Yemeni nationality, regardless of where the person resides. But territorial rootedness is also important, and may even trump the specifics of lineage, for whoever is born in Yemen to a mother who holds this nationality may also be legally considered Yemeni, as can an infant who is born to unknown parents in the nation-state's territory. As in many cases these days, transnational commitments do not necessarily override national ones, and this too is reflected in the law: emigrants may enjoy dual citizenship. Yemeni citizenship can also be "granted" to spouses of Yemeni citizens, to the child of a mother who holds Yemeni citizenship but was born abroad (if the child has lived in Yemen in "a legitimate manner for a period of ten successive years"), and so forth.

3. Key articles, in addition to Brubaker and Cooper's (2000), that raise some of these conceptual problems are Gleason (1996); Fearon (1999); and James Clifford's classic, "Identity in Mashpee" (1988). For a recent overview of the vast literature on identity, see Abdelal et al. (2008).

4. In much of the sociological and political science literature "framing" is the term used either to stress the importance of discourses or to describe the relationship between cognitive patterns and interpretations of political events. But this metaphor implies that language simply outlines or frames action rather than suffusing or being integral to it. Goffman (1974) gave the concept of framing its sociological formulation and made the metaphor famous. He drew on Bateson (1985 [1955]). See also Snow et al. (1986) and Snow and Benford (1988). In addition, Gamson and Modigliani (1989), Gamson (1992), and Esser (1999) have made important contributions to the literature, as has Brubaker, whose chap. 4 (2004) deals with the ethnic framing of violence. On the related concept of schema, see D'Andrade (1995).

5. For a discussion of criteria for analyzing "political identities in transition" see Courtney Jung's *Then I Was Black* (New Haven: Yale University Press, 2000). She looks at "historical precedence, political institutions, mobilizing discourse, material conditions, organization, available ideology, and resonance." I have preferred to streamline my analysis (some of her categories seem to overlap) and to highlight too the importance of events and everyday practices. As my argument makes clear, I assume that material conditions are important to many of these rubrics—to the possibilities of organization, for the interpretive construction of group affiliations, to the kinds of relationships among members of a particular organization, etc.

6. Thanks are owed to Rosalind C. Morris for helping me formulate this passage.

7. I am grateful to Linda Zerilli here. See also her discussion (2005, 16-21).

BIBLIOGRAPHY

ARABIC NEWSPAPERS

26 September
al-Ayyām
Fatāt al-jazīra
al-Ḥaqq
al-Ḥayāt
al-Īmān
Al-Jazeera.net
al-Quds al-'Arabī
Ra'y
al-Ra'y
al-Ṣaḥwa
al-Shumū'
al-Thawra
al-Thawrī
al-Umma
al-Waḥdawī
al-Wasaṭ
Newsyemen.net

ENGLISH NEWSPAPERS

New York Times
Observer
Yemen Observer
Yemen Times

AUDIOCASSETTE SERMONS

'Alī, 'Abd Allāh Aḥmad, "al-'Ashr al-Wājibāt lil-Fard al-Muslim."
'Alī, 'Abd Allāh Aḥmad, "al-Thabāt 'alā al-Mabādi'."
al-Ānisī, Muḥammad, "Saffāḥ Kulliyyat al-Ṭibb."
al-Ānisī, Muḥammad, "al-Tanṣīr fī al-Yaman."
al-Ānisī, Muḥammad, "Sakarāt al-Mawt."
al-Ānisī, Muḥammad, "al-Taskhīr wa al-Tadhlīl."
al-Duwaysh, Muḥammad, "Akhṭā'inā [*sic*] fī Mu'ālajat al-Akhṭā'."

al-Duwaysh, Muḥammad, "Kayfa Nata'āmal ma' Ma'āṣī al-Muslimīn?"
al-Duwaysh, Muḥammad, "Fann al-Taharrub min al-Mas'ūliyya."
al-Ḥazmī, Muḥammad ibn Nāṣir, "Layl al-Ẓālimīn."
al-Ḥazmī, Muḥammad ibn Nāṣir, "al-Ṭūfān al-Mudammir."
Kishk, "Mumayyizāt al-'Ālam al-'Āmil."
Kishk, "al-Qulūb Thalāthat Aqsām."
Kishk, "al-Ṣidq wa al-Kidhb."
al-Miswarī, Hazzā', "Risāla 'Ājila ilā Ḥukkām al-'Arab al-Mutakhādhila."
al-Miswarī, Hazzā', "Inna lil-Muttaqīna Mafāzan."
al-Miswarī, Hazzā', "Lā Ḥayā bi-dūn Īmān."
al-Qaranī, 'Ā'iḍ, "Lā Taḥzan."
al-Qaranī, 'Ā'iḍ, "Man Yaṣna' Majd al-Umma."
al-Qaranī, 'Ā'iḍ, "al-Ṭarīq ilā Allāh."
al-Qaṭṭān, "Ahammiyyat al-Istighfār."
al-Qaṭṭān, "al-Farāgh al-Rūḥī."
al-Qaṭṭān, Aḥmad, "al-Mawt wa 'Adhāb al-Qabr."
Ṣa'tar, "An Urīd lā [*sic*] al-Iṣlāḥ."
Ṣa'tar, "al-'Aqliyya al-Jāhiliyya."
Ṣa'tar, "Quwwat al-'Adl lā 'Adl lil-Quwwa."
al-Zindānī, 'Abd al-Majīd, "al-'Asal wa Āthāruh 'alā al-Amrāḍ."
al-Zindānī, 'Abd al-Majīd, "Sharī'a li-Kull Zamān."
al-Zindānī, 'Abd al-Majīd, "al-Īmān bil-Yawm al-Ākhir."

ARTICLES AND BOOKS

'Abd al-Fattāḥ, Fatḥī. *Tajribat al-thawra fī al-Yaman al-dīmuqrāṭiyya*. Beirut: Dār Ibn Khaldūn, 1974.

al-'Abdalī, Aḥmad Faḍl. *Hadiyyat al-zaman fī akhbār mulūk Laḥj wa-'Adan*. Beirut: Dār al-'Awda, 1931.

Abdelal, Rawi, Yoshika Herrera, Alastair Iain Johnston, and Rose McDermott, eds. *Identity as a Variable: Conceptualization and Measurement of Identity*. New York: Cambridge University Press, 2008.

Abdo, Geneive. *No God but God: Egypt and the Triumph of Islam*. New York: Oxford University Press, 2000.

Abu El-Haj, Nadia. *Facts on the Ground: Archaeological Practice and Territorial Self-Fashioning in Israeli Society*. Chicago: University of Chicago Press, 2001.

Abū Ghānim, Faḍl bin 'Alī. *al-Bunya al-qabaliyya fī al-Yaman bayna al-istimrār wa al-taghyīr*. Damascus: Maṭba'at al-Kātib al-'Arabī, 1985.

Abu-Lughod, Lila. *Dramas of Nationhood: The Politics of Television in Egypt*. Chicago: University of Chicago Press, 2005.

Abū Ṭālib, Ḥasan. *al-Waḥda al-yamaniyya: dirāsāt fī 'amaliyyat al-taḥawwul min al-tashṭīr ilā al-waḥda*. Beirut: Markaz Dirāsāt al-Waḥda al-'Arabiyya, 1994.

Adas, Michael. "South Asian Resistance in Comparative Perspective." In *Contesting Power: Resistance and Everyday Social Relations in South Asia*, edited by Douglas Haynes and Gyan Prakash. Berkeley: University of California Press, 1992.

Adcock, Robert, and David Collier. "Measurement Validity: A Shared Standard for Qualitative and Quantitative Research." *American Political Science Review* 95, no. 3 (September 2001): 529–46.

Adra, Najwa. "Dance and Glance: Visualizing Tribal Identity in Highland Yemen." *Visual Anthropology* 11 (1998): 55–102.

———. "Qabyallah: The Tribal Concept in the Central Highlands of the Yemen Arab Republic." PhD dissertation, Temple University, 1982.

———. "Tribal Dancing and Yemeni Nationalism: Steps to Unity." *RE.M.M.M.* 67, no. 1 (1993): 161–67.

'Afīf, Aḥmad Jābir. *al-Ḥaraka al-waṭaniyya fī al-Yaman*. Damascus: Dār al-Fikr, 1982.

Agrama, Hussein Ali. "Law Courts and Fatwa Councils in Modern Egypt: An Ethnography of Islamic Legal Practice." PhD dissertation, Johns Hopkins University, 2005.

———. "Theoretical Problems of Islamism." N.d. Available from the author, University of Chicago, Department of Anthropology.

Aḥmad, 'Izz al-Dīn Sa'īd, ed. *Dalīl al-munaẓẓamāt ghayr al-ḥukūmiyya fī al-Yaman*. Ta'izz: Human Rights Information and Training Center, 2003.

Aḥmad, Maḥmūd 'Ādil. *Dhikrayāt ḥarb al-Yaman, 1962–1967*. Cairo: Maṭba'at al-Ukhuwwa, 1992.

Althusser, Louis. "Ideology and Ideological State Apparatuses (Notes towards an Investigation)." In *Lenin and Philosophy, and Other Essays*. New York: Monthly Review Press, 1971.

al-'Amal al-niqābī al-'ummālī fī al-jumhuriyya al-yamaniyya: al-judhūr al-tārikhiyya, al-wāqi', āfāq al-mustaqbal. Ṣan'ā': al-Markaz al-Yamanī lil-Dirāsāt al-Istrātījiyya, 2004.

Amnesty International. "Yemen Report, 2005: Covering Events from January–December 2004." http: web.amnesty.org/report2005/yem-summar-eng.

Anderson, Benedict. *Imagined Communities: Reflections on the Origin and Spread of Nationalism*. London: Verso, 1991.

Anscombe, Elizabeth. *Intention*. Cambridge: Harvard University Press, 2000.

Antoun, Richard T. *Muslim Preacher in the Modern World: A Jordanian Case Study in Comparative Perspective*. Princeton: Princeton University Press, 1989.

Appadurai, Arjun. *Modernity at Large: Cultural Dimensions of Globalization*. Minneapolis: University of Minnesota Press, 1996.

Arendt, Hannah. *Between Past and Future*. New York: Penguin Books, 1993 [1954].

———. *The Human Condition*. Chicago: University of Chicago Press, 1958.

———. *On Revolution*. New York: Penguin Books, 1963.

Asad, Talal. *Formations of the Secular: Christianity, Islam, Modernity*. Stanford: Stanford University Press, 2003.

———. *Genealogies of Religion: Discipline and Reasons of Power in Christianity and Islam*. Baltimore: Johns Hopkins University Press, 1993.

———. *The Idea of an Anthropology of Islam*. Occasional Papers Series. Washington, D.C.: Georgetown University, Center for Contemporary Arab Studies, 1986.

Austin, J. L. *How to Do Things with Words*. Edited by J. O. Urmson. New York: Oxford University Press, 1965.

———. *Philosophical Papers*. Oxford: Clarendon Press, 1961.

Ayyūb, Muḥammad al-Sayyid. *al-Yaman bayna al-qāt wa-fasād al-ḥukm qabl al-thawra.* Cairo: Dār al-Ma'ārif, 1963.

Baaklini, Abdo I., Guilain Denoeux, and Robert Springborg. *Legislative Politics in the Arab World: The Resurgence of Democratic Institutions.* Boulder, Colo.: Lynne Rienner, 1999.

al-Bakrī, Ṣalāḥ. *Tārīkh Ḥaḍramawt al-siyāsī.* Cairo: Muṣṭafā al-Bābī al-Ḥalabī, 1935–36.

Balibar, Étienne. "The Nation Form: History and Ideology." In *Race, Nation, Class: Ambiguous Identities,* by Étienne Balibar and Immanuel Wallerstein. Balibar translated by Chris Turner. London: Verso, 1991.

al-Baraddūnī, 'Abd Allāh. *Min Arḍ Bilqīs.* Cairo: Maṭba'at al-Ma'rifa, 1961.

Barber, Benjamin R. *Jihad vs. McWorld: How Globalism and Tribalism Are Reshaping the World.* New York: Ballantine Books, 1996.

Barth, Frederik, ed. *Ethnic Groups and Boundaries: The Social Organization of Culture Difference.* Prospect Heights, Ill.: Waveland Press, 1998 [1969].

Bateson, Gregory. "A Theory of Play and Fantasy." In *Semiotics: An Introductory Anthology,* edited by Robert E. Innis. Bloomington: Indiana University Press, 1985.

Bauman, Richard. *Story, Performance and Event: Contextual Studies of Oral Narrative.* Cambridge: Cambridge University Press, 1986.

———. *Verbal Art as Performance.* With supplementary essays by Barbara A. Babcock. Rowley, Mass.: Newbury House, 1978.

Bauman, Richard, and Joel Sherzer, eds. *Explorations in the Ethnography of Speaking.* New York: Cambridge University Press, 1974.

Bayān al-mu'tamar al-sha'bī. al-Ṣaḥwa net. June 6, 2004.

———. al-Ṣaḥwa net. June 28, 2004.

Bayard de Volo, Lorraine, and Edward Schatz. "From the Inside Out: Ethnographic Methods in Political Research." *PS: Political Science and Politics* 37, no. 2 (2004): 267–71.

Beeston, A. F. L., and A. Ayalon. "Sha'b." In *The Encyclopedia of Islam.* Vol. 9. Leiden: E. J. Brill, 1995.

Beiner, Ronald. "Why Citizenship Constitutes a Theoretical Problem in the Last Decade of the Twentieth Century." In *Theorizing Citizenship,* edited by Ronald Beiner. Albany: State University of New York Press, 1995.

Beinin, Joel, and Joe Stork. *Political Islam: Essays from* Middle East Report. Berkeley: University of California Press, 1997.

Benhabib, Seyla. *Situating the Self: Gender, Community, and Postmodernism in Contemporary Ethics.* New York: Routledge, 1992.

———. ed. *Democracy and Difference: Contesting Boundaries of the Political.* Princeton: Princeton University Press, 1996.

Benjamin, Walter. *Illuminations.* London: Fontana, 1973.

Berlant, Lauren. *The Anatomy of National Fantasy: Hawthorne, Utopia, and Everyday Life.* Chicago: University of Chicago Press, 1991.

———. "The Subject of True Feeling: Pain, Privacy, and Politics." In *Cultural Studies and Political Theory,* edited by Jodi Dean. Ithaca: Cornell University Press, 2000.

Berman, Sheri. "Islamism, Revolution, and Civil Society." *Perspectives on Politics* 1, no. 2 (June 2003): 11–26.

Billig, Michael. *Banal Nationalism.* London: Sage, 1995.

Bloch, Maurice, ed. *Political Language and Oratory in Traditional Society*. London: Academic Press, 1975.

Boas, Taylor C., and Jordan Gans-Morse. "From New Liberal Ideology to Anti-Liberal Creed: The Problematic Evolution of the Term 'Neoliberalism.'" Unpublished paper, March 9, 2007. Available at author's website (under a slightly revised title), http://socrates.berkeley.edu/~tboas/.

Bobo, Lawrence D. "Racial Attitudes and Relations at the Close of the Twentieth Century." In *America Becoming: Racial Trends and Their Consequences*, edited by Neil Smelser, William Julius Wilson, and Faith Mitchell. Washington, D.C.: National Academy Press, 2001.

Bobo, Lawrence D., Camille L. Zubrinsky, James H. Johnson Jr., and Melvin L. Oliver. "Public Opinion Before and After a Spring of Discontent." In *The Los Angeles Riots: Lessons for the Urban Future*, edited by M. Baldassare. Boulder, Colo.: Westview Press, 1994.

Bohman, James. *Public Deliberation: Pluralism, Complexity, and Democracy*. Cambridge: MIT Press, 1996.

Boix, Carles. "Democracy and Inequality." *Centro de Estudios Sociales Avanzados Fundación Juan March Working Paper Series*. Madrid: January 2001.

———. *Democracy and Redistribution*. Cambridge: Cambridge University Press, 2003.

Boix, Carles, and Susan Stokes. "Endogenous Democratization." *World Politics* 55 (July 2003): 517–49.

Boix, Carles, and Milan Svolik. "Non-Tyrannical Autocracies." Unpublished manuscript. April 2007. Available from Boix, Department of Political Science, Princeton University.

Bollen, Kenneth A., and Robert W. Jackman. "Democracy, Stability, and Dichotomies." *American Sociological Review* 54, no. 4 (August 1989): 612–21.

Bourdieu, Pierre. *Language and Symbolic Power*. Translated by Gino Raymond and Matthew Adamson. Cambridge: Harvard University Press, 1991.

———. *The Logic of Practice*. Translated by Richard Nice. Cambridge: Polity, 1990.

———. *Outline of a Theory of Practice*. Translated by Richard Nice. Cambridge: Cambridge University Press, 1977.

Boxberger, Linda. *On the Edge of Empire: Hadhramawt, Emigration, and the Indian Ocean, 1880s–1930s*. Albany: State University of New York Press, 2002.

Boyd, Douglas A. *Broadcasting in the Arab World: A Survey of the Electronic Media in the Middle East*. Ames: Iowa State University Press, 1999.

Brass, Paul R. *Theft of an Idol: Text and Context in the Representation of Collective Violence*. Princeton: Princeton University Press, 1997.

Breuilly, John. *Nationalism and the State*. Chicago: University of Chicago Press, 1994.

Brown, Daniel. *Rethinking Tradition in Modern Islamic Thought*. Cambridge: Cambridge University Press, 1999.

Brownlee, Jason. *Authoritarianism in an Age of Democratization*. New York: Cambridge University Press, 2007.

Brubaker, Rogers. *Ethnicity without Groups*. Cambridge: Harvard University Press, 2004.

———. *Nationalism Reframed: Nationhood and the National Question in the New Europe*. Cambridge: Cambridge University Press, 1996.

Brubaker, Rogers, and Frederick Cooper. "Beyond 'Identity.'" *Theory and Society* 29, no. 1 (February 2000): 1–47.

Brubaker, Rogers, and David Laitin. "Ethnic and Nationalist Violence." In *Ethnicity without Groups*, by Rogers Brubaker. Cambridge: Harvard University Press, 2004.

Buckler, F. W. "The Oriental Despot." *Anglican Theological Review* 10, no. 3 (1927–28): 238–49.

———. "Two Instances of Khilat in the Bible." *Journal of Theological Studies* 23 (1922): 197–99.

Bujra, A. S. "Urban Elites and Colonialism: The National Elite of Aden and South Arabia." *Middle East Journal* 6 (1970): 189–211.

Bull, Michael. *Sounding Out the City: Personal Stereos and the Management of Everyday Life*. Oxford: Berg, 2000.

Burgat, François. "Les élections présidentielles de septembre 1999 au Yémen: Du 'pluralisme armé' au retour à la 'norme arabe.'" *Monde arabe Maghreb-Machrek* 168 (April–June 2000): 67–75.

Burgat, François, and Mohamed Sbitli. "Les Salafis au Yémen ou la modernization malgré tout." *Chroniques Yémenites* (2002): 123–52.

Burrowes, Robert D. *The Yemen Arab Republic: The Politics of Development, 1962–1986*. Boulder, Colo.: Westview Press; London: Croom Helm, 1987.

Butler, Judith. *Bodies That Matter: On the Discursive Limits of "Sex."* New York: Routledge, 1993.

———. *Excitable Speech: A Politics of the Performative*. New York: Routledge, 1997.

Calhoun, Craig. "Introduction: Habermas and the Public Sphere." In *Habermas and the Public Sphere*, edited by Craig Calhoun. Cambridge: MIT Press, 1992.

———. *Nationalism*. Minneapolis: University of Minnesota Press, 1997.

———. "The Problem of Identity in Collective Action." In *Macro-Micro Linkages in Sociology*, edited by Joan Huber. Newbury Park, Calif.: Sage, 1991.

Caraccioli, Louis Augustin. *Dictionnaire Critique, Pittoresque et Sentencieux, Propre à faire connaître les usages du Siecle, ainsi que ses bisarreries. Par l'Auteur de la Conversation avec Soi Même.* Vol. 1. Lyon: Chez Benoît Duplain, 1768.

Carapico, Sheila. *Civil Society in Yemen: The Political Economy of Activism in Modern Arabia*. Cambridge: Cambridge University Press, 1998.

———. "The Economic Dimensions of Yemeni Unity." *Middle East Report* 184 (1993): 9–14.

———. "From Ballotbox to Battlefield: The War of the Two 'Alis." *Middle East Report* 190, no. 25 (September–October 1994): 27.

———. "How Yemen's Ruling Party Secured an Electoral Landslide." *Middle East Report Online* (May 16, 2003).

———. "No Quick Fix: Foreign Aid and State Performance in Yemen." In *Short of the Goal: US Policy and Poorly Performing States*, edited by Nancy Birdsall, Milan Vaishnav, and Robert L. Ayres. Washington, D.C.: Center for Global Development, 2006.

———. "Yemen between Civility and Civil War." In *Civil Society in the Middle East*, vol. 2, edited by Augustus Richard Norton. Leiden: E. J. Brill, 1996.

Carapico, Sheila, and Richard Tutwiler. *Yemeni Agriculture and Economic Change: Case Studies of Two Highland Regions*. San'a: American Institute for Yemeni Studies, 1981.

Carothers, Thomas. "The End of the Transition Paradigm." *Journal of Democracy* 13, no. 1 (2002): 5–21.

Caton, Steven C. *"Peaks of Yemen I Summon": Poetry as Cultural Practice in a North Yemeni Tribe*. Berkeley: University of California Press, 1990.

Central Intelligence Agency (CIA). *The World Fact Book*. https://www.cia.gov/cia/publications/factbook/geos/ym.html (accessed November 29, 2006).

Chabal, Patrick, and Jean-Pascal Daloz. *Africa Works: Disorder as Political Instrument*. Bloomington: Indiana University Press, 1999.

Chakrabarty, Dipesh. *Provincializing Europe: Postcolonial Thought and Historical Difference*. Princeton: Princeton University Press, 2000.

Chandra, Kanchan. *Why Ethnic Parties Succeed: Patronage and Ethnic Headcounts in India*. Cambridge: Cambridge University Press, 2004.

Chatterjee, Partha. *The Nation and Its Fragments: Colonial and Postcolonial Histories*. Princeton: Princeton University Press, 1993.

———. "Religious Minorities and the Secular State: Reflections on an Indian Impasse." *Public Culture* 8, no. 1 (Fall 1995): 11–39.

———. "A Response to Taylor's 'Modes of Civil Society.'" *Public Culture* (Fall 1990): 119–32.

Chaudhry, Kiren Aziz. *The Price of Wealth: Economies and Institutions in the Middle East*. Ithaca: Cornell University Press, 1997.

Clark, Janine A. *Islam, Charity, and Activism: Middle-Class Networks and Social Welfare in Egypt, Jordan, and Yemen*. Bloomington: Indiana University Press, 2004.

Clifford, James. *The Predicament of Culture: Twentieth-Century Ethnography, Literature, and Art*. Cambridge: Harvard University Press, 1988.

Cohen, Cathy. *The Boundaries of Blackness: AIDS and the Breakdown of Black Politics*. Chicago: University of Chicago Press, 1999.

Cohen, Jean L. "American Civil Society Talk." *Report from the Institute for Philosophy and Public Policy* 18, no. 3 (Summer 1998).

Cohen, Joshua. "Deliberation and Democratic Legitimacy." In *The Good Polity: Normative Analysis of the State*, edited by Alan Hamlin and Philip Pettit. Oxford: Blackwell, 1989.

———. "Procedure and Substance in Deliberative Democracy." In *Democracy and Difference: Contesting the Boundaries of the Political*, edited by Seyla Benhabib. Princeton: Princeton University Press, 1996.

Cohen, Stanley. *Folk Devils and Moral Panics: The Creation of the Mods and Rockers*. London: MacGibbon and Kee, 1972.

Cohn, Bernard S. *Colonialism and Its Forms of Knowledge: The British in India*. Princeton: Princeton University Press, 1996.

Colburn, Marta. *The Republic of Yemen: Development Challenges in the 21st Century*. London: Stacey International, 2002.

Collier, David, and Robert Adcock. "Democracy and Dichotomies: A Pragmatic Approach to Choices about Concepts." *Annual Review of Political Science* 2 (1999): 537–65.

Collier, David, Fernando Daniel Hidalgo, and Andra Olivia Maciuceanu. "Essentially Contested Concepts: Debates and Applications." *Journal of Political Ideologies* 11, no. 3 (October 2006): 211–46.

Collier, David, and Steven Levitsky. "Democracy with Adjectives: Conceptual Innovation in Comparative Research." *World Politics* 49 (April 1997): 430–51.

Collier, Paul, and Anke Hoeffler. "Greed and Grievance in Civil War." *Oxford Economic Papers* 56, no. 4 (October 2004): 563–95.

Collier, Ruth B. *Paths toward Democracy: The Working Class and Elites in Western Europe and South America.* Cambridge: Cambridge University Press, 1999.

Colton, Nora. "The Silent Victims: Yemeni Migrants Return Home." *Oxford International Review* 3, no. 1 (1991): 23–37.

Comaroff, Jean. "The Politics of Conviction: Faith on the Neoliberal Frontier." Paper presented at an international conference on "Reasons on Faith." WISER, University of the Witwatersrand, October 10–17, 2005.

Comaroff, Jean, and John L. Comaroff. "Criminal Obsessions, After Foucault: Postcoloniality, Policing, and the Metaphysics of Disorder." *Critical Inquiry* 30, no. 4 (2004): 800–824.

———. *Ethnicity, Incorporated: On Identity, Culture, and the Commodity in the 21st Century.* Forthcoming.

———. "Millennial Capitalism: First Thoughts on a Second Coming." In *Millennial Capitalism and the Culture of Neoliberalism*, edited by Jean Comaroff and John L. Comaroff. Durham, N.C.: Duke University Press, 2001.

———. "Naturing the Nation: Aliens, Apocalypse and the Postcolonial State." *Journal of Southern African Studies* 27, no. 3 (September 2001a): 627–51.

———. "Occult Economies and the Violence of Abstraction: Notes from the South African Postcolony." *American Ethnologist* 26, no. 3 (1999): 279–301.

———. *Of Revelation and Revolution, Volume 1: Christianity, Colonialism, and Consciousness in South Africa.* Chicago: University of Chicago Press, 1991.

———. *Of Revelation and Revolution. Volume 2: The Dialectics of Modernity on a South African Frontier.* Chicago: University of Chicago Press, 1995.

———. "Policing the Occult in the Postcolony: Law and the Regulation of 'Dangerous' Cultural Practices, in South Africa and Elsewhere." Unpublished paper, 1998.

———. "Postcolonial Politics and Discourses of Democracy in Southern Africa: An Anthropological Reflection on African Political Modernities." *Journal of Anthropological Research* 53, no. 2 (Summer 1997): 123–46.

Connor, Walker. "Nation-Building or Nation-Destroying?" *World Politics* 24, no. 3 (April 1972): 319–55.

Cook, Michael. *Commanding Right and Forbidding Wrong in Islamic Thought.* Cambridge: Cambridge University Press, 2000.

Cooley, John K. *Unholy Wars: Afghanistan, America, and International Terrorism.* London: Pluto Press, 2000.

Cooper, Fredrick. *Colonialism in Question: Theory, Knowledge, History.* Berkeley: University of California Press, 2005.

Crone, Patricia. "The Tribe and the State." In *States in History*, edited by John A. Hall. Oxford: Blackwell, 1986.

Cunningham, Frank. *Democratic Theory and Socialism.* Cambridge: Cambridge University Press, 1987.

———. *Theories of Democracy: A Critical Introduction.* London: Routledge, 2002.

Dahl, Robert A. *Polyarchy: Participation and Opposition.* New Haven: Yale University Press, 1971.

D'Andrade, Roy G. *The Development of Cognitive Anthropology.* Cambridge: Cambridge University Press, 1995.

Davidson, Arnold I. *The Emergence of Sexuality: Historical Epistemology and the Formation of Concepts.* Cambridge: Harvard University Press, 2001.

Dawson, Michael C. *Behind the Mule: Race and Class in African-American Politics.* Princeton: Princeton University Press, 1994.

———. *Black Visions: The Roots of Contemporary African-American Political Ideologies.* Chicago: University of Chicago Press, 2001.

Debord, Guy. *The Society of the Spectacle.* New York: Zone Books, 1994.

De Certeau, Michel. *The Practice of Everyday Life.* Translated by Steven F. Rendall. Berkeley: University of California Press, 1984.

Derrida, Jacques. "Signature Event Context." In *Limited Inc.* Evanston, Ill.: Northwestern University Press, 1988.

Detalle, Renaud. "Ajuster sans douleur? La méthode yéménite." *Monde arabe Maghreb-Machrek* 155 (January–March 1997): 20–36.

———. "Les élections legislatives du 27 avril 1993." *Monde arabe Maghreb-Machrek* 141 (1993a): 3–36.

———. "The Yemeni Elections Up Close." *Middle East Report* 23, no. 6 (1993b): 8–12.

Deutsch, Karl Wolfgang. *Nationalism and Social Communication: An Inquiry into the Foundations of Nationality.* Cambridge: Technology Press of the Massachusetts Institute of Technology; New York: Wiley, 1953.

Diamond, Larry. *Developing Democracy: Toward Consolidation.* Baltimore: Johns Hopkins University Press, 1999.

Diamond, Larry, and Gary Marks, eds. *Reexamining Democracy: Essays in Honor of Seymour Martin Lipset.* Newbury Park, Calif.: Sage, 1992.

Dietz, Mary G. "Feminist Receptions of Hannah Arendt." In *Feminist Interpretations of Hannah Arendt,* edited by Bonnie Honig. University Park: Pennsylvania State University, 1995.

Dirks, Nicholas B., ed. *Castes of Mind: Colonialism and the Making of Modern India.* Princeton: Princeton University Press, 2001.

———. *Colonialism and Culture.* Ann Arbor: University of Michigan Press, 1992.

Dohrn-van Rossum, Gerhard. *History of the Hour: Clocks and Modern Temporal Orders.* Chicago: University of Chicago Press, 1996.

Dominguez, Virginia R. *White by Definition: Social Classification in Creole Louisiana.* New Brunswick, N.J.: Rutgers University Press, 1997.

Donner, Fred M. *Narratives of Islamic Origins: The Beginnings of Islamic Historical Writing.* Princeton: Darwin Press, 1998.

Douglas, J. Leigh. *The Free Yemeni Movement, 1935–1962.* Beirut: American University of Beirut, 1987.

Drake, St. Clair. *Race Relations in a Time of Rapid Social Change: Report of a Survey.* New York: National Federation of Settlements and Neighborhood Centers, 1966.

Dresch, Paul. *A History of Modern Yemen.* Cambridge: Cambridge University Press, 2000.

———. "Imams and Tribes: The Writing and Acting of History in Upper Yemen." In *Tribes and State Formation in the Middle East,* edited by Philip S. Khoury and Joseph Kostiner. Berkeley: University of California Press, 1990.

———. "The Tribal Factor in the Yemeni Crisis." In *The Yemeni War of 1994: Causes and Consequences*, edited by Jamal S. al-Suwaidi. London: Saqi Books, 1995.

———. *Tribes, Government, and History in Yemen*. Oxford: Clarendon Press, 1993.

Dresch, Paul, and Bernard Haykel. "Stereotypes and Political Styles: Islamists and Tribesfolk in Yemen." *International Journal of Middle East Studies* 27 (1995): 405–31.

Dryzek, John S. *Deliberative Democracy and Beyond: Liberals, Critics, Contestations*. Oxford: Oxford University Press, 2000.

———. *Discursive Democracy: Politics, Policy, and Political Science*. Cambridge: Cambridge University Press, 1990.

Duara, Prasenjit. *Rescuing History from the Nation: Questioning Narratives of Modern China*. Chicago: University of Chicago Press, 1995.

Duranti, Alessandro. *From Grammar to Politics: Linguistic Anthropology in a Western Samoan Village*. Berkeley: University of California Press, 1994.

al-Duwayhī, Shawqī. *Maqāhī Bayrūt al-Sha'biyya 1950–1990*. Beirut: Dār al-Nahār, 2005.

Eickelman, Dale F. "Mass Higher Education and the Religious Imagination in Contemporary Arab Societies." *American Ethnologist* 19, no. 4 (1992): 643–55.

Eickelman, Dale F., and John W. Anderson. "Print, Islam, and the Prospects for Civic Pluralism: New Religious Writings and Their Audiences." *Journal of Islamic Studies* 8, no. 1 (1997): 43–62.

———, eds. *New Media in the Muslim World: The Emerging Public Sphere*. Bloomington: Indiana University Press, 1999.

Eley, Geoff. "Historicizing the Global, Politicizing Capital: Giving the Present a Name." *History Workshop Journal* 63 (Spring 2007): 154–88.

Eley, Geoff, and Ronald Grigor Suny. *Becoming National: A Reader*. New York: Oxford University Press, 1996.

Elias, Norbert. *The Civilizing Process*. Translated by Edmund Jephcott. New York: Pantheon Books, 1982.

Esser, Frank. "'Tabloidization' of News: A Comparative Analysis of Anglo-American and German Press Journalism." *European Journal of Communication* 14, no. 3 (1999): 291–324.

Euben, Roxanne L. *Enemy in the Mirror: Islamic Fundamentalism and the Limits of Modern Rationalism; A Work of Comparative Political Theory*. Princeton: Princeton University Press, 1999.

Fahmy, Khaled. *All the Pasha's Men: Mehmed Ali, His Army and the Making of Modern Egypt*. Cambridge: Cambridge University Press, 1997.

Farah, Caesar E. *The Sultan's Yemen: Nineteenth-Century Challenges to Ottoman Rule*. London: I. B. Tauris, 2002.

Fearon, James D. "Deliberation as Discussion." In *Deliberative Democracy*, edited by Jon Elster. Cambridge: Cambridge University Press, 1998.

———. "What Is Identity (As We Now Use the Word)?" Unpublished essay. 1999. Available from the author, Department of Political Science, Stanford University.

Fearon, James D., and David D. Laitin. "Ethnicity, Insurgency, and Civil War." *American Political Science Review* 97, no. 1 (February 2003): 75–90.

———. "Violence and the Social Construction of Ethnic Identity." *International Organization* 54, no. 4 (Autumn 2000): 845–77.

Ferguson, James. *The Anti-Politics Machine: "Development," Depoliticization, and Bureaucratic Power in Lesotho*. Minneapolis: University of Minnesota Press, 1994.

Fishkin, James S. *Democracy and Deliberation: New Directions for Democratic Reform*. New Haven: Yale University Press, 1991.

Foreign Policy. Failing States Index, July–August 2005; 2006.

Foster, Robert J. *Materializing the Nation: Commodities, Consumption, and Media in Papua New Guinea*. Bloomington: Indiana University Press, 2002.

Foucault, Michel. *Discipline and Punish: The Birth of the Prison*. Translated by Alan Sheridan. New York: Vintage Books, 1979.

———. *Dits et écrits: 1954–1988*. Paris: Éditions Gallimard, 1994.

———. "Governmentality." In *The Foucault Effect: Studies in Governmentality*, edited by Graham Burchell, Colin Gordon, and Peter Miller. London: Harvester Wheatsheaf, 1991.

———. *The History of Sexuality, Volume One: An Introduction*. Translated by Robert Hurley. New York: Pantheon Books, 1978.

———. "The Subject and Power." In *Michel Foucault: Beyond Structuralism and Hermeneutics*, edited by Hubert L. Dreyfus and Paul Rabinow. Chicago: University of Chicago Press, 1982.

Fraser, Nancy. "Rethinking the Public Sphere: A Contribution to the Critique of Actually Existing Democracy." In *Habermas and the Public Sphere*, edited by Craig Calhoun. Cambridge: MIT Press, 1992.

Freitag, Ulrike. *Indian Ocean Migrants and State Formation in Hadhramaut: Reforming the Homeland*. Leiden: E. J. Brill, 2003.

Gaffney, Patrick D. "The Changing Voices of Islam: The Emergence of Professional Preachers in Contemporary Egypt." *Muslim World* 81, no. 1 (1991): 27–47.

———. *The Prophet's Pulpit: Islamic Preaching in Contemporary Egypt*. Berkeley: University of California Press, 1994.

Gambetta, Diego. *The Sicilian Mafia: The Business of Private Protection*. Cambridge: Harvard University Press, 1993.

Gamson, William A. *Talking Politics*. Cambridge: Cambridge University Press, 1992.

Gamson, William A., and Andre Modigliani. "Media Discourse and Public Opinion on Nuclear Power: A Constructionist Approach." *American Journal of Sociology* 95, no. 1 (July 1989): 1–37.

Gates, Robert M. *From the Shadows: The Ultimate Insider's Story of Five Presidents and How They Won the Cold War*. New York: Simon and Schuster, 1996.

Gause, F. Gregory. "The Idea of Yemeni Unity." *Journal of Arab Affairs* 6, no. 1 (1987): 55–81.

———. *Saudi-Yemeni Relations: Domestic Structures and Foreign Influence*. New York: Columbia University Press, 1990.

Gavin, R. J. *Aden under British Rule, 1839–1967*. London: Hurst, 1975.

Geertz, Clifford. "Centers, Kings, and Charisma." In *Local Knowledge: Further Essays in Interpretive Anthropology*. New York: Basic Books, 1983.

———. *Negara: The Theater State in Nineteenth-Century Bali*. Princeton: Princeton University Press, 1980.

Gellner, Ernest. *Nations and Nationalism*. Oxford: Blackwell, 1983.

Gelvin, James L. *Divided Loyalties: Nationalism and Mass Politics in Syria at the Close of Empire*. Berkeley: University of California Press, 1998.

Gerholm, Tomas. *Market, Mosque and Mafraj: Social Inequality in a Yemeni Town*. Stockholm: University of Stockholm, Department of Social Anthropology, 1977.

al-Ghafārī, 'Alī 'Abd al-Qawī. *al-Waḥda al-yamaniyya: al-wāqi' wa al-mustaqbal*. Ṣan'ā': Mu'assasat al-Kitāb al-Madrasī, 1997.

Giddens, Anthony. *The Consequences of Modernity*. Stanford: Stanford University Press, 1990.

———. *Runaway World: How Globalization Is Reshaping Our Lives*. New York: Routledge, 2003.

Gills, Barry, Joel Rocamora, and Richard Wilson, eds. *Low Intensity Democracy: Political Power in the New World Order*. London: Pluto Press, 1993.

Gilpin, Robert. *The Challenge of Global Capitalism: The World Economy in the 21st Century*. Princeton: Princeton University Press, 2000.

Gleason, Philip. "Identifying Identity: A Semantic History." In *Theories of Ethnicity: A Classical Reader*, edited by Werner Sollors. Washington Square, N.Y.: New York University Press, 1996.

Glosemeyer, Iris. "The First Yemeni Parliamentary Elections in 1993: Practising Democracy." *Orient* 34 (1993): 439–51.

———. "Local Conflict, Global Spin: An Uprising in the Yemeni Highlands." *Middle East Report* 34, no. 3 (Fall 2004): 44–47.

Goffman, Erving. "Footing." In *Forms of Talk*. Philadelphia: University of Pennsylvania Press, 1981.

———. *Frame Analysis: An Essay on the Organization of Experience*. New York: Harper and Row, 1974.

Golden, Miriam, and Michael Wallerstein. "Domestic and International Causes for the Rise of Pay Inequality: Post-Industrialism, Globalization, and Labor Market Institutions." Conference on "The Political Economy of Post-Industrial Societies," Yale University, February 24, 2006.

Goodman, Dena. *The Republic of Letters: A Cultural History of the French Enlightenment*. Ithaca: Cornell University Press, 1996.

Goodpaster, Gary. "On the Theory of American Adversary Criminal Trial." *Journal of Criminal Law and Criminology* 78, no. 1 (1987): 118–54.

Goswami, Manu. "From Swadeshi to Swaraj: Nation, Economy, and Territory in Colonial South Asia." *Comparative Studies in Society and History* 40, no. 4 (1998): 609–36.

———. *Producing India: From Colonial Economy to National Space*. Chicago: University of Chicago Press, 2004.

Gramsci, Antonio. *Selections from the Prison Notebooks*. Edited and translated by Quintin Hoare and Geoffrey Nowell Smith. New York: International Publishers, 1971.

Greene, Paul D. "Sound Engineering in a Tamil Village: Playing Audio Cassettes as Devotional Performance." *Ethnomusicology* 43, no. 3 (1999): 459–89.

Guha, Ranajit. *Elementary Aspects of Peasant Insurgency in Colonial India*. Delhi: Oxford University Press, 1983.

Gutmann, Amy, and Dennis Thompson. *Democracy and Disagreement*. Cambridge: Belknap Press of Harvard University Press, 1996.

Habermas, Jürgen. *Between Facts and Norms: Contributions to a Discourse Theory of Law and Democracy*. Translated by William Rehg. Cambridge: MIT Press, 1996.

——. *The Structural Transformation of the Public Sphere: An Inquiry into a Category of Bourgeois Society.* Translated by Thomas Burger and Fredrick Lawrence. Cambridge: MIT Press, 1996 [1962].

——. *The Theory of Communicative Action.* Vol. 1, *Reason and the Rationalization of Society.* Vol. 2, *Lifeworld and System: A Critique of Functionalist Reason.* Translated by Thomas McCarthy. Boston: Beacon Press, 1984, 1987.

Hacking, Ian. "Making Up People." In *Reconstructing Individualism: Autonomy, Individuality, and the Self in Western Thought,* edited by Thomas C. Heller, Morton Sosna, and David E. Wellbery. Stanford: Stanford University Press, 1986.

——. *Rewriting the Soul: Multiple Personality and the Sciences of Memory.* Princeton: Princeton University Press, 1995.

al-Ḥajrī, Muḥammad Aḥmad. *Majmūʻ buldān al-Yaman wa qabā'ilihā.* Ṣan'ā': Wizārat al-I'lām wa al-Thaqāfa, 1984.

Hall, Stuart. "The Toad in the Garden: Thatcherism among the Theorists." In *Marxism and the Interpretation of Culture,* edited by Cary Nelson and Lawrence Grossberg. Urbana: University of Illinois Press, 1988.

Hall, Stuart, Charles Critcher, Tony Jefferson, John Clarke, and Brian Robert. *Policing the Crisis: Mugging, the State, and Law and Order.* London: Macmillan, 1978.

Halliday, Fred. *Arabia without Sultans: A Political Survey of Instability in the Arab World.* New York: Vintage Books, 1975.

——. "The Formation of Yemeni Nationalism: Initial Reflections." In *Rethinking Nationalism in the Arab Middle East,* edited by Israel Gershoni and James Jankowski. New York: Columbia University Press, 1997.

——. *Revolution and Foreign Policy: The Case of South Yemen, 1967–1987.* Cambridge: Cambridge University Press, 1990.

——. *The World at 2000: Perils and Promises.* New York: Palgrave, 2001.

al-Hamdānī, al-Ḥasan ibn Aḥmad (d. 945 AD). *al-Iklīl (al-juz' al-thāmin).* Edited by Nabih Amin Faris. Princeton: Princeton University Press, 1940.

——. *Kitāb al-iklīl [al-juz' 1–2].* Edited by Muḥammad bin 'Alī bin al-Ḥusayn al-Akwaʻ al-Ḥawālī. Cairo: Maṭba'at al-Sunna al-Muḥammadiyya, 1963-1966.

——. *Kitāb al-iklīl min akhbār al-Yaman wa ansāb Ḥimyar: al-kitāb al-'āshir fī ma'ārif Hamdān wa ansābihā wa 'uyūn akhbārihā.* Edited by Muḥammad bin 'Alī bin al-Ḥusayn al-Akwaʻ al-Ḥawālī. Ṣan'ā': Maktabat al-Jīl al-Jadīd, 1990.

——. *Ṣifat jazīrat al-'Arab.* Edited by Muḥammad bin 'Alī al-Akwaʻ. Baghdad: Wizārat al-Thaqāfa wa al-I'lām, Dār al-Shu'ūn al-Thaqāfiyya al-'Āmma "Āfāq 'Arabiyya," 1989.

Hamzeh, Ahmad Nizar. *In the Path of Hizbullah.* Syracuse, N.Y.: Syracuse University Press, 2004.

Handler, Richard. *Nationalism and the Politics of Culture in Quebec.* Madison: University of Wisconsin Press, 1988.

Hansen, Thomas Blom. *The Saffron Wave: Democracy and Hindu Nationalism in Modern India.* Princeton: Princeton University Press, 1999.

Hansen, Thomas Blom, and Finn Stepputat, eds. *States of Imagination: Ethnographic Explorations of the Postcolonial State.* Durham, N.C.: Duke University Press, 2001.

Harvey, David. *A Brief History of Neoliberalism.* New York: Oxford University Press, 2005.

Haykel, Bernard. "Rebellion, Migration or Consultative Democracy? The Zaydis and Their Detractors in Yemen." In *Le Yémen contemporain*, edited by Remy Leveau, Franck Mermier, and Udo Steinbach. Paris: Éditions Karthala, 1999.

———. *Revival and Reform in Islam: The Legacy of Muhammad al-Shawkānī*. Cambridge: Cambridge University Press, 2003.

———. "The Salafis in Yemen at a Crossroad: An Obituary of Shaykh Muqbil al-Wadi'i of Dammaj." *Jemen Report* 33 (2002): 28–31.

———. "A Zaydi Revival?" *Yemen Update* 36 (1995): 20–21.

Held, David. "The Decline of the Nation State." In *Becoming National: A Reader*, edited by Geoff Eley and Ronald Grigor Suny. New York: Oxford University Press, 1996.

Held, David, and Anthony McGrew. "The Great Globalization Debate: An Introduction." In *The Global Transformations Reader: An Introduction to the Globalization Debate*, edited by David Held and Anthony McGrew. Malden, Mass.: Polity Press, 2000.

Henry, Clement M., and Robert Springborg. *Globalization and the Politics of Development in the Middle East*. Cambridge: Cambridge University Press, 2001.

Herbst, Jeffrey I. *States and Power in Africa: Comparative Lessons in Authority and Control*. Princeton: Princeton University Press, 2000.

al-Hilālī, Salīm bin 'Īd. *Limādhā ikhtarnā al-manhaj al-salafī?* Amman: Markaz al-dirāsāt al-Manhajiyya al-Salafiyya, 1999.

———. *Limādhā ikhtartu al-manhaj al-salafī*? Dammām: Dār Ibn al-Qayyim; Cairo: Dār Ibn 'Affān, 2001.

Hirsch, Susan F. *Pronouncing and Persevering: Gender and the Discourses of Disputing in an African Islamic Court*. Chicago: University of Chicago Press, 1998.

Hirschkind, Charles. "Civic Virtue and Religious Reason: An Islamic Counterpublic." *Cultural Anthropology* 16, no. 1 (2001): 3–34.

———. *The Ethical Soundscape: Cassette Sermons and Islamic Counterpublics*. New York: Columbia University Press, 2006.

———. "The Ethics of Listening: Cassette-Sermon Audition in Contemporary Cairo." *American Ethnologist* 28, no. 3 (2001a): 623–49.

———. "Tradition, Myth, and Historical Fact in Contemporary Islam." *ISIM Newsletter* 8 (September 2001b): 18.

———. "What Is Political Islam?" *Middle East Research and Information Project* 27, no. 4 (1997): 12–15.

Hirst, Paul, and Grahame Thompson. *Globalization in Question: The International Economy and the Possibilities of Governance*. Cambridge: Polity Press; Cambridge: Blackwell, 1996.

Ho, Engseng. *The Graves of Tarim: Genealogy and Mobility across the Indian Ocean*. Berkeley: University of California Press, 2006.

———. "Hadramis Abroad in Hadramawt: The Muwalladin." In *Hadhrami Traders, Scholars and Statesmen in the Indian Ocean, 1750s–1960s*, edited by Ulrike Freitag and William G. Clarence-Smith. Leiden: E. J. Brill, 1997.

———. "Yemenis on Mars: The End of Mahjar (Diaspora)?" *Middle East Report* 211 (Summer 1999): 29–31.

Hobsbawm, Eric. *The Age of Empire, 1875–1914*. New York: Pantheon Books, 1987.

———. *The Age of Extremes: A History of the World, 1914–1991*. New York: Pantheon Books, 1994.

——. *Nations and Nationalism since 1780: Programme, Myth, Reality.* Cambridge: Cambridge University Press, 1990.

Hobsbawm, Eric, and Terence Ranger, eds. *The Invention of Tradition.* Cambridge: Cambridge University Press, 1983.

Hollander, Isaac, ed. *Jews and Muslims in Lower Yemen: A Study in Protection and Restraint, ca. 1918–1949.* Leiden: E. J. Brill, 2005.

Honig, Bonnie. "Declarations of Independence: Arendt and Derrida on the Problem of Founding a Republic." *American Political Science Review* 85, no. 1 (March 1991): 97–113.

Hoogvelt, Ankie. *Globalization and the Postcolonial World: The New Political Economy of Development.* Baltimore: Johns Hopkins University Press, 2001.

Hopf, Ted. "Ethnography and Rational Choice in David Laitin: From Equality to Subordination to Absence." *Qualitative Methods: Newsletter of the APSA Organized Section on Qualitative Methods* 4, no. 1 (2006): 17–20.

Horowitz, Donald L. *Ethnic Groups in Conflict.* Berkeley: University of California Press, 1985.

Hroch, Miroslav. "From National Movement to the Fully-Formed Nation: The Nation-Building Process in Europe." *New Left Review* 198 (March–April 1993): 3–20.

Human Rights Watch. "Yemen." (2000): 420–24.

Huntington, Samuel P. *The Third Wave: Democratization in the Late Twentieth Century.* Norman: University of Oklahoma Press, 1991.

al-Ḥūthī, Ḥusayn Badr al-Dīn. *Risāla min al-Ḥūthī lil-Sīstānī: ta'thīr ḥarb bayānāt bayna 'ulamā' Ṣan'ā' wa Najaf.* www.newsyemen.net (May 7, 2005).

al-'Inān, Zayd. *Mudhakkirātī.* Cairo: al-Maktaba al-Salafiyya, 1983.

International Crisis Group. "Jordan's 9/11: Dealing with Jihadi Islamism." *Middle East Report* 47 (November 2005).

——. "Yemen: Coping with Terrorism and Violence in a Fragile State." *Middle East Report* 8 (January 2003).

International Monetary Fund. *Country Report* 02/61. 2001.

Ismail, Salwa. *Rethinking Islamist Politics: Culture, the State and Islamism.* London: I. B. Tauris, 2003.

'Izzān, Muḥammad, ed. *al-'Allāma al-Shāmī: ārā' wa mawāqif.* Amman: Maṭābi' Sharikat al-Mawārid al-Ṣinā'iyya al-Urduniyya, 1994.

Jackson, Robert H. *Quasi-States: Sovereignty, International Relations, and the Third World.* Cambridge: Cambridge University Press, 1990.

——. *Race, Caste, and Status: Indians in Colonial Spanish America.* Albuquerque: University of New Mexico Press, 1999.

Jallūl, Fayṣal. *al-Yaman: al-thawratān, al-jumhūriyyatān, al-waḥda, 1962–1994.* Beirut: Dār al-Jadīd, 1999.

al-Jirāfī, 'Abd Allāh. *al-Muqtaṭaf min tārīkh al-Yaman.* Cairo: 'Īsā al-Bābī al-Ḥalabī, 1951.

Johnsen, Gregory D. "Salih's Road to Reelection." *Middle East Report Online* (January 13, 2006).

Johnson, Chalmers. *Blowback: The Costs and Consequences of American Empire.* New York: Metropolitan Books, 2000.

Jung, Courtney. *Then I Was Black: South African Political Identities in Transition.* New Haven: Yale University Press, 2000.

Kalyvas, Stathis N. "Democracy and Religious Politics: Evidence from Belgium." *Comparative Political Studies* 31, no. 3 (1998): 291–319.

——. *The Logic of Violence in Civil War.* Cambridge: Cambridge University Press, 2006.

——. "The Ontology of 'Political Violence': Action and Identity in Civil Wars." *Perspectives on Politics* 1, no. 3 (2003): 475–94.

Kaplan, Sam. *The Pedagogical State: Education and the Politics of National Culture in post-1980 Turkey.* Stanford: Stanford University Press, 2006.

Karlström, Mikael. "Imagining Democracy: Political Culture and Democratisation in Buganda." *Africa* 66, no. 4 (1996): 485–505.

Kashani-Sabet, Firoozeh. *Frontier Fictions: Shaping the Iranian Nation, 1804–1946.* Princeton: Princeton University Press, 1999.

Keane, Webb. *Christian Moderns: Freedom and Fetish in the Mission Encounter.* Berkeley: University of California Press, 2007.

Kelly, John D., and Martha Kaplan. *Represented Communities: Fiji and World Decolonization.* Chicago: University of Chicago Press, 2001.

Kepel, Gilles. *Jihad: The Trail of Political Islam.* Cambridge: Belknap Press of Harvard University Press, 2002.

——. *Muslim Extremism in Egypt: The Prophet and the Pharaoh.* Berkeley: University of California Press, 1993.

Khalidi, Rashid. *Palestinian Identity: The Construction of Modern National Consciousness.* New York: Columbia University Press, 1997.

Khoury, Philip S., and Joseph Kostiner. "Introduction." In *Tribes and State Formation in the Middle East,* edited by Philip S. Khoury and Joseph Kostiner. London: I. B. Tauris, 1991.

Kohn, Hans. *The Idea of Nationalism: A Study in Its Origins and Background.* New York: Macmillan, 1967 [1944].

Koselleck, Reinhart. *Futures Past: On the Semantics of Historical Time.* Translated by Keith Tribe. New York: Columbia University Press, 2004 [1979].

Krämer, Gudrun. "Islamist Notions of Democracy." In *Political Islam: Essays from* Middle East Report, edited by Joel Beinin and Joe Stork. Berkeley: University of California Press, 1997.

Kühn, Thomas. "An Imperial Borderland as Colony: Knowledge Production and the Elaboration of Difference in Ottoman Yemen, 1872–1914." *MIT Electronic Journal of Middle East Studies* 3 (Spring 2003): 5–17.

——. "Ordering the Past of Ottoman Yemen, 1872–1914." *Turcica* 34 (2002): 189–220.

Kundera, Milan. *The Book of Laughter and Forgetting.* New York: Penguin Books, 1980.

Lackner, Helen. *P.D.R. Yemen: Outpost of Socialist Development in Arabia.* London: Ithaca Press, 1985.

Laitin, David D. *Identity in Formation: The Russian-Speaking Populations in the Near Abroad.* Ithaca: Cornell University Press, 1998.

——. "National Revivals and Violence." *Archives Européennes de Sociologie* 36, no. 1 (Spring 1995): 3–43.

——. "The Perestroikan Challenge to Political Science." *Politics and Society* 31, no. 1 (2003): 163–84.

Landes, David S. *Revolution in Time: Clocks and the Making of the Modern World.* Cambridge: Belknap Press of Harvard University Press, 1983.

Lee, Benjamin. "Textuality, Mediation, and Public Discourse." In *Habermas and the Public Sphere,* edited by Craig Calhoun. Cambridge: MIT Press, 1992.

Linz, Juan J., and Alfred Stepan. *Problems of Democratic Transition and Consolidation: Southern Europe, South America, and Post-Communist Europe*. Baltimore: Johns Hopkins University Press, 1996.

Lipset, Seymour Martin. "Some Social Requisites of Democracy: Economic Development and Political Legitimacy." *American Political Science Review* 53, no. 1 (1959): 69–105.

Little, Tom. *South Arabia: Arena of Conflict*. London: Pall Mall Press, 1968.

Lloyd, David, and Paul Thomas. *Culture and the State*. New York: Routledge, 1998.

Lomnitz, Claudio. *Deep Mexico, Silent Mexico: An Anthropology of Nationalism*. Minneapolis: University of Minnesota Press, 2001.

Lugard, Frederick. *The Dual Mandate in British Tropical Africa*. London: Frank Cass, 1965.

Lust-Okar, Ellen. "Elections under Authoritarianism: Preliminary Lessons from Jordan." *Democratization* 13, no. 3 (2006): 456–71.

———. *Structuring Conflict in the Arab World: Incumbents, Opponents, and Institutions*. Cambridge: Cambridge University Press, 2005.

Lynch, Marc. "Beyond the Arab Street: Iraq and the Arab Public Sphere." *Politics and Society* 31, no. 1 (2003): 55–91.

———. *Voices of the New Arab Public: Iraq, Al-Jazeera, and Middle East Politics Today*. New York: Columbia University Press, 2006.

MacIntyre, Alasdair. *After Virtue: A Study in Moral Theory*. Notre Dame: University of Notre Dame Press, 1981.

Magaloni, Beatriz. *Voting for Autocracy: Hegemonic Party Survival and Its Demise in Mexico*. New York: Cambridge University Press, 2006.

Mahmood, Saba. *The Politics of Piety: The Islamic Revival and the Feminist Subject*. Princeton: Princeton University Press, 2005.

———. "Rehearsed Spontaneity and the Conventionality of Ritual: Disciplines of Salat." *American Ethnologist* 28, no. 4 (2001): 827–53.

Makdisi, Ussama. *The Culture of Sectarianism: Community, History, and Violence in Nineteenth-Century Ottoman Lebanon*. Berkeley: University of California Press, 2000.

Makram, Fayṣal. "al-Aḥzāb: 'al-liqā' al-mushtarak' fī muwājahat ikhtirāq al-ra'īs al-yamanī ṣufūfahā: 'Alī Ṣāliḥ baghat mu'āriḍīh al-islāmiyyīn min yamīnihim wa bāshar ḥamlatahu al-intikhābiyya fī Jāmi'at al-Īmān." www.daralhayat.com (September 15, 2005).

Mamdani, Mahmood. *Citizen and Subject: Contemporary Africa and the Legacy of Late Colonialism*. Princeton: Princeton University Press, 1996.

———. *Good Muslim, Bad Muslim: America, the Cold War, and the Roots of Terror*. New York: Pantheon Books, 2004.

Mann, Michael. "A Political Theory of Nationalism and Its Excesses." In *Notions of Nationalism*, edited by Sukumar Periwal. Budapest: Central European University Press; New York: Oxford University Press, 1995.

———. *The Sources of Social Power*. Vol. 2. Cambridge: Cambridge University Press, 1993.

Mansbridge, Jane. "Feminism and Democratic Community." In *Democratic Community*, edited by John W. Chapman and Ian Shapiro. New York: New York University Press, 1993.

Manuel, Peter. *Cassette Culture: Popular Music and Technology in North India*. Chicago: University of Chicago Press, 1993.

Mares, Isabella. "The Great Divergence in Social Protection." Paper presented at the Comparative Politics Workshop, University of Chicago, 2006.

Markell, Patchen. *Bound by Recognition*. Princeton: Princeton University Press, 2003.

———. "Contesting Consensus: Rereading Habermas on the Public Sphere." *Constellations* 3, no. 3 (1997): 377–400.

Marks, Susan. *The Riddle of All Constitutions: International Law, Democracy, and the Critique of Ideology*. Oxford: Oxford University Press, 2000.

Marx, Anthony W. *Faith in Nation: Exclusionary Origins of Nationalism*. New York: Oxford University Press, 2003.

Matoesian, Gregory M. *Law and the Language of Identity: Discourse in the William Kennedy Smith Rape Trial*. Oxford: Oxford University Press, 2001.

Maza, Sarah. *The Myth of the French Bourgeoisie: An Essay on the Social Imaginary, 1750–1850*. Cambridge: Harvard University Press, 2003.

———. *Private Lives and Public Affairs: The Causes Célèbres of Prerevolutionary France*. Berkeley: University of California Press, 1993.

Mead, George Herbert. *Mind, Self, and Society: From the Standpoint of a Social Behaviorist*. Chicago: University of Chicago Press, 1967 [1934].

Medani, Khalid. "Funding Fundamentalism: The Political Economy of an Islamist State." In *Political Islam: Essays from* Middle East Report, edited by Joel Beinin and Joe Stork. Berkeley: University of California Press, 1997.

Meissner, Jeffrey R. "Tribes at the Core: Legitimacy, Structure and Power in Zaydi Yemen." PhD dissertation, Columbia University, 1987.

Meneley, Anne. *Tournaments of Value: Sociability and Hierarchy in a Yemeni Town*. Toronto: University of Toronto Press, 1996.

Mermier, Franck. "L'islam politique au Yémen ou la 'Tradition' contre les traditions?" *Monde arabe Maghreb-Machrek* 155 (1997a): 6–19.

———. "Yémen, les héritages d'une histoire morcelée." In *Le Yémen contemporain*, edited by Remy Leveau, Franck Mermier, and Udo Steinbach. Paris: Éditions Karthala, 1999.

———. "Yemen: L'état en face à la démocratie." *Monde arabe Maghreb-Machrek* 155 (1997b): 3–5.

Messick, Brinkley. *The Calligraphic State: Textual Domination and History in a Muslim Society*. Berkeley: University of California Press, 1993.

———. "Cover Stories: A Genealogy of the Legal Public Sphere in Yemen." In *Religion, Social Practice, and Contested Hegemonies: Reconstructing the Public Sphere in Muslim Majority Societies*, edited by Armando Salvatore and Mark LeVine. New York: Palgrave Macmillan, 2005a.

———. "Madhhabs and Modernity." In *The Islamic School of Law: Evolution, Devolution, and Progress*, edited by Peri Bearman, Rudolph Peters, and Frank E. Vogel. Cambridge: Islamic Legal Studies Program, Harvard Law School, distributed by Harvard University Press, 2005b.

———. "Written Identities: Legal Subjects in an Islamic State." *History of Religions* 38, no. 1 (August 1998): 25–51.

Migdal, Joel S. *State in Society: Studying How States and Societies Transform and Constitute One Another*. Cambridge: Cambridge University Press, 2001.

———. *Strong Societies and Weak States: State-Society Relations and State Capabilities in the Third World*. Princeton: Princeton University Press, 1988.

Miller, Daniel. *Capitalism: An Ethnographic Approach*. Oxford: Berg, 1997.

Miller, W. Flagg. "Inscribing the Muse: Political Poetry and the Discourse of Circulation in the Yemeni Cassette Industry." PhD dissertation, University of Michigan, 2001.

———. *The Moral Resonance of Arab Media: Audiocassette Poetry and Culture in Yemen*. Cambridge: Harvard University, Center for Middle East Studies, 2007.

Mitchell, Timothy. *Colonising Egypt*. Cambridge: Cambridge University Press, 1988.

———. "The Limits of the State: Beyond Statist Approaches and Their Critics." *American Political Science Review* 85, no. 1 (March 1991): 77–96.

———. "McJihad: Islam in the U.S. Global Order." *Social Text* 20, no. 4 (Winter 2002a): 1–18.

———. *Rule of Experts: Egypt, Techno-Politics, Modernity*. Berkeley: University of California Press, 2002b.

Moore, Barrington, Jr. *Liberal Prospects under Soviet Socialism: A Comparative Historical Perspective*. New York: Columbia University, W. Averell Harriman Institute for Advanced Study of the Soviet Union, 1989.

Morris, Rosalind C. "All Made Up: Performance, Theory, and the New Anthropology of Sex and Gender." *Annual Review of Anthropology* 24 (1995): 567–92.

———. "Legacies of Derrida." *Annual Review of Anthropology* 36 (2007): 355–89.

Mouffe, Chantal. "Deconstruction, Pragmatism and the Politics of Democracy." In *Deconstruction and Pragmatism*, edited by Chantal Mouffe. London: Routledge, 1996.

———. *The Democratic Paradox*. London: Verso, 2000.

Mumford, Lewis. *Technics and Civilization*. New York: Harcourt, Brace and Company, 1934.

Mundy, Martha. *Domestic Government: Kinship, Community, and Polity in North Yemen*. London: I. B. Tauris, 1995.

———. "Land and Family in a Yemeni Community." PhD dissertation, University of Cambridge, 1991.

Munson, Ziad W. "Islamic Mobilization: Social Movement Theory and the Egyptian Muslim Brotherhood." *Sociological Quarterly* 42, no. 4 (2001): 487–510.

Mu'tamar al-waḥda wa al-salām: al-qarārāt wa al-tawṣiyāt. Ṣan'ā': Maṭābi' Ṣan'ā' al-Ḥadītha, 1993.

al-Mutawakkil, Muḥammad 'Abd al-Malik. *al-Ṣaḥāfa al-yamaniyya: nash'atuhā wa taṭawwuruhā*. Ṣan'ā': Maṭābi' al-Tubjī al-Tijāriyya, 1983.

———. "al-Shar'iyya al-mafqūda . . . wa al-shar'iyya al-muḥtamala." *al-Waḥdawī* (October 5, 1999).

Muthannā, Muṣliḥ Aḥmad. "Hunāka thalāthat malāyīn mariḍ bi-fayrūs al-kabid lan yushārik fī al-intikhābāt." *al-Waḥdawī* (September 21, 1999).

Nairn, Tom. "Scotland and Europe." In *Becoming National: A Reader*, edited by Geoff Eley and Ronald Grigor Suny. New York: Oxford University Press, 1996.

Nājī, Sulṭān. *al-Tārīkh al-'askarī lil-Yaman: dirāsa siyāsiyya tabḥath irtibāṭ nushū' wa taṭawwur al-mu'assasāt wa al-anshiṭa al-'askariyya bil-awḍā' wa al-mutaghayyirāt al-siyāsiyya*. Kuwait: Sharikat Kāẓima lil-Nashr wa al-Tarjama wa al-Tawzī', 1976.

Najmabadi, Afsaneh. *Women with Mustaches and Men without Beards: Gender and Sexual Anxieties of Iranian Modernity*. Berkeley: University of California Press, 2005.

Al-Naqeeb, Khaldoun Hasan. *Society and State in the Gulf and Arab Peninsula: A Different Perspective.* New York: Routledge, 1991.

Nozick, Robert. *Anarchy, State, and Utopia.* New York: Basic Books, 1974.

Obermeyer, Gerald J. "*al-Īmān* and al-Imām: Ideology and State in the Yemen, 1900–1948." In *Intellectual Life in the Arab East 1890-1939*, edited by Marwan R. Buheiry. Beirut: Center for Arab and Middle East Studies, American University of Beirut, 1981.

O'Donnell, Guillermo, and Philippe C. Schmitter. *Transitions from Authoritarian Rule: Tentative Conclusions about Uncertain Democracies.* Baltimore: Johns Hopkins University Press, 1986.

Öniş, Ziya. "Turgut Özal and His Economic Legacy: Turkish Neo-Liberalism in Critical Perspective." *Middle Eastern Studies* 40, no. 4 (July 2004): 113–34.

Pachirat, Timothy. "Ethnography from Below? Reflections from an Industrialized Slaughterhouse on Perspective, Power, and the Ethnographic Voice." Prepared for delivery at the Annual Meeting of the APSA, Philadelphia, August 30–September 3, 2006.

Pader, Ellen. "Seeing with an Ethnographic Sensibility: Explorations beneath the Surface of Public Policies." In *Interpretation and Method: Empirical Research Methods and the Interpretive Turn*, edited by Dvora Yanow and Peregrine Schwartz-Shea. Armonk, N.Y.: M. E. Sharpe, 2006.

Paley, Julia. *Marketing Democracy: Power and Social Movements in Post-Dictatorship Chile.* Berkeley: University of California Press, 2001.

———. "Toward an Anthropology of Democracy." *Annual Review of Anthropology* 31 (2002): 469–96.

Peet, Richard. "Ideology, Discourse and the Geography of Hegemony: From Socialist to Neoliberal Development in Post-Apartheid South Africa." *Antipode* 34, no. 1 (2002): 54–84.

Peterson, J. E. *Yemen: The Search for a Modern State.* Baltimore: Johns Hopkins University Press, 1982.

Phillips, Anne. *The Enigma of Colonialism: British Policy in West Africa.* London: James Currey; Bloomington: Indiana University Press, 1989.

Phillips, Sarah. "Cracks in the Yemeni System." *Middle East Report Online* (July 28, 2005).

Pierson, Paul. *Politics in Time: History, Institutions, and Social Analysis.* Princeton: Princeton University Press, 2004.

Pincus, Steven. "Nationalism, Universal Monarchy, and the Glorious Revolution." In *State/Culture: State-Formation after the Cultural Turn*, edited by George Steinmetz. Ithaca: Cornell University Press, 1999.

Pitkin, Hanna. *The Attack of the Blob: Hannah Arendt's Concept of the Social.* Chicago: University of Chicago Press, 1998.

———. *The Concept of Representation.* Berkeley: University of California Press, 1967.

———. *Wittgenstein and Justice: On the Significance of Ludwig Wittgenstein for Social and Political Thought.* Berkeley: University of California Press, 1993.

Pocock, John G. A. *The Machiavellian Moment: Florentine Political Thought and the Atlantic Republican Tradition.* Princeton: Princeton University Press, 1975.

Pontusson, Jonas. *Inequality and Prosperity: Social Europe vs. Liberal America.* Ithaca: Cornell University Press, 2005.

Posner, Daniel N. *Institutions and Ethnic Politics in Africa.* New York: Cambridge University Press, 2005.

Postone, Moishe. *Time, Labor, and Social Domination: A Reinterpretation of Marx's Critical Theory.* Cambridge: Cambridge University Press, 1993.

Povinelli, Elizabeth A. "Consuming Geist: Popontology and the Spirit of Capital in Indigenous Australia." In *Millennial Capitalism and the Culture of Neoliberalism,* edited by Jean Comaroff and John L. Comaroff. Durham, N.C.: Duke University Press, 2001.

———. *The Cunning of Recognition: Indigenous Alterities and the Making of Australian Multiculturalism.* Durham, N.C.: Duke University Press, 2002.

Powell, G. Bingham, Jr. *Elections as Instruments of Democracy: Majoritarian and Proportional Visions.* New Haven: Yale University Press, 2000.

Przeworski, Adam. *Democracy and the Market: Political and Economic Reforms in Eastern Europe and Latin America.* Cambridge: Cambridge University Press, 1991.

Przeworski, Adam, Michael E. Alvarez, Jose Antonio Cheibub, and Fernando Limongi. *Democracy and Development: Political Institutions and Well-Being in the World, 1950–1990.* Cambridge: Cambridge University Press, 2000.

Przeworski, Adam, and Fernando Limongi. "Modernization: Theories and Facts." *World Politics* 49, no. 2 (January 1997): 155–83.

Putnam, Robert D., with Robert Leonardi and Rafaella Y. Nanetti. *Making Democracy Work: Civic Traditions in Modern Italy.* Princeton: Princeton University Press, 1993.

al-Qāt fī ḥayāt al-Yaman wa al-yamaniyyīn: raṣd wa dirāsāt wa taḥālīl. Ṣan'ā': Markaz al-Dirāsāt wa al-Buḥūth al-Yamanī; Beirut: Maktabat al-Jamāhīr, 1981–82.

Qureshi, Regula Burckhard. "Recorded Sound and Religious Music: The Case of Qawwali." In *Media and the Transformation of Religion in South Asia,* edited by Lawrence A. Babb and Susan S. Wadley. Philadelphia: University of Pennsylvania Press, 1995.

Rabinow, Paul, and William M. Sullivan, eds. *Interpretive Social Science: A Second Look.* Berkeley: University of California Press, 1987.

Ramadan, Tariq. *Les Musulmans de l'Occident et l'avenir de l'islam.* Arles: Sindbad-Actes Sud, 2003.

al-Rasheed, Madawi. *Contesting the Saudi State: Islamic Voices from a New Generation.* Cambridge: Cambridge University Press, 2007.

Renaud, E., and C. Fayein, eds. *Poèmes de la révolution yéménite.* Paris: Éditions Recherches, 1979.

Republic of Yemen. *Poverty Reduction Strategy Paper* (PRSP). San'a': Ministry of Planning and International Cooperation, 2002.

Robinson, William I. *Promoting Polyarchy: US Intervention, Globalization, and Hegemony.* Cambridge: Cambridge University Press, 1996.

Rodinson, Maxime. "Esquisse d'une monographe du qat." *Journal Asiatique* 265 (1977): 71–96.

Rogers, Susan. "Batak Tape Cassette Kinship: Constructing Kinship through the Indonesia National Mass Media." *American Ethnologist* 13, no. 1 (February 1986): 23–42.

Roland, Gérard. *Transition and Economics: Politics, Markets, and Firms.* Cambridge: MIT Press, 2000.

Rosaldo, Michelle Z. "The Things We Do with Words: Ilongot Speech Acts and Speech Act Theory in Philosophy." *Language in Society* 11 (1982): 203–37.

Rose, Sonya O. "Cultural Analysis and Moral Discourses: Episodes, Continuities, and Transformations." In *Beyond the Cultural Turn: New Directions in the Study of Society and Culture*, edited by Victoria E. Bonnell and Lynn Hunt. Berkeley: University of California Press, 1999.

Rosenberg, Justin. *The Follies of Globalization Theory: Polemical Essays*. London: Verso, 2000.

Ross, Michael. "Does Oil Hinder Democracy?" *World Politics* 53, no. 3 (2001): 325–61.

Rougier, Bernard. "Yémen 1990–1994: La logique du pact politique mise en échec." In *Le Yémen contemporain*, edited by Rémy Leveau, Franck Mermier, and Udo Steinbach. Paris: Éditions Karthala, 1999.

Roy, Olivier. *The Failure of Political Islam*. Translated by Carol Volk. Cambridge: Harvard University Press, 1996.

———. *Globalized Islam: The Search for a New Ummah*. New York: Columbia University Press, 2004.

Rubin, Barnett R. *Fragmentation of Afghanistan: State Formation and Collapse in the International System*. New Haven: Yale University Press, 2002.

Rustow, Dankwart A. "Transitions to Democracy: Toward a Dynamic Model." *Comparative Politics* 2, no. 3 (April 1970): 337–63.

Rutherford, Danilyn. *Raiding the Land of the Foreigners: The Limits of the Nation on an Indonesian Frontier*. Princeton: Princeton University Press, 2003.

———. "Why Papua Wants Freedom: The Third Person in Contemporary Nationalism." *Public Culture* 10, no. 1. Forthcoming.

al-Sa'dī, 'Abbās Fāḍil. *al-Qāt fi al-Yaman: dirāsa jughrāfiyya*. Kuwait: Waḥdat al-Baḥth wa al-Tarjama, Qism al-Jughrāfiyā bi-Jāmi'at al-Kuwayt, al-Jam'iyya al-Jughrāfiyya al-Kuwaytiyya, 1983.

Sadowski, Yahya. "Egypt's Islamist Movement: A New Political and Economic Force." *Middle East Insight* (1987): 37–45.

Sahlins, Marshall. *Historical Metaphors and Mythical Realities: Structure in the Early History of the Sandwich Islands Kingdom*. Ann Arbor: University of Michigan Press, 1981.

———. *Islands of History*. Chicago: University of Chicago Press, 1987.

Sahlins, Peter. *Boundaries: The Making of France and Spain in the Pyrenees*. Berkeley: University of California Press, 1991.

Sālim, Sayyid Muṣṭafā. *Takwīn al-Yaman al-ḥadīth: al-Yaman wa al-imām Yaḥyā*. 2nd edition. Cairo: Ma'had al-Buḥūth wa al-Dirāsāt al-'Arabiyya, 1971.

Salvatore, Armando, and Mark LeVine, eds. *Religion, Social Practice, and Contested Hegemonies: Reconstructing the Public Sphere in Muslim Majority Societies*. New York: Palgrave Macmillan, 2005.

Sambanis, Nicholas. "What Is Civil War? Conceptual and Empirical Complexities of an Operational Definition." *Journal of Conflict Resolution* 48, no. 6 (2004): 819–58.

Sandel, Michael. *Democracy's Discontent: America in Search of Public Philosophy*. Cambridge: Belknap Press of Harvard University Press, 1996.

Sanders, Lynn. "Against Deliberation." *Political Theory* 25, no. 3 (June 1997): 347–76.

al-Saqqāf, Abū Bakr. *al-Waḥda al-yamaniyya: min al-indimāj al-fawrī ilā al-isti'mār al-dākhilī*. London: Bareed al-Janūb, 1996.

———. "The Yemeni Unity: Crisis in Integration." In *Le Yémen contemporain*, edited by Rémy Leveau, Franck Mermier, and Udo Steinbach. Paris: Éditions Karthala, 1999. [Note: transliterated in this work as Abou Bakr.]

al-Ṣarrāf, 'Alī . *al-Yaman al-Janūbī: al-ḥayā al-siyāsiyya min al-isti'mār ilā al-waḥda*. London: Riad El-Rayyes Books, 1992.

Sassen, Saskia. *The Global City: New York, London, Tokyo*. Princeton: Princeton University Press, 2001.

———. *Globalization and Its Discontents: Essays on the New Mobilization of People and Money*. New York: New Press, 1998.

Schaffer, Frederic. *Democracy in Translation: Understanding Politics in an Unfamiliar Culture*. Ithaca: Cornell University Press, 1998.

Schmidt, D.A. *Yemen: The Unknown War*. London: Bodley Head, 1968.

Schmitter, Philippe C., and Terry Lynn Karl. "What Democracy Is . . . and Is Not." *Journal of Democracy* 2, no. 3 (1991): 75–88.

Schumpeter, Joseph. *Capitalism, Socialism, and Democracy*. New York: Harper and Row, 1962 [1950].

Schwedler, Jillian. "Democratization in the Arab World? Yemen's Aborted Opening." *Journal of Democracy* 13, no. 4 (2002): 48–55.

———. *Faith in Moderation: Islamist Parties in Jordan and Yemen*. Cambridge: Cambridge University Press, 2006.

Scott, David. "Norms of Self-Determination: Thinking Sovereignty Through." N.d. Essay available from author, Department of Anthropology, Columbia University.

———. *Refashioning Futures: Criticism after Postcoloniality*. Princeton: Princeton University Press, 1999.

Scott, James C. *Seeing Like a State: How Certain Schemes to Improve the Human Condition Have Failed*. New Haven: Yale University Press, 1998.

Seif, Huda. "The Accursed Minority: The Ethno-Cultural Persecution of Al-Akhdam in the Republic of Yemen: A Documentary and Advocacy Project." *Muslim World Journal of Human Rights* 2, no. 1 (2005).

———. "Moralities and Outcasts: Domination and Allegories of Resentment." PhD dissertation, Columbia University, 2003.

Serjeant, R. B. "The Market, Business Life, Occupations, the Legality and Sale of Stimulants." In *Ṣan'ā': An Arabian Islamic City*, edited by R. B. Serjeant and R. Lewcock. London: World of Islam Festival Trust, 1983.

Seton-Watson, Hugh. *Nations and States: An Enquiry into the Origins of Nations and the Politics of Nationalism*. Boulder, Colo.: Westview Press, 1977.

Sewell, William H., Jr. "The Concept(s) of Culture." In *Beyond the Cultural Turn: New Directions in the Study of Society and Culture*, edited by Victoria E. Bonnell and Lynn Hunt. Berkeley: University of California Press, 1999.

———. "The French Revolution and the Emergence of the Nation Form." In *Revolutionary Currents: Transatlantic Ideology and Nationbuilding, 1688–1821*, edited by Michael Morrison and Melinda Zook. Lanham, Md.: Rowman and Littlefield, 2004.

———. "Three Temporalities: Toward an Eventful Sociology." In *The Historic Turn in the Human Sciences*, edited by Terrence J. McDonald. Ann Arbor: University of Michigan Press, 1996.

Shafir, Gershom. "Introduction: The Evolving Tradition of Citizenship." In *The Citizenship Debates: A Reader*. Minneapolis: University of Minnesota Press, 1998.

al-Shamāḥī, 'Abd Allāh. *al-Yaman: al-insān wa al-ḥaḍāra*. Cairo: Dār al-Hanā', 1972.

Shapiro, Ian. *Democratic Justice*. New Haven: Yale University Press, 1999.

al-Shawkānī, Muḥammad bin 'Alī (1759–1839). *al-Sayl al-jarrār al-mutadaffiq 'alā ḥadā'iq al-azhār*. Vol. 3. Edited by Muḥammad Ṣubḥī ibn Ḥasan Ḥallāq. Damascus: Dār Bin Kathīr, 2000.

Silverstein, Michael. "The Three Faces of 'Function': Preliminaries to a Psychology of Language." In *Social and Functional Approaches to Language and Thought*, edited by Maya Hickmann. Orlando: Academic Press, 1987.

Silverstein, Michael, and Greg Urban. "The Natural History of Discourse." In *Natural Histories of Discourse*, edited by Michael Silverstein and Greg Urban. Chicago: University of Chicago Press, 1996.

Singerman, Diane. *Avenues of Participation: Family, Politics, and Networks in Urban Quarters of Cairo*. Princeton: Princeton University Press, 1995.

Smith, Rogers. "The Politics of Identities and the Tasks of Political Science." In *Problems and Methods in the Study of Politics*, edited by Ian Shapiro, Rogers M. Smith, and Tarek E. Masoud. Cambridge: Cambridge University Press, 2004.

Snow, David A., and Robert D. Benford. "Ideology, Frame Resonance, and Participant Mobilization." *International Social Movement Research* 1 (1988): 197–217.

Snow, David A., E. Burke Rochford Jr., Steven K. Worden, and Robert D. Benford. "Frame Alignment Processes, Micromobilization, and Movement Participation." *American Sociological Review* 51, no. 4 (August 1986): 464–81.

Somers, Margaret R. "The Narrative Constitution of Identity: A Relational and Network Approach." *Theory and Society* 23, no. 5 (October 1994): 605–49.

Starrett, Gregory. *Putting Islam to Work: Education, Politics, and Religious Transformation in Egypt*. Berkeley: University of California Press, 1998.

Stevens, Jacqueline. "The Political Science of Love and Death." Prepared for presentation at the annual meetings of the American Political Science Association, Chicago, August 30–September 2, 2007.

Stevenson, Thomas B. *Social Change in a Yemeni Highlands Town*. Salt Lake City: University of Utah Press, 1985.

———. "Yemeni Workers Come Home: Reabsorbing One Million Migrants." *Middle East Report* 181 (March–April 1993): 15–20.

Stiglitz, Joseph E. *Globalization and Its Discontents*. New York: W. W. Norton, 2002.

Stoler, Ann Laura. *Carnal Knowledge and Imperial Power: Race and the Intimate in Colonial Rule*. Berkeley: University of California Press, 2002.

Stookey, Robert W. *Yemen: The Politics of the Yemen Arab Republic*. Boulder, Colo.: Westview Press, 1978.

Strong, Roy. *The Cult of Elizabeth: Elizabethan Portraiture and Pageantry*. London: Thames and Hudson, 1977.

Sunstein, Cass R. "Deliberative Trouble? Why Groups Go to Extremes." *Yale Law Journal* 110, no. 1 (October 2000): 71–119.

———. *Designing Democracy: What Constitutions Do*. New York: Oxford University Press, 2001.

Suny, Ronald Grigor. *The Revenge of the Past: Nationalism, Revolution, and the Collapse of the Soviet Union*. Stanford: Stanford University Press, 1993.

Suny, Ronald Grigor, and Michael D. Kennedy, eds. *Intellectuals and the Articulation of the Nation*. Ann Arbor: University of Michigan Press, 2001.

al-Suwaidi, Jamal S., ed. *The Yemeni War of 1994: Causes and Consequences*. London: Saqi Books, 1995.

Tambar, Kabir. Dissertation Proposal for the Social Science Research Council. 2005. Available from the author, Department of Anthropology, University of Chicago.

Tambiah, Stanley. *Culture, Thought, and Social Action: An Anthropological Perspective*. Cambridge: Harvard University Press, 1985.

Ṭarābulsī, Fawwāz. *Wu'ūd 'Adan: riḥlāt yamaniyya*. Beirut: Riad el-Rayyes Books, 2000.

Taylor, Charles. *Modern Social Imaginaries*. Durham, N.C.: Duke University Press, 2004.

———. "Modes of Civil Society." *Public Culture* 3, no. 1 (Fall 1990): 95–118.

Tétreault, Mary Ann. *Stories of Democracy: Politics and Society in Contemporary Kuwait*. New York: Columbia University Press, 2000.

Thompson, E. P. "Time, Work-Discipline, and Industrial Capitalism." *Past and Present* 38, no. 1 (1967): 56–97.

Tilly, Charles, ed. *Coercion, Capital and European States, AD 990–1990*. Cambridge, Mass.: Blackwell, 1990.

———. *Durable Inequality*. Berkeley: University of California Press, 1998.

———. *The Formation of National States in Western Europe*. Princeton: Princeton University Press, 1975.

———. "War Making and State Making as Organized Crime." In *Bringing the State Back In*, edited by Peter B. Evans, Dietrich Rueschemeyer, and Theda Skocpol. Cambridge: Cambridge University Press, 1985.

Turner, Victor. *From Ritual to Theater: The Human Seriousness of Play*. New York: Performing Arts Journal, 1982.

———. *The Ritual Process: Structure and Anti-Structure*. Chicago: Aldine, 1969.

Tutwiler, Richard. "Tribe, Tribute, and Trade: Social Class Formation in Highland Yemen." PhD dissertation, State University of New York at Binghamton, 1987.

'Umar, Jār Allāh. "The Importance and Position of Political Pluralism within the Framework of Political Reform." (Typescript) memorandum submitted to the YSP central committee, 1989. Available through Lisa Wedeen, Department of Political Science, University of Chicago.

United Nations Development Programme (UNDP). *Human Development Report* (2004). New York: UNDP.

———. *Yemen Country Profile* (2002). New York: UNDP.

Urbinati, Nadia. *Representative Democracy: Principles and Genealogy*. Chicago: University of Chicago Press, 2006.

Vail, Leroy, ed. *The Creation of Tribalism in Southern Africa*. London: Currey; Berkeley: University of California Press, 1989.

Van Hear, Nicholas. "The Socio-economic Impact of the Involuntary Mass Return to Yemen in 1990." *Journal of Refugee Studies* 7, no. 1 (1994): 18–38.

Varisco, Daniel Martin. "On the Meaning of Chewing: The Significance of qat (*Catha edulis*) in the Yemen Arab Republic." *International Journal of Middle East Studies* 18 (1986): 1–13.

Varisco, Daniel Martin, and Najwa Adra. "Affluence and the Concept of the Tribe in the Central Highlands of the Yemen Arab Republic." In *Affluence and Cultural Survival*, edited by Richard F. Salisbury and Elizabeth Tooker. Washington, D.C.: American Ethnological Society, 1984.

Vitalis, Robert. "Black Gold, White Crude: An Essay on American Exceptionalism, Hierarchy, and Hegemony in the Gulf." *Diplomatic History* 26, no. 2 (2002): 185–213.

———. "Introduction to Part Two." In *Political Islam: Essays from* Middle East Report, edited by Joel Beinin and Joe Stork. Berkeley: University of California Press, 1997.

vom Bruck, Gabriele. "Being a Zaydi in the Absence of an Imam: Doctrinal Revisions, Religious Instruction, and the (Re)invention of Ritual." In *Le Yémen contemporain*, edited by Rémy Leveau, Franck Mermier, and Udo Steinbach. Paris: Éditions Karthala, 1999.

———. "Evacuating Memory in Postrevolutionary Yemen." In *Counter-Narratives: History, Contemporary Society, and Politics in Saudi Arabia and Yemen*, edited by Madawi al-Rasheed and Robert Vitalis. New York: Palgrave Macmillan, 2004.

al-Wādi'ī, Muqbil bin Hādī. *al-Makhraj min al-fitna*. (A manifesto), 1982.

Walkowitz, Judith R. *City of Dreadful Delight: Narratives of Sexual Danger in Late-Victorian London*. Chicago: University of Chicago Press, 1992.

Ward, C., and A. al-Thawr, F. Qasem, and A. No'man. "Qat. Yemen Agricultural Strategy." Working Paper No. 8. Sa'a': Ministry of Agriculture and Irrigation, 1998.

Warner, Michael. *Publics and Counterpublics*. New York: Zone Books; Cambridge: Distributed by MIT Press, 2002.

al-Wāsi'ī, 'Abd al-Wāsi' bin Yaḥyā. *Tārīkh al-Yaman*. Cairo: al-Maṭba'a al-Salafiyya, 1927–28.

———. *Tārīkh al-Yaman*. 2nd edition. Ṣan'ā': Maktabat al-Yaman al-Kubrā, 1991 [1948].

Waterbury, John. "Democracy without Democrats?: The Potential for Political Liberalization in the Middle East." In *Democracy without Democrats? The Renewal of Politics in the Muslim World*, edited by Ghassan Salamé. London: I. B. Tauris, 1994.

———. *The Egypt of Nasser and Sadat: The Political Economy of Two Regimes*. Princeton: Princeton University Press, 1983.

Waters, Delores. "Perceptions of Social Inequality in Yemen." PhD dissertation, New York University, 1987.

Weber, Eugen. *Peasants into Frenchmen: The Modernization of Rural France, 1870–1914*. Stanford: Stanford University Press, 1976.

Wedeen, Lisa. *Ambiguities of Domination: Politics, Rhetoric, and Symbols in Contemporary Syria*. Chicago: University of Chicago Press, 1999.

———. "Beyond the Crusades." *Items and Issues: Social Science Research Council* 4, nos. 2–3 (Spring–Summer 2003a): 1–6.

———. "Concepts and Commitments in the Study of Democracy." In *Problems and Methods in the Study of Politics*, edited by Ian Shapiro, Rogers Smith, and Tarek E. Masoud. Cambridge: Cambridge University Press, 2004.

———. "Conceptualizing Culture: Possibilities for Political Science." *American Political Science Review* 96, no. 4 (December 2002): 713–28.

———. "Ethnography as Interpretive Enterprise." In preparation.

———. "Seeing Like a Citizen, Acting Like a State: Exemplary Events in Unified Yemen." *Comparative Studies in Society and History* 45, no. 4 (October 2003b): 680–713.

Weir, Shelagh. "A Clash of Fundamentalisms: Wahhabism in Yemen." *Middle East Report* 204 (July–September 1997): 22–26.

———. *Qāt in Yemen: Consumption and Social Change*. London: British Museum Publications, 1985.

———. "Trade and Tribal Structures in North West Yemen." *Arabie du Sud: Cahiers du GREMAMO* 10 (1991): 87–101.

———. *A Tribal Order: Politics and Law in the Mountains of Yemen*. Austin: University of Texas Press, 2007.

———. "Tribe, Hijrah and Madina in North-West Yemen." In *Middle Eastern Cities in Comparative Perspective: Points de vue sur les villes du Maghreb et du Machrek*, edited by Kenneth Brown, Michael Jole, Peter Sluglett, and Sami Zubaida. London: Ithaca Press, 1986.

Wenner, Manfred W. *Modern Yemen, 1918–1966*. Baltimore: Johns Hopkins University Press, 1967.

West, Paige, and James G. Carrier. "Ecotourism and Authenticity." *Current Anthropology* 45, no. 4 (August–October 2004): 483–98.

White, Jenny B. *Islamist Mobilization in Turkey: A Study in Vernacular Politics*. Seattle: University of Washington Press, 2002.

Whitrow, G. J. *The Nature of Time*. Harmondsworth: Penguin, 1975.

Wickham, Carrie Rosefsky. "Islamic Mobilization and Political Change: The Islamist Trend in Egypt's Professional Associations." In *Political Islam: Essays from* Middle East Report, edited by Joel Beinin and Joe Stork. Berkeley: University of California Press, 1997.

———. *Mobilizing Islam*. New York: Columbia University Press, 2002.

Wiktorowicz, Quintan. *Islamic Activism: A Social Movement Theory Approach*. Bloomington: Indiana University Press, 2004.

Williams, Raymond. *Marxism and Literature*. Oxford: Oxford University Press, 1977.

Willis, John M. "Leaving Only Question Marks: Geographies of Rule in Modern Yemen." In *Counter-Narratives: History, Contemporary Society, and Politics in Saudi Arabia and Yemen*, edited by Madawi al-Rasheed and Robert Vitalis. New York: Palgrave Macmillan, 2004.

———. "Unmaking North and South: Spatial Histories of Modern Yemen." PhD dissertation, New York University, 2007.

Willis, Paul. *Learning to Labor: How Working Class Kids Get Working Class Jobs*. New York: Columbia University Press, 1981.

Wilson, William J. *The Declining Significance of Race: Blacks and Changing American Institutions*. Chicago: University of Chicago Press, 1980.

Winichakul, Thongchai. *Siam Mapped: A History of the Geo-Body of a Nation*. Honolulu: University of Hawaii Press, 1994.

al-Wīsī, Ḥusayn bin ʿAlī. *al-Yaman al-kubrā: kitāb jughrāfī chiyūlūchī tārīkhī*. Cairo: Maṭbaʿat al-Nahḍa al-ʿArabiyya, 1962.

———. *al-Yaman al-kubrā: kitāb jughrāfī jiyūlūjī tārīkhī*. 2nd edition. Ṣanʿāʾ: Maktabat al-Irshād, 1991.

Wittgenstein, Ludwig. *Philosophical Investigations*. Translated by G. E. M. Anscombe. Malden, Mass.: Blackwell, 1958.

Wood, Elisabeth Jean. *Insurgent Collective Action and Civil War in El Salvador*. Cambridge: Cambridge University Press, 2003.

World Bank. *World Bank Report* (1999). Sustainable Development Department, Middle East and North Africa Region.

———. *World Bank Report* (2002). Sustainable Development Department, Middle East and North Africa Region.

———. "Yemen—Comprehensive Development Review" (2000). Sustainable Development Department, Middle East and North Africa Region.

———. *Yemen Economic Monitoring Update* (2004). Sustainable Development Department, Middle East and North Africa Region.

———. *Yemen, Towards Qat Demand Reduction.* Report No. 39738-YE. Country Department III, Sustainable Development Department, Middle East and North Africa Region, June 2007.

Würth [Wuerth], Anna. "Employing Islam and Custom against Statutory Reform: Bayt at-Ta' in Yemen." In *Le cheikh et le Procureur: Systèmes coutumiers, centralisme étatique et pratiques juridiques au Yémen et en Egypte*, edited by Baudouin Dupret and François Burgat. Brusells: Complexe (coll. Egypte-Monde arabe), 2005.

Yamani, Mai. *Changed Identities: Challenge of the New Generation.* Washington, D.C.: Brookings Institution, 2002.

Yanow, Dvora. "Neither Rigorous Nor Objective? Interrogating Criteria for Knowledge Claims in Interpretive Science." In *Interpretation and Method: Empirical Research Methods and the Interpretive Turn*, edited by Dvora Yanow and Peregrine Schwartz-Shea. Armonk, N.Y.: M. E. Sharpe, 2006.

Yāqūt ibn 'Abd Allāh al-Ḥamawī (1179?–1229 AD). *Jacut's Geographisches Wörterbuch / Mu'jam al-buldān.* Edited by Ferdinand Wüstenfeld. Leipzig: In Commission bei F.A. Brockhaus, 1866–73.

———. *Mu'jam al-buldān.* Beirut: Dār Ṣādir, 1955–57.

Yates, Frances A. *Astraea: The Imperial Theme in the Sixteenth Century.* Boston: Ark Paperbacks, 1975.

Young, Crawford. *The Politics of Cultural Pluralism.* Madison: University of Wisconsin Press, 1976.

Young, Iris Marion. "Communication and the Other: Beyond Deliberative Democracy." In *Democracy and Difference: Contesting the Boundaries of the Political*, edited by Seyla Benhabib. Princeton: Princeton University Press, 1996.

———. *Inclusion and Democracy.* Oxford: Oxford University Press, 2000.

———. *Justice and the Politics of Difference.* Princeton: Princeton University Press, 1990.

Young, Jock. *The Drugtakers: The Social Meaning of Drug Use.* London: MacGibbon and Kee, 1971.

Zabāra, Muḥammad bin Muḥammad. *A'immat al-Yaman bil-qarn al-rābi' 'ashar.* Cairo: al-Maṭba'a al-Salafiyya, 1956.

———. *Nuzhat al-naẓar fī rijāl al-qarn al-rābi' 'ashar.* Ṣan'ā': Markaz al-Dirāsāt wa al-Abḥāth al-Yamaniyya, 1979.

Zerilli, Linda M. G. *Feminism and the Abyss of Freedom.* Chicago: University of Chicago Press, 2005.

Zolondek, Leon. "*Ash-Sha'b* in Arabic Political Literature of the 19th Century." *Die Welt des Islams* 10 (1965): 1–16.

Zubaida, Sami. *Law and Power in the Islamic World.* London: I. B. Tauris, 2005.

INDEX